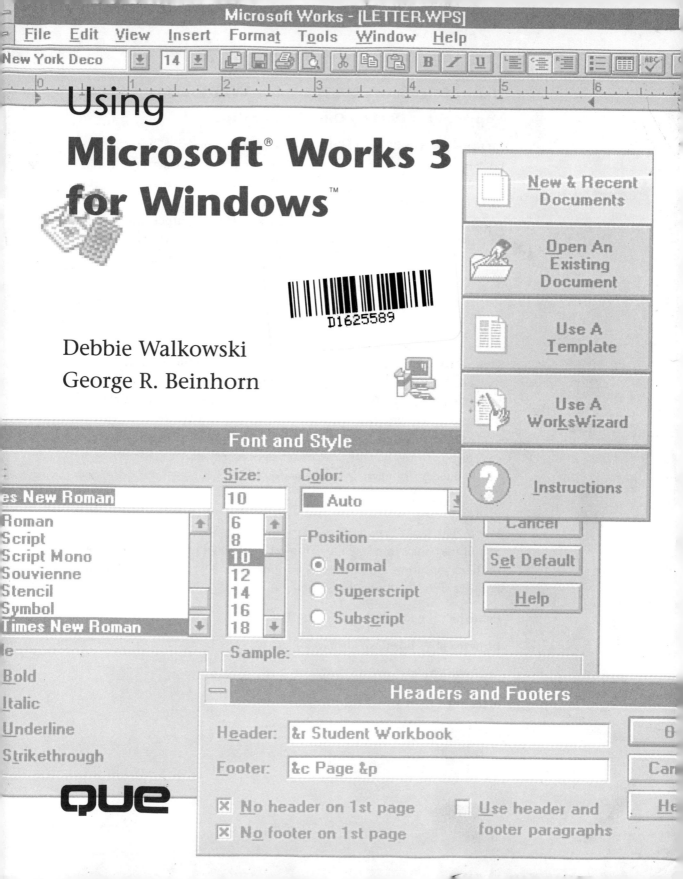

Microsoft Works - [LETTER.WPS]

File   Edit   View   Insert   Format   Tools   Window   Help

New York Deco   14

Using
Microsoft® Works 3
for Windows™

Debbie Walkowski

George R. Beinhorn

D1625589

New & Recent Documents

Open An Existing Document

Use A Template

Use A WorksWizard

Instructions

Font and Style

Size: 10   Color: Auto

es New Roman

Roman
Script
Script Mono
Souvienne
Stencil
Symbol
Times New Roman

6
8
10
12
14
16
18

Position
● Normal
○ Superscript
○ Subscript

Cancel
Set Default
Help

Sample:

Bold
Italic
Underline
Strikethrough

Headers and Footers

Header: &r Student Workbook

Footer: &c Page &p

☒ No header on 1st page
☒ No footer on 1st page

☐ Use header and footer paragraphs

que

Using Microsoft Works 3 for Windows

Copyright © 1994 by Que® Corporation

Library of Congress Catalog No.: 93-87569

ISBN: 1-56529-303-7

97 96 95 94   6 5 4 3 2 1

Interpretation of the printing code: the rightmost double-digit number is the year of the book's printing; the rightmost single-digit number, the number of the book's printing. For example, a printing code of 94-1 shows that the first printing of the book occurred in 1994.

Publisher: David P. Ewing

Director of Publishing: Michael Miller

Managing Editor: Corinne Walls

Marketing Manager: Ray Robinson

Dedication

To Aunt Aline, who, since the sixteenth summer of my life, has inspired me in more ways than she will ever know.

Credits

Publishing Manager
Lisa A. Bucki

Acquisitions Editor
Thomas F. Godfrey III

Product Directors
Stephanie D. Gould
Kathie-Jo Arnoff

Production Editors
Anne Owen
Heather Kaufman

Editors
Thomas F. Hayes
Patrick Kanouse
Phil Kitchel
Christine Prakel
Linda Seifert

Technical Editor
Jeff Adams

Figure Specialist
Wilfred R. Thebodeau

Book Designer
Amy Peppler-Adams

Cover Designer
Karen Ruggles

Production Team
Angela Bannan
Claudia Bell
Danielle Bird
Katie Bodenmiller
Paula Carroll
Julie Cook
Stephanie Gregory
Carla Hall
Bob LaRoche
Beth Lewis
Tim Montgomery
Nanci Sears Perry
Marc Shecter
Dennis Sheehan
Greg Simsic
Carol Stamile
Amy L. Steed
Michael Thomas
Tina Trettin
Mary Beth Wakefield
Sue VandeWalle
Jennifer Willis
Donna Winter
Lillian Yates

Indexer
Charlotte Clapp

Editorial Assistance
Jill Stanley
Michelle Williams

About the Author

Debbie Walkowski has worked in the computer industry since 1981 writing documentation, designing user interfaces, and teaching computer courses. Her company, The Writing Works, specializes in writing computer self-help books and providing writing services to companies such as Microsoft Corporation and Digital Equipment Corporation. Debbie has a degree in scientific and technical communication and has authored and coauthored ten books on popular computer software, including Microsoft Excel, WordPerfect, Microsoft PowerPoint, Lotus 1-2-3, Microsoft Works, Microsoft Project, Quicken, and Professional Write Plus.

Acknowledgments

No author ever writes a book completely alone. My appreciation and thanks to two terrific acquisitions editors, Nancy Stevenson and Tom Godfrey; to coauthor George Beinhorn for picking up the sections I didn't have time to squeeze in; and to Kathie-Jo Arnoff, Stephanie Gould, and Jeff Adams, for their watchful eyes and discerning questions, comments, and suggestions. These professionals and many others behind the scenes *all* contribute to the quality of this book.

A special thanks to Frank, the most terrific husband on earth, for putting up with horrendous schedules and frozen dinners, and for sacrificing many precious woodworking hours.

Trademarks

All terms mentioned in this book that are known to be trademarks or service marks have been appropriately capitalized. Que Corporation cannot attest to the accuracy of this information. Use of a term in this book should not be regarded as affecting the validity of any trademark or service mark.

Contents at a Glance

Enhancing Documents

Integrate & Communicate

Appendixes

Contents

6 Enhancing the Appearance of a Document   87

7 Working with Tables, Columns, and Inserted Objects   115

8 Adding Headers, Footers, Footnotes, and Bookmarks to a Document   131

9 Checking Your Document 149

III Spreadsheets and Charting 167

10 Creating, Saving, and Printing a Spreadsheet 169

11 Working with Formulas and Functions   205

12 Enhancing the Appearance of a Spreadsheet   219

IV Databases   297

16 Creating and Saving a Database File   299

17 Creating and Editing a Database Form   315

21 Retrieving Database Information   401

22 Creating a Database Report   421

Introduction

In a world where personal computer software is becoming increasingly complex and sophisticated, Microsoft Works for Windows 3.0 is a breath of fresh air. Not only is Works easy to use, but it combines four of the most popular types of software—word processing, spreadsheet, database, and communications—into one package.

The word processor allows you to create any type of text document, from a simple interoffice memo or letter to a proposal or other document complete with a title page, footnotes, and automatic page numbers. The spreadsheet lets you create financial reports for your business, prepare forecasts or budgets, and compute complex scientific, statistical, or mathematical calculations. The database helps you keep track of important information about clients, employees, products, inventories, or any other data that lends itself to a list format. The communications tool gives you contact with the outside world so that you can send, receive, and share information with other computer users and computer information services.

In addition to the four basic tools, Works includes four additional tools that help you create truly professional looking documents. *Microsoft Draw* is a drawing package you can use to create your own illustrations. If you prefer to use prepared art, you can choose an illustration from the *ClipArt* gallery to include in your documents. With *WordArt*, you can jazz up a document by including fancy, "stylized" text that bends, curves, or conforms to a particular shape, and *Note-It* lets you annotate documents with eye-catching icons, and when you click the icon, a note or comment appears.

If all this isn't enough, WorksWizards make it easy for you to accomplish more challenging tasks such as compiling a database of names and addresses, and creating form letters or mailing labels. Just by answering a few simple questions, the WorksWizards do the job for you.

Who Should Use This Book?

If you have ever tried to learn a computer program using a software manual, you know how frustrating it can be. Often software manuals are full of every detail about a computer program but are organized in such a way that they are virtually useless to the reader. Until you've learned a program, a manual that's organized alphabetically by command name is of little value to you. On the other end of the spectrum are manuals that seem to leave out the important details and give just enough information to get into trouble.

Using Microsoft Works 3 for Windows is for anyone who wants to learn how to use Works in a practical way. This book leads you through the basic steps involved in creating documents, spreadsheets, and databases and then builds on that foundation by teaching you more sophisticated features. You then learn how to use the extra tools Works provides such as Microsoft Draw, WordArt, ClipArt, and Note-It. You discover how to put pieces from various tools together and integrate them into a single document. Finally, you learn how to connect to other computers to read and gather information you can use in the Works documents you create.

How To Use This Book

You can read selected chapters in *Using Microsoft Works 3 for Windows*, or you can work through the book from beginning to end. This book opens with an introduction to the four components of Works and the basic steps for getting started with the program. It then leads you through beginning and advanced chapters for the word processing, spreadsheet, and database. Next you learn how to use Microsoft Draw, WordArt, ClipArt, and Note-It, and the communications tool.

Following is a brief look at the contents of each chapter in *Using Microsoft Works 3 for Windows*:

Chapter 1, "Introducing Works for Windows," describes the four basic Works tools as well as the Works accessories: Microsoft Draw, WordArt, ClipArt, and Note-It. This chapter also describes how you can integrate information from any of the four Works tools into a single document.

Chapter 2, "Getting Started with Works for Windows," tells you how to start and exit the program. You also get a tour of the basic Works window, instructions for using the mouse, keyboard, dialog boxes, and toolbars. In addition, you learn how to get help when you need it.

In Chapter 3, "Working with Files, Templates, and WorksWizards," you discover how to create, save, copy, and retrieve files and how to use AutoStart templates and WorksWizards to help you create documents. You also learn how to automatically open files that you use regularly when you start Windows.

Chapter 4, "Creating, Saving, and Printing a Word Processing Document," introduces you to the basic skills required to create a word processor document, move around in the document, correct minor errors, and then save and print the document once it's complete.

Chapter 5, "Editing a Document," teaches you how to select and change text by inserting, deleting, and overtyping. You also learn to move and copy text and undo changes that you make.

In Chapter 6, "Enhancing the Appearance of a Document," you learn all the tricks for making a document more attractive and readable, including changing the style and font of text, changing the alignment of paragraphs, indenting paragraphs and setting tab stops, and changing the line spacing in a document. You also learn about inserting page breaks in a document.

Chapter 7, "Working with Tables, Columns, and Inserted Objects," shows you how to create tables using tab stops and format a document for multiple columns of text. You also learn how to move, size, and wrap text around inserted objects in a document.

Chapter 8, "Adding Headers, Footers, Footnotes, and Bookmarks to a Document," describes how to add repetitive text at the top and bottom of each page. You also learn how to cite references or add a comment to a document using footnotes and how to find your place in a document using a bookmark.

In Chapter 9, "Checking Your Document," you learn how to change your view of a document by zooming in and out, wrapping text within a window, viewing hidden characters, and turning the toolbar and ruler on and off. You also learn how to search for text, replace text, how to check your document for spelling errors, and how to use the thesaurus.

Chapter 10, "Creating, Saving, and Printing a Spreadsheet," introduces you to the basic steps for creating a spreadsheet file, moving around in the worksheet, and entering text and numbers in the cells. You also learn how to make changes to spreadsheet entries, enter simple formulas, save, and print a spreadsheet.

Chapter 11, "Working with Formulas and Functions," examines relative and absolute cell addressing, creating formulas using functions, and naming ranges of cells. You also learn the effects of moving, copying, and deleting formulas.

Chapter 12, "Enhancing the Appearance of a Spreadsheet," describes how to make a spreadsheet more attractive by applying number formats, changing alignment of entries, choosing a font, size, color, and style for entries, and adjusting row height. You also learn how to add borders and patterns to cells. Finally, you see how to add repetitive text at the top and bottom of spreadsheet pages.

In Chapter 13, "Searching, Viewing, and Sorting a Spreadsheet," you discover how to find specific information in a spreadsheet and sort data in different ways. You also learn different viewing options, including zooming in and out, hiding rows or columns, freezing row and column headings, and displaying formulas in a spreadsheet rather than spreadsheet values.

Chapter 14, "Creating Charts," teaches you how to generate charts from spreadsheet data. You learn about the basic elements of a chart, and you learn how to create different chart types (for example, pie, bar, and XY). You also learn how to save, name, and recall a chart, and how to print a chart.

Chapter 15, "Editing and Enhancing a Chart," describes how to change the data plotted in a chart and how to enhance a chart with features such as titles, borders, gridlines, droplines, legends, data markers, colors, and patterns.

Chapter 16, "Creating and Saving a Database File," introduces you to databases and database terminology. You learn basic skills for creating and saving a database file, using and customizing the Database toolbar, and switching between database views.

In Chapter 17, "Creating and Editing a Database Form," describes how to lay out a database form and create data entry fields.

Chapter 18, "Enhancing a Database Form," shows you how to spruce up your database forms with labels, fonts, rectangles, borders, colors, shading, drawings, pictures, Note-Its, and WordArt.

In Chapter 19, "Entering and Editing Data," you learn how to type data and save records. In addition, you learn to copy and move information and hide records.

Chapter 20, "Expanding Your Database Skills," teaches you how to sort and print records, use dates, times, math formulas and functions, protect your data, and format data in fields.

Chapter 21, "Retrieving Database Information," describes how to retrieve information from a database using specific criteria.

Chapter 22, "Creating a Database Report," tells you how to print database information in neatly formatted lists.

Chapter 23, "Customizing a Report," illustrates how to produce reports that require customized formatting and data selection and to print reports for use with other applications.

Chapter 24, "Using Microsoft Draw and ClipArt," introduces you to creating your own drawings by using Microsoft Draw or including prepared art in your files by choosing a file from the ClipArt gallery.

Chapter 25, "Using WordArt and Note-It," shows you how to create stylized text for your documents by choosing a unique font for your text, then bending, shaping, or curving it, and adding other effects like borders, color, and patterns. You also learn about Note-It, a tool that lets you add distinctive notes and annotations to your documents.

Chapter 26, "Using the Works Tools Together," teaches you how to copy information from one tool to another. You also learn how to *link* information, which causes data in one location to be updated automatically when the source data is changed.

Chapter 27, "Printing Form Letters, Envelopes, and Mailing Labels," describes how to merge database and word processor files to create and print form letters, mailing labels, and envelopes.

Chapter 28, "Communicating with Other Computers," first examines communications terms and then describes how to specify all the required settings to establish a communications session. You learn how to save the settings in a file so you can use them again later. Also in this chapter are instructions for sending and receiving text and files.

Appendix A, "Installing Microsoft Works for Windows," describes how to install Works on a hard disk computer system.

Appendix B, "Works for Windows Functions," lists all of the functions included in Works, describes the arguments, and provides an example of each.

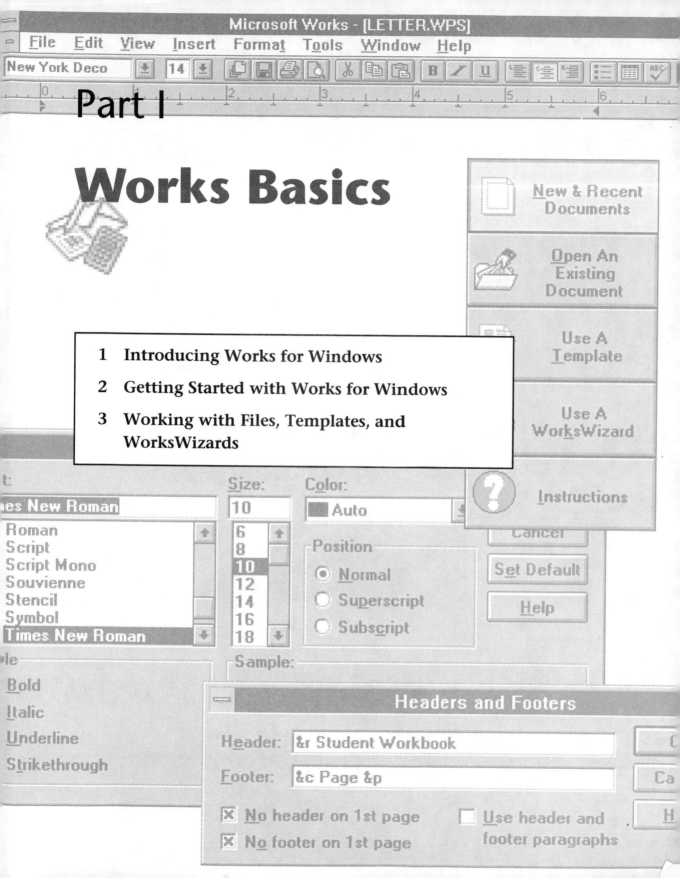

Part I

Works Basics

1   Introducing Works for Windows

2   Getting Started with Works for Windows

3   Working with Files, Templates, and
    WorksWizards

Chapter 1

Introducing Works
for Windows

If you have already purchased Works for Windows, you know its greatest advantage: it contains four software packages in one. The four components, or *tools*, are a *word processor* with a drawing package, a *spreadsheet* with a charting package, a *database*, and a *communications package*. Each component is designed to help you create, present, illustrate, organize, sort, report on, and print your data in the ways that are most important to you. Works for Windows is referred to as an *integrated* software program because all four tools are designed to work together.

Integrated software programs offer two distinct advantages over stand-alone programs. First, they offer *consistency*, enabling you to use the same methods from tool to tool for performing basic tasks, such as saving a file or printing. Second, integrated programs also allow you to share data effortlessly among the tools. For example, you can easily include a spreadsheet or chart in a word processing document. Another benefit of Works for Windows (not necessarily true of other integrated programs) is that, because it is a Windows program, you can work with multiple documents on-screen at the same time.

The Word Processor

A word processor is a tool you use to create documents that primarily contain text. You can use a word processor to create a letter, memo, report, legal document, proposal, article, or book. The greatest advantage to using a word processor is your ability to change what you have written before you print. If you make an error, you can erase and retype it; if you decide to rearrange paragraphs, you can move or copy them easily.

In this chapter, you learn about the following:

- Works tools: the word processor, spreadsheet, database, and communications

- Accessories: Microsoft Draw, ClipArt, and WordArt

- Timesavers: WorksWizards and AutoStart templates

- Integration of Works tools

Using a word processor, you are in complete control of how your document looks. You can choose from a wide variety of character styles and sizes and add features like bold, underline, or italic. You can set margins and tabs anywhere you like, adjust line spacing, specify text alignment, and alter the page size. Other sophisticated features in the word processor allow you to insert footnotes in a document, add repetitive text at the top and bottom of each page, check your spelling, replace a word with a synonym, and search the document for a word or phrase and replace it with other text.

A sample word processing document is shown in figure 1.1. The logo was created by using a clip art illustration, described later in this chapter. In Part II, "Word Processing," you learn how to work with the word processor and in Part V, "Enhancing Documents," you learn how to create drawings by using Microsoft Draw.

Fig. 1.1
A word processing document with a clip art logo.

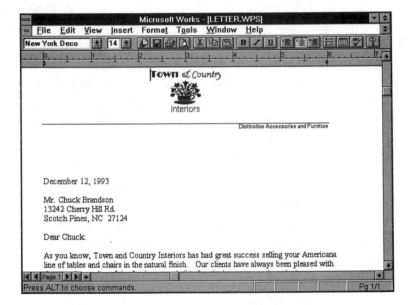

The Spreadsheet

A spreadsheet is like an electronic version of a paper worksheet that performs numeric calculations automatically. Spreadsheets are generally used to calculate financial data, although they can also be used to calculate and analyze mathematical and scientific data as well. Spreadsheets are most commonly used for tasks such as budgets, balance sheets, income statements, and sales forecasts. An example is shown in figure 1.2.

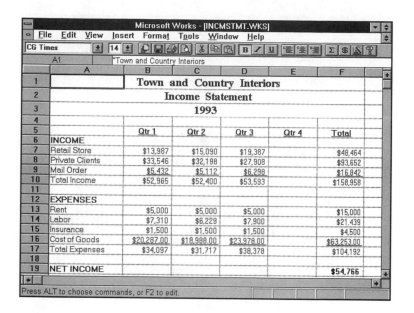

Fig. 1.2
A sample
spreadsheet.

Works Basics

A spreadsheet is arranged in rows and columns, just like a paper worksheet. In each *cell* (the intersection of a row and column), you enter text, numbers, or formulas. Text describes the data in each row or column, numbers represent the raw data, and formulas perform the calculations you specify. When you change a number in a formula, the spreadsheet automatically recalculates the correct result. You can create your own formulas, or you can use special formulas called *functions*. Functions are designed to perform a specific type of calculation, such as computing the monthly payment amount for a loan.

Like a word processing document, the electronic spreadsheet's advantage over its paper counterpart is that it allows you to change and rearrange data easily and all the calculations are done for you automatically. You can also enhance a worksheet by adding bold, underline, or italic to selected data, or by changing the size and style of the characters you use. Before printing, add a title or file name that appears at the top or bottom of each page and add page numbers that appear at the bottom of each page.

Spreadsheet information can be difficult to interpret sometimes without the aid of a graph or chart, so the spreadsheet in Works for Windows lets you create a chart based on the data in a worksheet. You can choose from several chart styles, including variations of bar, line, and pie charts. Once you create a chart, you can incorporate it into the spreadsheet or into a word processing document. A sample chart appears in figure 1.3. Chapters 10 through 15 discuss how to create spreadsheets and charts.

Fig. 1.3
A sample chart
representing
data from a
spreadsheet.

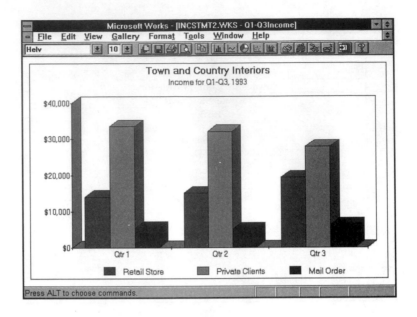

Fig. 1.3
A sample chart
representing
data from a
spreadsheet.

The Database

A database is nothing more than a collection of related information. You may think that you have never used a database, but you probably have. The telephone book—a common item that many people use every day—is an example of a database of names, addresses, and phone numbers. You can use the database in Works for Windows to create a database of client's or supplier's names, addresses, and phone numbers. Other examples of databases include a product list that contains item numbers, descriptions and prices, or an inventory list that contains items and quantities.

In Works for Windows, you can display a database in *List* view or *Form* view. In List view, all the items in the database are displayed at once (see fig. 1.4). In Form view, each record in the database is displayed individually in an appealing format that's easy to work with (see fig. 1.5).

Databases are not only handy for cataloging information, they can also be sorted by category and queried for specific information. For instance, records in a database are often entered at random, but you can put the records in alphabetic order by sorting the database. Or, if your database includes your clients' receivables, you can query the database to display all accounts that are 90 days past due.

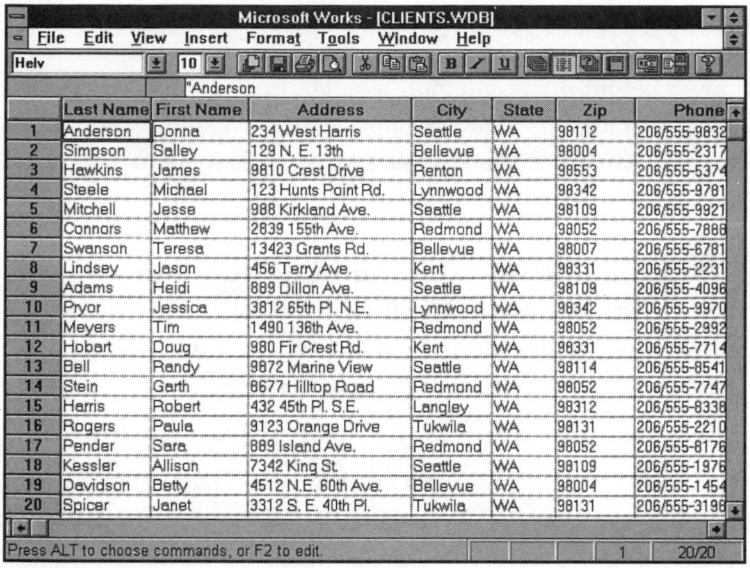

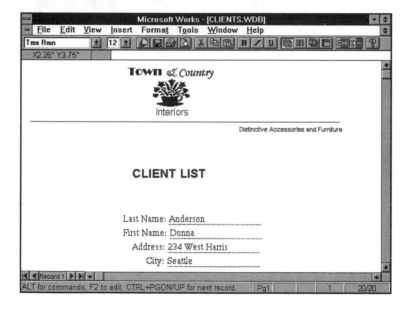

Fig. 1.4
A database
displayed in List
view.

Fig. 1.5
Record one of
a database is
displayed in
Form view with
a ClipArt Logo.

Databases often contain a great deal of information, whether it's about clients, products, or inventory. Works allows you to print different types of database reports so that you have the information you need at your fingertips. You can select the data you want to include in a report, summarize columns of figures, and give the report a polished appearance by adding a title and other special formatting. You learn how to create a database and work with database reports in Chapters 16 through 23.

Communications

As computers become more and more a part of everyday life, the ability to communicate from one computer to another becomes more important. With a modem and communications software on your computer, you can use your personal computer to log on to your computer at the office, read your electronic mail, and send and receive files. Communications software also enables you to dial up to an information service such as CompuServe and have a wealth of information at your fingertips—from current stock quotes to travel and shopping services. The communications software in Works for Windows provides the capability to do all of these tasks.

You can incorporate any of the information you receive from other computers into your Works for Windows documents. For instance, you may want to collect a history of stock prices from an information service, copy the data into a spreadsheet, and create a chart that depicts the stock's performance over the previous year. Chapter 28, "Communicating with Other Computers," teaches you how to use the Communications tool in Works.

Integration

Because Works for Windows is an integrated product, you can easily move or copy information from one tool to another. For example, you can include text from a word processor document in a spreadsheet; or you can insert a spreadsheet table or a chart in a letter or report. Through a process called *linking*, information that you include in one document is automatically updated when the information in another document is changed.

The integration feature of Works also allows you to merge information from a database with a word processing document. For example, suppose that you want to send collection letters to all of your clients whose accounts are 90 days past due. By including the proper code in your collection letter, Works can automatically insert each client's name, address, and the dollar amount due in individual letters. The merge feature between the word processor and database also allows you to print mail labels or envelopes for each letter. In Chapters 26 and 27, you learn how to integrate information from various Works tools into a single document.

Works for Windows Accessories and Other Timesavers

Most documents have more visual appeal when they include illustrations. To help you enhance your word processor documents and database forms, Works provides four accessories:

- *Microsoft Draw* is a special drawing tool that lets you create your own color drawings. Using Draw, you can create illustrations, then insert them easily into your word processor files or database forms.

- *ClipArt* is a collection of prepared drawings included in Works for Windows. The collection includes illustrations across a wide variety of categories—from sports to animals to business. If you don't want to create your own drawing by using Microsoft Draw, you may want to include a prepared clip art drawing in your document (refer to fig. 1.1).

- *WordArt* lets you dress up your documents with stylized text. Choose from a variety of font styles and sizes, then curve, slant, bend, or rotate the text and add shadows, borders, and shading. Use WordArt to create a professional-quality logo for your letterhead or an eye-catching banner for your monthly newsletter.

- *Note-It* provides a distinctive and unique way for you to annotate your documents. An *icon* (a picture of a notepad, envelope, file folder, or other item) appears in your document indicating the location of a note. Double-click the icon to display the contents of the note, then click anywhere in the document to close the note.

If you have never used Works for Windows and you're in a hurry to complete a task, you will appreciate WorksWizards and AutoStart templates.

- *WorksWizards* make it easy to complete a task, such as creating an address book, a home inventory log, or a form letter. You answer some simple on-screen questions related to the task you want to accomplish, then Works takes off and completes the task for you.

- *AutoStart templates* are preformatted documents such as a fax cover sheet, a purchase order, or a check register. When you choose a template, Works opens a new document that already contains text and placeholders. After making the appropriate changes, you give the document a unique name and save the file.

From Here...

■ Chapter 2, "Getting Started with Works for Windows," discusses how to start and exit Works; how to use the mouse, keyboard, dialog boxes, menus, and toolbars; and how to get help when you need it.

■ Chapter 3, "Working with Files, Templates, and WorksWizards," describes how to create, save, copy, and retrieve files, and how to use AutoStart templates and WorksWizards to help you create documents. You also learn how to automatically open files that you use regularly when you start Works.

Chapter 2

Getting Started with Works for Windows

Before you begin using the individual tools in Works for Windows, you need to learn the basics of using the program. To make the program as easy to use as possible, Microsoft provides consistency from tool to tool. For example, menus, commands, dialog boxes, and toolbars are elements that appear in each of the tool windows. Although the choices among each of these elements vary, the method for working with them is the same from tool to tool. The goal of this chapter is to teach you about all the elements that are consistent from tool to tool so that you can interact comfortably with *any* of the tools in Works.

Using the Mouse

Works for Windows is designed to be used with a mouse. If your computer is not equipped with a mouse, you can use the keyboard to accomplish every action or command you might initiate using a mouse, but you cannot access the toolbars.

The mouse is indicated on your screen by a mouse pointer that changes shape depending on the location of the mouse (see Table 2.1). In a word processor, communications, or database form document, the mouse pointer is an I-beam. In a spreadsheet or database list document, the mouse pointer is a cross. In all of the Works tools, the mouse pointer changes to the shape of an arrow when you point to the toolbar, menu bar, or scroll bars. The arrow tracks your movement of the mouse on the mouse pad.

In this chapter, you learn how to:

- Start and close Works

- Work with the mouse and the keyboard

- Work with menus, commands, dialog boxes, and toolbars

- Arrange multiple document windows

- Get help when you need it

Table 2.1 Mouse Point Shapes	
Shape	**Description**
▷	The mouse pointer is an arrow when you point to a toolbar, menu, scroll bar, or anywhere in a database form.
I	The mouse pointer is an I-beam in a word processor document.
✚	The mouse pointer is a cross in a spreadsheet or database list document.

In general, you use the mouse to move, resize, or otherwise manipulate document windows or the Works window, and to select menu commands. Table 2.2 lists the terms used to describe mouse techniques.

Table 2.2 Mouse Techniques	
Technique	**Description**
Point	Move the mouse pointer to a specific location on-screen.
Click	Press and release the left mouse button once.
Double-click	Press and release the left mouse button twice quickly.
Click and drag	Point to an object on the screen, press and hold the left mouse button, then move the mouse to a new location before releasing the mouse button.

Unless otherwise noted, the left mouse button is used almost exclusively in Works; middle and right mouse buttons are not implemented. When using the mouse in Works, most actions are as simple as "point and click." To make an inactive window active, for example, you simply point anywhere in the window and click.

Starting Works for Windows

Works for Windows must be installed on your computer before you can start the program. If you have not yet installed Works, refer to Appendix A, "Installing Microsoft Works for Windows." During the installation process, the Works for Windows files are copied on to your computer's hard drive in the

C:\MSWORKS directory (or any other directory that you specify). Also at that time, a startup icon is added to the Microsoft Works for Windows program group in the Windows program manager (see fig. 2.1).

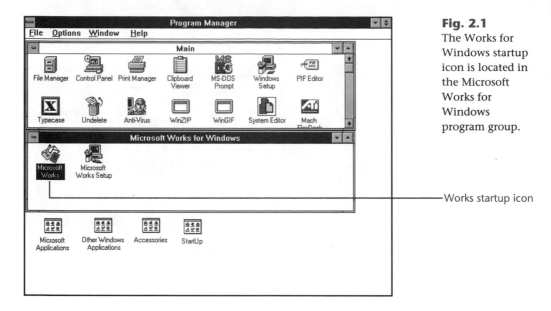

Fig. 2.1
The Works for Windows startup icon is located in the Microsoft Works for Windows program group.

Works startup icon

The first time you start Works for Windows, a welcome window appears asking if you want to take a guided tour of Works or start the Works program. You also are given the option of skipping the welcome screen the next time you start the program.

To start Works for Windows, follow these steps:

1. Turn your computer on and start Windows. The Windows Program Manager is displayed on-screen. If the Microsoft Works for Windows group window is closed, double-click the left mouse button on the Microsoft Works for Windows icon to open the window.

2. In the Microsoft Works for Windows program group, double-click the left mouse button on the Microsoft Works icon. The Welcome to Microsoft Works window is displayed.

3. To start Works now, click the Start Works Now button or press **W**. To bypass the Welcome box the next time you start Works, click the left mouse button on the Skip Welcome Screen button or press **S**. In either case, the Works Startup dialog box shown in figure 2.2 is displayed.

Fig. 2.2
The Works Startup
Dialog Box

Command buttons

Tool buttons

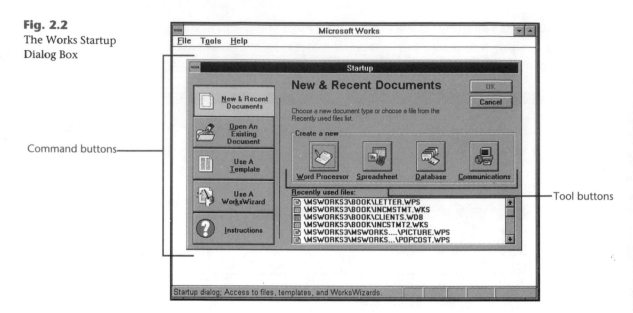

The Startup dialog box is a central element in Works; you use it frequently to start new documents, open existing ones, and to access templates and WorksWizards. The options on the left side of the window let you choose a task. When the Startup window is displayed, the first button, **N**ew & Recent Documents, is highlighted, indicating that you can open a Works tool and create a new document by clicking on the **W**ord Processor, **S**preadsheet, **D**atabase, or Communications tool buttons.

When you click the **O**pen an Existing Document option, Works displays a dialog box from which you can choose a file to open. To use a Works template file, choose the Use A **T**emplate option, which displays a dialog box listing available templates. When you click the Use a Wor**k**sWizard option, Works displays a dialog box from which you choose a WorksWizard. (Refer to Chapter 3, "Working with Files, Templates, and WorksWizards," for more information about templates and WorksWizards.)

To move directly into the Works window without starting a Works tool or a new document, click the Cancel button in the upper right corner of the window (see fig. 2.3). To recall the Startup dialog box at any time, click the File menu, then click the Create New File option.

Troubleshooting

I can't find the Microsoft Word for Windows group in my Program Manager.

If you can't find the Microsoft Works for Windows group in your Program Manager, the installation may not have been completed successfully. Try reinstalling the program and watch your screen to see that the installation is completed successfully. The Microsoft Works for Windows group and the Microsoft Works icon are set up automatically by the installation program.

Learning About the Standard Works Window

The Works window shown in figure 2.3 contains several standard window elements: a title bar, menu bar, status bar, control menu box, and maximize and minimize buttons. The title bar contains the name of the program, Microsoft Works. The menu bar contains only three menu names: **F**ile, **T**ools, and **H**elp.

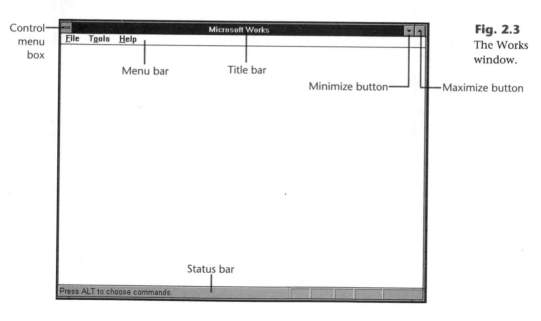

Fig. 2.3
The Works window.

About Document Windows

When you start one of the tools in Works (the word processor, spreadsheet, database, or communications), Works opens a separate *document* window inside of the initial Works window (refer to fig. 2.3). The document window contains its own title bar, control menu box, maximize and minimize buttons, and scroll bars. The title bar for the document window reflects the name of the tool; for example, Word1 appears in the title bar of the word processor document window (see fig. 2.4). Notice also that the menu bar changes to reflect the tool you are using, and a toolbar now appears just beneath the menu bar.

Fig. 2.4

A word processor document window appears inside of the Works window.

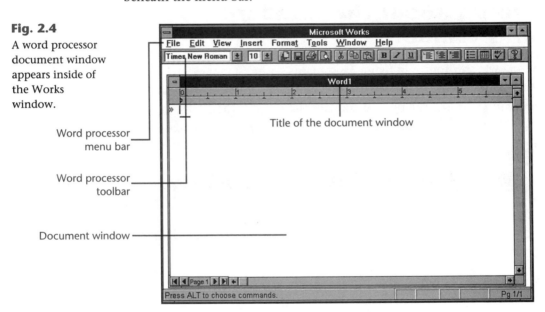

Initially, the document window is slightly smaller than the Works window. When you maximize the document window by clicking its maximize button, the two windows blend together and share a title bar (see fig. 2.5). Notice that Microsoft Works - [Word1] now appears in the title bar. The restore button for the document window appears at the far right end of the menu bar. More information on minimizing windows is contained in the section "Arranging Multiple Document Windows" later in this chapter.

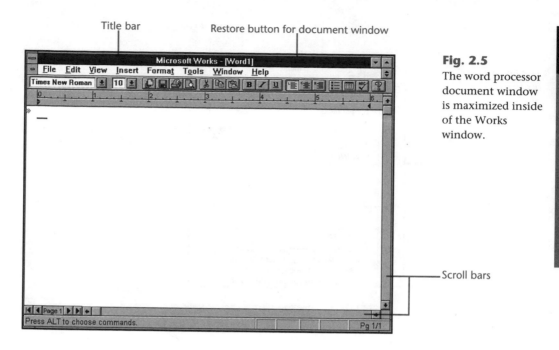

I

Works Basics

Fig. 2.5
The word processor
document window
is maximized inside
of the Works
window.

Moving Around in a Document Window

Regardless of the tool you are using, all Works document windows contain
vertical and horizontal scroll bars (refer to fig. 2.5). When a document is too
long to be displayed completely in a window, use the vertical scroll bar to
move the document up and down. When a document is too wide to be displayed in a window, use the horizontal scroll bar to move the document from
side to side. The Word Processor and Database document windows contain
buttons on the horizontal scroll bar that allow you to move to a specific page
(word processor) or record (database) in the file. See Chapters 4 and 15 for
more information about moving around in a window.

Selecting Menus and Commands

Select a command when you're ready to tell Works what you want to do
next. Commands are grouped by categories and are listed on menus. Commands that pertain to files appear on the File menu, and so on (see fig. 2.6).
To select a command, click the menu name, and then click the command
name on the menu.

Fig. 2.6
The File Menu
for the word
processor.

Commands

Selection
character

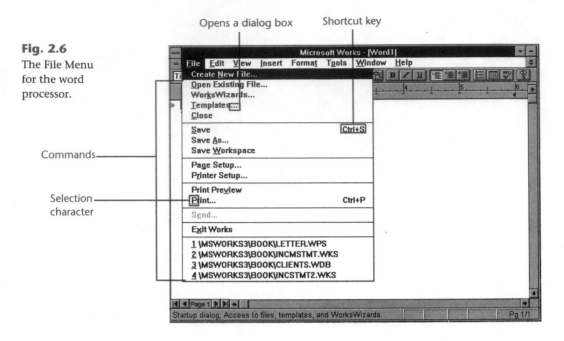

Opens a dialog box   Shortcut key

Some menu commands take immediate action, some toggle on and off, some open dialog boxes, and some appear grayed on the menu. When a toggle command is turned on, or *selected*, a check mark appears to the left of the command name on the menu. When a command opens a dialog box, the command name is followed by an ellipsis on the menu. When a command doesn't apply to the task you are performing at the time, the command is shaded on the menu and you cannot select it.

The underlined letter in each menu name and menu command is known as the selection letter, or hot key. If you are using the keyboard, you open a menu by pressing Alt plus the selection letter in the menu name. To open the File menu, for example, press Alt+F. To select a command after a menu is open, simply type the selection letter in the command name.

Some menu commands have keyboard shortcuts assigned to them. Keyboard shortcuts allow you to bypass the menu command, saving you the time of opening the menu and selecting the command. Shortcut keys appear to the right of the command name on the menu. For example, the keyboard short-cut for the Move command on the File menu is F7; you can select the Move command just by pressing F7.

Troubleshooting

I keep trying to select a menu command, and nothing happens.

The menu command might be grayed, meaning it isn't available at this time. Make sure you have completed the command (such as entering information in a database form) you are currently using before trying to select another. Or, check Help to see if you need to select text before using the command you are selecting.

When I press Alt plus a selection letter (hot key) to select a command, Works beeps and doesn't carry out the command.

To select a command once a menu is already open, just type the selection letter (hot key); don't press Alt again.

Working with Dialog Boxes

A dialog box is a special window that appears on the screen when you select any menu command that is followed by an ellipsis (...). In the dialog box, you provide more information about the command you have chosen by typing an entry, making a selection, or specifying an option. The dialog box is displayed on top of the window in which you are working and remains on-screen until you close it.

Learning Dialog Box Elements

Because dialog boxes often contain many different choices, they are sometimes divided into named sections containing different elements. The most common dialog box elements are described next.

- *Command buttons* such as OK and Cancel appear in every dialog box. To activate a command, click the button. Command buttons that are followed by an ellipsis open another dialog box.

- *List boxes* contain a list of items from which to choose. You can select only one item in a list box.

- *Check boxes* are options that toggle on and off. To select an option, click the check box and an X will appear in the box; to cancel an option, click the check box to remove the X. When multiple check boxes appear in a dialog box, you can select more than one.

■ *Drop-down lists* are similar to list boxes, but the list is hidden until you reveal it. To reveal the list, click the downward-pointing arrow at the right end of the box. Select one list item by clicking it. The list closes automatically.

■ *The Save As dialog box* shown in figure 2.7 illustrates command buttons as well as check boxes, drop-down boxes, and list boxes. (In fig. 2.7 the Save File as Type drop-down box is open.)

Fig. 2.7
Use Command buttons, check boxes, list boxes, and drop-down lists to make your selections in a dialog box.

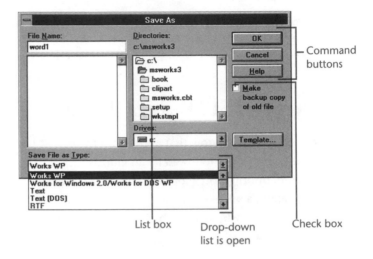

■ *Text boxes* allow you to enter specific information, such as a file name. Click the box, then type the information you are asked to supply.

■ *Option buttons* represent either/or choices; you can choose only one option button when multiple option buttons are displayed. Clicking one cancels the option that is currently selected.

■ *The Print dialog box* shown in figure 2.8 illustrates text boxes and option buttons.

Fig. 2.8
Use option buttons and text boxes to specify your selections in a dialog box.

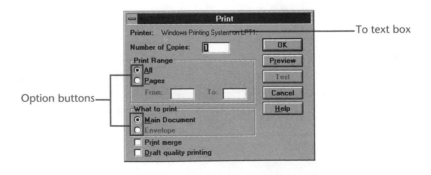

Making Selections in Dialog Boxes

Changing dialog box settings is as easy as clicking the option or command button, check box, or list item you want to select. For a text box, click in the box, and then type the appropriate text. A dotted rectangle, a highlight, or both indicate the option in the dialog box that is currently selected.

If you are using the keyboard, you can move forward through the sections of a dialog box by pressing the Tab key. Each time you press Tab, Works highlights an item in the current section of the dialog box. To highlight a different item within a section, use the up- and down-arrow keys. You can also press Shift+Tab to move backward through the sections of a dialog box.

Almost all dialog boxes have Cancel, OK, and Help buttons. Select OK to accept and carry out the changes you make and close the dialog box. Click Cancel to cancel all changes you made in the dialog box and use the previous settings. If you select a dialog box by mistake, close it without making changes by selecting Cancel. Click the Help button when you want help specific to the choices in the dialog box. (For more information, see the section "Getting Help," later in this chapter.)

Working with Tabbed Dialog Boxes

A tabbed dialog box looks similar to a regular dialog box but contains tabs along the top, similar to the tabs you might find in an index or recipe box. Each tab represents a category of choices in the dialog box. Because some dialog boxes contain a wide variety of options, the choices are categorized to make them easier to find. An example of a tabbed dialog box is shown in figure 2.9. In this Paragraph dialog box, Quick Formats, Indents and Alignment, and Breaks and Spacing are the three tab categories.

To use a tabbed dialog box, click the tab you want to use to bring it to the foreground, and then choose options just like you would in any other dialog box. Click another tab to set more options, or click OK to close the dialog box. If you are using the keyboard, select a dialog box tab by pressing Alt plus the selection character (hot key) for the tab.

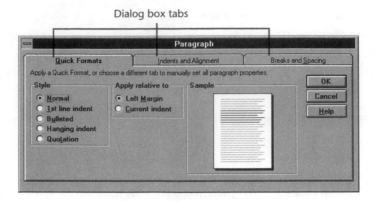

Dialog box tabs

Fig. 2.9
Tabs in a dialog
box represent
categories of
choices.

Troubleshooting

I want to select two option buttons but can't.

The selections that option buttons represent, such as the Style group under Quick
Formats in the Paragraph box, are usually in conflict with one another and, therefore,
only one can be selected at a time. For instance, in figure 2.8, you can't choose **A**ll
and **P**ages at the same time because one option prints every page, the other option
prints a selection of pages.

I want to select a shaded item in a dialog box but can't.

Just as menu commands are sometimes shaded when they don't apply to the task
you are performing, dialog box items sometimes are shaded when they don't apply
to the task you are performing. For instance, in figure 2.8, the Envelope option is
shaded because the document that was active when the Print command was selected
does not include information for printing envelopes.

Using Toolbars

A toolbar is a convenient feature that allows you to initiate an action quickly.
The toolbar contains *buttons*—small icons that represent menu commands.
For example, the third button shown on the toolbar is a printer. To begin
printing a file, you can click this button rather than selecting the Print command on the File menu.

Each Works tool uses a different toolbar with buttons that pertain to that
particular tool. The spreadsheet toolbar, for example, contains a button for
formatting numbers with a dollar sign. This feature would be meaningless in
the word processor window, so its toolbar contains different buttons that

pertain to text documents. Likewise, the database toolbar contains a button for creating database reports—a feature that has no meaning in either the word processor or spreadsheet tools—so the database toolbar contains buttons specific to database tasks. The toolbars for each of the four tools are shown in figure 2.10. The individual tools are identified and described in Chapters 4, 10, 16, and 27.

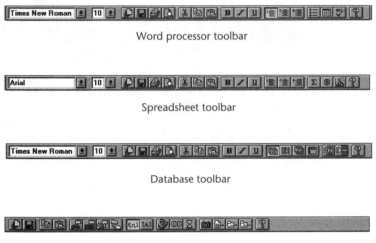

Word processor toolbar

Spreadsheet toolbar

Database toolbar

Communications toolbar

Fig. 2.10
The toolbars that appear in the word processor, spreadsheet, database, and communications windows.

Identifying Toolbar Buttons

Although the icons used on toolbar buttons are designed to reflect the commands they represent (such as a printer for the Print command), it would be difficult to remember what each toolbar button is for—especially if you've never used Works for Windows. When you're not sure which command a button represents, point to it with the mouse pointer but don't click the mouse. The name of the button is displayed just below the button and disappears when you move the mouse pointer (see fig. 2.11). Works for Windows calls this feature "Tool Tips." If you don't want to use tool tips, you can disable this feature by following the steps in the next section.

Customizing the Toolbars

The toolbars in Works contain buttons that represent the most commonly used commands; they do not include a button for *every* Works command. As you become more familiar with Works for Windows, you will discover the commands you use most often, and some of these commands will not be available on the standard toolbar. However, you can customize the toolbar for each of the Works tools. For example, if your work requires that you insert the current date or time in all your word processor documents, you might want to add the Insert Current Date or Insert Current Time buttons to your word processor toolbar. These buttons do not appear on the standard word processor toolbar but are available if you want to add them to your toolbar. You use the Customize Works Toolbar dialog box shown in figure 2.12 to add buttons to a toolbar.

Fig. 2.11
Works displays
Tool Tips when
you point to a
toolbar button
without clicking.

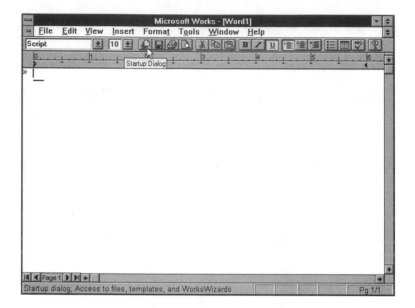

Fig. 2.12
You can add and
remove buttons
on the toolbar
with the Custom-
ize Works Toolbar
dialog box.

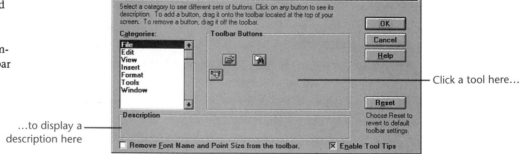

...to display a
description here

Click a tool here...

In the dialog box, you choose a category of buttons (Edit, Insert, View, and so on), and then choose the button you want to add to the toolbar. To display a button's function, click the button. The description appears in the Descrip-tion box.

To customize a toolbar, follow these steps:

1. Open the Works tool (Word Processor, Spreadsheet, Database, or Communications) for which you want to customize the toolbar.

2. From the Tools menu, choose the Customize Toolbar command. The Customize Works Toolbar dialog box appears (refer to fig. 2.12).

3. In the Categories box, choose a category from the list. The buttons displayed in the Toolbar Buttons area reflect the category you choose.

4. To see a description of a button, click the button once. The button's function is displayed in the Description box.

5. To add a button, click and drag the button from the dialog box to the toolbar, and then release the mouse button. You can place the button anywhere on the toolbar you choose. (To insert a button, drag it between two existing buttons, and then release the mouse button.)

6. To remove a button from the toolbar, click and drag the button from the toolbar into the Toolbar Buttons area of the dialog box.

7. Choose OK to accept the changes.

At the bottom of the Customize Works Toolbar dialog box are two check boxes. To remove the Font Name and Font Size buttons from a toolbar, click in the Remove Font Name And Point Size From The Toolbar check box to place an X in the box. To disable Tool Tips, click the Enable Tool Tips check box to remove the X.

Tip
To display the Customize Works Toolbar dialog box, double-click in any blank area of the toolbar.

Works Basics

Troubleshooting

I have added and removed many toolbar buttons and now I don't remember the standard buttons. How can I restore them?

In the Customize Works Toolbar dialog box, click on the Reset button, then click OK. When you restore the standard buttons, your customized toolbar is lost.

I would like to rearrange the buttons on my toolbar. Is there a way to do this?

Yes, choose the Customize Toolbar command on the Tools menu, which displays the Customize Works Toolbar dialog box. (You don't actually use the dialog box to rearrange buttons, but you must display it.) On the toolbar, drag the button you want to move to a new location, then release the mouse button. Works moves existing buttons aside and inserts the button you moved. Continue dragging other buttons to new locations to rearrange them. When you are finished rearranging buttons, click OK to close the Customize Works Toolbar dialog box.

Working with Multiple Document Windows

You already learned that a Works document window is displayed inside of the initial Works window. You can open up to eight files of any type at one time; each is displayed in a separate document window and the windows can be various sizes. However, only one document at a time can be active, indicated by the highlighted title bar. The menu and toolbar automatically reflect the active window.

Opening Several Document Windows at Once

Earlier in this chapter you were introduced to the Startup dialog box (refer to fig. 2.2). When Works is running, you use the Startup dialog box to start a new word processor, spreadsheet, database, or communications document. If you're already working on one document—for example, a database—you can create additional documents without closing the current one. When you create a new document, Works opens an additional document window on top of the window you are currently using and the new window becomes the active window. In figure 2.13, three document windows appear in the Works program window.

Fig. 2.13
Three separate document windows are open at once.

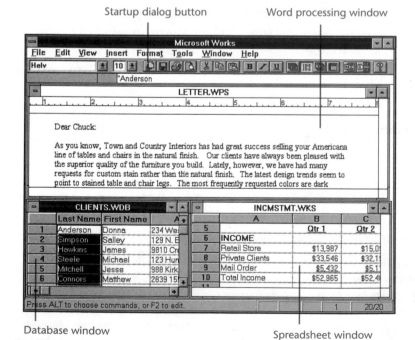

Startup dialog button   Word processing window

Database window   Spreadsheet window

To create a new document of any type when one is already open, follow these steps:

1. From the **F**ile menu, choose Create **N**ew File. The Startup dialog box is displayed.

2. Click the tool button for the type of document you want to create. Works opens a new document window on-screen.

Switching Among Document Windows

When several document windows are open at once, you can switch the active window simply by clicking another visible window. In figure 2.13, for example, the database window is active, but the title bars for all other open windows are visible so you could choose any window simply by clicking it. Depending on the arrangement of windows, however, sometimes the window you want isn't visible. When a window is completely obscured by other windows, you can restore the window by using the **W**indow menu. At the bottom of the Window menu, the names of all open documents are listed. Click a document name, or press the number next to the file you want. The window immediately becomes the active window and appears on top of all other open windows.

Arranging Multiple Document Windows

Your screen can become very cluttered when you have several documents open at once. Fortunately, Works gives you an easy way to arrange open documents. You can choose to *cascade* all open windows (see fig. 2.14), an arrangement that stacks the windows and leaves the title bar of each window visible. Or you can *tile* all open windows (see fig. 2.15). This arrangement varies depending on the number of document windows that are open at once. To choose an arrangement, select the **C**ascade or **T**ile command from the **W**indow menu.

You also can arrange open windows by resizing and moving them to new locations on-screen. To resize a window, click and drag any of the window borders. To resize in two dimensions at once and maintain the height-to-width proportions of the window, click and drag any of the window corners. To move a window, click and drag the title bar to a new location, then release the mouse button.

Tip

To instantly display the Startup dialog box, click the Startup Dialog box button on the toolbar

Tip

Another way to activate a lost window is by pressing Ctrl+F6, which activates the next open document window. Press Ctrl+F6 repeatedly until the document window you want is active, or press Shift+Ctrl+F6 to move backwards through open windows.

Works Basics

Fig. 2.14
All open document windows are cascaded.

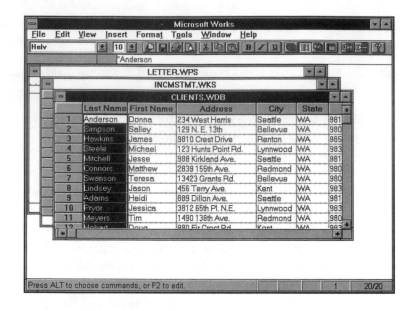

Another way to arrange open windows on-screen is to minimize them. Minimizing a window shrinks it to an icon but leaves the document open. Minimizing a window gets it out of your way but leaves it quickly accessible when you need it. In figure 2.16, the word processor window is active and the database, spreadsheet, and communications windows are minimized.

Fig. 2.15
All open document windows are tiled.

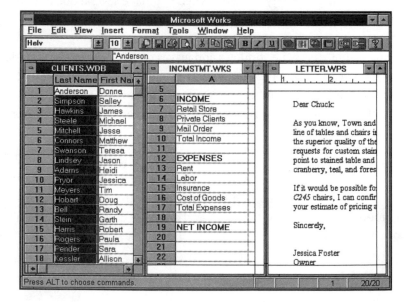

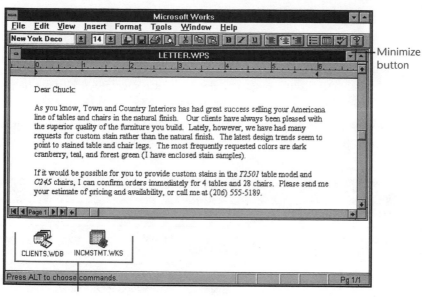

Fig. 2.16

Minimized document windows appear as icons along the bottom of the Works program window.

Icons for minimized document windows

To minimize a window, click the document window's minimize button. To make a minimized window active again, double-click the icon. The window is restored to its previous size and position on-screen.

> **Caution**
>
> Don't confuse the document window's minimize button with the Works program window's minimize button. (If you do, you will shrink the Works window instead of just the document window.) When a document window is maximized, its minimize button appears at the far right end of the menu bar.

Closing a Document Window

There are several ways to close a document window. First click the window to make sure the window is active. Then choose the **C**lose command on the **F**ile menu or double-click the document window's control menu box. (If you click only once rather than double-click, the Control menu appears, from which you choose the **C**lose command.) You can also press Ctrl+F4, the shortcut key, for closing a window.

Regardless of the method you choose, if you haven't saved recent changes to your file, a reminder message appears. Click Yes to save changes, No to abandon the changes, or Cancel to return to the document without saving changes.

Getting Help

When you first begin using Works or you're learning a new feature, there will be times when you wish you had the answer to a quick question right at your fingertips. With on-line help, you do. There are several ways to get help as you're working. One is to click the Help menu to reveal the list of help commands shown in Table 2.3. Each command brings up a separate help window.

Table 2.3 Help Menu Commands and Their Functions	
Help Command	**Displays**
(Overview)	An overview of the Works for Windows tool you were using when you opened the Help window.
Contents	A table of contents listing all help topics in the help file, categorized by Works for Windows tools.
Search for Help on...	A Search dialog box in which you can choose a specific topic on which you want help.
How to Use Help	Step-by-step instructions for using Help.
Basic Skills	Basic skills topics, such as getting started with Works, working with windows, working with documents, and so on.
C**ue** Cards	Step-by-step instructions for performing basic tasks in a separate Cue Cards window on your screen. Keep Cue Cards on your screen as long as you need them; close the Cue Cards window when you don't need them any more.
Tutorial	A tutorial, or on-line lesson, in which you get hands-on experience learning basic skills by working with practice documents.
About Microsoft Works	Works for Windows copyright and version information.

When you select the **C**ontents, **H**ow to Use Help, and **B**asic Skills commands, the Help window displays a list of help topics. The topics shown are first-level help topics—indicated by green underlined characters on-screen. To select a help topic, move your mouse pointer to the topic you want to view. The arrow pointer changes to a pointing hand. Click the topic. A list of second-level topics is displayed, also indicated by green underlined characters. Continue clicking the topics you want to view until a help information screen like the one shown in figure 2.17 is displayed.

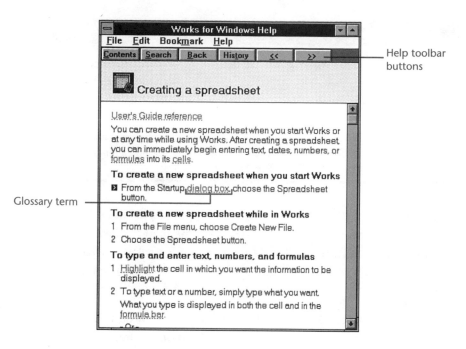

Fig. 2.17
A typical help topic
window.

Works Basics

Help toolbar
buttons

Glossary term

Help screens often include *glossary terms* that appear in green dotted-underlined characters. At any time you can click a glossary term to display a definition in a pop-up window. To dismiss the definition, click anywhere on the Help window or press any key on the keyboard.

Once you display a topic, you can use the toolbar buttons pointed out in figure 2.17 to navigate the Help files. You might also need to use the scroll bars or Page Up and Page Down keys to view all information on a topic. Table 2.4 lists the function of each of these buttons.

Table 2.4 Command buttons available in Help windows	
Command Button	**Use**
Contents	Displays the Works for Windows Help index.
Search	Displays a Search dialog box in which you can specify the topic you're looking for or choose from a list of keywords.
Back	Displays the previous help topic you viewed.

(continues)

Table 2.4 Continued

Command Button	Use
History	Displays up to the last 40 help topics you viewed in the current Works session.
<<	Lets you browse backwards through a series of related topics.
>>	Lets you browse forward through a series of related topics.

When you're looking for help on a specific help topic, it's often more efficient to use the **S**earch command on the Help menu or the **S**earch button in a Help information window. The Search command displays a separate Search window in which you can type any word or topic. To use Search, follow these steps:

1. Choose the **S**earch command on the Help window or, from any Help information window, click the Help button on the toolbar. Help displays a separate Search dialog box and the cursor is blinking in a text box in the upper half of the dialog box.

2. In the text box, type a word or phrase for which to search and press Enter, or click an item in the list shown. You can move quickly to an alphabetic section in the list by typing a letter of the alphabet. For instance, type **L** to move to the beginning of the topics that begin with L.

3. Click the Show Topics button. In the lower half of the dialog box, a list of subtopics appears.

4. Click a subtopic, then click the **G**o To button, or simply double-click the subtopic. Help displays the topic you choose.

Help windows stay open on-screen until you close them. If you want Help to be easily accessible, you can keep the Help window open while you work. To close a Help window, double-click the Help window's control menu box, or choose the Close command on the control menu.

Aside from the Help menu, there are many ways to get help in Works. One method of getting help is to press the F1 key. When you press F1 as you're working, Help displays the Help overview for the Works tool you are currently using. For example, when the active document is a database, pressing F1 displays the Database Overview help topic. If you want help on a specific menu command, you also can highlight the command name, and then press F1. Works automatically displays the correct help topic for the command. You can get help on specific dialog box options by clicking the Help button located in the dialog box. (Every dialog box in Works has a Help button.) A final way to get help is by clicking the Help button (a question mark), the final button on the standard toolbar in each of the Works tools. This button gives you access to Cue Cards, Help files, tutorials, and WorksWizards.

Exiting Works for Windows

When you're finished using Works, choose the Exit Works command on the File menu to close the program. If you still have open document files that have not yet been saved, Works displays a dialog box for each file asking if you want to save the changes. Click Yes to save the most recent changes, click No to abandon the most recent changes, or click Cancel to return to Works. When Works is closed, the Windows Program Manager returns to your screen.

Tip
To exit Works quickly, press Alt+F4. If open documents have not been saved, Works displays a reminder message asking if you want to save changes.

From Here...

In this chapter, you learned some basic skills to get you started using Works. Refer to the following chapters to learn how to work with files, and to get an introduction to each of the Works tools.

- Chapter 3, "Working with Files, Templates, and WorksWizards," shows you how to create, save, copy, and retrieve files, and how to use AutoStart templates and WorksWizards to help you create documents. You also learn about how to automatically open files that you use regularly when you start Windows.

- Chapter 10, "Creating, Saving, and Printing a Spreadsheet," introduces you to the basic steps for creating a spreadsheet file and entering text and numbers in the cells. You also learn how to make changes to spreadsheet entries, enter simple formulas, save, and print a spreadsheet.

Works Basics

■ Chapter 16, "Creating and Saving a Database File," introduces you to databases and database terminology. You learn how to start a new database file, how to use the database menus and toolbar, how to work with different views of the database, and how to name and save a database file.

■ Chapter 28, "Communicating with Other Computers," first examines communications terms, then describes how to specify all the required settings to establish a communications session and save the settings in a file. Also in this chapter are instructions for sending and receiving text and files.

Chapter 3

Working with Files, Templates, and WorksWizards

As you begin to use the tools in Works for Windows, you will create documents that you want to save and reuse, perhaps many times. There are several ways to create documents using Works: from "scratch," by using a template as a model, or by using a WorksWizard to create a document's custom framework for you. Whichever method you use, it's important to understand how Works handles files and how to save, rename, copy, and recall a file whenever necessary.

Working with Files

A file is a collection of information that is stored on your computer's hard disk or a diskette. As you use Works—regardless of the tool you use—you create, name, save, and copy files as well as open existing files.

Creating New Files

In Chapter 2, "Getting Started with Works for Windows," you are introduced to the Startup dialog box, which appears when you start the Works program. At this point, you know that you create a new Works file by clicking on one of the tool buttons in the Startup dialog box (see fig. 3.1). If you are already working on a document and want to create a new one, you access the Startup dialog box by choosing the Create **N**ew File command on the **F**ile menu or by clicking on the Startup Dialog button on the toolbar, which displays the Startup dialog box instantly.

In this chapter, you learn:

- How to create, save, duplicate, open, and close files

- How to create specialized documents using AutoStart templates

- How to use WorksWizards to accomplish specific tasks

Fig. 3.1
The Startup dialog
box.

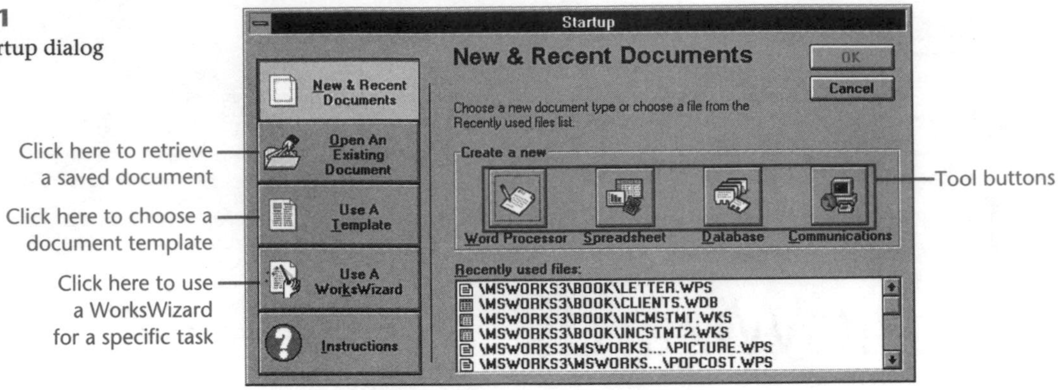

Click here to retrieve — a saved document

Click here to choose a — document template

Click here to use — a WorksWizard for a specific task

Tool buttons

Before you name and save a document, the title bar contains a temporary file name that reflects the tool you are using. For instance, when you create a new word processor document, it is called Word1 until you name and save the document. Subsequent new word processor documents that you create are called Word2, Word3, and so on. Spreadsheet documents are called Sheet1, Sheet2, Sheet3. New database and communications documents are called Data1 and Comm1 respectively where the number is incremented with each subsequent document you create. You rename a file when you save it, as described in the next section.

Naming and Saving Files

Every file has a file name that consists of two parts: a title that describes the contents of the file, and a file extension that identifies the *file type*. File titles can contain up to eight alphanumeric characters; file extensions can contain up to three characters. For example, BUDGET93.WKS is a file name for a 1993 budget spreadsheet file. Works uses the following file types for files created in each of its tools:

.WPS	For word processor files
.WKS	For spreadsheet files
.WDB	For database files
.WCM	For communications files

As you begin doing real work with the tools in Works, you will want to save the information you type. When you save a file, you assign it a permanent file name and choose other options such as the file type and the drive and directory where the file will be stored.

In all four of the Works tools, there are two commands for saving files: **S**ave and Save **A**s. Generally, you use the **S**ave command to save a file; you use the Save **A**s command only when you want to change how or where the file is saved. The Save As command displays the Save As dialog box shown in figure 3.2. The first time you save a file, you can choose either the **S**ave or Save **A**s command. In either case, the Save As dialog box is always displayed if the file has not yet been saved.

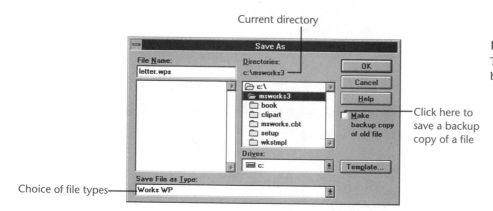

Current directory

Choice of file types

Click here to save a backup copy of a file

Fig. 3.2
The Save As dialog box.

In the **D**irectories box, notice that an open file folder icon appears to the left of the MSWORKS3 directory (your directory is MSWORKS unless you chose a different directory when you installed Works). Works automatically chooses this directory each time you save a file. If you want to save the file in a different directory, click on a directory name in the **D**irectories list. If you want to save the file on a different disk drive, choose a disk drive from the Dri**v**es list.

> **Note**
>
> If you are not familiar with using and creating directories, consult your Microsoft Windows documentation. To create or delete a directory, you must use the Windows File Manager.

In most cases, you will want to save your Works files with the default file type—that is, .WPS for word processor files, .WKS for spreadsheet files, .WDB for database files, and .WCM for communications files. However, if you will be using the file on another computer or in a different program, you might want to save a file using a different file type. The Save File as **T**ype drop-down list shows a variety of file types you can use to save your file. For example, you can save a word processor file as a WordPerfect for DOS or WordPerfect for Windows file. The choices vary depending on the Works tool you are using. If you save a file using the default Works file type, you don't need to type the file extension when you specify the file name; Works will do it for you automatically.

By checking the **M**ake backup copy check box, you can specify that Works save a backup copy of your file. When you make changes to a file and save it, the backup copy is a copy of the file as it was before you made changes. Backup files are saved under the same descriptive file name but have a B in place of the W in the file extension:

.BPS	For word processor files
.BKS	For spreadsheet files
.BDB	For database files
.BCM	For communications files

To save a Works file for the first time, follow these steps:

1. From the **F**ile menu, choose the **S**ave or Save **A**s command, or click the Save button (the 3-1/2 inch diskette) on the toolbar. The Save As dialog box shown in figure 3.2 is displayed. The file's temporary file name appears in the File **N**ame text box.

2. To save the file in a directory other than msworks, click a directory name in the **D**irectories box.

3. To save a file to a different disk drive, choose a drive from the Dri**v**es drop-down list.

4. To choose a different file type, select a type from the Save File as **T**ype drop-down list.

5. In the File **N**ame text box, enter a name for the file. (*Don't* type the file extension; Works will do it for you automatically.)

6. If you want to save a backup copy of the file, check the **M**ake backup copy check box.

7. Choose OK.

While you're working on a document, it's a good idea to save the file frequently—every ten minutes or so, especially when you're making extensive changes. If power to your computer is interrupted or if you have an equipment failure, the changes you made to the file since you last saved are lost.

To save a file that has already been saved, use the **S**ave command. Because you have already named the file, the file is automatically saved using its current name, location, and file type, so the Save As dialog box does not appear. If you want to save the file under a different name, file type, drive, or directory, choose the Save **A**s command rather than **S**ave to display the Save As dialog box again.

> **Note**
>
> When you save an already-saved file to a different drive, directory, or with a new file type or name, the previous file remains saved and unchanged in its original location and file format; the changes are saved only to the new name, drive, directory, or file type you specify.

Closing Files

After you save a file for the first time, the file continues to be displayed on-screen so you can continue working on it. The title bar now reflects the file name you specified when you saved the file. When you are finished working with a file and have saved the most recent changes, you remove the file from the window by choosing the **C**lose command on the **F**ile menu. When you close a file, other open files, if any, are still visible on-screen. When you close the last open file, the initial blank Works window is displayed.

If you forget to save a file before closing it, don't worry about losing your work. Works displays a dialog box asking if you want to save the file. Choose **Y**es to save the most recent changes, choose **N**o to abandon the changes, or choose Cancel to return to the document window without saving the file.

Retrieving Files

You can reopen a saved file at any time, whether you want to make changes to it or just review it. To open a saved Works file, click the Startup Dialog button on the toolbar, then click the **O**pen an Existing Document button to display the Open dialog box shown in figure 3.3. Or, choose the **O**pen Existing File command on the **F**ile menu. The Open dialog box is very similar to the Save As dialog box shown in figure 3.3.

Tip

It doesn't matter which tool you're using when you display the Open dialog box; you can open any type of file from the Open dialog box.

Works Basics

I

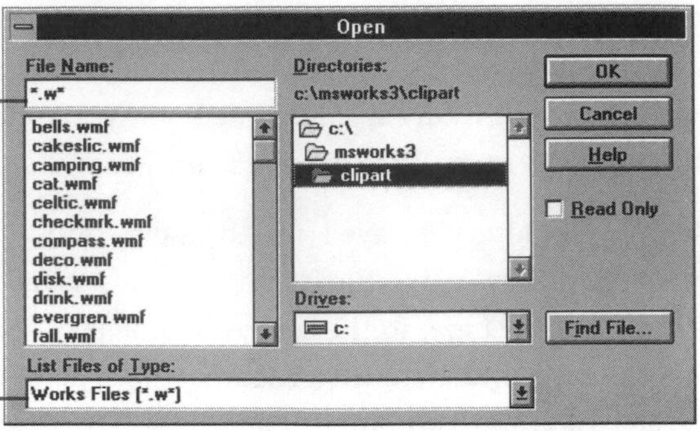

Fig. 3.3
The Open dialog
box.

Displays all files
whose extension ———
begins with W

Choice of file types to display ———

In the File **N**ame box, the entry *.w* appears. This entry determines which files are shown in the files list. The asterisks are *wild cards*, or placeholders, that represent any number of characters in a file name. Since all Works file extensions begin with w and end in two different letters, the entry *.w* allows for every Works file to be shown in the files list. If you wanted only database files to be listed, for example, you would change the *.w* entry to *.wdb. A quick way to specify the types of files you want to list is by choosing an option from the List Files of **T**ype drop-down list.

To open a saved Works file, follow these steps:

1. From the **F**ile menu, choose the **O**pen Existing File command. Or, click on the Startup Dialog button on the toolbar, then click the **O**pen an Existing Document button. The Open dialog box shown in figure 3.3 appears.

2. If desired, type a new file specification in the File **N**ame text box, or click a file type in the List Files of Type drop-down box. The list of files is updated to reflect your specification.

3. If the file you want to open is stored in a different directory or drive, click the correct directory and drive in the **D**irectories and Dri**v**es lists.

4. In the files list, click the name of the file you want to open and press Enter, or double-click the file name. The file is opened in the appropriate document window.

Note

To prevent you from changing two separate versions of the same file at once, Works will not allow you to open more than one copy of a file at once. If you try to open an additional copy of a file that is already open, Works displays an error message.

Works makes it easy for you to reopen a file you recently worked on. The four files you most recently opened are always listed at the bottom of the **F**ile menu. To quickly open a file that you used recently, double-click the file name on the **F**ile menu, or highlight the file name and press Enter. Remember, also, that the Startup dialog box lists the eight most recently used files. You can also select a file to open from this list. If the file you choose was created with a different tool than the current one, Works opens the appropriate tool and the file.

Duplicating Files

When you duplicate a file, you make an exact copy of a file and save it under a different name. Once duplicated, the two files are entirely separate; if you make changes in one file, the other file is not affected. Duplicating can be especially helpful when you need to create two or more similar—but not exactly the same—copies of a document. Suppose you're sending a similar letter to two clients. You can save yourself the time of typing two separate letters by creating one, duplicating it, then making the appropriate changes to the second letter. Or, suppose you prepare a monthly sales spreadsheet that is identical in structure and format each month; only the numbers change from month to month. You can prepare the spreadsheet the first month, then duplicate it each following month and change only the numbers.

To duplicate a file, follow these steps:

1. Open the file you want to duplicate.

2. From the **F**ile menu choose the Save **A**s command. The Save As dialog box is displayed (refer to fig. 3.2).

3. In the Directories and Drives boxes, choose the appropriate directory and drive where you want to store the duplicate file.

4. In the File **N**ame box, type a unique name for the file.

5. Choose OK. Works closes the original file and leaves the new file open on-screen.

Opening Files Automatically When You Start Works

If you frequently work with the same documents each time you use Works, you'll find the Save **W**orkspace command on the **F**ile menu a handy feature. Using this command, Works automatically saves the documents you specify as a group and reopens them each time you start the program. The document windows are displayed on-screen in the same size and arrangement in which you saved them. This feature saves you the trouble of reopening each file individually and arranging each document window. You can save up to eight open documents of any time (word processor, spreadsheet, database, or communications) as a workspace.

To save a workspace, follow these steps:

1. Open all the documents you want to save.

2. Arrange the document windows on-screen just as you want them.

3. From the **F**ile menu, choose the Save **W**orkspace command.

The next time you start Works, the documents you save as a workspace are automatically reopened.

You can save a new workspace at any time by following the preceding steps with a new set of documents on-screen. If at some point you choose not to use the saved workspace, select the **O**ptions command on the T**o**ols menu to display the Options dialog box. In the box, remove the x from the **U**se Saved Workspace check box.

Troubleshooting

I named my spreadsheet file BUDGET but Works didn't add the .WKS file extension.

You named the file "BUDGET." rather than "BUDGET". If you type the period that Works uses as a separator between the file name and file extension and don't include a file extension, Works saves the file without a file extension.

I named my database file CLIENTS.WDB but I can't find it in the MSWORKS directory.

You might have inadvertently selected a different directory or drive, or typed the file name incorrectly when you saved the file. To find the file, choose the F**i**nd File button in the Open dialog box, then follow the WorksWizard instructions on-screen. Or, use the **F**ile Searc**h** command in the Windows File Manager to find the file, then move it to the correct directory.

I made some changes to an existing file, then duplicated the file by saving it under a different name, but the changes I made weren't saved in the original file.

You didn't save the changes you made to the original file before you duplicated it. Before you duplicate a file, *always* save the changes you make if you want them saved in both files.

Using AutoStart Templates

Before you've had time to master the tools in Works, you might find yourself up against a deadline to complete a three-column newsletter, an accounts receivable report, a job estimate, or a weekly time sheet. These are just a few examples of the many common documents used every day in the business world. Sometimes the effort involved in setting up the layout of a newsletter, report, estimate, or time sheet can be more time-consuming than supplying the data or information itself.

To help you create the document you need quickly, Microsoft Works for Windows includes a variety of *AutoStart templates*, prepared documents that serve as a model for a specific type of document you need to create. The dozens of templates included in Works are divided into three groups: business, personal, and education. (A fourth group, custom, allows you to create your own templates.)

Within each group are categories. For example, in the business group, categories include billing, planning, documents, expenses, inventory, management, and sales. Within each category are specific types of documents. You choose a group, then a category, then a specific document template to use (see fig. 3.4). On-screen, Works opens a new document that is a copy of the template you choose. You make the appropriate changes to the document, then save it under a new name.

Tip

AutoStart templates are an important feature to remember when you're in a crunch for time. You can create your document in a fraction of the time it might have taken to create it from scratch—and with any luck, you meet your deadline.

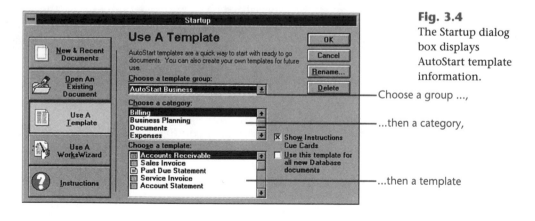

Fig. 3.4
The Startup dialog box displays AutoStart template information.

Choose a group ...,

...then a category,

...then a template

To use an AutoStart template, follow these steps:

1. In the Startup dialog box, click the Use a **T**emplate button, or, from any Works tool, choose the **T**emplates command on the **F**ile menu. The Startup dialog box displays template information.

2. From the **C**hoose a template group list, select a group.

3. From the C**h**oose a category list, select a category.

4. From the Choo**s**e a template list, select a template.

5. If you want Cue Cards to help you fill in the template document, make sure the Sho**w** Instructions Cue Cards box is checked.

6. If the template you choose is one you want to use for all new documents you create with the specified tool, select the **U**se this template for all new Word Processor (or Spreadsheet or Database) documents button.

7. Choose OK. Works opens a new document that is a copy of the template.

8. Follow the instructions on the Cue Cards for filling in the document with your own information.

9. When the document is complete, use the Save **A**s command to save the file with a new file name.

Works allows you to create your own templates, too. Suppose your company requires you to use a specialized FAX cover sheet rather than the template supplied with Works. You can create a document that meets all your company's requirements, then save it as a template.

To save a file as a template, follow these steps:

1. Create the document exactly as you want the template to appear.

2. Choose the Save **A**s command on the **F**ile menu. The Save As dialog box is displayed.

3. Select the Tem**p**late command button. The Save As Template dialog box is displayed.

4. In the Template **N**ame box, enter a name for the template file, then choose OK.

5. Choose OK to close the Save As dialog box. The template you create is automatically added to the Custom Group in the Template Startup dialog box.

Using WorksWizards

WorksWizards are guided on-line scripts that help you accomplish specific tasks, such as creating a form letter, designing a personalized letterhead, or finding a lost file. They are different from AutoStart templates in that they are not prepared documents; rather, they are tools for creating custom documents or accomplishing specific tasks. A WorksWizard provides step-by-step instructions on-screen that you respond to interactively. Using the information you supply, the WorksWizard either completes a task or creates a document for you. The complete list of WorksWizards can be seen in the list box in figure 3.5.

Highlight a WorksWizard in the list to display a description here

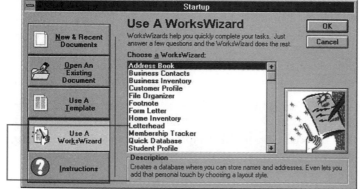

Fig. 3.5
The Startup dialog box displays WorksWizard choices.

To use a WorksWizard click on the Use A WorksWizard button in the Startup dialog box (refer to fig. 3.1) or, from any tool in Works, choose the WorksWizards command on the File menu. The Startup dialog box shown in figure 3.5 is displayed. Choose the WorksWizard you want to use from the list that appears, then click OK and follow the instructions on-screen.

From Here...

In this chapter, you learned how to manage Works files and how to use AutoStart templates and WorksWizards. Now you are ready to begin learning about the individual tools in Works, described in the following chapters.

- Chapter 4, "Creating, Saving, and Printing a Word Processing Document," introduces you to the basic skills required to create a word processor document, move around in the document, correct minor errors, then save and print the document once it's complete.

- Chapter 10, "Creating, Saving, and Printing a Spreadsheet," introduces you to the basic steps for creating a spreadsheet file and entering text and numbers in the cells. You also learn how to make changes to spreadsheet entries, enter simple formulas, and save and print a spreadsheet.

- Chapter 16, "Creating and Saving a Database File," introduces you to databases and database terminology. You learn how to start a new database file, how to use the database menus and toolbar, how to work with different views of the database, and how to name and save a database file.

- Chapter 28, "Communicating with Other Computers," first examines communications terms and then describes how to specify all the required settings to establish a communications session and save the settings in a file. Also in this chapter are instructions for sending and receiving text and files.

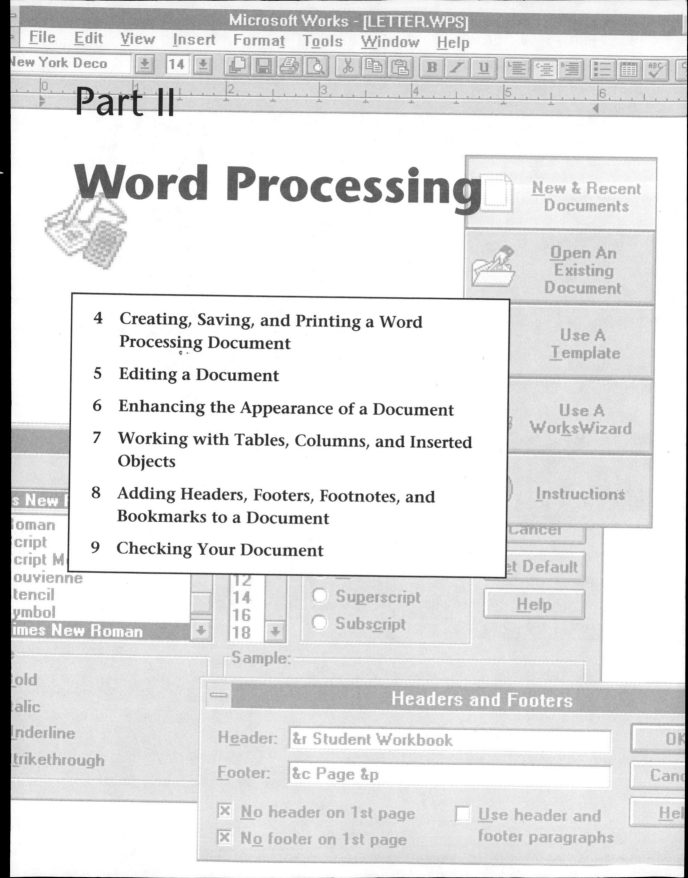

Part II

Word Processing

Microsoft Works - [LETTER.WPS]

File Edit View Insert Format Tools Window Help

New York Deco | 14 |

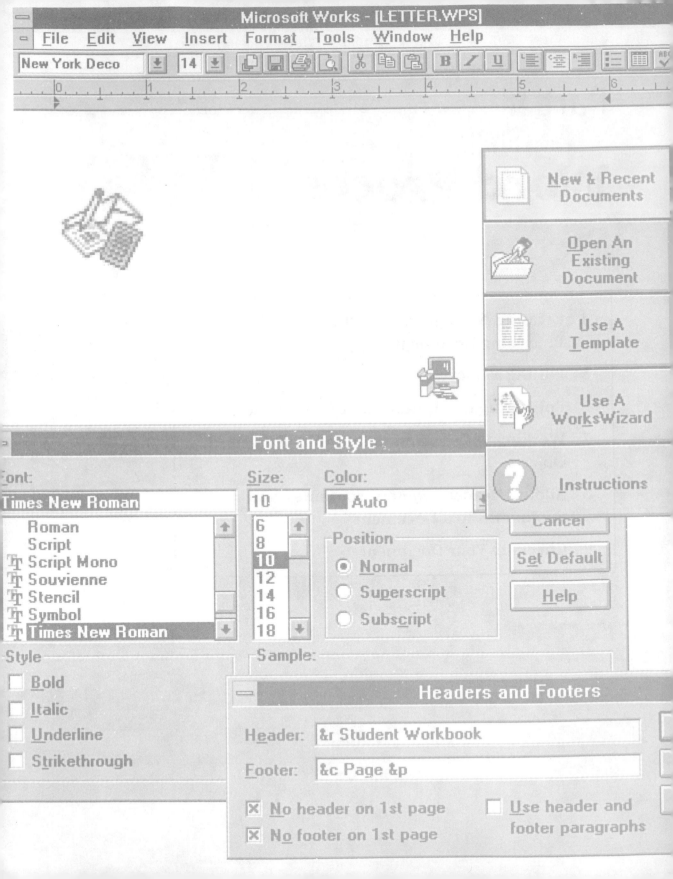

New & Recent Documents

Open An Existing Document

Use A Template

Use A WorksWizard

Instructions

Font and Style

Font:

Times New Roman

- Roman
- Script
- Script Mono
- Souvienne
- Stencil
- Symbol
- **Times New Roman**

Size: 10

- 6
- 8
- **10**
- 12
- 14
- 16
- 18

Color: Auto

Position
- Normal
- Superscript
- Subscript

Cancel

Set Default

Help

Style
- Bold
- Italic
- Underline
- Strikethrough

Sample:

Headers and Footers

Header: &r Student Workbook

Footer: &c Page &p

- X No header on 1st page
- X No footer on 1st page
- Use header and footer paragraphs

Chapter 4

Creating, Saving, and Printing a Word Processing Document

In Chapters 1, 2, and 3, you learn about the components of Works, how to get around in the program, how to work with menus, toolbars, and windows, and how to get help when you need it. You also learn how to create, name, save, duplicate, open, and close files. Now you're ready to actually start creating files using the word processor.

The Word Processor Window

As you learn in Chapter 2, "Getting Started with Works for Windows," each of the tools in Works displays a unique window inside the overall Works window. The window shown in figure 4.1 is the basic word processing window that opens when you choose the Word Processor tool from the Startup dialog box. In the figure, the window is maximized so that the Works window and the word processing window blend together to become one. The title bar, (shared by both windows) indicates the temporary file name, Word1.

The text area is where you enter the text of your document. The blinking vertical bar is the *insertion point*, the point at which characters are inserted when you type. The double right-pointing arrow in the left margin is a page marker that marks the beginning of the document. When a document becomes longer than one page, Works inserts additional page markers in the left margin in the appropriate locations.

The main topics covered in this chapter are:

- Using the word processing window

- Entering text

- Moving around in a document

- Correcting minor errors

- Saving and printing a document

II

Word Processing

Fig. 4.1

The word processor window.

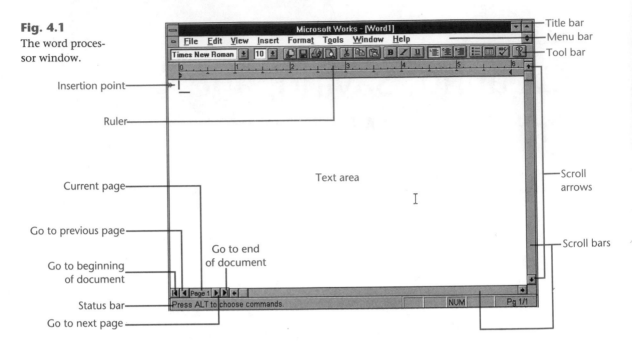

Insertion point

Ruler

Current page

Go to previous page

Go to beginning of document

Status bar

Go to next page

Go to end of document

Title bar

Menu bar

Tool bar

Scroll arrows

Scroll bars

Like all other document windows, the word processor window has both a vertical and a horizontal scroll bar so you can scroll a long document up and down or a wide document right to left. As usual, click on the scroll arrows at either end of the scroll bar to shift your view of the document in the direction of the arrow. To the left of the horizontal scroll bar are navigation buttons that allow you to move quickly to the beginning of the document, the end of the document, back one page, or forward one page. Also displayed is the number of the current page.

The ruler, which appears just below the word processor toolbar, illustrates the width of a document and indicates where right and left margins, indents, and tabs are located. You'll learn more about using the ruler in Chapter 6, "Enhancing the Appearance of a Document." If you do not see the ruler on your screen, the ruler option is probably turned off. To display the ruler, choose the **R**uler command on the **V**iew menu. The ruler is displayed when a check mark appears next to the **R**uler command on the **V**iew menu.

At the bottom of the window, the far right end of the status bar indicates the current page where the insertion point is located and the total number of pages (as in page 5 of 10, noted as 5/10). The left end of the status bar provides brief instructions (such as `Press ALT to choose commands.`), or describes the current menu command that is highlighted. For instance, if you highlight the Save **W**orkspace command on the **F**ile menu, the status bar reads: `Saves the names and positions of all open documents.` When you're first learning to use Works, the messages in the status bar can be a handy feature to help you remember command functions. When you press the Num Lock and Caps Lock keys, indicators also appear on the status bar to the left of the page indicator.

The Word Processor Menus

As you learn in Chapter 2, "Getting Started with Works for Windows," each Works tool has its own set of menus. Some menus, such as **F**ile, **E**dit, **V**iew, **W**indow, and **H**elp, appear in every tool but may contain slightly different commands from tool to tool. Table 4.1 describes the types of commands you find on the word processor menus.

Table 4.1 The Word Processor Menus	
Menu Name	**Command Functions**
File	On this menu you find all the commands necessary for creating, opening, saving, and printing files. Recall from Chapter 3, "Working with Files, Templates, and WorksWizards," that the four most recently opened files are always listed at the bottom of the File menu, providing a quick way to open a file.
Edit	This menu contains commands for cutting, copying, and pasting text and for undoing the most recent change to a document.
View	The commands on the View menu determine how a document is displayed, for instance, in draft view or page layout view. Use this menu also to display or turn off the ruler, the toolbar, hidden characters, and so on. Commands for displaying footnotes, headers, and footers also appear on this menu.
Insert	Use this menu to insert any type of graphics object (such as a drawing, clip art, word art, chart, or spreadsheet) in a document. This menu also contains commands for inserting page breaks, special characters, footnotes, bookmarks, and so on.
Forma**t**	On the Format menu you find commands that allow you to choose a font and text style, specify a paragraph's format, set tabs, add a border to selected text, create columns of text, and format a picture.

(continues)

II

Word Processing

Table 4.1 Continued	
Menu Name	**Command Functions**
Tools	This menu contains special tools for working with a word processor document. Here you have access to the spell checker, thesaurus, hyphenation, and word count features in Works. You also use this menu to customize the toolbar and other Works options.
Window	Use the commands on this menu to help you arrange all open documents on your screen and to select the active window.
Help	The Help menu lists a variety of help topics, including an overview of the word processor tool.

The Word Processor Toolbar

As with menus, each Works tool has a unique toolbar as well. Each tool on the toolbar represents a particular command. Just click on the tool to activate the command. Table 4.2 describes the function of each of the word processor tools.

Table 4.2 The Tools on the Word Processor Toolbar	
Tool	**Function**
Times New Roman	Displays a drop-down list of all available fonts.
10	Displays a drop-down list of all available point sizes for the current font.
	Displays the Startup dialog box.
	Saves the file using the current file name and settings. If the document has not yet been saved, the Save As dialog box appears.
	Prints the current document using the current print settings.

Tool	Function
	Click this tool to preview your document before printing.
	Removes the selected text to the Clipboard.
	Copies the selected text to the Clipboard.
	Inserts the contents of the Clipboard in a document at the location of the insertion point.
	Applies bold to selected text.
	Applies italics to selected text.
	Applies underline to selected text.
	Left-aligns selected text.
	Centers the selected text between the left and right margins.
	Right-aligns selected text.
	Places a bullet to the left of the selected paragraph.
	Displays a dialog box in which you specify a spreadsheet or table to insert in your document.
	Begins spell checking the current document.

II

Word Processing

Troubleshooting

I don't see a toolbar in my word processor window.

In Works, you can choose to display the toolbar or turn it off. If the toolbar isn't visible in the word processor window, choose the Toolbar option on the **V**iew menu. (The toolbar is visible in the window when a check mark appears to the left of the Toolbar option on the **V**iew menu.)

On my toolbar, I can't find all of the tools listed in Table 4.2.

The tools listed in Table 4.2 appear on the standard toolbar. If the toolbar has been customized, some of the standard tools might not be shown. To reset the toolbar to the standard tools, choose the Customize Toolbar command on the Tools menu. When the Customize Works Toolbar dialog box appears, choose the Reset tool, and then choose OK. Works resets the toolbar to its standard tools.

Entering Text

Entering text in a word processing document is one of the simplest things you can do; you just start typing. Characters appear on the screen to the left of the insertion point, and the insertion point moves to the right as you type. When you reach the end of the first line, continue typing. Works automatically *wraps* text to the next line so you don't have to press Enter at the end of each line. The only time you need to press Enter is when you want to return the insertion point to the left margin to begin a new line or paragraph.

As you type a document on a word processor, the characters you type appear on the lines that are visible in the display area of the window. When you fill those lines, the document scrolls upward to reveal a larger blank working area. For example, if you typed three pages of text without stopping, the window would display the third page and the insertion point would be located to the right of the last character you typed. Before you can make changes in a document, you must know how to move the insertion point to any location, as you learn in the next section.

Moving Around in a Document

If you type a letter on a typewriter and realize you made an error on the first line, you roll the platen backward to the first line to correct the error. In a sense, you do the same thing on a word processor, except that you move the insertion point. Once you move the insertion point, you can insert new text, erase existing text, or select text that you want to move or copy.

Using the Keyboard, Mouse, and Scroll Bars

The easiest way to move the insertion point is with the arrow keys. The up- and down-arrow keys move the insertion point up or down one line at a time. The left- and right-arrow keys move the insertion point right or left one character at a time. You can press and hold any of these keys to repeat the action. But the arrow keys do not always provide the most efficient way to move through a document. For instance, what if you want to move the insertion point five pages back? It could take a while using just the up-arrow key. You can take larger jumps using the Page Up and Page Down keys, which move the insertion point one window back and one window forward respectively. These keys also repeat when held down.

Another way to move the insertion point a long distance is to use the scroll bars and the mouse. To the left of the horizontal scroll bar in the word processor window are four navigation buttons, two on either side of the current page number. To the left of the current page number are the First and Previous buttons, which move the insertion point to the first page in the document or the previous page. To the right of the current page number are the Next and Last buttons, which move the insertion point to the next page or the last page in the document. Click on any of these buttons to move quickly through a document.

The scroll box, inside the vertical scroll bar, indicates your approximate position in a document. For example, if a document is 10 pages long and the scroll box is located half way down the vertical scroll bar, you are probably viewing page 5. Using the mouse, drag the scroll box to the approximate location in the document you want to view, then click anywhere within the working area to move the insertion point. You can also move the document up or down one line at a time by clicking the scroll arrows at either end of the vertical scroll bar.

> **Note**
>
> Scrolling alone does not move the insertion point; you must click inside the window as well.

You can also use the keys listed in Table 4.3 to move the insertion point in a document.

Word Processing   II

Table 4.3 Keys for Moving the Insertion Point	
Keys	**Moves Insertion Point**
Home	To the beginning of the current line
End	To the end of the current line
Ctrl+Home	To the beginning of the document
Ctrl+End	To the end of the document
Ctrl+right arrow	To the previous word
Ctrl+left arrow	To the next word
Ctrl+up arrow	To the previous paragraph
Ctrl+down arrow	To the next paragraph
Right arrow	One character to the right
Left arrow	One character to the left
Up arrow	One line up
Down arrow	One line down
PgUp	Up one window
PgDn	Down one window

Using the Go To Command

When you want to move to a specific page in a document, the **G**o To command on the **E**dit menu is a handy feature. When you choose this command, the Go To dialog box shown in figure 4.2 is displayed. Type the page number you want in the **G**o To box, then click OK. Works moves the insertion point to the beginning of the page you specify.

Tip
The shortcut key for the **G**o To command is F5.

If your document contains bookmarks, you can use the Go To dialog box to move directly to the bookmark you specify rather than to a page. Chapter 8, "Adding Headers, Footers, Footnotes, and Bookmarks to a Document," discusses how to insert bookmarks in a document.

Fig. 4.2
The Go To dialog
box.

Correcting Minor Errors

When you're entering new text, it's easiest to correct minor errors as you type. Minor errors are those that you become aware of quickly and therefore can change quickly and easily without moving around in the document too much. These include typing mistakes, punctuation errors, or a minor change to a word or phrase. (To make major changes, such as extensive editing of a document, refer to Chapter 5, "Editing a Document," for more efficient methods of changing existing text.) To correct minor errors, you use the Backspace or Delete key.

To delete the character to the left of the insertion point, press the Backspace key. Like the arrow keys, the Backspace key repeats when held down, so you can delete a sequence of characters quickly. If you prefer, you can use the Delete key to delete the character to the right of the insertion point. Use the arrow keys to position the insertion point, then press Delete. Like the arrow and Backspace keys, the Delete key also repeats when held down. Be careful when holding down either the Backspace or Delete key! On a fast computer, these keys can delete very quickly and, in a matter of seconds, remove more characters than you intend.

Saving Your Work

Once you begin creating real documents with Works, it's important to save your work. As you learn in Chapter 3, "Working with Files, Templates, and WorksWizards," you choose a permanent name for a document, a location to store it, and the file type, the first time you save a document. Until you save a document, any text that you enter is vulnerable. An interruption of power or

II

Word Processing

an equipment failure will cause an unsaved file to be lost, so it's important to remember to save a file frequently. For specific information about how to save a file, refer to Chapter 3, "Working with Files, Templates, and WorksWizards."

If you anticipate using your document with another word processing program, such as Word for Windows, WordPerfect, or Works 3.0 for Macintosh, you can save the file in the appropriate file format. Works also offers Text and Text (DOS) formats that allow you to save the text along with spaces, paragraph markers, punctuation, and sometimes with tab settings. However, enhancements such as bold, underline, italics, subscript, superscript, and special fonts are not saved.

Printing a Document

No matter what kind of document you create using the word processor, printing is something you do quite often. Short, simple documents, you might print only once. For longer, more complex documents that must be reviewed in draft stages, you might print several times before the final product is produced. In any case, you should review the document's page and print settings before printing.

Use the Page Setup command on the File menu to display the Page Setup dialog box. In this dialog box you specify the page, header, and footer margins; the source, size, and orientation for the paper you are printing on; page numbering and footnote options, and other standard settings for your particular printer. (You learn how to create headers, footers, and footnotes in Chapter 8, "Adding Headers, Footers, Footnotes, and bookmarks to a Document.") When all page settings are correct, you preview the document to make a final check before printing. In the following section you learn how to specify page settings.

> **Note**
>
> The settings you choose in the Page Setup dialog box affect only the current document.

Setting Margins

Page margins are the white spaces that surround the text on the printed page. To set page margins for the document you are printing, you use the Page

Setup dialog box shown in figure 4.3. (Notice that Page Setup is a tabbed dialog box. In the figure, the Margins tab is selected and the default margin settings are displayed.) Unless you change margin settings, the Page Setup dialog box shows the default margins that Works uses: 1 inch for top and bottom margins, and 1.25 inches for left and right margins. The Sample area of the dialog box displays a graphic representation of these settings. The default margin settings shown are fairly standard for most types of documents—from letters and memos to reports and resumes—you seldom need to change these settings.

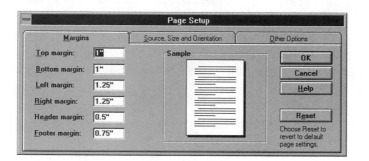

Fig. 4.3
The Page Setup dialog box displays margin settings for the current document.

For certain documents, however, you will change the default margin settings. For example, suppose you want all documents that you print on your company letterhead to align with the logo, name, address, and other graphic elements on your letterhead. After some careful measuring, you might find that the left and right margins need to be 1 inch, the top margin 1.25 inches, and the bottom margin .75 inch. Or, suppose that when you print your resume using default margin settings, the last two lines get bumped to a second page. If you want your resume to be a single page, you can probably get all of the text on one page by altering the page margins slightly.

To change margin settings for the current document, follow these steps:

1. From the **F**ile menu, choose the Page Setup command. The Page Setup dialog box is displayed.

2. In the dialog box, choose the **M**argins tab. The dialog box shown in figure 4.3 is displayed.

3. In the appropriate margin boxes, type the setting you want to use in inches. Type a decimal for fractions of an inch (such as **1.25** for 1-1/4 inches). The Sample area of the dialog box changes to reflect the settings you choose.

4. When all margin settings are correct, choose OK. Works automatically reformats your document using the new margin settings.

If you decide to include a header or footer in your document, you change the header and footer margins the same way you change any other margin. Determining whether or not you need to alter header and footer margins is discussed in Chapter 8, "Adding Headers, Footers, Footnotes, and Bookmarks to a Document."

Note

If you commonly work with centimeters or another unit of measure rather than inches, you can change the Works default units setting. Choose the **O**ptions command on the **T**ools menu to display the Options dialog box. In the Units box, choose a unit of measure, then choose OK. Note that the unit of measure you choose applies to *all* tools in Works.

Setting Paper Source, Size, and Orientation

Before printing a document, you must specify in Works which paper source to use, the size of the paper you're printing on, and the direction you want the print to appear on the page. To change the paper source, paper size, and print orientation, you use the Page Setup dialog box shown in figure 4.4. In the figure, the Source, Size, and Orientation tab is selected and the default settings are displayed. The page in the Sample area reflects the current paper size and orientation settings.

Fig. 4.4
The Page Setup dialog box displays paper source, size, and orientation settings for the current document.

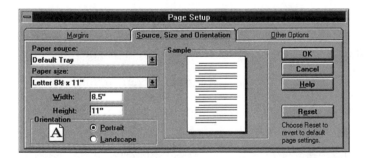

Depending on the type of printer you are using, you can choose the correct paper source (such as the default paper tray, second paper tray, envelope feeder) from the Paper Source drop-down list. The Paper Size list offers a variety of standard paper and envelope sizes. Choose a size from the list or enter the correct size in the **W**idth and Hei**g**ht boxes.

Paper orientation refers to the direction the document is printed on the paper. Most documents printed on standard 8-1/2 x 11 inch paper are printed in *portrait* orientation, or using the 11-inch dimension as the *height* of the paper. For documents that are printed in landscape orientation, the paper is rotated 90 degrees so that the 8-1/2 dimension is used as the height of the paper. (Of course, the paper is not actually rotated in your printer, your printer simply prints the image "sideways.") The default orientation is **P**ortrait; to print in landscape mode, choose the **L**andscape option button. The paper in the Sample area of the dialog box is rotated. Notice, also, that for the paper size you specified, the settings in the **W**idth and Hei**g**ht boxes are automatically reversed.

To change source, size, and orientation settings, follow these steps:

1. From the **F**ile menu, choose the Pa**g**e Setup command. The Page Setup dialog box is displayed.

2. In the dialog box, choose the **S**ource, Size, and Orientation tab. The dialog box shown in figure 4.4 is displayed.

3. Choose a paper source from the Paper source drop-down list. Choose a paper size from the Paper Size drop-down list, or specify a custom size in the **W**idth and Hei**g**ht boxes. Choose a paper orientation by clicking either the **P**ortrait or **L**andscape option button. The Sample area of the dialog box reflects the settings you choose.

4. When all settings are correct, choose OK.

Setting Other Page Options

The third tab in the Page Setup dialog box is Other Options (see figure 4.5.) Use the settings on this tab to specify the page number on the first page of the document, and where you want footnotes to be printed.

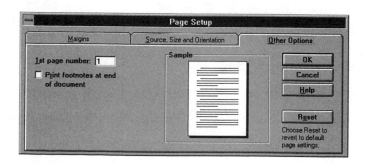

Fig. 4.5
The Page Options dialog box displays miscellaneous page settings.

The page number on the first printed page of your document can be a number other than 1. To start page numbering with the number 5, for instance, enter 5 in the **1**st page number box. When you include footnotes in your document, they generally appear at the bottom of each page where they are inserted. If you prefer, you can print all footnotes at the end of a document by checking the P**r**int footnotes at end of document check box. After choosing page number and footnote settings, select OK. You learn more about using page numbers and footnotes in Chapter 8, "Adding Headers, Footers, Footnotes, and Bookmarks to a Document."

Previewing a Document

One of the most important steps you can take before printing a document is to *preview* it. Previewing allows you to see on the screen how your document will look on the printed page. When you preview a document, Works displays a full-page view, one page at a time, of the document. This is your chance to see that margins are the appropriate size, line spacing is good, page separations are correct, header and footer text is positioned correctly, inserted objects appear in the proper locations, and so on. When included in a document, all of these elements appear on the preview screen.

To preview a document, choose the Print Pre**v**iew command on the **F**ile menu. The current document is displayed in a preview screen like the one shown in figure 4.6.

Fig. 4.6
Previewing a document shows you how the document will appear when printed.

Current page number

Preview command buttons

Full-page view of document

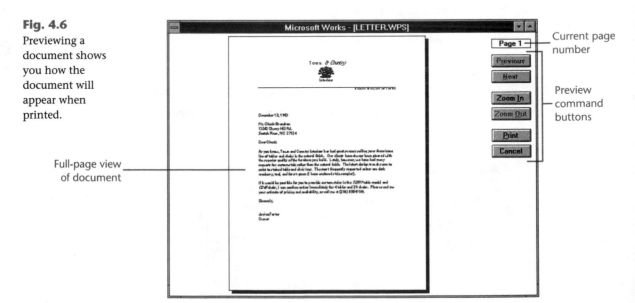

The actual text displayed in the preview screen can be difficult to read because it is reduced, but reading the text isn't the important consideration here; checking the document's layout is. If you think you spot a problem, however, you can zoom in on the document. Notice that the mouse pointer changes to a magnifying glass when it is pointing anywhere on the page. Click the left mouse button once anywhere on the page to zoom in on the document, or click the Zoom In button. If you need to magnify the document further, click the left mouse button once more anywhere on the page, or click the Zoom In button again. To zoom back out, click the mouse button a third time, or click the Zoom Out button.

If your document is longer than one page, display the page you want to preview by clicking the **P**revious or **N**ext button, or use the Page Up and Page Down keys on the keyboard. When you're ready to print the document, you can print directly from the preview screen by choosing the **P**rint button. This button displays the Print dialog box shown in figure 4.7. You learn how to use the Print dialog box in the next section. To close the preview screen, click the Cancel button.

Printing

When you're ready to print a document, choose the **P**rint command on the **F**ile menu, which displays the Print dialog box shown in figure 4.7. You use the Print dialog box to specify the number of copies you want to print, the particular pages you want to print, and the quality of printing you want to use. The printer that is currently selected is shown at the top of the dialog box. If the printer shown is not correct, select the correct printer using the Printer Setup command on the **F**ile menu.

> **Note**
>
> If you have access to more than one printer on your computer, you need to check the settings in the Printer Setup dialog box. This is where you specify which printer you want to use. To display the Printer Setup dialog box, choose the Printer Setup command on the **F**ile menu. The printer that is currently selected is highlighted in the Printer Setup dialog box. To choose a different printer, highlight the name, then choose OK.

Fig. 4.7
The Print dialog
box.

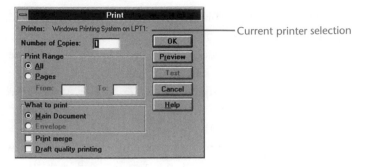

Current printer selection

Notice that a Preview command button is available in the Print dialog box. If you forget to preview a document before choosing the Print command on the File menu, you can choose the Preview button in the Print dialog box. The Test button is used when you merge documents, as you learn in Chapter 27, "Creating and Printing Form Letters, Envelopes, and Mailing Labels." Table 4.4 describes the options in the Print dialog box.

Table 4.4 Options in the Print dialog box	
Option	**Description**
Number of Copies	The default setting is 1; to print more than one copy of the current document, enter a number.
Print Range: All	The default setting is to print all pages of the current document.
Print Range: Pages	To print selected pages, choose the Pages option button, then enter the first page to print in the From box and the last page to print in the To box.
Main Document	Prints the main document rather than an envelope. This is the default setting.
Envelope	Choose this option to print envelopes.
Print merge	Allows you to merge a word processor document with a database document.
Draft quality printing	If your printer is capable of printing draft quality, choose this setting to print more quickly but at a lower print quality.

To print a document, follow these steps:

1. Open the document you want to print.

2. Specify print margins, paper source, size, orientation, and other print settings, as described earlier.

3. Preview the document, as described earlier.

4. From the **F**ile Menu choose the **P**rint command. The Print dialog box shown in figure 4.7 is displayed.

5. Choose the appropriate print settings, then choose OK.

Closing a Document

When you're finished working with a document, you can close it using the **C**lose command on the **F**ile menu. Closing a file closes only the current document window so you can continue using Works. If you prefer to exit Works altogether, choose the E**x**it Works command on the **F**ile menu. Refer to Chapter 3, "Working with Files, Templates, and WorksWizards," for a discussion of closing and opening files.

From Here...

In this chapter, you learned the basic skills for creating, saving, and printing a word processor document. To learn other word processing skills, refer to the following chapters:

- Chapter 5, "Editing a Document," teaches you how to select and change text by inserting, deleting, and overtyping. You also learn to move and copy text and undo changes that you make.

- Chapter 6, "Enhancing the Appearance of a Document," describes all the tricks for making a document more attractive and readable, including changing the style and font of text, changing the alignment of paragraphs, indenting paragraphs and setting tab stops, and changing the line spacing in a document. You also learn about inserting page breaks in a document.

Tip
If you haven't saved your most recent changes to the document, Works displays a message asking if you want to save your file. Choose Yes to save your changes, No to abandon changes, or Cancel to return to your document without saving.

II

Word Processing

- Chapter 7, "Working with Columns, Tables, and Inserted Objects," shows you how to create tables using tab stops and how to format a document for multiple columns of text. You also learn how to move, size, and wrap text around inserted objects in a document.

- Chapter 8, "Adding Headers, Footers, Footnotes, and Bookmarks to a Document," describes how to add repetitive text at the top and bottom of each page. You also learn how to cite references or add a comment to a document using footnotes, and how to find your place in a document using a bookmark.

- In Chapter 9, "Checking Your Document," you learn how to change your view of a document by zooming in and out, wrapping text within a window, viewing hidden characters, and turning the toolbar and ruler on and off. You also learn how to search for text, replace text, how to check your document for spelling errors, and how to use the thesaurus.

Chapter 5

Editing a Document

The beauty of using a word processor to create text documents is that you can change a document as often as you change your mind. You can insert new text, delete existing text, rearrange sentences or paragraphs, and copy portions of text anywhere within a document.

II

Word Processing

Opening an Existing Document

When you use a word processor to type letters, memos, reports, and other text documents, you don't have to finish the document all in one session. You can enter as much text as you like (including mistakes), save the document and close it, then come back to it again later. You might reopen a document a dozen or more times before it's finally complete.

As you learn in Chapter 3, "Working with Files, Templates, and WorksWizards," there are four ways you can open an existing file. You can select from the Startup Dialog Box either the **O**pen an Existing Document Option or one of the eight most recently used files. Alternatively, in the Word Processor window you can select either **O**pen Existing File from the **F**ile menu, or one of the four most recently used word processing files. To review how to retrieve existing files, refer to Chapter 3, "Working with Files, Templates, and WorksWizards."

Selecting Text

Whenever you want to make changes to text—whether you're deleting, moving, or copying—you must select it first so that Works knows what portion of text you want to change. When you select—or *highlight*—text, the background color behind the text changes color so that the text appears highlighted (see fig. 5.1). There are a variety of methods for selecting text using the mouse, the keyboard, or both. The method you choose depends on your own personal preference and the amount of text you are selecting.

Fig. 5.1
The selected text is highlighted.

Selected text —

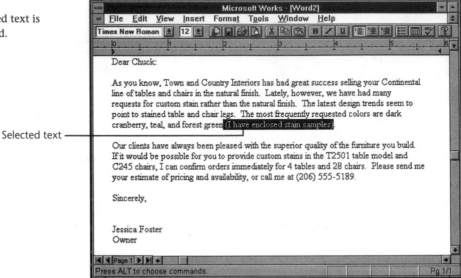

Using the Mouse

One method of selecting text is to click and drag the mouse pointer over the portion of text you want to select. (Recall from Chapter 1, "Introducing Works for Windows," that "click and drag" means to click the left mouse button and hold it down as you move the mouse pointer.) This is the best method to use when you are selecting irregular areas of text. As you move the mouse, the text that you drag the pointer across is automatically highlighted. If you move the mouse vertically through lines of text, one line at a time is added to the selection. If you move the mouse horizontally across words on the same line, one word at a time is added to the selection. When the portion of text you want to select is highlighted, release the mouse button.

> **Note**
>
> Works selects entire words at a time because the **A**utomatic Word Selection setting on the **O**ptions menu is selected by default. If you prefer to have Works select a character at a time rather than an entire word, you can turn off the Automatic Word Selection option. Choose the **O**ptions command on the **To**ols menu to display the Options dialog box, then remove the check from this option.

Another way to select text is with a single click or a double-click in the right location. To select a single line of text, click in the left margin next to the line; to select an entire paragraph, double-click in the left margin next to the paragraph. Be sure to release the mouse button to avoid selecting unwanted text. To select an entire word, double-click anywhere on the word. To select an entire document, press and hold the Ctrl key, then click anywhere in the left margin. By pressing and holding the Shift key, you can also select text from the location of the insertion point to the location where you click. These methods are summarized in Table 5.1.

Table 5.1 Selecting Text by Clicking the Mouse	
To Select	**Do This**
One word	Double-click anywhere on the word
One line	Click in the left margin next to the line
One paragraph	Double-click in the left margin next to the paragraph
The entire document	Press and hold the Ctrl key, then click anywhere in the left margin
From insertion point to any other point	Press and hold the Shift key, then click where you want the selection to end

Using the Shift Key

If you prefer not to select text using the mouse, you can select text using a combination of the Shift key and the Page Up, Page Down, Home, End, and arrow keys. When the text you want to select is highlighted, release all keys on the keyboard. Using the "Shift" method to select text is sometimes easier than using the mouse because you don't need to reach for the mouse and take your hands away from the keyboard. Again, the method you use often comes down to personal preference. The Shift key methods of selecting text are summarized in Table 5.2.

Table 5.2 Using the Shift Key To Select Text	
To Select	**Press and hold the Shift key, then...**
One word	Press the right- or left-arrow key
One line	Press the up- or down-arrow key
To the beginning of the current line	Press Home
To the end of the current line	Press End
To the previous paragraph	Press Ctrl+up arrow
To the next paragraph	Press Ctrl+down arrow
To the beginning of the document	Press Ctrl+Home key
To the end of the document	Press Ctrl+End key

If you select the wrong text, or decide you don't need to select text, you can cancel a selection by pressing any of the arrow keys or clicking anywhere in the document. Before canceling a selection, however, be sure to release the mouse button and any keyboard keys that you pressed while making the selection, otherwise you might inadvertently extend the selection.

Deleting and Inserting Text

In Chapter 4, "Creating, Saving, and Printing a Word Processing Document," you learn about two simple keys that help you change text: Backspace and Delete. These keys are useful for making minor changes in a document such as correcting a word or phrase. But sometimes you need to make major changes—like deleting several paragraphs, or rewording several sentences. These types of changes call for more efficient methods of revising text.

Deleting Large Areas of Text

If the Backspace and Delete keys were the only keys you could use to delete large areas of text, you could spend a great deal of time deleting! Fortunately, the ability to select text makes it easy to delete large amounts of text; you select the text first, then delete it using the Cut command on the Edit menu.

Using the Cut command removes the selected text from the document— much the same way you might remove a section of text using scissors. If the text you remove is in the middle of a paragraph, the text that follows the selection is automatically realigned with the surrounding text. Although the text that you cut is removed from the document, it isn't permanently lost. It is stored on the Clipboard, a temporary storage area for text that you cut or copy. The Clipboard is a convenient "safety net" because there might be times when you delete the wrong text by mistake. When this happens, you can bring the text back, as you'll learn later in this chapter.

To select the text to cut, use any of the selection methods you learned earlier in this chapter. Be sure to select the appropriate lines and spaces surrounding the text that you want to cut. For instance, if you are cutting a paragraph, you need to select the blank line that precedes or follows the paragraph, otherwise you'll be left with two blank lines between the two remaining paragraphs. If you are selecting several sentences, be sure to select the space or spaces that follow the last sentence (see fig. 5.2).

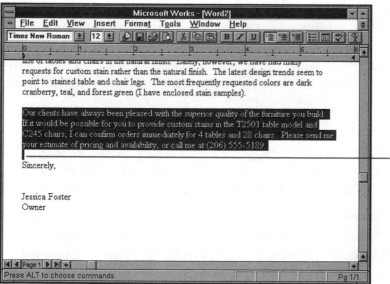

Fig. 5.2
The paragraph is selected to be cut. Notice that the blank line following the paragraph is selected as well.

— Blank line selected

Word Processing

To delete text from a document, follow these brief steps:

1. Select the text you want to delete, including the appropriate blank lines and spaces.

2. From the **E**dit menu choose the **Cu**t command.

Tip
The keyboard shortcut for the **Cu**t command on the **E**dit menu is Ctrl+X.

> ### Caution
>
> Don't use the Delete key on the keyboard in place of the **Cu**t command. The Delete key deletes selected text from your document, but does *not* place it on the Clipboard. Using the Delete key permanently removes the selected text from the document and you cannot retrieve it.

Inserting Text and Typing Over Text

The Works word processor operates in *insert mode*. In this mode, any new text you type in a document is automatically inserted beginning at the insertion point. For example, if the insertion point is located in the middle of a paragraph when you begin typing, existing text is shifted to the right to make room for the new text you type. Insert mode is the "safest" mode in which to work because you don't risk changing or losing any existing text. You don't have to set the word processor to operate in insert mode; it operates automatically in insert mode.

The alternative to insert mode is *overtype* mode. In this mode, any text to the right of the insertion point is automatically replaced by new text that you type. Overtyping is a method you might choose when you know you want to replace an existing phrase, sentence, or paragraph with new text. Overtyping saves you the trouble of selecting and deleting existing text, then inserting new text.

Tip
If you just want to delete text without replacing it, using the **Cu**t command is the best option.

In contrast to insert mode, overtype mode is riskier to use because it automatically replaces existing text. If you forget that you are using overtype mode and begin typing in the middle of a sentence or paragraph, you can't retrieve the original text; it is permanently replaced by the new text you type.

To use overtype mode, choose the **O**ptions command on the **To**ols menu. In the Options dialog box, choose the O**v**ertype check box, then click OK. The OVR indicator appears near the right end of the status line. To switch back to insert mode, turn off the O**v**ertype option in the **O**ptions dialog box.

Automatically Replacing Selected Text

Another check box you can choose in the Options dialog box is Typing Replaces Selection. Using this option, all text that you select is automatically replaced by new text that you type. For instance, if you select a sentence, then begin typing, the sentence is automatically removed from the document and replaced by the new text that you type. This feature saves you the trouble of deleting selected text before you type new text. However, if you are new to word processing or if other word processors you've used did not operate this way, you might want to get comfortable with Works before using this feature. Although it is a time-saver, it is somewhat risky to use because it automatically deletes selected text.

Moving and Copying Text

When you use a word processor to create and revise documents, moving and copying are editing changes you make frequently. With a few simple keystrokes, you can move or copy any selection of text, anywhere in a document. These features make it easy for you to completely rearrange a document—without losing any of its original text.

You can move and copy text using menu commands or using a special mouse technique called drag-and-drop. You learn both methods in the following sections.

When you move text in a document, you must select it first, then choose a new location for it. The selected text is *inserted* at the location you choose, and the existing text is shifted to make room for the new text. The text surrounding the area from which you removed the text is automatically realigned as if the text you removed never existed.

When you copy text, you must select it first, then choose the location where you want the text to be duplicated. The original text that you select remains intact in its original location in the document. The new text that you copy is inserted at the location you choose.

Whether you're moving or copying text, it's important to remember to select the proper spacing along with the text you select. For example, when you want to move or copy an entire paragraph, select the blank line that precedes or follows the paragraph when you make your selection. Otherwise, the spacing will be incorrect when you insert the text in its new location. The same is

Tip

You can quickly turn overtype mode on by pressing the Insert key on your keyboard. Again, the OVR indicator appears on the status line. The Insert key toggles on and off, so press it again to turn overtype mode off.

II

Word Processing

true when you are moving or copying a word, phrase, or sentence. Select the space before or after the word, phrase, or sentence along with the text itself.

Moving and Copying Using Menu Commands

When you move text, you use the Cu**t** command on the **E**dit menu to remove the text from its original location, then you use the **P**aste command to insert the text in its new location (see fig. 5.3 and fig. 5.4). While you're in the process of moving text, Works uses the Clipboard as a temporary storage area for the selected text.

Fig. 5.3
A sentence is
highlighted for
moving.

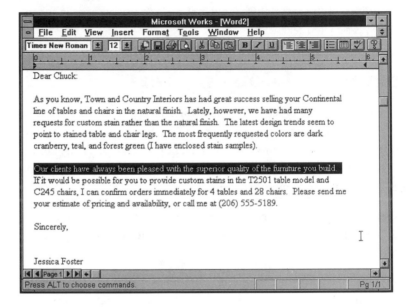

Follow these steps to move text:

1. Select the text you want to move, including the appropriate spaces and blank lines surrounding the text.

2. From the **E**dit menu, select the Cu**t** command; or press Ctrl+X. The selected text is removed from the document and placed on the Clipboard.

3. Move the insertion point to the location where you want to move the text.

4. From the **E**dit menu, select the **P**aste command; or press Ctrl+V. Works inserts the selected text where the insertion point is located.

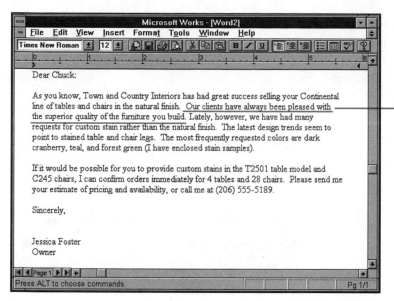

Fig. 5.4
The sentence in its
new location.

—The moved sentence

When you copy text, you use the **C**opy and **P**aste commands on the **E**dit menu. Again, Works uses the Clipboard to store a copy of the selected text until you choose a location to paste it. Here's how to copy a selection:

1. Select the text you want to copy, including the appropriate spaces and blank lines surrounding the text.

2. From the **E**dit menu, select the **C**opy command; or press Ctrl+C. The selected text is copied to the Clipboard.

3. Move the insertion point to the location where you want to copy the text.

4. From the **E**dit menu, select the **P**aste command, or press Ctrl+V. Works inserts the selected text where the insertion point is located. The original text you selected remains intact in its previous location.

Caution

When you move or copy text in a document, be sure to complete the operation before doing any other editing. That is, paste the selection somewhere in the document immediately after you cut or copy it, otherwise you might lose it. The Clipboard can hold only one selection of text at a time. If you cut a paragraph, then cut a sentence without first pasting the paragraph, the sentence replaces the paragraph on the Clipboard.

Word Processing

Moving and Copying Using Drag-and-Drop

Tip

If you prefer not
to use drag-and-
drop, you can turn
the feature off in
the **O**ptions dialog
box (select the
Options command
on the T**o**ols
menu).

If you prefer to use the mouse rather than menu commands to move and
copy text, you can use the drag-and-drop method. Using this technique, you
select the text to move or copy, then drag it to its new location. This feature
is turned on by default when you start Works.

To use drag-and-drop, you must first select the text you want to move or
copy. When you point to the highlighted text, notice that the standard arrow
mouse pointer changes to an arrow labeled DRAG (see fig. 5.5). This lets you
know that Works is ready for you to drag the selection to a new location.

Fig. 5.5

The *DRAG* label
indicates Works is
ready for you to
move or copy the
selection.

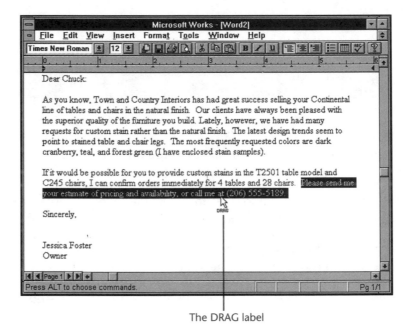

The DRAG label

To move text, you simply click anywhere on the selection (remember to hold
down the mouse button), then drag the selection to a new location. When
you click on the selection, the mouse pointer label changes to MOVE. Once
the text is positioned properly in the new location, release the mouse button.
The selected text is moved automatically.

To copy text, you use the same procedure, but you must press and hold the
Ctrl key as you drag the selection. When you click in the selection with the
Ctrl key pressed, the mouse pointer label says COPY rather than MOVE.

To use drag-and-drop to move or copy text, follow these steps:

1. Select the text you want to move or copy.

2. To move text, click anywhere on the selected text until you see the MOVE label. To copy text, press and hold the Ctrl key, then click anywhere on the selected text until you see the COPY label.

3. Drag the selection to its new location, then release the mouse button and the Ctrl key, if you are copying. Works moves or copies the text to its new location.

Troubleshooting

I tried to move a paragraph to another page in my document, but when I chose the Paste command, Works pasted a word. What happened?

You cut your paragraph from the document, then cut a word before you pasted your paragraph in the new location. When moving text, you must complete the move before you cut additional text, because the Clipboard holds only one selection at a time.

I tried to use the drag-and-drop method to move some text, but I don't see the DRAG label when I point to the selected text.

You may have one of two problems: drag-and-drop is not turned on, or the helpful mouse pointers setting is not turned on. To verify that both of these options are turned on, choose the **O**ptions command on the **T**ools menu, which displays the Options dialog box. If an X does not appear in the Dra**g** and Drop and Help**f**ul Mouse Pointers check boxes, select both boxes, then choose OK.

Undoing Changes

Fortunately, Works provides a way for you to undo changes that you make by using the **U**ndo command on the **E**dit menu. This command reverses the most recent editing changes you make in a document. Editing changes include typing, replacing text, deleting, moving, and copying. (Note that you *cannot* undo overtyping.) Although Undo is useful in all these cases, you'll probably most appreciate Undo when you delete text by mistake. For example, if you select and delete several paragraphs by mistake, you can bring them back by using the Undo command.

The most important thing to remember about Undo is that you must use it *immediately* after the editing change you make. If you delete several paragraphs, then type a new word, using Undo will remove the new word you typed; it will not bring back your paragraphs. You must select Undo immediately after deleting the paragraphs in order to bring them back.

Suppose you delete a paragraph by mistake, retrieve it using **U**ndo, then decide you really do want to delete the paragraph. You could select and delete the paragraph again, or you could just choose **U**ndo again. The **U**ndo command toggles between **U**ndo and **R**edo for cases when you undo a change by mistake. You can change your mind back and forth as many times as you like using **U**ndo and **R**edo (for instance, deleting and retrieving a paragraph), but once you make a *new* editing change, the previous change becomes part of the document and the Undo command is no longer available.

> **Note**
>
> In the word processor, the Undo command also works to reverse formatting changes, including changes to the font, size, style (such as bold, underline, italics), color, alignment, and so on. You learn more about using these features in Chapter 6, "Enhancing the Appearance of a Document."

From Here...

In this chapter, you learned various techniques for making changes to the *content* of a document. The following chapters teach you other features of the word processing tool:

- Chapter 6, "Enhancing the Appearance of a Document," describes all the tricks for making a document more attractive and readable, including changing the style and font of text, changing the alignment of paragraphs, indenting paragraphs and setting tab stops, and changing the line spacing in a document. You also learn about inserting page breaks in a document.

■ Chapter 7, "Working with Tables, Columns, and Inserted Objects," shows you how to create tables using tab stops and how to format a document for multiple columns of text. You also learn how to move, size, and wrap text around inserted objects in a document.

■ Chapter 8, "Adding Headers, Footers, Footnotes, and Bookmarks to a Document," describes how to add repetitive text at the top and bottom of each page. You also learn how to cite references or add a comment to a document using footnotes and how to find your place in a document using a bookmark.

■ In Chapter 9, "Checking Your Document," you learn how to change your view of a document by zooming in and out, wrapping text within a window, viewing hidden characters, and turning the toolbar and ruler on and off. You also learn how to search for text, replace text, how to check your document for spelling errors, and how to use the thesaurus.

II

Word Processing

Chapter 6

Enhancing the Appearance of a Document

Have you ever noticed how difficult it is to read a document that has characters all the same width, makes no size or style distinction between body text and headings, and uses no special styles such as bold, italic, or underlining for emphasis? Not only is staying awake difficult while reading such a document, you often have trouble grasping what you're reading. You may find yourself reading sentences over and over again. Enhancing the appearance of a document makes the document more visually appealing and also easier to read and comprehend.

This chapter is about enhancing the appearance of your documents. You can change the text of a document by changing the font, size, color, style, or position of text. And you can change entire paragraphs by selecting indent and alignment styles, as well as paragraph breaks and line spacing.

Working with Text

Changes you make to enhance the appearance of a document often are known as *format* changes. The word processor in Works includes a Format menu that contains a variety of format commands. Using these commands, you can change the *character style* of selected text (the style for individual characters, words, or a specific selection of text), or you can change the format of entire paragraphs. In this section, you learn how to change the character style of selected text.

This chapter discusses the following topics:

- Adding and removing character styles

- Copying a character style

- Choosing preset and custom paragraph styles

- Bordering paragraphs

- Setting paragraph breaks and line spacing

- Copying a paragraph style

- Inserting page breaks

You can use several methods to change the character style of selected text: menu commands, toolbar buttons, or keyboard shortcuts. This section discusses menu commands first. Figure 6.1 shows the Font and Style dialog box, which opens after you choose the Font and Style command on the Format menu.

Fig. 6.1
The Font and Style
dialog box.

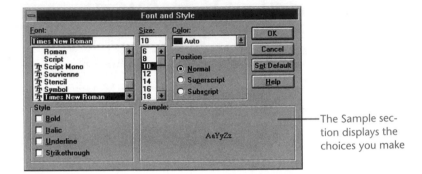

The Sample section displays the choices you make

Choosing a Character Style

In the Font and Style dialog box shown in figure 6.1, you see settings for the font, size, color, style, and position of text. The following list describes these attributes:

- *Font.* In Works a *font* refers to a specific style or design for a set of characters that Works displays on-screen and prints on paper. Each font has a particular shape or other characteristics that distinguish the font from other fonts. For example, this sentence appears in the Avant Garde font.

> **Note**
>
> In addition to the fonts Works provides, you can add additional fonts through Windows or other programs. When you add other fonts, they are included in the Font list in the dialog box. Some printers can print only a limited number of fonts. Whether or not you can print all of the screen fonts available through Works is entirely dependent on the capabilities of your printer.

- *Size.* Most fonts are available in different sizes and generally are measured in points. (A point is equal to 1/72 of an inch.) The most common point sizes for body text in a typical document (such as a letter or report) are 10 or 12. Other elements in a document, such as titles or headings, often appear in larger sizes, such as 14, 16, 18, or 24 points.

- *Color.* If you have a color monitor, you can display selected text in a variety of colors. If you have a color printer, you also can print the colors that you display in your document.

- *Style.* In Works, a text style refers to bold, italic, underline, or strikethrough. Bold, italic, and underline are common styles used to emphasize text. Strikethrough is a special style often used in legal documents. Strikethrough prints a line through text, indicating that the text is marked for deletion, but the text still is readable.

- *Position.* The position of text refers to its placement on the line. The superscript option raises a selected character slightly above the normal line level. Superscript often is used in documents that contain mathematical notations such as 10.218×7^3. In contrast, the subscript option drops a selected character slightly below the normal line level, as in H_2O, the symbol for water.

In the Font and Style dialog box, font, size, and color choices are available from list boxes. Option buttons represent positions because you can select only one position at a time. However, check boxes represent text styles (bold, italic, underline, and strikethrough) because you can select more than one style simultaneously. As you make font, size, color, style, and position choices, the Sample section of the dialog box displays the choices you make. The Sample section is especially helpful for viewing the unique design of a particular font and the relative size of characters.

Changing the Character Style of Existing Text

You often may type all the text of a document before you apply any character styles, especially if the document goes through several draft phases before final printing. (You don't want to spend time formatting a document only to change or cut portions.)

To apply a character style to existing text using menu commands, follow these steps:

1. Select the text you want to format.

2. From the Format menu, choose the Font and Style command. The Font and Style dialog box opens.

3. From the Font, Size, and Color lists, select one option.

4. From the Position section, select one option.

5. From the Style section, select any styles you want to apply to the selected text.

6. When the text shown in the Sample section appears as you want, choose OK. Works automatically reformats the selected text.

The *toolbar* helps you execute commands quickly and avoid using dialog boxes. When choosing a character style for text, using the buttons on the toolbar can speed up your work. The word processor toolbar has buttons for font and size, as well as bold, italic, and underline (see fig. 6.2).

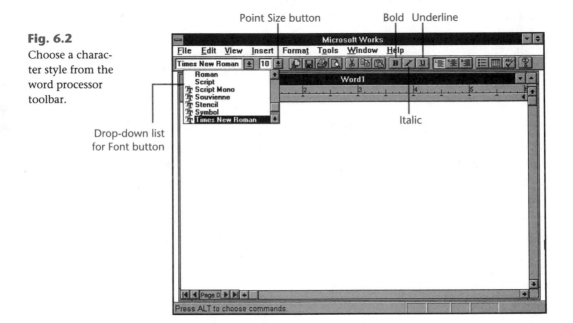

Fig. 6.2
Choose a character style from the word processor toolbar.

The Font and Size buttons contain drop-down lists from which you select a font and point size. (The disadvantage of using the toolbar rather than the menu command is that you cannot preview the font and size like you can in the Sample section of the Font and Style dialog box.) To change a font or size, select the text you want to change then select an item from each drop-down list. To add bold, italic, or underline to text in a document, select the text first then click the appropriate button. Note that the bold, italic, and underline buttons toggle on and off, so if you want to remove an attribute, select the affected text, then click the appropriate button again.

If you choose to customize your word processor toolbar, you can add buttons for strikethrough, subscript, and superscript. To customize your toolbar, refer to Chapter 2, "Getting Started with Works for Windows."

If you use your keyboard more than your mouse, you may apply some character styles using keyboard shortcuts, listed in Table 6.1. To use a keyboard shortcut, select the text you want to format, then press the key sequence shown in Table 6.1. Note that all the shortcuts listed except Ctrl+space bar (for plain text) toggle on and off.

Table 6.1 Keyboard Shortcuts for Character Styles	
Key Combinations	**Character Style**
Ctrl+B	Bold
Ctrl+U	Underline
Ctrl+I	Italic
Ctrl+Plus Sign (+)	Superscript
Ctrl+Equal Sign (=)	Subscript
Shift+F7	Repeat character style
Ctrl+space bar	Plain text (remove all character styles)

Note

Although the toolbar and keyboard shortcuts for character styles are helpful, they do not replace all menu commands for text character styles. For instance, if you want to change the color of text, you still must use the Font and Style dialog box because color has no toolbar button or keyboard shortcut.

Choosing a Character Style for New Text

Because character styles are attributes you can apply and remove from text, you can select styles before you enter new text just as easily as you can add styles to existing text. The time at which you choose to apply character styles is purely a matter of personal preference. Sometimes when you create a new document, you don't know the character style you want to use, so you apply the character style later. If you already know the character style you want to use, you may want to apply the character style as you type.

Except for selecting the text first, you apply a character style to new text the same way you apply a character style to existing text. Place the insertion point where you want the new character style to begin, select the character style options you want to use, then begin typing. All new text you type conforms to the character style you specify until you perform one of the following actions:

- Change the character style

- Move the insertion point to an area of the document that uses a different character style

Suppose that your document contains one paragraph typed in Helvetica 14-point bold, then you select CG Times 12 point for new text. CG Times 12 point remains in effect for all new text until you change the character style again or move the insertion point back into the paragraph typed in Helvetica.

Removing Character Styles from Existing Text

Tip
When text contains several attributes, you can remove all attributes quickly by selecting the text then pressing Ctrl+space bar. This keyboard shortcut changes all selected text back to plain text and saves you the trouble of removing each attribute individually.

As you begin experimenting with character styles, you may change your mind many times. You may decide to change character styles you have applied, or you may decide to remove character styles altogether. Attributes you add to text (such as bold, italic, underline, strikethrough, subscript, and superscript) toggle on and off, whether you select the setting using the Font and Style dialog box, toolbar, or a keyboard shortcut. To remove any of these character styles, select the affected text. Then select the dialog box option, the toolbar button, or the keyboard shortcut to remove the attribute.

Unlike attributes that are added to text, attributes such as font, size, and color change the *characteristics* of text. Technically, you cannot remove these attributes from text, but you can change them. Select the affected text then choose the **F**ont and Style command on the Forma**t** menu to change any or all of these attributes.

Copying a Character Style

In Chapter 5, "Editing a Document," you learn how to copy a selection of text from one location in a document to another. Instead of copying text, however, sometimes you may want to copy a character style from one selection to another. For example, suppose that you are creating a report that contains special cautions and notes. You want to identify each caution and note paragraph easily in the text, so you use a special font, size, color, and style to distinguish cautions and notes from the body text. Without the ability to copy a character style, you would need to select and apply the font, size, color, and style each time you typed a new caution or note paragraph.

Works enables you to copy attributes from the first caution or note paragraph you type, offering you several advantages. First, copying saves you the trouble of remembering (or checking each time) the attributes you assigned to the first paragraph. Second, this method is fast because it copies all attributes at one time. And third, copying eliminates the likelihood of errors; you cannot possibly get the character style wrong when you copy it.

To copy a character style, follow these steps:

1. Select the text that uses the character style you want to copy. (You don't need to select all the text like an entire paragraph. Just select any portion that uses all the attributes you want to copy.)

2. From the **E**dit menu, choose the **C**opy command.

3. Select *all* the text to which you want to copy the character style.

4. From the **E**dit menu, choose the Paste **S**pecial command. Works displays the Paste Special dialog box shown in figure 6.3.

5. Select the **C**haracter Style option then choose OK. Works applies the copied character style to the selected text.

Fig. 6.3
The Paste Special
dialog box.

You also can copy a character style to a blank line where you intend to enter new text. Follow the preceding steps, but instead of selecting text in step 3, move the insertion point to where you want the copied character style to take effect. Complete steps 4 and 5 then begin typing. All new text you type conforms to the copied character style until you change the character style or move the insertion point to text that uses a different style.

Troubleshooting

I set a specific character style for a new paragraph I typed, but now I don't know how to turn it off.

When you set a character style for new text, the style remains in effect until you change it. You don't turn off a character style; you define a new one. If you want to switch to a style you used previously in the document, copy the character style to the location where you want the style to begin.

I selected some text then pressed Ctrl+space bar to remove all style characteristics. Works removed the bold, underline, and color, but not the special font I used.

Bold, underline, italic, subscript, superscript, and color are attributes you can add to text; therefore, you can remove them from text. Technically, you cannot remove a font from text, but you can change the font. Select the text, then choose a new font from the **F**ont and Style command or from the Font toolbar button.

I changed some text from Times New Roman 12 to Coronet 12, but now the text is much smaller than it was before. Why?

Even though you chose 12 point for both fonts, they don't necessarily appear the same size. Because fonts have unique designs with unique style characteristics, they often vary greatly in size from font to font. Use whatever point size seems appropriate for the particular document.

Working with Paragraphs

In the first half of this chapter you learned how to change the format or character style of text. You select the text then apply certain attributes to enhance the text's appearance or convey a specific meaning (as with subscript and superscript). In the next half of this chapter, you learn about certain attributes you can apply to paragraphs rather than to selected text. These attributes, such as indentation, bullets, alignment, line spacing, borders, and so on, often are known as the *paragraph format*.

Paragraph formats not only improve the appearance of your document, they make the information more accessible by defining some structure within the text and distinguishing particular types of text. You can apply a variety of formats to paragraphs, and you can copy paragraph formats just like you can copy character styles. Before examining the types of formats you can use, this section first describes an element that plays an important role in paragraph formatting—the *ruler* in the word processor window.

Examining the Ruler in the Document Window

The ruler in the word processor window serves as a guide to the width of a document. Unless you change the Page Setup, which determines margin settings, Works uses left and right margins of 1.25 inches each. (Refer to Chapter 4, "Creating, Saving, and Printing a Word Processing Document," for a discussion of page setup.) On standard 8 1/2-by-11-inch paper, 6 inches remain across the paper for text; therefore, you see markers at the 0 and 6-inch points on the ruler (see fig. 6.4).

First-line indent marker

Left-indent marker

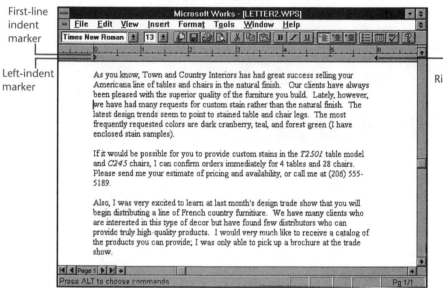

Fig. 6.4

Ruler markers guide the format of a paragraph.

Right-indent marker

The markers you see are not margin markers; however, they are *indent markers*. Indent markers indicate the points at which text indents from the left and right margins. Two indent markers are on the left side of the ruler; the left indent marks the indentation of the entire paragraph and the first-line indent marks the indentation of only the first line of a paragraph (again see fig. 6.4). The right-indent marker indicates the point at which text indents from the right margin. In figure 6.4, you see the default settings: left indent at 0, first-line indent at 0, and right indent at 6.

In figure 6.5, you see an example of a paragraph that indents from both the right and left margins; the first line indents as well. Notice that the left-indent marker appears at the 1/2-inch point, the first-line indent marker appears at the 1-inch point, and the right-indent marker is at the 5-inch point on the ruler.

Fig. 6.5
Indent markers move
along the ruler to
reflect the format of a
paragraph.

First-line indent marker

Left-indent
marker

Right-indent
marker

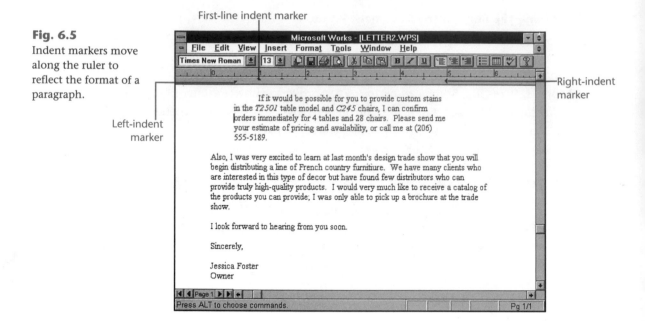

Specifying Paragraphs To Format

Before you can format a paragraph, you first must indicate the paragraph to which you want to apply a format. You mark the paragraph by positioning the insertion point anywhere in the paragraph. Or you can select any text in the paragraph; selecting the entire paragraph isn't necessary. The placement of the insertion point or the selected text tells Works which paragraph to format.

Quite often, you may want to apply the same format to several paragraphs in a document. When the paragraphs are contiguous, you can apply a format to all paragraphs at one time by selecting at least a portion of text in all paragraphs. For example, if you want to format three consecutive paragraphs, you can select the last line in the first paragraph, all the second paragraph, and the first line of the third paragraph, as shown in figure 6.6. You can select all text in all three paragraphs if you like, but that step isn't necessary. When paragraphs are not contiguous, you must apply the format to each paragraph individually or copy the format from one paragraph to another. (Copying a format is discussed later in this section.)

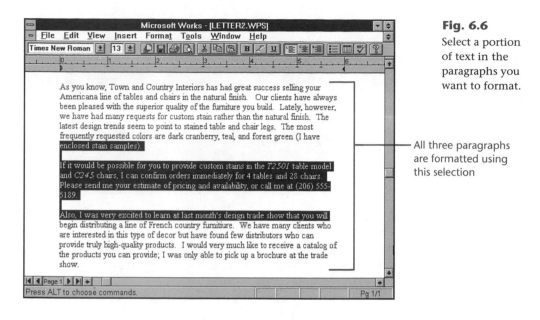

Fig. 6.6
Select a portion
of text in the
paragraphs you
want to format.

All three paragraphs
are formatted using
this selection

Choosing a Preset Paragraph Format

Several paragraph formats are used so commonly in text documents that
Works predefines the formats for you. For instance, bullets often are used to
set off specific points in a document. A bullet generally aligns with body text
at the left margin, and the bullet text usually indents 1/4 inch from the bullet. When a document includes quotations, they usually indent 1/2 inch on
both the right and left sides to distinguish them from body text. Other common paragraph formats include indentation of the first line in a paragraph
and a specific style of indentation called a *hanging indent*, which left-aligns
the first line and indents the remaining lines. Hanging indents are often used
to format numbered lists, among other things.

When you want to use one of these common formats—or *quick formats*, as
Works calls them—you simply select the format as an option in the Paragraph dialog box. By predefining formats for you, Works takes the guesswork
and experimentation out of creating these formats from scratch.

To display the Paragraph dialog box, choose the P**a**ragraph command on the
Forma**t** menu (see fig. 6.7). Choose the first tab in the dialog box labeled
Quick Formats.

Choose this tab to select quick formats

Fig. 6.7

Use a quick format to speed up your work.

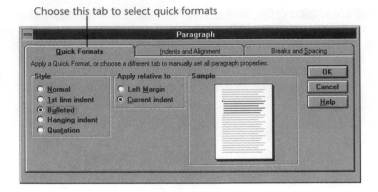

- The Style area of the dialog box lists the four predefined formats. The **1**st line indent setting indents the first line of the current paragraph 1/2 inch.

- The **B**ulleted setting inserts a bullet at the left margin then aligns the bullet text 1/4 inch from the left margin.

- The Han**g**ing Indent setting aligns the first line in the paragraph at the left margin and indents the remainder of the paragraph 1/2 inch (the first line *hangs* to the left of the remainder of the paragraph).

- This setting is used most often to format numbered lists. Finally, the Quo**t**ation setting indents the current paragraph 1/2 inch from both the left and right margins.

- The **N**ormal setting lets you reset the paragraph to conform to standard right and left margin settings.

In the Apply Relative To section, you select whether to apply a format relative to the left margin or relative to the current indentation of the paragraph. For instance, suppose that your paragraph already is indented 1/2 inch from the left margin. You want the paragraph to remain indented, but you also want to indent the first line. To do so, you would select the **1**st Line Indent option in the Style section and the **C**urrent Indent setting in the Apply Relative To section. Selecting these options means the first line indents 1 inch and the remainder of the paragraph indents 1/2 inch. If you select the Left **M**argin setting instead, Works moves the entire paragraph back to the left margin and indents the first line 1/2 inch.

The Sample section of the Paragraph dialog box illustrates the quick format you select. The grayed lines in the area represent text that conforms to the standard right and left margins in a document. The dark lines represent the format of the current paragraph (the paragraph you have chosen to format). After you select one of the Style options, the Sample section displays how the format will affect the current paragraph. This preview lets you see the style before you apply it to your paragraph. Notice that in figure 6.7 the Sample section of the dialog box illustrates the bulleted format style. If you're not familiar with the format styles listed, experiment by selecting each of the Style options to see how each one looks in the Sample section.

To use a quick format, follow these steps:

1. Place the insertion point anywhere in the paragraph you want to format. To format more than one paragraph at a time, select at least a portion of text in each paragraph.

2. From the Format menu, choose the Paragraph command. The Paragraph dialog box shown in figure 6.6 opens. (If the **Q**uick Formats tab is not selected, choose it now.)

3. In the Style area, select a quick format option.

4. In the Apply Relative To section, select the Left **M**argin or **C**urrent Indent option.

5. When the Sample section displays the correct format, choose OK. Works automatically reformats the current paragraph.

Creating Custom Paragraph Formats

Quick formats are excellent time-savers when your requirements are simple, but in some cases, quick formats don't provide the format you need. For example, suppose that you want to create a bulleted list, but you want the bullet text to indent 1/2 inch from the left margin rather than 1/4 inch. Or suppose that you want your quotations to indent 1 inch from each margin rather than 1/2 inch. You cannot customize the settings used in quick formats, so the alternative is to set up a format yourself using the **I**ndents and Alignment tab in the Paragraph dialog box. This tab is highlighted in figure 6.8.

Tip
To quickly format a paragraph with a bullet, select the paragraph and click the Bullets button on the toolbar.

Word Processing

II

Fig. 6.8

Create custom paragraph formats using the Indents and Alignments tab in the Paragraph dialog box.

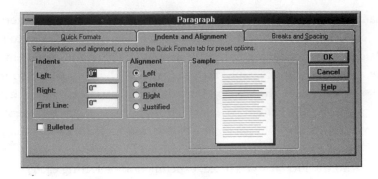

In the Indents section, you can specify Left, Right, and First Line indent settings; these settings are the indents that quick formats alter. When you change these settings manually, you have control over the width of the settings. The Left indent setting indicates how many inches (or what fraction of an inch) you want a paragraph to indent from the left margin. The Right indent setting does just the opposite; it specifies the number of inches or fraction of an inch you want a paragraph to indent from the right margin. The First Line indent is a little tricky because it indicates the number of inches or fraction of an inch you want the first line to indent *relative to the left indent.* This positioning makes a hanging indent a little more difficult to set up than, say, a quotation that's indented 1 inch from each margin.

Suppose, for example, that you want to set up the table shown in figure 6.9. In the figure, each paragraph uses a hanging indent format; that is, the first line of each paragraph *hangs* to the left of the rest of the paragraph by 2 inches. Because of the way the text aligns with the ruler markings, the First Line indent may appear to be set at 0 and the Left indent set at 2 inches. Actually, the First Line indent is set at -2 and the Left indent is set at 2—the First Line indent is applied *relative to* the Left indent setting. In other words, Works measures the First Line indent setting from the Left indent setting, not from the 0 point on the ruler. If you find this concept confusing, think of the Left indent setting you select as the new 0 point on the ruler, then measure the First Line Indent setting to the *left* of that zero point. Therefore, in a hanging indent, the First Line indent setting must always be a negative number.

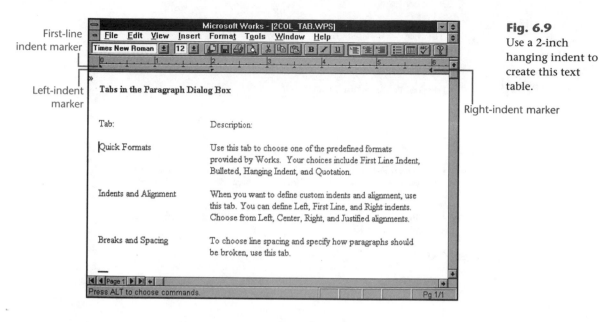

First-line indent marker

Left-indent marker

Fig. 6.9
Use a 2-inch hanging indent to create this text table.

Right-indent marker

To set up a custom paragraph format, follow these steps:

1. Place the insertion point anywhere in the paragraph you want to format. To format more than one paragraph at a time, select at least a portion of text in each paragraph.

2. From the Forma**t** menu, choose the P**a**ragraph command. The Paragraph dialog box opens. (If the **I**ndents and Alignment tab is not selected, choose it now.)

3. In the Indents section, set the L**e**ft, Ri**g**ht, and **F**irst Line indent settings.

4. When the Sample section displays the correct format, choose OK. Works automatically reformats the current paragraph.

Bulleted lists use a format similar to a hanging indent because the bullet on the first line hangs to the left of the rest of the paragraph. To create a custom bulleted list, specify the L**e**ft indent and **F**irst Line indent settings as described in the preceding steps, then click the **B**ulleted check box in the Paragraph dialog box shown in figure 6.8. The bulleted list shown in figure 6.10 was created using a .5-inch L**e**ft indent and a –.5-inch **F**irst Line indent.

Left-indent marker

Fig. 6.10
Create custom
bulleted lists using
the same prin-
ciples as a hanging
indent.

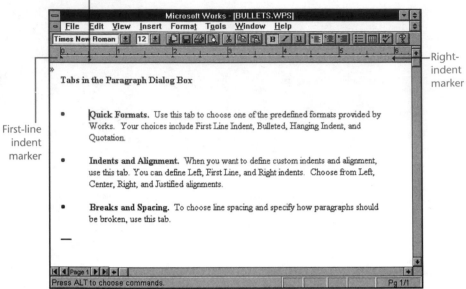

First-line
indent
marker

Right-
indent
marker

As an alternative to using the Paragraph dialog box, the quickest—and possibly easiest—way to set left, right, and first-line indents is by dragging the
markers on the ruler. By dragging indent markers, you can determine visually
where you want paragraph text to align. When setting up custom paragraph
formats (a hanging indent in particular), this method often is easier than
trying to remember how Works calculates a first line indent relative to a left
indent.

When you create a new document, the first-line indent and left-indent markers both appear at 0 on the ruler; the right indent marker appears at 6 inches.
You can drag any of these markers toward the center of the ruler and drop
them at any point. (You cannot drag the left and first line indent markers to
the left, outside the 0 point, and you cannot drag the right marker to the
right, outside the 6-inch point.)

To create a hanging indent of 1/2 inch, for example, position the left-indent
marker at the 1/2 inch point on the ruler and the first-line indent marker at
the 0 point on the ruler. Press and hold Shift and click and drag the left indent marker to the 1/2 inch mark on the ruler and release the mouse button.
The first-line indent marker already is positioned correctly, so you don't need
to move it.

Table 6.2 Keyboard Shortcuts for Indentation	
Press	**To**
Ctrl+H	Create a simple hanging indent of 1/2 inch.
Ctrl+G	Remove a hanging indent from the selected paragraph.
Ctrl+N	Indent the current paragraph 1/2 inch from the left margin. Press repeatedly to indent the selected paragraph in 1/2-inch increments.
Ctrl+M	Move the indentation of the current paragraph to the left in 1/2- inch increments.

Setting Paragraph Alignment

Alignment refers to the way the left and right edges of a paragraph line up. For instance, the paragraph you are reading is left-aligned because the characters at the left margin are aligned vertically and the characters at the right margin are ragged. Left-aligned text is most commonly used in business documents because it is considered easy to read and not too stiff or formal. In Works, you can left-align, right-align, center, or justify paragraphs. A right-aligned paragraph is just the opposite of a left-aligned paragraph—characters at the right margin are aligned vertically and characters at the left margin are ragged. Right alignment sometimes is used in brochures, flyers, or other advertising literature for its stylistic effect. Each line of a centered paragraph is positioned at the midpoint between margins, leaving ragged left and right edges. In a justified paragraph, characters at both the right and left margins are aligned vertically by adjusting the space between letters on each line. Justified text conveys a more formal appearance than left-aligned text. An example of each of these alignment styles is shown in figure 6.11.

You can use menu commands, toolbar buttons, or keyboard shortcuts to align paragraphs. To set alignment of a paragraph using menu commands, follow these steps:

1. Place the insertion point anywhere in the paragraph you want to align. To align two or more contiguous paragraphs at a time, select at least a portion of text in each paragraph.

2. From the Forma**t** menu, choose the **P**aragraph command to open the Paragraph dialog box. (If the **I**ndents and Alignment tab is not selected, choose it now.)

II

Word Processing

3. From the Alignment section, select **L**eft, **C**enter, **R**ight, or **J**ustified.

4. Choose OK. Works realigns the current paragraph.

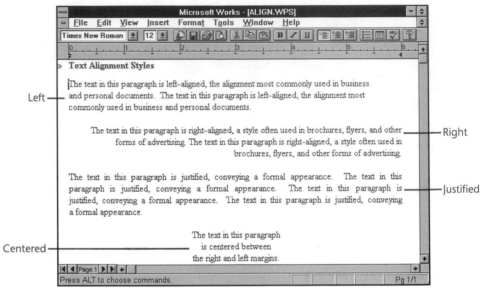

Because alignment is a feature frequently used in documents, the word processor toolbar contains the following alignment buttons:

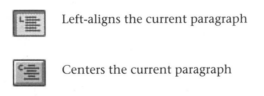

Left-aligns the current paragraph

Centers the current paragraph

Right-aligns the current paragraph

Aligning a paragraph using a toolbar button is easy. Place the insertion point anywhere in the paragraph then click an alignment button. Works immediately realigns the paragraph without displaying any dialog boxes. Also, remember that you can customize the toolbar by choosing the Customize Toolbar command on the Tools menu. When you choose the Format category in the Customize Works Toolbar dialog box, one of the buttons you can add to the toolbar is for justified text. Refer to Chapter 2, "Getting Started with Works for Windows," for complete instructions on customizing the toolbar.

If you prefer to use the keyboard, you can set paragraph alignment using a keyboard shortcut. Move the insertion point anywhere in the paragraph you want to align, then press one of the following key sequences:

Key Sequence	Function
Ctrl+L	Left-aligns the current paragraph
Ctrl+E	Centers the current paragraph
Ctrl+R	Right-aligns the current paragraph
Ctrl+J	Justifies the current paragraph

Setting Line Spacing and Paragraph Breaks

Two additional factors that affect the appearance of a document are line spacing and paragraph breaks. *Line spacing* refers to the amount of space between lines. A *paragraph break* is the point where a paragraph divides when it falls near the bottom of a page. In this section, you learn how to adjust both of these settings using the Breaks and **S**pacing tab in the Paragraph dialog box, shown in figure 6.12.

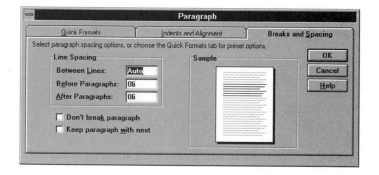

Fig. 6.12
You can control space between lines, before and after paragraphs, and the location of paragraph breaks.

Most common business documents such as letters and memos are single-spaced documents; the amount of space between lines is just enough to make the document readable. Single-spaced documents, however, do not allow much room for writing between the lines, which is why most draft documents are double-spaced. For example, reports and proposals often are double-spaced—at least in the beginning stages—because many people may review the document. In addition to being easier to read, a double-spaced document is much easier to review, edit, and add comments to than a single-spaced document.

In Works, you have complete control over the line spacing used in your documents; you aren't limited to single or double spacing. In the Paragraph dialog box in figure 6.12, the setting in the Between Lines section is represented in number of lines. The default setting is *Auto*, which means the line space is equal to the height of the largest character in the current font and size. (If you change the font and size of the current text, Works automatically adjusts the line spacing.) You can enter any whole positive number in the Between Lines section (2, 5, 10, and so on) or any number fraction (1.3, 3.2, 5.8, and so on). To return to the default setting, enter Auto in the Between Lines section.

> **Note**
>
> If you prefer to set line spacing using a different unit of measurement, you can type a designator following the number you enter, such as 3 cm for 3 centimeters. You can enter *in* or " for inches, *cm* for centimeters, *mm* for millimeters, *pi* for picas, or *pt* for points.

You can set a paragraph to single, double, or one-and-one-half spaced lines quickly by placing the insertion point anywhere in the paragraph then pressing one of the following key sequences:

Key Sequence	Function
Ctrl+1	Single spaces the current paragraph
Ctrl+2	Double spaces the current paragraph
Ctrl+5	Sets the spacing of the current paragraph to one-and-one-half

Works also enables you to specify the number of lines that precede and follow a paragraph. This setting is especially helpful for chapter names, titles, headings, opening paragraphs, and so on. Often you want these document elements set off with extra space, and the Before Paragraphs and After Paragraphs settings enable you to define this space. Like the Between Lines setting, the Before Paragraphs and After Paragraphs settings are measured in number of lines. For example, if you want one blank line to precede a document heading and two blank lines to follow the heading, enter **1** and **2** respectively in these settings boxes.

The two check boxes below the Line Spacing box are concerned with how paragraphs break in a document. You can select not to break a particular paragraph (Don't Brea**k** Paragraph), and you can select to keep a paragraph together with the paragraph that follows (Keep Paragraph **W**ith Next). For example, suppose that the letter you are writing includes an address near the bottom of the page where the reader can write for more information. If a page break causes the first line of the address to appear at the bottom of the page and the rest of the address appears at the top of the next page, you want to use the Don't Brea**k** Paragraph setting to keep all lines of the address together. Or suppose that the last paragraph on a page in your document ends in a colon and has a bulleted list of items following. You don't want a page break to occur between these two paragraphs, so highlight the first paragraph then select the Keep Paragraph **W**ith Next setting.

Keep your eye on the Sample section as you select your settings in the Paragraph dialog box. The settings you choose are reflected in the Sample section. For instance, if you set line spacing to 2, the sample paragraph switches to double-spaced text. When you select the Don't Brea**k** Paragraph setting, a bracket appears to the left of the sample paragraph in the Sample section indicating the paragraph should not be broken.

Use the following steps to set line spacing and paragraph breaks:

1. Place the insertion point in the paragraph you want to format. To format contiguous paragraphs, select at least a portion of text in each paragraph.

2. From the Forma**t** menu, choose the P**a**ragraph command. The Paragraph dialog box opens. If the Breaks and **S**pacing tab is not selected, choose it now.

3. In the Line Spacing section, set the amount of space in the Between **L**ines, **B**efore Paragraphs, and **A**fter Paragraphs boxes.

4. If you want to prevent the current paragraph from splitting in a page break, select the Don't Brea**k** Paragraph check box.

5. If you want to keep the current paragraph together with the paragraph that follows, select the Keep Paragraph **W**ith Next check box.

6. Choose OK. Works adjusts line spacing and page breaks according to the choices you make.

II

Word Processing

Bordering a Paragraph

Often documents contain special types of text that need to be very visible and accessible. One way to make a paragraph stand out is to place a border around it. For example, the notes and cautions in this book contain important information you don't want to overlook. To make sure you don't miss them, each note and caution has a border. Using Works, you can create a border using a single line, double line, bold line, or a color.

The term *border* is somewhat misleading because it implies that a line completely surrounds a paragraph. This type of border is called an *outline* border. But in Works, you also can create *partial* borders that fall on the top, bottom, left, or right sides of a paragraph. Or you can use any combination of the four partial borders. For example, you may want to use a bottom border to set off chapter names in a multi-chapter document, or you may want to use right and left borders to set off notes and cautions. A creative way to use a left or right border in a draft document is to mark all paragraphs in which a change has occurred. This type of border commonly is called a *change bar* or *revision mark*. Figure 6.13 illustrates some sample border styles.

Fig. 6.13
Use borders creatively to add style, draw attention, or mark revised text.

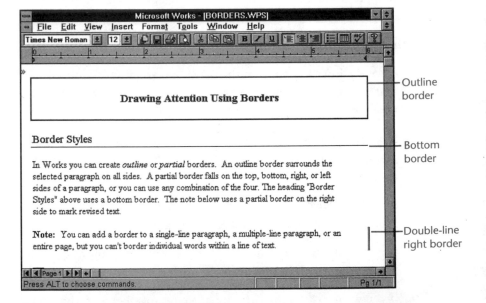

Note

You can add a border to a single-line paragraph, a multiple-line paragraph, several contiguous paragraphs, or an entire page, but you cannot border individual words within a line of text.

You use the Border dialog box shown in figure 6.14 to define a border, style, and color. To create an outline border, select the **O**utline check box. To create a partial border, select any combination of the **T**op, Botto**m**, **L**eft, and **R**ight check boxes. In the Line Style box, select **N**ormal for a single-line border, **B**old for a darker single-line border, or **D**ouble for a double-line border. To create a colored border, select a color from the **C**olor list. Note that unless you have a color printer, the color is visible only on-screen.

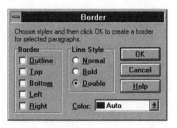

Fig. 6.14
Use the Border dialog box to select a border, style, and color.

Use the following steps to add a border to text:

1. Place the insertion point anywhere in the paragraph you want to border. To border contiguous paragraphs, select a portion of text in each paragraph.

2. From the Forma**t** menu, choose the **B**order command. The Border dialog box shown in figure 6.14 opens.

3. Select the **O**utline check box to create an outline border. Select any combination of the **T**op, Botto**m**, **L**eft, and **R**ight check boxes to create a partial border.

4. Select a style from the Line Style section.

5. Select a color from the **C**olor list.

6. Choose OK. Works adds the specified border to the current paragraph.

To remove a border, use the preceding steps but remove the *x* from all border check boxes.

Copying a Paragraph Style

Just as copying a character style can save you time and ensure consistency, copying a paragraph style can do the same. When you have spent time setting up indent markers, choosing paragraph alignment, defining line spacing, and specifying paragraph breaks for a single paragraph, you can copy the style to another paragraph faster than redefining it. When you copy a paragraph style, the paragraph to which you copy takes on all the indents, alignment, spacing, and paragraph breaks of the paragraph from which you copy.

You copy a paragraph style in much the same way you copy a character style. Follow these steps:

1. Select a portion of the paragraph that you want to copy the paragraph style.

2. From the **E**dit menu, choose the **C**opy command.

3. Select the paragraph to which you want to copy the paragraph style.

4. From the **E**dit menu, choose **P**aste Special. The Paste special dialog box opens.

5. Select the **P**aragraph Format option then choose OK. Works applies the copied paragraph style to the selected text.

Troubleshooting

When I drag the left-indent marker on the ruler, the first-line indent marker moves with it. Why?

The first-line indent is positioned relative to the left indent; therefore, when you move the left-indent marker, the first-line indent marker moves with it. To move the first-line indent marker by itself, press and hold Shift as you drag the marker.

Can I quickly set up the paragraph formats required to type a typical three- or four-level outline (I, II, III, A, B, C, 1, 2, 3, a, b, c, and so on)?

Yes. For the I. section of your outline, select the Hanging Indent quick format from the Paragraph dialog box, which creates a 1/2-inch hanging indent. When you're ready to type section A at the next outline level, press Ctrl+N to move the hanging indent 1/2 inch to the right. Ctrl+N is a keyboard shortcut for what Works calls a *nested* indent, an indent identical to the preceding indent except bumped 1/2 inch to the right. When you're ready to type point 1 under section A., press Ctrl+N again. Works moves the hanging indent to the right 1/2 inch. To move back to the preceding outline level, press Ctrl+M, which moves the hanging indent back to the left 1/2 inch. Press Ctrl+M again to move the hanging indent back another 1/2 inch.

I used an outline border on a paragraph that split between two pages. Now half the border appears at the bottom of the first page and the other half appears at the top of the next page. Why did this happen?

A border around a paragraph doesn't prevent the paragraph from splitting if it falls near a page break. To avoid this situation, select the bordered paragraph then select the Don't Break Paragraph setting in the Paragraph dialog box under the Breaks and Spacing tab.

Inserting Page Breaks in a Document

As you create a document, Works keeps track of the number of lines you type relative to the page size and margin settings you are using. The program calculates where page breaks should occur and inserts a page break marker (a chevron character, shown in figure 6.15) at the proper location in the left margin. The page breaks that Works inserts are called *automatic* page breaks.

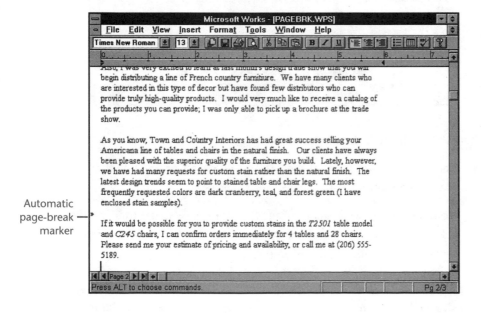

Automatic page-break marker

Fig. 6.15
A chevron character marks automatic page breaks in the left margin.

II

Word Processing

Because Works does not always break a page where you want, you can insert page breaks anywhere in a document. For instance, suppose that Works inserts a page break following a section heading and the first paragraph in the section bumps to the next page. You probably want to insert a page break just before the section heading so the heading and the first paragraph appear on the same page.

Page breaks that you insert are called *manual* page breaks and are indicated on-screen by a dashed line that runs horizontally across the document (see fig. 6.16). Manual page breaks are sometimes called *hard* page breaks. Works cannot adjust hard breaks; only you can move or delete them. When you insert a manual page break, Works automatically adjusts automatic page breaks throughout the document.

Fig. 6.16
A dashed line across the document indicates manual page breaks.

Manual page-break marker

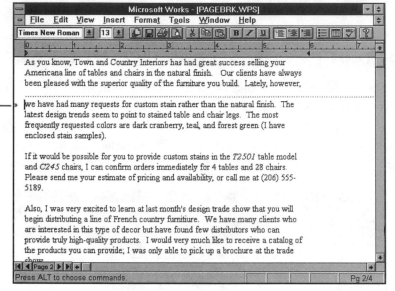

Follow these steps to insert a manual page break:

1. Place the insertion point at the leftmost character on the line that you want to appear on the new page.

2. From the **I**nsert menu, choose Page **B**reak; or press Ctrl+Enter. Works inserts a manual page break marker (a dashed line) in the document above the line with the insertion point.

To remove a manual page break, move the insertion point to the beginning of the dashed line, then press the Del key. When you delete a manual page break, Works automatically adjusts all automatic page breaks.

Troubleshooting

How can I delete an automatic page break that Works inserts in my document?

You cannot delete an automatic page break, but you can insert a manual break, which causes the automatic page break to readjust.

Why does the document I just printed contain many misplaced page breaks?

The document may contain manual page breaks you inserted before you revised the document. When a document undergoes extensive revision—large amounts of text are added or deleted—Works automatically adjusts the automatic page breaks but not the manual page breaks. Only you can move or delete manual breaks. When you know a document will undergo extensive revisions, don't insert manual page breaks until the content and structure of the document are stable. Also, don't forget to preview your document before printing so you can see where page breaks occur.

From Here...

For information related to enhancing the appearance of a document, refer to the following chapters of this book:

- Chapter 7, "Working with Tables, Columns, and Inserted Objects." You can use columns as an alternate format for a document, use tables to present certain types of information, and dress up documents with inserted objects.

- Chapter 8, "Adding Headers, Footers, Footnotes, and Bookmarks to a Document." Headers and footers make the pages of your document easier to manage and identify.

- Chapter 24, "Using Microsoft Draw and ClipArt." Creating a drawing or adding clip art can help you illustrate points in a document.

- Chapter 25, "Using WordArt and Note-It." Jazz up the text in your documents using WordArt or add a pop-up reminder or comment using Note-It.

II

Word Processing

Chapter 7

Working with Tables, Columns, and Inserted Objects

In Chapter 6, "Enhancing the Appearance of a Document," you learn how to enhance the appearance of text in a document by adding attributes such as special fonts, bold, italic, underline, and color. You also learn how to improve the appearance of paragraphs with special indentation, bullets, borders, and alignment styles. In this chapter, you learn some techniques that affect the layout of a document. For instance, certain types of documents lend themselves well to multi-column text rather than full-page text. Newsletters are a good example, and they often include pictures that blend comfortably into surrounding text. In other documents such as reports, manuals, or proposals, multi-column tables are appropriate. These features all affect the layout of a document and enhance its appearance.

This chapter discusses the following topics:

- Creating multi-column tables

- Formatting a document in multiple columns

- Inserting objects in a document

- Wrapping text around objects

Word Processing

Working with Tables

What is a table? Many ideas may come to mind, but in Works, a table consists of rows and columns of text or data arranged in a way that makes the information easy to understand. Some types of information in a document are best presented in a table rather than text. In Chapter 6, "Enhancing the Appearance of a Document," you learn how to create a two-column text table using the hanging indent format. But often, two columns are not enough. Your text or data may require 3, 4, 6, or more columns. An example of a 4-column text table is shown in figure 7.1.

Fig. 7.1
Some types of
information are
more accessible
when formatted as
a table.

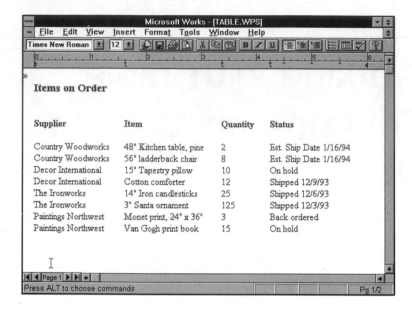

Because spreadsheets are fundamentally tables—they consist of rows and columns of data—Works enables you to include spreadsheets in word processor documents. In Works, you can incorporate spreadsheets using one of several methods. You can *embed* a spreadsheet, which gives you full access to the Works spreadsheet functions from inside the word processor window. Or you can *link* an existing spreadsheet, which ensures that the spreadsheet in your word processor document updates automatically when you change the spreadsheet in the window. To use either of these methods, refer to Chapter 26, "Using the Works Tools Together," which discusses linking and embedding.

A third method for incorporating a table in a word processor document is to create the table using *tabs*. A tab is a location to which the insertion point moves on the current line when you press the Tab key. Tabs enable you to align data or text in columns. In Works, you can set your own custom tabs or use default tab settings. Although the ruler doesn't display them, default tabs are at half-inch intervals on the ruler. Custom tabs always appear on the ruler, and you can set a custom tab at any ruler location.

Works offers four types of custom tabs: left, center, right, and decimal. The names refer to the alignment of text or data in a column. For instance, when you type data at a left tab, all data in the column is left-aligned at the tab location; when you type decimal numbers at a decimal tab, the decimal points in the column are aligned. Notice that all the data in the table in figure 7.1 is left-aligned. Left-alignment seems to work well for the Supplier and Item columns; however, the Quantity column is difficult to read because numbers are not generally left-aligned. In figure 7.2, the table is reset using a decimal tab for the numbers in the Quantity column and a right tab for the data in the Status column.

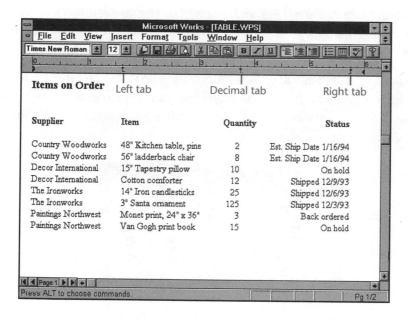

Fig. 7.2
Left-aligned, decimal, and right-aligned tabs change the alignment of data in a table.

Notice in figure 7.2 that tab marks for each type of tab appear on the ruler. Works uses the following marks on the ruler for each type of tab:

Right tab mark

Center tab mark

Left tab mark

Decimal tab mark

Creating a Table by Using Tabs

Tip
You can quickly open the Tabs dialog box without highlighting a tab by double-clicking to the left of the zero point on the ruler.

To create a table using tabs, first decide how many columns you need, the approximate width of each column, and the type of tab that's appropriate for the data in your table. To set a left tab, click on the ruler in the proper location. Works inserts left tabs wherever you click on the ruler. To set a right, center, or decimal tab, choose the **T**abs command on the Forma**t** menu to open the Tabs dialog box shown in figure 7.3. The **P**osition text box indicates the exact position of a tab, such as 1.62" or 3.37". Select from **L**eft, **C**enter, **R**ight, and **D**ecimal in the Alignment box.

You can set a left tab and open the Tabs dialog box all in one step by double-clicking the ruler in the location where you want the tab to be set. When the Tabs dialog box appears, the tab you set is highlighted and you can change its alignment, if necessary.

Fig. 7.3
Use the Tabs dialog box to specify tab settings for a table.

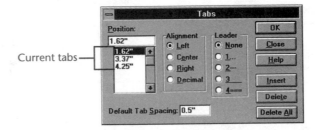

To set tabs for the columns in a table, follow these steps:

1. Move the insertion point to the line where you want your table to begin.

2. To set left tabs, click the proper location on the ruler. Works inserts a left tab marker on the ruler.

3. To set center, right, or decimal tabs, double-click the ruler or choose the **T**abs command on the Forma**t** menu to open the Tabs dialog box.

4. In the **P**osition box, enter a number in inches indicating the location of the tab on the ruler.

5. In the Alignment box, select **L**eft, **C**enter, **R**ight, or **D**ecimal.

6. Choose the **I**nsert button.

7. To set additional tabs, repeat steps 4-6.

8. After you set all tabs correctly, choose the **C**lose button.

Note

Because inches often convert to unfamiliar decimal numbers (such as 1.62 for 1 5/8 inches), you may have difficulty positioning a tab correctly when you type a setting in the **P**osition box. You may make several guesses before getting the tab in exactly the position you want. To save time and avoid experimenting with different settings, double-click on the ruler where you want to set the tab. The Tabs dialog box opens and the tab you set is highlighted so that you can change its alignment, if necessary.

The tabs you set apply to the line containing the insertion point. Begin typing the data for your table, pressing Enter to begin a new line. Like character style and paragraph formats, tabs remain in effect until you change or remove them.

Moving and Deleting Tabs

Sometimes after you enter all the data for a table, you may want to move tabs that are not positioned correctly. Or you may decide to add or delete a column of data, requiring that you add or delete a tab. Works makes moving and deleting tabs easy because you can drag the tab mark right on the ruler.

Before you move or delete a tab, you must select the lines that the ruler tabs affect. For instance, if your table contains 1 line of column headings, 1 blank line, and 8 lines of data, select all 10 lines before changing tab settings. If you forget to select the table, your tab changes affect only the line containing the insertion point; the remainder of the table continues to use the original tab settings. If you select only a portion of the table, the changes you make apply only to the text you select.

To move a tab, click and drag the tab to a new location on the ruler then release the mouse button. The tab automatically assumes its new position on the ruler. To delete a tab, click and drag the tab off the ruler (up or down) then release the mouse button. Works automatically realigns the data in the table based on the new tab settings. If you move or delete a tab by mistake, you can restore it by choosing the **U**ndo command on the **E**dit menu or by pressing Ctrl+Z.

Tip

If you work frequently with tabs, think about customizing your toolbar to add the Left, Center, Right, and Decimal tab tools. To use a toolbar tab, click the tool to highlight it, then click anywhere on the ruler to insert a tab of that type.

Note

Before deleting a tab, you may want to delete the data in the column first. If you delete the tab first, the table reformats using one less tab, and the alignment of columns is thrown off. Finding the correct data to delete then becomes difficult. You can avoid this problem by deleting the data first then deleting the tab.

You also can use the Tabs dialog box to move or delete tabs. To move a tab, highlight the tab in the Position list. Move the insertion point into the **P**osition box and type a new setting for the tab. For instance, to move a tab from 3" to 3.5", highlight the 3" tab in the Position list then change the 3" entry in the **P**osition box to 3.5". Choose the **I**nsert button to save the new setting then choose **C**lose.

To delete a tab, highlight the tab in the Position list then choose the **D**elete button. Works removes the tab from the Position list. Repeat these steps to delete additional tabs then choose **C**lose to return to your document.

Using Leaders in a Table

Sometimes using a leader can make the data in a table easier to read and follow. A *leader* is a dotted line (or other character) that fills the space between columns in a table. Leaders help your eye track a row of data from one column to another. Figure 7.4 illustrates a dot leader.

Fig. 7.4
A leader helps your eye track a row in a table.

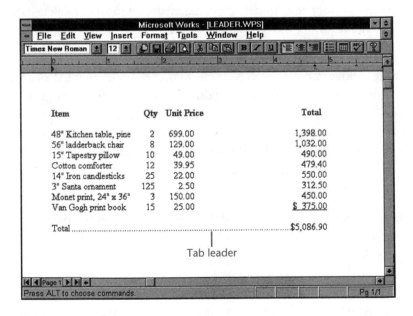

To add a leader to a tab, select a style from the Leader box after you set the tab (refer to fig. 7.3). Works automatically fills the space preceding the tab with the leader character you select.

Troubleshooting

I changed the tab position of several tabs in my table, but only part of my table reformatted. What happened?

You didn't select the entire table before you moved the tabs. If you haven't made any other changes to the document, use the **U**ndo command on the **E**dit menu to restore the original settings. If you aren't able to use Undo, select the entire table then reset all tabs to the new positions you want to use.

How can I center my column headings above the tables in my columns?

Works doesn't have a feature that automatically centers headings above columns. To make the headings appear centered over the columns, type the table first then type the headings using different tab settings than the table. You may need to experiment a little to find the correct position. Be sure to set the font and size you want to use before setting the tabs then preview the document before printing.

Creating Columns of Text

Certain types of documents lend themselves well to multiple columns of text. Newspapers and magazines use this style almost exclusively; you can use the same style to create newsletters, articles, brochures, or other types of documents.

When you format a document for multiple columns, you determine the number of columns and the amount of space between columns. The columns apply to the entire document except headers and footers. (You cannot use multiple columns on selected pages of a document.) Based on the number of columns you specify, the page size, and the margin settings, Works automatically calculates the width of the columns. You also can add a vertical line between columns. An example of a multi-column document is shown in the Preview screen in figure 7.5.

Choosing Column Specifications

To create a multi-column document, choose the **C**olumns command on the Forma**t** menu, which displays the Columns dialog box shown in figure 7.6. You don't need to select text in the document before formatting columns; Works applies the columns to the entire document. In the Columns dialog box, you specify the number of columns and the space between columns. You also can choose to insert a vertical line between columns. The Sample area shows how your document will look based on the specifications you use.

Fig. 7.5
The Preview screen
shows how a
multi-column
document looks.

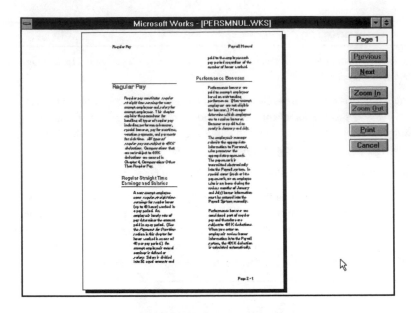

Fig. 7.6
The Columns
dialog box.

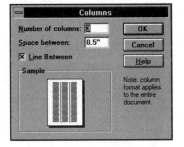

To specify columns in a document, follow these steps:

1. From the Format menu, choose the Columns command. The Columns
dialog box shown in figure 7.6 is displayed.

2. In the **N**umber of Columns box, enter the number of columns to use.

3. In the **S**pace Between box, enter a measurement in inches for the space
you want between columns.

4. To print a vertical line between columns, select the **L**ine Between check
box.

5. Click OK. Works displays a message suggesting that you switch to page
layout view to view the document.

6. Choose **Y**es. Works displays the columns on your screen.

Viewing and Moving through a Multi-Column Document

When you switch to Page Layout view, as Works suggests, the columns appear side by side on your screen. Notice that the right and left indent markers on the ruler now are much closer together than normal—the markers define the width of a single column. If you specify a line between columns, you don't see it in Page Layout view, but the line is visible when you preview the document.

To move the insertion point using the mouse, click anywhere on the page. Using the keyboard, press the right- and left-arrow keys to move the insertion point within the current column. When you reach the bottom of the first column, press the right-arrow key to bring the insertion point up to the top of the next column. Use the scroll bars, the page navigation buttons, and the Page Up and Page Down keys as you normally would. For more information about working with Page Layout view, refer to Chapter 9, "Checking Your Document."

If you choose to continue working in Normal rather than Page Layout view, multiple columns do not appear side by side. Instead, you see only one column of text along the left edge of the page. In Normal view, you cannot tell where a new column begins.

Troubleshooting

What is the maximum number of columns I can use in a document?

Works doesn't really have a maximum number because the program calculates the placement of columns based on the space between columns and the margin widths. If your margins are narrow and the space between columns is minimal, obviously Works can create more columns. The maximum number is entirely dependent on these factors. Works displays an error message when it is unable to create the number of columns you specify.

I want to format my document with two columns, but I want the left column to be wider than the right one. How can I do this?

In Works, all columns have uniform width; you cannot make one column wider or narrower than another.

I want to enter a title across the full page of my multi-column newsletter. How can I create this title if Works applies multiple columns to the entire document?

You can enter the title of your newsletter in a header. Multi-column formatting does not affect headers. For information about creating headers, refer to Chapter 8, "Adding Headers, Footers, Footnotes, and Bookmarks to a Document."

II

Word Processing

Removing Columns

Multiple columns are as easy to remove from a document as they are to define. Open the Columns dialog box, type a number in the **N**umber of Columns box, then choose OK. Works reformats the document according to the number of columns you specify.

Working with Inserted Objects

One of the most dramatic ways to make a document more visually appealing is to include graphic elements and illustrations. As discussed in Chapter 1, "Introducing Works for Windows," Works provides a variety of ways to include such items. Using ClipArt, you can include a prepared drawing to add humor, draw attention, or illustrate a point. With Microsoft Draw, you can create your own drawings that are custom-designed to achieve the same purpose. WordArt's unique capability to bend and shape text offers a creative way to dress up and stylize titles, banners, headlines, or logos. And finally, the Note-It feature in Works enables you to insert eye-catching icons into a document that reveal a hidden note when you click the icon.

Inserting Objects in a Document

All four of the mini-applications mentioned in the preceding section insert *objects* into your document. The method for inserting an object varies from application to application. For instance, when you create a drawing using Microsoft Draw, a separate drawing window appears on-screen. You use the drawing commands and tools to create your drawing, then insert the object into your document. Like Microsoft Draw, WordArt uses a separate window as well as its own menu bar and tool bar. To insert a note in a document, you use the Note-It dialog box to select a note style and enter the note text. ClipArt also uses its own dialog box from which you can preview and choose the file to insert.

Because the method for inserting objects varies from one application to another, the focus of this section is not to describe in detail how to insert objects—later chapters discuss these details. Rather, the important thing to understand is what actually happens when you insert an object. Because an object has height and width, it disrupts the surrounding text when placed at the insertion point. The insertion point may be on a blank line, at the end of a line of text, or in the middle of a paragraph. Regardless of the insertion point's position, the height of the current line increases to accommodate the height of the object. Therefore, you must determine the best size and position for the object then specify how you want to format the surrounding text.

Refer to Chapter 24, "Using Microsoft Draw and ClipArt," for details about creating and inserting Microsoft Draw drawings and choosing ClipArt files. Refer to Chapter 25, "Using WordArt and Note-It," for information about using WordArt and Note-It.

Selecting, Sizing, and Moving Objects

After you insert an object in a document, the object occupies space in the document. Because all objects have height and width, they generally occupy more space than a single line of text. Before you can determine how to format the surrounding text, you need to know how to select, move, and resize an object, if necessary.

To select an object, click anywhere on the object. The object's *frame* (the rectangular shape that surrounds the object) becomes visible. Regardless of the size of a particular object, all objects have a rectangular shape when you select them. At the corners and midpoints around the frame are *handles*, used for resizing the object (see fig. 7.7.).

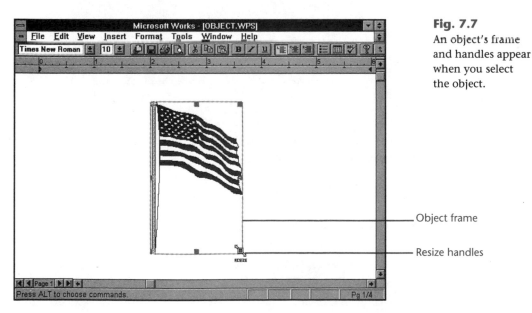

Fig. 7.7
An object's frame and handles appear when you select the object.

Object frame

Resize handles

You can resize an object in several ways. First select the object so its frame and handles are visible. When you place the mouse pointer on any of the handles, the pointer changes to a resize arrow (refer to figure 7.7). Click and drag a side, top, or bottom handle to resize in one dimension only. For instance, drag the top or bottom handle to make the object longer or shorter. Release the mouse button when the object is the size you want. To resize an object while maintaining its height-to-width ratio, click and drag any of the corner handles. The object resizes in two dimensions at the same time.

An alternative to sizing an object using the mouse is to specify exact dimensions for the object. To specify dimensions or to scale an object from its original size, choose the Picture/Object command on the Format menu, which displays the Picture/Object dialog box from the Format menu, shown in figure 7.8. (If the Size tab is not selected, click it or type Alt+S.)

The Original Size section lists the original width and height of the object. In the Size section, you can enter numbers in the **W**idth and **H**eight boxes. Or if you prefer to scale the object, enter percentages in the W**i**dth and Hei**g**ht boxes in the Scaling section. After you size the object correctly, choose OK.

Fig. 7.8
Use the Picture/
Object dialog box
to specify an
object's exact
dimensions and
scale.

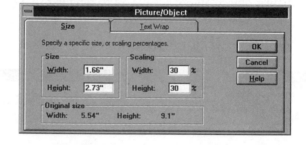

To move an object, you simply drag it to the proper location. When you point anywhere on the object, the I-beam mouse pointer changes to an arrow labeled DRAG. Click the object and hold down the left mouse button; the DRAG label changes to MOVE. Drag the object in any direction until it is where you want. Don't worry yet about the surrounding text.

Wrapping Text around Inserted Objects

Because most objects occupy more space than a single line of text in a document, you must make choices about how you want to format the surrounding text. Works offers two options for formatting the text that borders an inserted object: *in-line* or *absolute*. These options are illustrated in figure 7.9, where the Picture/Object dialog box is shown with the **T**ext Wrap tab selected.

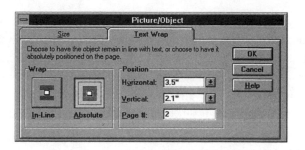

Fig. 7.9
The Picture/Object dialog box illustrates text wrap options.

The **In**-line wrap option positions an object on the same line as the text that immediately precedes and follows the object. The height of the object determines the height of that line because Works treats the object as if it were a character on the line. The **A**bsolute wrap option surrounds all sides of the object with text (see fig. 7.10).

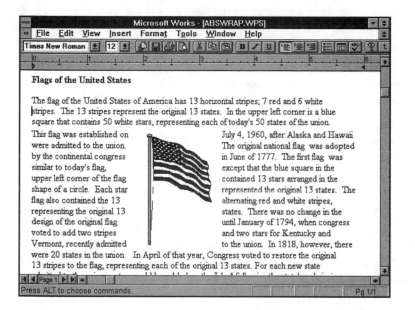

Fig. 7.10
The Absolute setting causes text to surround an object.

The settings in the Position box are available only when you select the **Abso**lute wrap option. Initially, the **Ho**rizontal box shows where the object is positioned relative to the left edge of the paper; the **V**ertical box shows where the object is positioned relative to the top edge of the paper. The **P**age # box shows the page number where the object is located. In figure 7.9, for example, the object is 3.5" from the left edge of the paper and 2.1" from the top of the paper.

If you prefer, you can use the H**o**rizontal and **V**ertical boxes to position an object for you. Each box is a drop-down list that contains the choices Left, Center, and Right. If you want your object to appear in the exact center of the page, for instance, you can select the Center setting in both the H**o**rizontal and **V**ertical boxes. If you want the object to appear in the lower left corner of the page, select the Left setting in the H**o**rizontal box and the Bottom setting in the **V**ertical box. To change the page on which the object appears, enter a new page number in the **P**age # box.

Troubleshooting

How can I place text only above and below my object and center the object horizontally? (I don't want any text on the line with the object.)

Works doesn't have an automatic setting for this arrangement, but you can achieve it. Place the object on a line of its own between the two lines of text that you want to border the object. Select the In-line wrap option. In the document, select the object then select the Center alignment button on the toolbar. The object is centered and bordered on top and bottom by text.

Sometimes when I select the Absolute setting, my screen shows a large space between lines of text at the top of my object. Will this cause a problem when I print my document?

No. If you preview your document, you see that the spacing between lines adjusts correctly.

From Here...

The topics discussed in this chapter affect the layout and overall appearance of a document. For more information about features that enhance the appearance of a document, refer to the following chapters:

- Chapter 6, "Enhancing the Appearance of a Document," includes information about choosing fonts, sizes, styles, and setting indentation, alignment, and spacing in a document.

- Chapter 8, "Adding Headers, Footers, Footnotes, and Bookmarks to a Document," explains how to add repetitive information at the top and bottom of pages to make a document easier to navigate.

- Chapter 24, "Using Microsoft Draw and ClipArt," describes how to create your own drawings or use prepared drawings in your documents.

- Chapter 25, "Using WordArt and Note-It," describes how you can spruce up your documents with flashy text and insert pop-up notes.

- Chapter 26, "Using the Works Tools Together," describes how to incorporate spreadsheets into a document as an alternative to creating tables with the word processor.

II

Word Processing

Adding Headers, Footers, Footnotes, and Bookmarks to a Document

Chapter 6, "Enhancing the Appearance of a Document," and Chapter 7, "Working with Tables, Columns, and Inserted Objects," discuss how to enhance documents by using various character and paragraph styles, alignment, borders, columns, tables, and inserted objects. All these features enhance the appearance of a document. The features discussed in this chapter also are enhancements, but they enhance the *readability* of a document.

This chapter discusses the following topics:

- Inserting headers and footers

- Adding footnotes

- Using a bookmark to mark a location in a document

Using Headers and Footers in a Document

Before you print a document, you may want to include a title, page number, date, or other information that prints at the top or bottom of each page. Repetitive text that appears at the top of each page is called a *header*. Text that appears at the bottom of the page is called a *footer*. You can add a header, footer, or both to any document and include any information relevant to the particular document. (For example, you may want to include a reminder such as *Company Confidential* at the top of each page.) If your document includes a title page, you may eliminate the header and footer from the first page if you want. Headers and footers print within the top and bottom margin areas of your document.

Choosing a Standard or Paragraph Header or Footer

In Works you can create two types of headers and footers: *standard* or *paragraph*. A standard header or footer cannot be longer than one line of text. You can insert special codes that print the current date, current time, page numbers, file name, and so on. However, you cannot change the font or add effects such as bold, underline, or italic. You enter a standard header or footer in the Headers and Footers dialog box, displayed by selecting the **H**eaders and Footers command on the **V**iew menu. After you close the dialog box, the header or footer is visible on-screen only in Page Layout view. When using Normal or Draft view, headers and footers are visible when you preview the document. Use a standard header or footer when you know the text will not be longer than one line and you don't have any special formatting, font, or enhancement requirements. Standard headers and footers are illustrated in figure 8.1.

A paragraph header or footer can be longer than one line of text. You also can include a picture or apply formatting, font, and style characteristics just like you do to regular text in a document. Paragraph headers and footers are visible in the document window. In Normal and Draft views, the header and footer appear only at the top of the first page of the document. In Page Layout view, the header appears at the top of every page, and the footer appears at the bottom of every page. Use a paragraph header or footer rather than a standard header or footer when you know the text will be longer than one line, when you want to include a picture, or when you want to format and enhance the header or footer. An example of paragraph headers and footers is shown in figure 8.2.

For information about inserting a picture in a header or footer, refer to Chapter 7, "Working with Tables, Columns, and Inserted Objects," and Chapter 24, "Using Microsoft Draw and ClipArt." For more information about using Draft and Page Layout views, refer to Chapter 9, "Checking Your Document."

Creating a Standard Header or Footer

To create a standard header, footer, or both, choose the **H**eaders and Footers command from the **V**iew menu to open the dialog box shown in figure 8.3. Enter the header text in the H**e**ader box; enter the footer text in the **F**ooter box. In either case, you can enter only as many characters that fit on one line of text. The number of characters varies depending on the font and point size you use in your document. The header and footer font and point size always match the font and point size used throughout the document. Headers and footers are always centered by default.

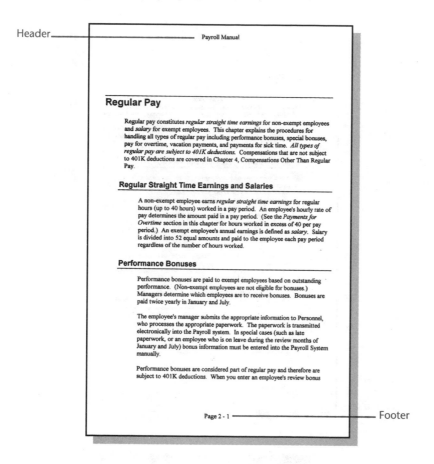

Fig. 8.1
Standard headers and footers cannot be longer than one line of text.

Because you cannot format standard header or footer text the way you normally format text in a document, Works provides some codes you can include with the header or footer text (refer to fig. 8.3). Some codes format text and other codes insert special text such as a page number, file name, or current date. For codes that format text, you must enter the code immediately preceding the text. For example, you can specify that Works right-align your text by entering **&r** immediately preceding the text you want right-aligned. For codes that insert text, you type the code, such as **&f**, which prints the file name in the header or footer. You also can combine codes where appropriate.

For instance, if you want Works to insert the file name of the current document and center the name, type **&c&f**. To make the codes easier to read, you can separate them with a space if you like (as in **&c &f**). You can also enter combinations of codes (such as centering and bolding) in any order.

Fig. 8.2
Paragraph headers
and footers can be
more than one line
and can include
character and
paragraph
enhancements.

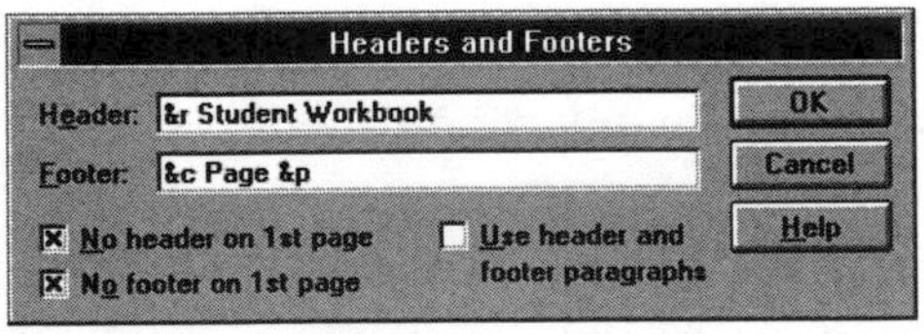

Header in
different font
from text and
with bottom
border

Footer in same
font as header
and with top
border

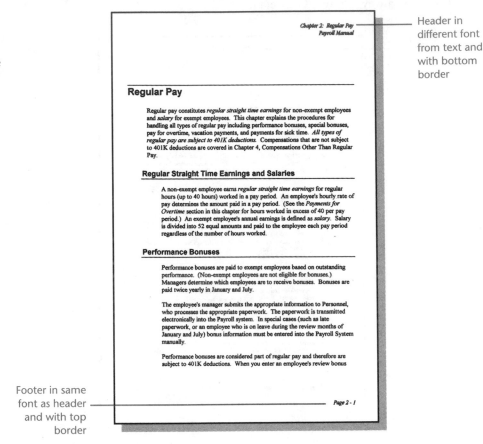

Fig. 8.3
Type the text for
a header, footer,
or both in the
Headers and
Footers dialog box.

The complete list of codes is shown in Table 8.1.

Code	Function
&l	Left-align the text that follows the code
&r	Right-align the text that follows the code
&c	Center the text that follows the code
&f	Print the file name
&p	Print page numbers
&t	Insert the time of printing
&d	Insert the date at time of printing (such as 3/2/94)
&n	Insert the long form date at time of printing (such as 2 March 94)
&&	Print an ampersand (&)

Table 8.1 Alignment and Special Character Codes

To create a header, footer, or both, follow these steps:

1. From the **V**iew menu, choose the **H**eaders and Footers command. The Headers and Footers dialog box shown in figure 8.3 opens.

2. In the He**a**der box, enter the text and any codes you want to use for the header.

3. In the **F**ooter box, enter the text and any codes you want to use for the footer.

4. To eliminate a header or footer on the first page of your document, select the **N**o Header on 1st Page or N**o** Footer on 1st Page check boxes.

5. Choose OK.

Changing and Deleting a Standard Header or Footer

At any time in a document, you can change the content of a standard header or footer, as well as the format or any special text you included. To change a header or footer, recall the Headers and Footers dialog box then make the appropriate changes in the **H**eader and **F**ooter text boxes.

Tip
If you are using Page Layout view, you can instantly display the Headers and Footers dialog box by double-clicking the header or footer text in your document.

Word Processing

Creating a Paragraph Header or Footer

To create a paragraph header or footer, choose the **H**eaders and Footers command on the **V**iew menu to open the Headers and Footers dialog box. After you select the **U**se Header and Footer Paragraphs check box, Works returns to your document and places an H at the far left position on the first line. You use this line to type the header text. On the line just below the H, Works places an F at the far left position to designate the footer line. (Notice that the H and the F are visible on-screen in normal and draft view; in page layout view, you see the actual text you enter.) At the center of this line is the notation Page - *page*. The Page - part of this notation indicates that Works will print the word *Page* followed by a hyphen on the footer line. The *page* portion of the notation is a code that inserts the proper page number on each page. So the footer on page 1 of a document reads Page - 1 using this notation. Below the F designating the footer line is the chevron symbol indicating the beginning of the page. The H and F appear above the chevron symbol because they are not part of the regular page of text; the text for the header and footer print within the top and bottom margin areas of the page.

Because page numbers are used so commonly in footers, the Page - *page* notation is automatically included when you create a paragraph footer. However, you can remove the footer or place the page numbers in the header if you want. An example of the header and footer as Works creates them is shown in figure 8.4.

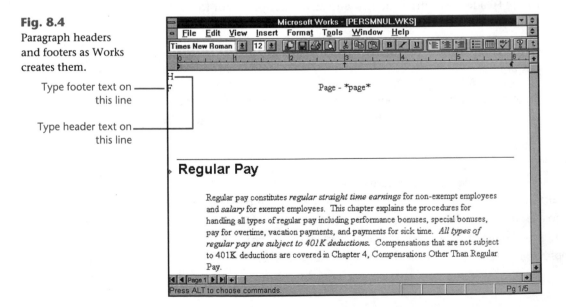

Fig. 8.4
Paragraph headers and footers as Works creates them.

Type footer text on this line

Type header text on this line

Because header and footer designators (H and F) appear in the working area of the word processor window, you can edit, format, and enhance a header or footer just like you can modify any other lines of body text. You can choose a different font, point size, or text color, and you can apply bold, underline, or italic. However, some restrictions apply. The alignment style you select applies to an entire header or footer; you cannot use one style on the first line and a different style on the next line. Likewise, borders apply to an entire header or footer; you cannot border individual lines.

Just as with standard headers and footers, paragraph headers and footers can include special text (such as the file name or the current time) that Works inserts for you automatically. However, rather than including &+codes with the text as you do with standard headers and footers, you insert special text by using the Special Character dialog box, displayed by selecting the Special Character command on the Insert menu (see fig. 8.5).

Fig. 8.5
Use the Special Character dialog box to insert special text in a paragraph header or footer.

When you select an option in the Special Character dialog box, Works inserts a code for the special text in the header or footer then substitutes the correct information when the document prints. The code is a word preceded and followed by an asterisk. You already have seen an example of such a code— the *page* notation is a special character code that Works inserts automatically in footers. Although the notation appears to be a simple *asterisk-word-asterisk*, the notation actually is a code. For example, you cannot simply type the characters ***page***. You must use the Special Character dialog box to insert the code. If you type ***page***, Works interprets the characters literally and prints **page** rather than the correct page number.

Works provides shortcut keys for inserting special character codes in paragraph headers and footers. These keys are shown in Table 8.2. (Notice that not all character codes have shortcut keys.)

Table 8.2 Shortcut Keys for Special Character Codes	
Code	**Function**
Ctrl+A	Insert the file name in a paragraph header or footer
Ctrl+;	Insert the current date in a paragraph header or footer
Ctrl+Shift+;	Insert the current time in a paragraph header or footer
Ctrl+D	Insert the date at time of printing
Ctrl+T	Insert the time of printing

To create a paragraph header or footer, follow these steps:

1. From the **V**iew menu choose the **H**eaders and Footers command. Works displays the Headers and Footers dialog box.

2. If you want, select the **N**o Header on 1st Page or the N**o** Footer on 1st Page check boxes.

3. Select the **U**se Header and Footer Paragraphs check box and choose OK. Works returns to your document and inserts an H (for header) on the first line of the document and an F (for footer) on the second line. The notation Page - *page* also appears on the footer line.

4. Move the insertion point to the H line and type the text for the header. Press Enter to add more lines to the header, if necessary.

5. Move the cursor to the F line and type the text for the footer. Press Enter to add more lines to the footer if necessary. (You may delete the Page - *page* notation if you want.)

6. Apply any fonts, point sizes, alignment styles, or character styles to selected header or footer text.

7. To have Works insert special text in the header or footer, place the insertion point in the correct position then choose the **S**pecial Character command from the **I**nsert menu. The Special Character dialog box opens. Select a special character option then choose OK. Works inserts a special character code in the header or footer.

8. After the header and footer are complete, move the insertion point back into the main body of the document and continue working.

Tip

You can use only a header in a document by clearing the footer line and leaving it blank. You can use only a footer by leaving the header line blank.

Removing a Paragraph Header or Footer

After setting up a standard or paragraph header or footer, you may decide you don't need it. To delete a standard header or footer, recall the Headers and Footers dialog box by choosing the **H**eaders and Footers command on the **V**iew menu. Delete all text in the He**a**der and **F**ooter boxes then choose OK. To delete a paragraph header and footer, recall the Headers and Footers dialog box, remove the *x* from the **U**se Header and Footer Paragraphs check box, then choose OK. Works automatically deletes the header and footer text from the document.

Altering Header and Footer Margins

As you learned earlier in this chapter, headers and footers print within the top and bottom margin areas of the document. The default top and bottom margin settings are 1 inch. Within that space are default header and footer margins of 1/2 inch. Therefore, a header or footer must fit within 1/2 inch to print correctly. Because the one-line standard header or footer always fits within a 1/2-inch margin, you never need to adjust margins for a standard header or footer. However, paragraph headers and footers can be multiple lines and therefore, margins may require adjustment.

Figure 8.6 illustrates how Works measures margins. The top margin is the distance from the top of the paper to the point where you want body text to begin. The header margin is the distance from the top of the paper to the first line of text in the header. The bottom margin is the distance from the bottom of the paper to the point where you want the last line of body text to fall. The footer margin is the distance from the bottom of the paper to the first line of text in the footer. Notice that the header and footer margins are different.

> **Note**
>
> *The footer margin includes the footer text itself, but the header margin does not.* This point is important to remember when adjusting header and footer margins. Also, because header and footer margins fit within top and bottom margins, header and footer margin measurements must be less than or equal to top and bottom margin measurements.

In Chapter 4, "Creating, Saving, and Printing a Word Processing Document," you learn how to adjust top, bottom, left, and right margins using the Page Setup dialog box (see fig. 8.7). In the same dialog box, you use the He**a**der Margin and **F**ooter Margin text boxes to adjust header and footer settings.

Fig. 8.6
Headers and
footers must fit
within top and
bottom margins.

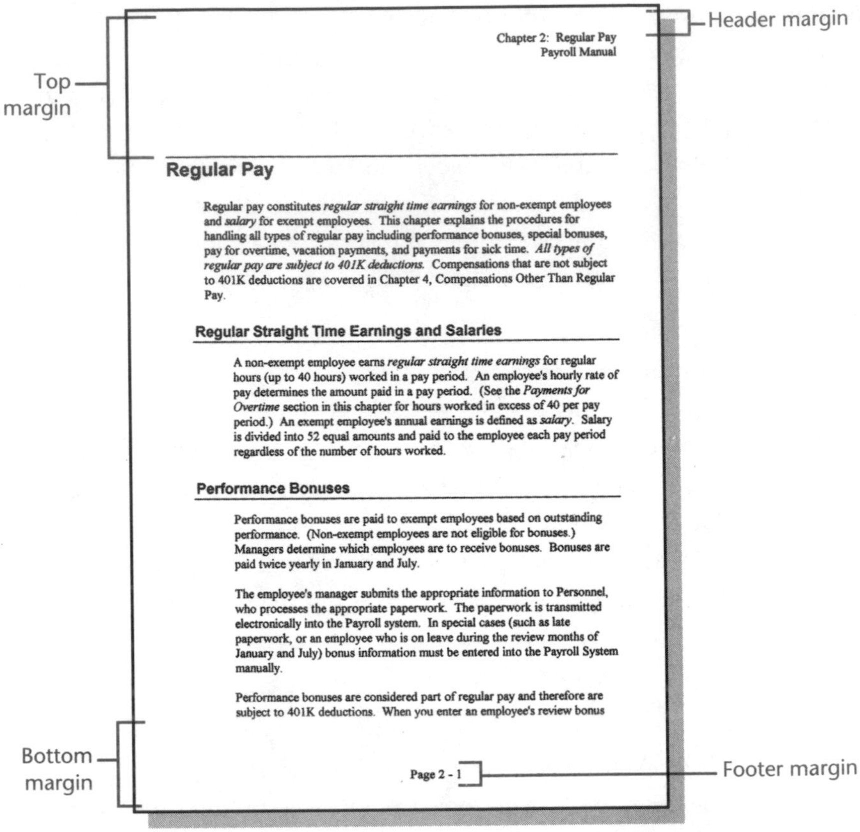

Fig. 8.7
Use the Page Setup
dialog box to
adjust header and
footer margins.

Enter header and
footer margins here

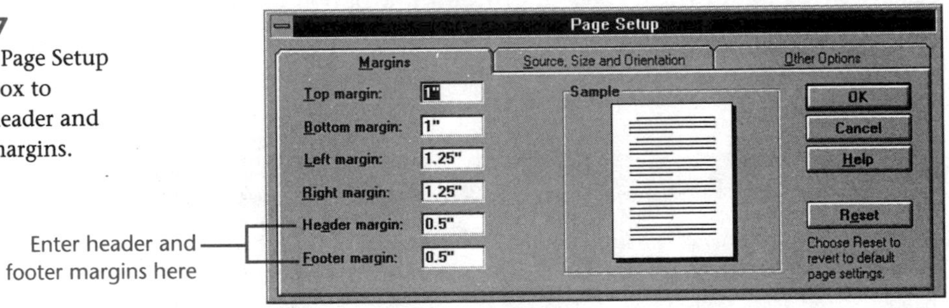

To adjust top, bottom, header, and footer margins, use the following steps:

1. From the **F**ile menu, choose the Pa**g**e Setup command. The Page Setup dialog box opens.

2. In the dialog box, choose the **M**argins tab. The dialog box shown in figure 8.7 opens.

3. In the **T**op Margin, **B**ottom Margin, He**a**der Margin, and **F**ooter Margin boxes, type the setting you want to use in inches. Type a decimal for fractions of an inch (such as 1.25 for 1 1/4 inches).

4. After all margin settings are correct, choose OK.

Troubleshooting

In my standard header, I entered the codes &r &f to right-align the document's file name, but when I printed the document, the header read "& f" at the right margin. What happened?

You typed the &r code correctly, but you typed a space between the & and f, so Works interpreted the two characters literally. When inserting codes, you can put a space between separate codes to make them easier to read, but be careful not to put a space within a code itself.

I removed a paragraph header and footer by mistake; can I restore it?

Yes. If you accidentally delete paragraph headers and footers by removing the x from the **U**se Header and Footer Paragraphs check box, just check the **U**se Header and Footer Paragraphs check box again. Works saves the paragraph header and footer text.

My two-line header is printing correctly, but my two-line footer is printing too close to the bottom of the page. My top and bottom margins are set at 1.25 inches, and my header and footer margins are set at .5 inch. What's wrong?

Remember that the footer margin is the space from the bottom of the page to the top of the footer—the footer margin includes the footer text, unlike the header margin. Try increasing the footer margin to .75 inches.

Adding Footnotes to a Document

Footnotes often are used in reports, proposals, and other business documents to cite the source of information or to provide additional information, comments, or remarks about a topic in the body. A footnote marker appears in the body of the document where you place the marker, and the actual footnote text prints at the bottom of the page or at the end of the document. You can use numbered footnote markers, or you can specify another character to mark the location of a footnote.

When you insert a footnote in Normal or Draft view, Works displays a footnote pane at the bottom of the document window (see fig. 8.8). Works inserts the matching footnote marker and places the insertion point next to the marker in the footnote pane. In this pane, you can enter, edit, and format the footnote text just like any other text in the document. After you complete the footnote, move the insertion point back into the body of the document and continue working. You can close the footnote pane by choosing the **F**ootnotes command on the **V**iew menu. This command toggles the footnote pane on and off; choose the command another time to view footnotes again.

Fig. 8.8

Enter, edit, and format footnote text in the footnote pane when using Normal or Draft views.

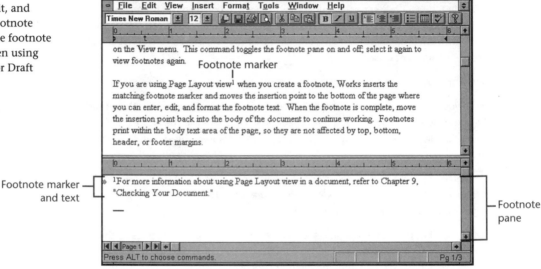

If you are using Page Layout view when you create a footnote, Works inserts the matching footnote marker and moves the insertion point to the bottom of the page where you can enter, edit, and format the footnote text. After you complete the footnote, move the insertion point back into the body of the document to continue working. Footnotes print in the body text area of the page, so they are not affected by top, bottom, header, or footer margins.

For more information about using different views in a document, refer to Chapter 9, "Checking Your Document."

Creating a Footnote

To insert a footnote in a document, you use the Footnote dialog box shown in figure 8.9. In this dialog box you select the **N**umbered or **C**haracter Mark style for the footnote marker. If you want help creating a footnote, you can choose the **U**se WorksWizard button.

Fig. 8.9
Use the Footnote dialog box to choose a footnote marker style.

Follow these steps to create a footnote:

1. Move the insertion point to the location in the document where you want to insert the footnote marker.

2. From the **I**nsert menu, choose the Foo**t**note command. The Footnote dialog box shown in figure 8.9 opens.

3. Select the **N**umbered or **C**haracter Mark option. If you select the **C**haracter Mark, type the character in the Mark box.

4. Choose OK. Works returns to your document. In Page Layout view, the insertion point moves to the bottom of the page. In Normal or Draft view, the insertion point moves into a footnote pane at the bottom of the document window. You now can enter, edit, and format the footnote text.

5. After you complete the footnote, move the insertion point back into the body of the document to continue working.

Moving or Copying a Footnote

Sometimes you may want to move a footnote in a document from one location to another, or you may want to copy a footnote to another page. You can move and copy footnotes in Works just like you move or copy any other text in a document. The important thing to remember is to select and move or copy the footnote *marker* in the body of the text rather than the footnote text itself. After you select the marker and move or copy it, Works removes the footnote marker and footnote text from the original location. In the case of a move, Works places the footnote marker and the footnote text in the location where you paste it. If the order of footnotes changes, Works automatically renumbers footnotes appropriately.

Deleting a Footnote

You cannot delete a footnote by selecting and cutting the footnote text from the bottom of the page or the footnote pane. If you try to delete the footnote, Works displays an error message. You must delete a footnote by selecting the footnote *marker* in the body of the document then deleting the marker. (Use the Cut command on the Edit menu or press Del.) Works removes the text and marker from the list of footnotes and, in the case of numbered footnotes, automatically renumbers all remaining footnotes.

Printing Footnotes at the End of a Document

By default, Works assumes you want to print footnotes at the bottom of the appropriate page in a document. For some documents, however, you may decide to print all footnotes at the end of a document. To choose this option, choose the Page Setup command on the File menu to display the Page Setup dialog box shown in figure 8.10. If the Other Options tab is not selected, click it or type Alt+O.

Fig. 8.10
The Other Options tab in the Page Setup dialog box.

Check this box to print footnotes at end of document

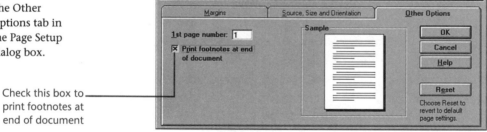

Follow these steps to print footnotes at the end of a document:

1. Before printing your document, from the File menu choose the Page Setup command. Works displays the Page Setup dialog box.

2. Choose the Other Options tab to open the dialog box shown in figure 8.10.

3. Select the Print Footnotes at End of Document check box.

4. Choose OK.

5. Print your document as you usually do.

To restore footnotes to their respective pages, clear the Print Footnotes at End of Document check box before printing again.

Troubleshooting

How many footnotes can I print on one page?

Because footnotes print in the body text area of a document, Works doesn't have a maximum number of footnotes. However, to maintain some balance on a page, you probably don't want footnotes to occupy more than half the page.

I created numbered footnotes in my document. Can I change them to character foot-notes?

Yes. Select the footnote marker in the body of the document then choose the Foot-note command on the Insert menu to insert a new footnote, changing the marker to a character. If you switch to character footnote markers, however, you should change all footnote markers throughout the document. If you mix numbered and character footnotes within a document, Works counts the character footnotes in sequence with the numbered ones.

Using Bookmarks

Just as you can place a paper bookmark in a book to mark the last page you read, you can insert an electronic *bookmark* in a document to mark a location where you want to return later. Using a bookmark lets you return instantly to the location you mark. Without using a bookmark, you can search for a location, but if you don't remember a particular word or phrase to search for, you may spend a long time looking for your place.

In Works, you assign a name to a bookmark using the Bookmark Name dialog box shown in figure 8.11. To find the bookmark in the document, you use the Go To dialog box, which lists the names of all bookmarks.

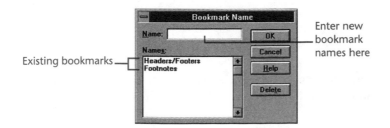

Fig. 8.11
Define bookmarks in the Bookmark Name dialog box.

Creating and Returning to a Bookmark

To create a bookmark, follow these steps:

1. Move the insertion point to the location in the document where you want to place a bookmark.

2. From the **I**nsert menu, choose the Bookmark **N**ame command. Works displays the Bookmark Name dialog box.

3. In the **N**ame text box, enter the name for the bookmark. Other existing bookmarks are listed in the Name**s** list box.

4. Choose OK.

Works invisibly marks the location in the document; you don't see bookmarks on-screen. To return to a bookmark, choose the **G**o To command on the **E**dit menu; or press F5. In the Go To dialog box that opens, double-click the bookmark name in the Name**s** list, or highlight the bookmark name and choose OK. Works immediately moves the insertion point in the document to the location of the bookmark.

Removing a Bookmark

When you no longer want to use an existing bookmark, you can delete it by following these steps:

1. From the **I**nsert menu choose the Bookmark **N**ame command. The Bookmark name dialog box opens.

2. In the Name**s** list, highlight the bookmark you want to delete.

3. Choose the Dele**t**e button. Works deletes the bookmark.

4. Repeat steps 2 and 3 to delete additional bookmarks.

5. After you finish deleting bookmarks, choose **C**lose.

From Here...

In this chapter, you learned how to make documents easier to read and manage by including headers, footers, footnotes, and bookmarks. For topics related to improving the appearance of a document, refer to the following chapters:

■ Chapter 6, "Enhancing the Appearance of a Document," includes information about choosing fonts, sizes, and styles, and setting indentation, alignment, and spacing in a document.

■ Chapter 7, "Working with Tables, Columns, and Inserted Objects," discusses using columns as an alternate format for a document, using tables to present certain types of information, and dressing up documents with inserted objects.

■ Chapter 24, "Using Microsoft Draw and ClipArt," describes how to create your own drawings or use prepared drawings in your documents.

■ Chapter 25, "Using WordArt and Note-It," describes how you can spruce up your documents with flashy text and insert pop-up notes.

II

Word Processing

Chapter 9

Checking Your Document

Nothing is worse than reading a printed document that contains spelling mistakes, formatting errors, and words used too frequently. Works contains several tools to assist you in producing clean, error-free documents. In addition, Works enables you to view a document in several ways, find and replace text, and count the words in a document. The best time to perform many of these checking tasks is after the content of the document is stable and before you print it; however, you are free to perform these tasks any time.

Changing Your View of a Document

A *view* defines the way Works displays a document on-screen. If you have read sequentially through the chapters in this book, you have seen many examples of documents in the figures. Most of these examples appear in *Normal* view, although you have seen a few examples of *Page Layout* view as well. A third view you have not yet seen is *Draft* view. In this section you can learn about these views and when to choose one view or another. Each view has its advantages and unique characteristics:

- *Normal view*. Works uses this view by default; unless you choose another view, Works displays all documents in Normal view. Normal view reflects most aspects of your document as they will appear when printed. That is, Works displays accurate font and point sizes, text alignment and paragraph formats, and any inserted pictures or drawings. Missing from Normal view are margins, headers, footers, footnotes, and columns in their proper locations.

Look for the following topics in this chapter:

- Using Normal, Draft, Page Layout, Zoom, and Wrap for window views

- Maximizing your working area

- Viewing hidden characters

- Searching for and replacing characters, words, or phrases

- Checking spelling and word usage

- Counting words

- *Page Layout view.* To view headers, footers, footnotes, and columns on-screen, use Page Layout view. This view presents all aspects of your document on-screen as they will appear when printed. The top, bottom, right, and left page margins are presented accurately on-screen. Headers and footers appear at the top and bottom of every page, footnotes appear at the bottom of the appropriate pages, and if you use multiple columns in a document, they appear on-screen as well.

- *Draft view.* In contrast to Normal and Page Layout views, Draft view presents the bare-bones view of a document. In Draft view, Works displays all text in only one font and one point size: Times New Roman 10. You don't see any character styles, paragraph formats, alignment, columns, headers, footers, footnotes, or other enhancements. If a document contains inserted objects, only a blank frame appears as a place holder.

Tip

You can add Normal, Draft, and Page Layout tools to your toolbar by customizing it. Refer to Chapter 2, "Getting Started with Works for Windows," for instructions on customizing the toolbar. The Normal, Draft, and Page Layout tools are located under the View category in the Customize Works Toolbar dialog box.

The more document enhancements, features, and special effects you choose to display on-screen, the more computer resources Works requires. Page Layout view requires the most computer resources and may cause slow response on a computer lacking adequate memory. Draft view, on the other hand, requires few computer resources and may be the best view to use on a slow or low-memory computer. Normal view falls somewhere in between. In most cases, you can enter and edit a document in Normal view. Use Draft view when speed of editing is a primary consideration. Use Page Layout view when you're doing final editing of a document and you want to view all document elements in their proper locations. An example of Draft view is shown in figure 9.1.

To change your view of a document, follow these steps:

1. Choose the **V**iew menu. A check mark appears to the left of the view you currently are using.

2. To select another view, choose **N**ormal, Pa**g**e Layout, or Dr**a**ft view. Works places a check mark next to the view you select and immediately switches your document to that view.

Using Zoom

Another feature Works offers that changes your view of a document is *Zoom.* Often you may find Zoom helpful to magnify a particular area of a document. Zoom also can reduce the displayed size of a document. The Zoom dialog box (displayed by choosing the Zoom command on the View menu) contains five preset magnification/reduction levels: **4**00%, **2**00%, **1**00%, **7**5%, and **5**0% (see fig. 9.2). You also can use the **C**ustom text box to specify a custom magnification level. In the **C**ustom text box, you can enter any number from 25 to 1000.

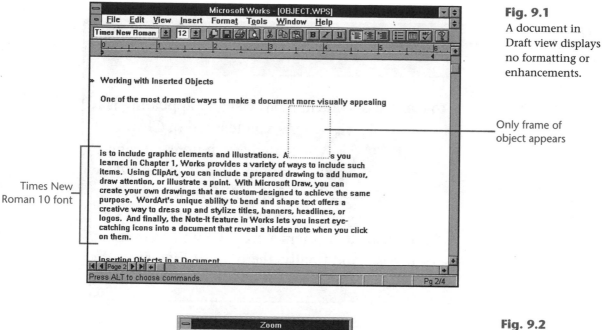

Fig. 9.1
A document in Draft view displays no formatting or enhancements.

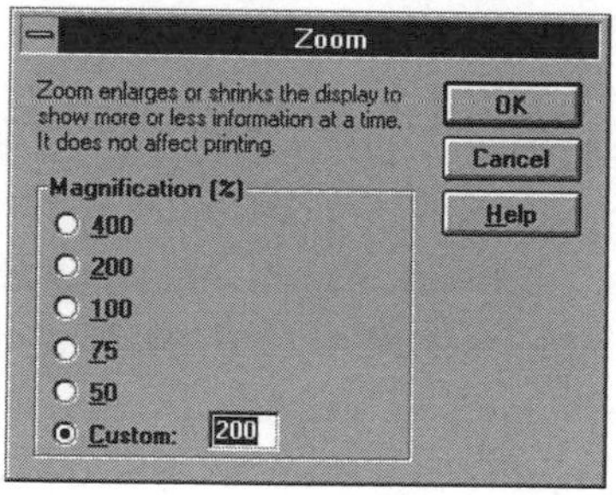

Only frame of object appears

Times New Roman 10 font

Fig. 9.2
The Zoom dialog box offers preset magnification levels of 400, 200, 100, 75, and 50.

Word Processing

To use the Zoom feature in Works, follow these steps.

1. From the **V**iew menu, choose the **Z**oom command. Works displays the Zoom dialog box shown in figure 9.2.

2. Select a magnification level or enter a number from 25 to 1000 in the **C**ustom text box.

3. Choose OK. Works displays the current document at the magnification level you choose.

An example of a magnified document is shown in figure 9.3. To return to 100% magnification (a normal view), use the preceding steps, choosing the 100% option.

Fig. 9.3
This document appears at 200% magnification.

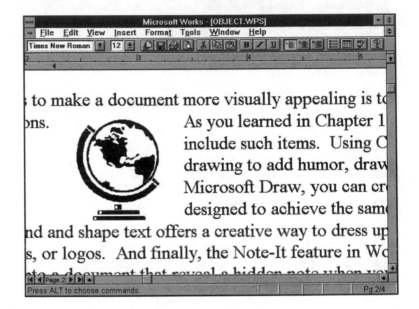

Wrapping Text in a Window

Previous chapters of this book have shown examples of word processor documents displayed in *maximized* document windows. When you maximize a document window, you create the maximum area in which to enter document text. In a maximized window, the right-indent marker is usually visible on-screen, and characters that you type always wrap at that point. But what about when you are using several document windows at one time? Chapter 2, "Getting Started with Works for Windows," described tiling as one option for arranging multiple document windows on-screen. An example is shown in figure 9.4.

Now, look closely at the text in each of these windows. Displaying all three documents on-screen at one time is useful, but the narrow document windows in the current configuration make the text difficult to read and manage. You can see only one-third of the width of each document.

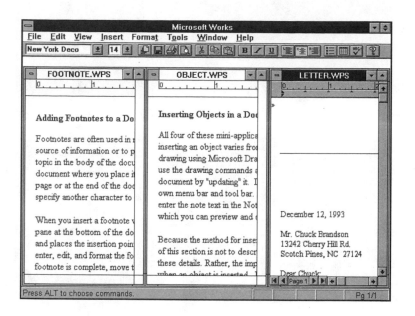

Fig. 9.4
Three word processor documents tiled on-screen.

The Wra**p** for Window option on the **V**iew menu enables you to easily work with all three documents at one time. Using this option, Works wraps text at the right edge of each window rather than at the right-indent marker. This option makes a document much easier to read and work with because the text flows from one line to the next within the width of the window (see fig. 9.5). The Wra**p** for Window option affects only how documents appear on-screen; it doesn't change the word wrap or the right-indent marker within the document itself.

To use the Wra**p** for Window option, choose the command from the **V**iew menu. This feature affects all open windows on-screen. After you finish using the Wrap for Window option, choose the command on the **V**iew menu again. Like many of the commands on the **V**iew menu, the Wra**p** for Win-dow command toggles on and off.

> **Note**
>
> The Wra**p** for Window option is available only in **N**ormal or Dr**a**ft views.

Tip
You can add a Wrap for Window tool to your toolbar by customizing it. Refer to Chapter 2, "Getting Started with Works for Windows," for instructions on customizing the toolbar. The Wrap for Window tool is located under the View category in the Customize Works Toolbar dialog box.

II

Word Processing

Fig. 9.5
Multiple documents are easier to read and work with when you use the Wrap for Window option.

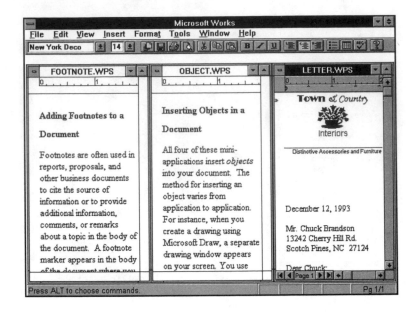

Turning Off the Toolbar and Ruler

Throughout this book, most of the figures that illustrate documents include the *toolbar* and the *ruler* in the document window. You may have thought that the toolbar and ruler were permanent fixtures of the document window, but they are not. You can remove the toolbar, the ruler, or both from the screen. Like maximizing the document window, removing the toolbar and ruler gives you the maximum working area on-screen. Often when you create a new document, you're more concerned about entering the text than about applying character styles, paragraph formats, or other enhancements, so you don't need the toolbar or ruler. Hiding the toolbar and ruler enables Works to display more lines of text in your document.

To control the toolbar and ruler, you use the Tool**b**ar and **R**uler commands on the **V**iew menu. When these features are visible on-screen, a check mark appears next to the Tool**b**ar and **R**uler commands on the **V**iew menu. To hide the toolbar or ruler, choose the Tool**b**ar or **R**uler command on the **V**iew menu, removing the check mark. Both commands toggle on and off; choose the command again to make the toolbar or ruler visible on-screen.

Viewing Hidden Characters

As you create a document, Works inserts *invisible* characters whenever you press the Tab key, the Enter key, or insert other special characters that are not visible on-screen. As discussed in Chapter 7, "Working with Tables, Columns, and Inserted Objects," pressing the Tab key moves the insertion point in your document to the location of the tab. The area between the tab and the original location of the insertion point does not contain spaces; the entire area is a special character that Works records in your document as a tab. Works inserts another invisible character, the paragraph marker, when you press Enter. And when you press Shift+Enter, Works inserts an end-of-line marker in your document.

As you check the format and spacing of a document, you may want to see these invisible characters. For example, suppose you created a table using tabs, and the data in the table is not lining up correctly. Viewing the hidden tabs can help you correct the alignment problem; you may have a tab in the wrong location. Or suppose you notice a short line in the middle of a paragraph. The line may contain an end-of-line marker rather than a space. Examples of these errors and other invisible characters are shown in figure 9.6.

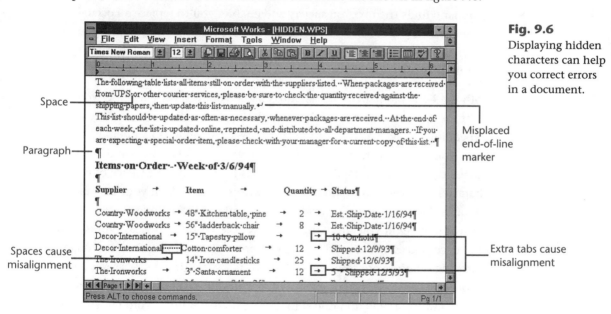

Fig. 9.6
Displaying hidden characters can help you correct errors in a document.

Word Processing

To display hidden characters in a document, choose the **All** Characters command on the **V**iew menu. The command affects all open documents and any documents that you open or create after choosing the command. This command remains in effect until you change it. A check mark appears next to the All Characters command on the View menu when the option is selected. To remove hidden characters from the screen display, choose the **All** Characters command again, which also removes the check mark from the command name on the menu.

Finding and Replacing Text in a Document

One of the most useful features of a word processor is its capability to search for and replace characters in a document. Imagine typing a 50-page sales proposal on a typewriter then discovering that you misspelled the client's company name throughout the document. Correcting every occurrence of the company name would be trouble enough, but *finding* every occurrence of the company name would take a great deal of time. With Works, you can find every occurrence easily, replace all occurrences, or replace only selected occurrences.

The two commands that enable you to search for and replace text in a document are **F**ind and Rep**l**ace, both located on the **E**dit menu. The **F**ind command enables you to search for text without replacing it. The Rep**l**ace command finds the text you specify and enables you to replace all occurrences or selected occurrences. Whether you are finding or replacing, you can specify a single character, word, phrase, or any string of characters, such as a part number like 120-NB98.

Both the **F**ind and Rep**l**ace commands enable you to specify whether you want Works to search for the whole word only or match the case of the word. Depending on the text you are searching for, these options can help you zero in on your search text. For example, if you want to replace the word *in* with the word *on* throughout a document, Works finds every occurrence of the characters *in*, even if they are contained within a word. So if your document contains the words *within*, *searching*, *again*, and *instance*, Works finds all these words. However, if you check the Match **W**hole Word Only box, Works finds only occurrences of the word *in*. Use this option when the characters you are searching for often are contained within other words. If you are searching for a word like *tomorrow*, you probably will not find these characters contained within a word, so you don't need to use the Match **W**hole Word Only option.

In some situations, you may want to specify that Works match the case of a word you're searching for. For example, if you are searching for the name *Young* in a document, you may want to check the Match **C**ase box if the document is about children and also contains occurrences of the word *young*. By checking the Match **C**ase box, Works finds only the occurrences of the name *Young* because it is capitalized.

Finding Text

The **F**ind command displays the Find dialog box shown in figure 9.7. Use the **F**ind command to find any type of text in a document. For instance, suppose that in the sales proposal you are creating, you know you mentioned training costs, but you cannot find it anywhere in the text. Using the **F**ind command, you can search for the word *training* and find the page that discusses this topic. You don't want to replace text; you simply want to find a specific topic in a document.

Fig. 9.7
Find any word, phrase, or character string using the Find dialog box.

When you find text in a document, Works locates the first occurrence of the text and highlights it, leaving the Find dialog box on-screen. To find additional occurrences, choose the **F**ind Next button. When the last occurrence is found, Works displays a message saying it reached the end of the document.

> ### Note
>
> If you begin searching in mid-document, Works offers to continue searching from the beginning of the document when you reach the end.

To find text in a document, follow these steps:

1. Move the insertion point to the beginning of the document.

2. From the **E**dit menu, choose the **F**ind command. The Find dialog box shown in figure 9.7 opens.

3. In the Fi**n**d What text box, enter the word, phrase, or character string to find.

4. To match the whole word or the case of the text, check the appropriate check box.

5. Choose the **F**ind Next button. Works finds the first occurrence of the text.

Word Processing

6. Repeat step 5 to find additional occurrences.

7. After you finish searching, close the **F**ind dialog box by choosing the Cancel button.

Tip

Pressing F7 causes Works to search for the last text you entered in the Find dialog box. This keyboard shortcut can be useful when you have finished a search, closed the Find dialog box, then realized you wanted to continue searching.

You can add a Find tool to your toolbar by customizing it. Refer to Chapter 2, "Getting Started with Works for Windows," for instructions on customizing the toolbar. The Find tool is located under the Edit category in the Customize Works Toolbar dialog box.

Replacing Text

The **Re**place command displays the Replace dialog box shown in figure 9.8. In the dialog box, you specify the text you're looking for as well as the replacement text. You can choose to replace all occurrences of the text you're looking for (using the Replace **A**ll button), you can replace occurrences selectively, or you can skip the occurrence and go on to the next.

Fig. 9.8
Use the Replace dialog box to specify the text to find as well as the replacement text.

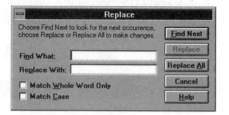

To replace text in a document, follow these steps:

1. Move the insertion point to the beginning of the document.

2. From the **E**dit menu, choose the Re**p**lace command. The Replace dialog box shown in figure 9.8 opens.

3. In the Fi**n**d What text box, enter the word, phrase, or character string to find.

4. In the Re**p**lace With text box, enter the replacement text.

5. To match the whole word or case of the text Works searches for, check the appropriate check box.

6. Choose the **F**ind Next button. Works finds the first occurrence of the text.

7. If you want to replace all occurrences of the text, choose the Replace **A**ll button. If you want to replace only the current occurrence, choose the **R**eplace button. If you want to find the next occurrence without replacing the current one, choose the **F**ind Next button.

8. Repeat step 7 until you finish searching for and replacing text. A message appears after Works has searched the entire document.

9. Close the Replace dialog box by choosing the Cancel button.

> **Note**
>
> Unlike the Find command, the Replace command does not go back to the start of the document if Replace is started in mid-document. Also, the text that was last entered in the Find What box (whether in the Find or Replace dialog box) remains in the Find What box whenever you use the Find or Replace command again.

Using Wild Cards and Special Characters in a Search

When you're uncertain about the spelling of a word in a document, you can use a wild card to represent any single character. For instance, if you search for *t?p*, Works finds *tap*, *tip*, and *top*. If you enter *t???p*, Works finds all five-letter words that begin with *t* and end with *p*. Wild cards can be very useful for finding names like Anders*o*n or Anders*e*n when you're not sure of the spelling.

In addition to searching for unknown characters with wild cards, searching for special characters in a document can be extremely useful. For instance, earlier in this chapter you learned how a misplaced tab or end-of-line marker can throw off the alignment of a table or paragraph. If a document contains many of these errors, searching for these special characters can save you a great deal of clean-up time. Table 9.1 lists all wild cards and special characters that you can enter in the Find or Replace dialog boxes.

Table 9.1 Wild Cards and Special Character Codes

To find this character	Type this code
Any single character	?
Question mark	^?

(continues)

Word Processing

Table 9.1 Continued	
To find this character	**Type this code**
End-of-line marker	^n
Paragraph mark	^p
Tab marker	^t
Page break	^d
White space (space between words)	^w
Optional hyphen	^-
Non-breaking space	^s

Troubleshooting

I know I typed the word "reflection" in my document, but when I used the Find command to search for it, Works found nothing. Why?

Works can miss a word for several reasons. If you select text before you choose the **F**ind command, Works searches only the selection. Or you may have misspelled the word, in which case Works would not find it. You may want to search for only a portion of the word such as *reflec*, or use wild cards to search for the word.

Checking Your Spelling

The spell checker in Works checks all the words in your document against a dictionary file that contains 110,000 words. When the spell checker finds a word not in the dictionary file, Works highlights the word in your document and displays the Spelling dialog box shown in figure 9.9.

When Works finds an unrecognized word, the word may have one of the following problems:

- Misspelling

- An unknown word (not in the dictionary)

- Incorrect hyphenation

- Irregular capitalization (such as wOrks)

- A repeated word

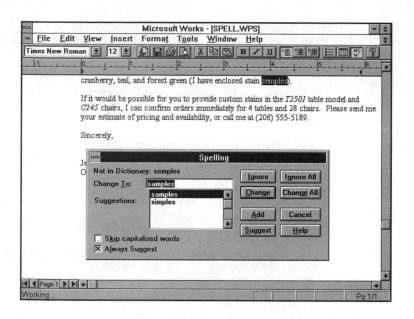

Fig. 9.9
The Spelling dialog box displays the unrecognized word and suggested replacement words.

The word in question appears highlighted in the document, and the word also appears at the top of the Spelling dialog box. If the Always Suggest check box is checked, the Suggestions list shows words you may use as replacement words. Of these words, the spell checker picks the most likely replacement word and places it in the Change To text box. (You may choose a different word if you like.) If a word is completely unrecognized, the Suggestions and Change To areas remain blank. The command buttons on the right side of the dialog box offer eight options to correct the error found in the document (see Table 9.2).

Table 9.2 Spell Checker Command Buttons

Button	Description
Ignore	If the highlighted word is spelled correctly, use this button to leave the word unchanged and continue checking the document.
Ignore All	If the highlighted word is spelled correctly and it occurs frequently in the document, use this button to leave the highlighted word and all subsequent occurrences of the word unchanged.
Change	Choose this button if you want to replace the highlighted word with the word shown in the Change To box.

(continues)

Table 9.2 Continued	
Button	**Description**
Change All	Choose this button if you want to replace the highlighted word and all other occurrences of the same word throughout the document with the word shown in the Change To box.
Add	If you want to add a word to the dictionary, choose this button. For instance, if the name of your company is Smithson Tool Works, the dictionary will always question *Smithson* as a misspelled word unless you add it to the dictionary file.
Suggest	If the Always Suggest check box is not selected, choose this button to see a list of suggested replacement words.
Cancel	Close the spell checker without checking the remainder of the document.
Help	Display the help topic that describes the spell checker dialog box.

To use the spell checker, follow these steps:

1. Move the insertion point to the beginning of the document.

2. Choose the **S**pelling command on the T**o**ols menu or click the Spell Checker button on the toolbar. The Spelling dialog box shown in figure 9.9 opens. The first unrecognized word is highlighted in the document and shown at the top of the dialog box.

3. If the word is spelled correctly, choose the **I**gnore, I**g**nore All, or **A**dd button.

   If the word is spelled incorrectly, select a replacement word from the Su**g**gestions list or use the word shown in the Change **T**o box. (If the A**l**ways Suggest check box is not checked, you can display a list of suggested words by choosing the **S**uggest button.) If no words are suggested, type the correct spelling in the Change **T**o box, then choose the **C**hange or Chang**e** All button.

4. After you choose a command button, Works highlights the next unrecognized word in the document. Repeat step 3 until Works displays a message saying it has reached the end of the document.

5. Choose OK to dismiss the message and return to your document.

If you start the spell checker anywhere other than at the beginning of a document, Works checks spelling from the location of the insertion point to the end of the document. Works then displays a message signaling the end of the document and asks if you want to continue checking from the beginning of the document. Choose OK to continue or Cancel to close the spell checker.

You also can use the spell checker to check only a selection of text in a document. Select the text you want to check, then choose the **S**pelling command on the **T**ools menu.

Finding the Right Word with the Thesaurus

A *thesaurus* is a list of synonyms and related words. A thesaurus helps you find just the right word to use in a particular context; it also helps you improve the style and readability of a document by eliminating overuse of the same word. To use the thesaurus, you place the insertion point in or next to a word in a document for which you want to find a synonym, then choose the **T**hesaurus command on the **T**ools menu. The Thesaurus dialog box shown in figure 9.10 opens.

On the left side of the dialog box, the **M**eanings box lists possible meanings for the selected word. Because some words often have several meanings, you begin by selecting the appropriate meaning then selecting a synonym from the **S**ynonyms box. The list of synonyms changes depending on the meaning you choose. Use the **C**hange button to change the selected word to the synonym you highlight in the **S**ynonyms list. Use the **S**uggest button to see a new list of synonyms for any word you select in the **M**eanings or **S**ynonyms box.

To use the thesaurus, follow these steps:

1. In the document, move the insertion point in or near the word for which you want to find a synonym.

2. From the **T**ools menu, choose the **T**hesaurus command or click the Thesaurus button on toolbar. The Thesaurus dialog box shown in figure 9.10 opens.

Tip
If you use the Thesaurus frequently, consider adding the Thesaurus button to your toolbar. Refer to Chapter 2, "Getting Started with Works for Windows," for instructions on customizing the toolbar. The Thesaurus button is available in the Tools category in the Customize Works Toolbar dialog box.

Word Processing

Fig. 9.10

The Thesaurus
dialog box lists
synonyms for a
particular word.

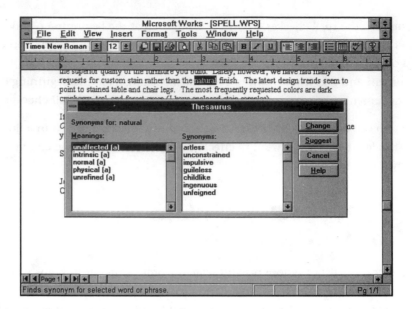

3. In the **M**eanings box, highlight the word that most closely resembles
   the meaning of the selected word in its context. If none of the
   meanings are correct, click the **S**uggest button until an appropriate
   meaning appears, then highlight the meaning.

4. In the S**y**nonyms list, highlight the word you want to use as the replacement. If none of the synonyms are acceptable, click the **S**uggest
   button until an appropriate synonym appears, then highlight the
   synonym.

5. Choose the **C**hange button to change the selected word in the document to the highlighted synonym. Works returns to your document
   and changes the highlighted word.

Counting Words in a Document

In some situations, you may want to count the number of words in a document. For instance, if you are writing a 500-word essay or submitting a 1000-
word article for publication, Works can tell you how close you are to your
limit. To count the number of words in an entire document, choose the
Word **C**ount command on the T**o**ols menu. Works displays a message indicating the total number of words in the document, including footnotes,
header text, and footer text. You also can count the number of words in a

selection of text by first selecting the text before you choose the Word **C**ount command. Note that Works counts the exact number of words and does not estimate word length.

From Here...

In this chapter, you learned how to perform some final checks on your document before printing a finished copy. At this point, you have completed the word processor section in this book. To review word processing topics, refer to any of the chapters listed below.

- Chapter 4, "Creating, Saving, and Printing a Word Processing Document," describes how to get started using the word processor.

- Chapter 5, "Editing a Document," describes how to make changes to a document after you have created and saved it.

- Chapter 6, "Enhancing the Appearance of a Document," includes information about choosing fonts and setting indentation, alignment, and spacing in a document."

- Chapter 7, "Working with Tables, Columns, and Inserted Objects," describes how to create tables, how to format the text of your document into columns, and how to create visual interest in a document with inserted objects.

- Chapter 8, "Adding Headers, Footers, Footnotes, and Bookmarks to a Document," explains how to add repetitive information at the top and bottom of pages, how to add footnotes to a document, and how to mark your place in a document using a bookmark.

Tip

If you count words frequently in a document, consider adding the Word Count button to your toolbar. Refer to Chapter 2, "Getting Started with Works for Windows," for instructions on customizing the toolbar. The Word Count button is available in the Tools category in the Customize Works Toolbar dialog box.

Word Processing

Part III

Spreadsheets and Charting

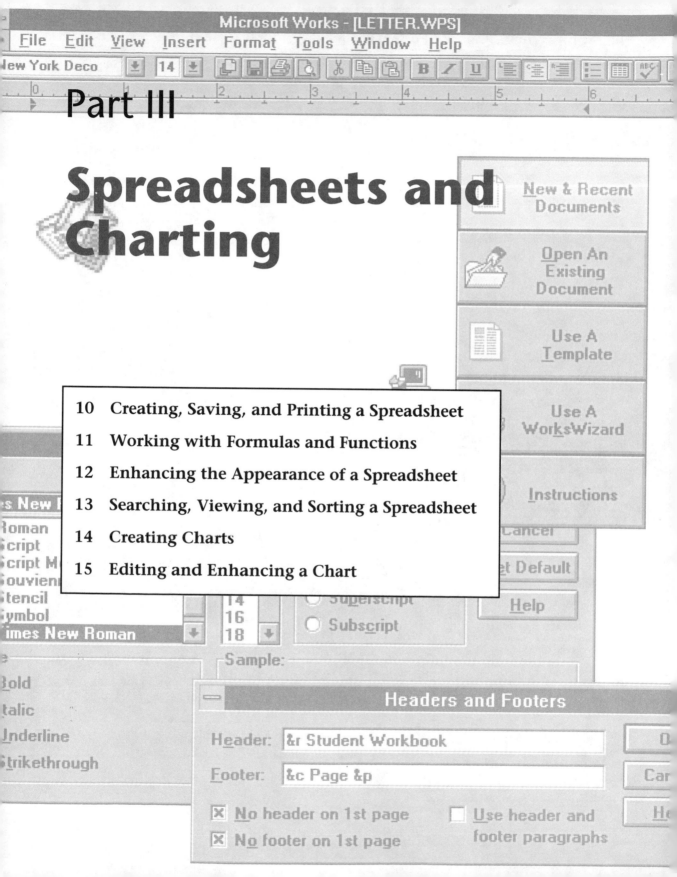

Microsoft Works - [LETTER.WPS]

File **Edit** **View** **Insert** **Format** **Tools** **Window** **Help**

New York Deco | 14 |

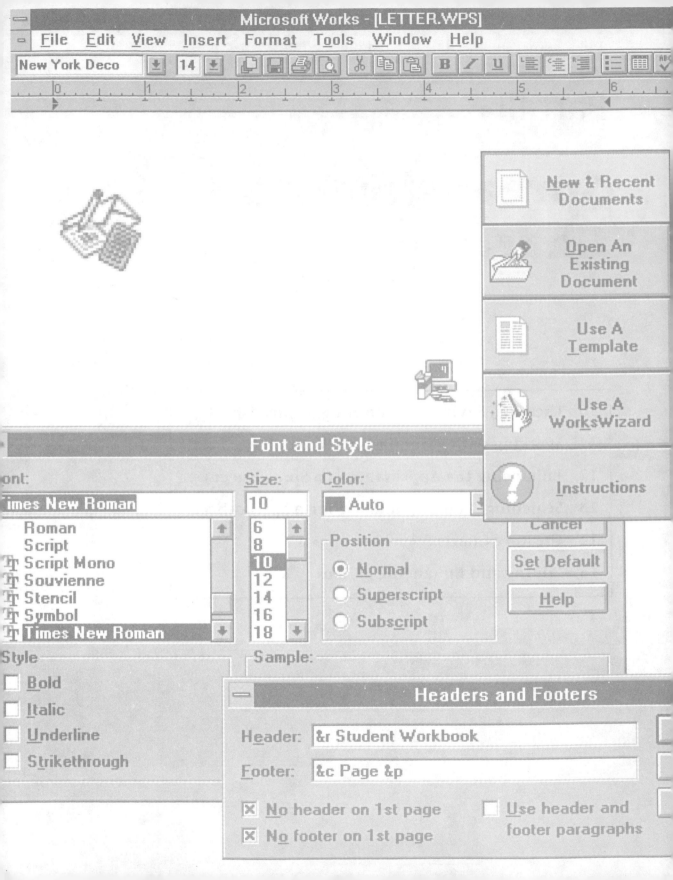

New & Recent Documents

Open An Existing Document

Use A Template

Use A WorksWizard

Instructions

Font and Style

Font:

Times New Roman

Roman
Script
T Script Mono
T Souvienne
T Stencil
T Symbol
T Times New Roman

Style
- [ ] **Bold**
- [ ] **Italic**
- [ ] **Underline**
- [ ] **Strikethrough**

Size: 10

6
8
10
12
14
16
18

Color: Auto

Position
- (•) **Normal**
- ( ) **Superscript**
- ( ) **Subscript**

Cancel

Set Default

Help

Sample:

Headers and Footers

Header: &r Student Workbook

Footer: &c Page &p

[X] **No header on 1st page**   [ ] **Use header and**
[X] **No footer on 1st page**   **footer paragraphs**

Chapter 10

Creating, Saving, and Printing a Spreadsheet

A spreadsheet is an electronic version of a paper worksheet that performs numeric calculations automatically. You can use a spreadsheet to create standard financial reports such as income statements, balance sheets, and cash flow statements, or to perform scientific and statistical calculations. If you want a refresher on the basic capabilities of the spreadsheet, refer to Chapter 1, "Introducing Works for Windows." The topics covered in this chapter help you to get started creating, saving, and printing spreadsheets.

Examining the Spreadsheet Window

As discussed in Chapter 2, "Getting Started with Works for Windows," each of the tools in Works displays a unique document window inside the overall Works window. When you maximize the document window, the two windows blend together and share the title bar. A sample spreadsheet is shown in figure 10.1. You open a new spreadsheet window by choosing the Spreadsheet icon from the Startup dialog box.

In this chapter, you learn:

- What's behind spreadsheet menus and the toolbar

- How to move around in a spreadsheet

- How to enter and edit text and numbers into spreadsheet cells

- How to create simple formulas

- How to save and print a spreadsheet

III

Spreadsheets and Charting

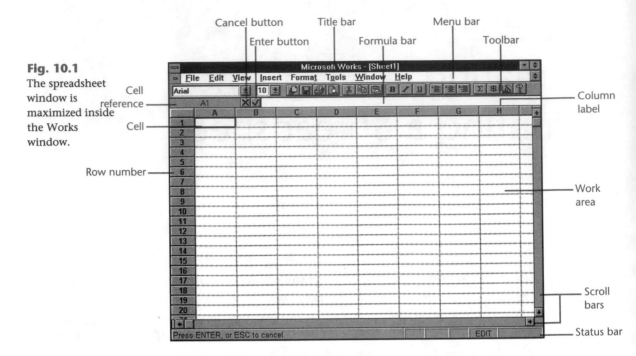

Fig. 10.1
The spreadsheet window is maximized inside the Works window.

The working area of the spreadsheet window is divided into rows and columns. The spreadsheet is bordered on the bottom and right sides by scroll bars. It is bordered on the left with row numbers and on the top with column labels. Above the working area are the title bar, menu bar, and toolbar. The various elements of the spreadsheet window are described in detail next:

■ *Work area, row numbers, and column labels.* The work area in a spreadsheet file is a grid of rows and columns. On average, the spreadsheet window displays 7 or 8 columns and up to 20 rows at a time. (The exact number depends on your monitor and the resolution you are using, the width of columns, and the height of rows.) Although the portion of the spreadsheet that you see may seem rather small, the entire spreadsheet is actually quite large: 256 columns by 16,384 rows. The columns are labeled A through Z, then are labeled AA, AB, AC...AZ; BA, BB, BC...BZ; CA, CB, CC...CZ; and so on until the last column, IV. Row numbers run consecutively from 1 to 16,384.

■ *Cell.* A cell is the point at which columns and rows intersect; it is the "box" into which you enter data. A cell is referenced by its *address*, the column letter and row name. For example, C19 is the address for the cell at the intersection of column C and row 19. The cell you are currently using is called the *active* cell and is easily identified by its bold border. When you select a cell *range*—two or more cells—Works highlights the range.

- *Mouse pointer.* When pointing anywhere within the work area, the mouse pointer in the spreadsheet tool is a large, bold cross that's easy to find anywhere on-screen. When you point to a menu command or a tool on the toolbar, the mouse pointer changes to an arrow. When you point to the formula bar (described later in this list), the mouse pointer changes to an I-beam so you can enter text or numbers.

- *Title bar.* The title bar in the spreadsheet displays the name Microsoft Works followed by the name of the current file. In figure 10.1, the file name is Sheet1. New spreadsheet files are named SHEET1, SHEET2, SHEET3, and so on, until you rename and save the files. The file extension Works adds to spreadsheet files is .wk1.

- *Menu bar.* The menu bar displays the names of the menus that hold spreadsheet commands. For instance, the File menu contains commands for working with files, like Print and Save. Menus are described in more detail later in this chapter under "The Spreadsheet Menus."

- *Toolbar.* The buttons on the toolbar represent spreadsheet commands that are used frequently. If you use a mouse, you can click on a toolbar button rather than selecting a command from a menu. The toolbar buttons are described in detail later in this chapter under "The Spreadsheet Toolbar."

- *Scroll bars.* Use the horizontal and vertical scroll bars to display different parts of the worksheet. Click the arrows on the vertical scroll bar to display one more row at a time; click the arrows on the horizontal scroll bar to display one more column at a time.

- *Cell reference, Cancel button, Enter button, Formula bar.* These four items appear just below the toolbar and above the column labels. In the cell reference area, Works displays the address of the active cell or cell range. In the formula bar, Works displays the entry in the active cell. If the cell contains a formula, the result of the formula is shown in the cell itself, and the formula is shown in the formula bar. You use the formula bar to enter and edit information in cells. Use the cancel button to cancel the entry shown in the formula bar; use the enter button to accept the entry.

■ *Status bar.* The status bar provides brief instructions (such as "Press ALT to choose commands or F2 to edit.") or describes the current menu command that is highlighted.

The Spreadsheet Menus

The menu names in the spreadsheet are identical to many of those used in other Works tools. The commands on each menu, however, perform unique functions in the spreadsheet. The spreadsheet menus are described in Table 10.1.

Table 10.1 The Spreadsheet Menus	
Menu Name	**Command functions**
File	On this menu you find all the commands necessary for creating, opening, saving, and printing files. The four most recently opened files are always listed at the bottom of the File menu, providing a quick way to open a file. (Refer to Chapter 3, "Working with Files, Templates, and WorksWizards," for information on working with files.)
Edit	This menu contains commands for cutting, copying, and pasting data and for undoing the most recent change to a spreadsheet. You also use this menu to select rows and columns, to find and replace data in a spreadsheet, and to fill a range of cells with data.
View	The commands on the View menu determine how a spreadsheet is displayed; for instance, with gridlines or showing formulas in place of data. Also, use this menu to create headers and footers for a spreadsheet, and to switch between Chart and Spreadsheet views.
Insert	Use this menu to insert page breaks, rows and columns, functions, and range names into a spreadsheet.
Format	On the Format menu you find commands for font and style, number formats, borders, alignment, patterns, row height, and column width. From the Format menu, The AutoFormat command lets you apply specially designed formats to spreadsheets. Use the Format menu as well to set the print area so you can print only a selected portion of a larger spreadsheet.

Menu Name	Command functions
Tools	This menu contains special tools for working with a spreadsheet. Use these menu commands to check the spelling in a spreadsheet, sort a spreadsheet, calculate a spreadsheet, and work with charts. You also use this menu to customize the toolbar and other Works options. A special command on this menu, Dial This Number, automatically dials a phone number for you if contained in a cell of the spreadsheet.
Window	Use the commands on this menu to help you arrange all open documents on-screen and to select the active window.
Help	The Help menu lists a variety of help topics, including an overview of the spreadsheet tool.

The Spreadsheet Toolbar

Just as each Works tool has unique menus, each tool has unique buttons on the toolbar. Each tool on the toolbar represents a particular command. Just click the tool to activate the command. Table 10.2 describes the function of each of the default spreadsheet tools.

Table 10.2 The Tools on the Word Processor Toolbar

Tool	Function
	Displays a drop-down list of all available fonts.
10	Displays a drop-down list of all available point sizes for the current font.
	Displays the Startup dialog box.
	Saves the file using the current file name and settings. If a spreadsheet has not yet been saved, the Save As dialog box appears.
10	Prints the current spreadsheet using the current print settings.
	Previews your spreadsheet before printing.
	Removes the selected text to the Clipboard.
	Copies the selected text to the Clipboard.
	Inserts the contents of the Clipboard into the spreadsheet at the location of the insertion point.

III

Spreadsheets and Charting

(continues)

Tool	Function
Table 10.2 Continued	
Tool	**Function**
B	Applies bold to the entry in the selected cell.
I	Applies italics to the entry in the selected cell.
<u>U</u>	Applies underline to the entry in the selected cell.
⬐	Left-aligns selected cell entry.
⬆	Centers the contents of the selected cell.
⬏	Right-aligns selected entry.
Σ	Automatically sums the nearest row of numbers or column of numbers.
$	Automatically formats the data in selected cells using the dollar symbol ($) and two decimal places.
⬚	Click this button to create a new chart using data in the current spreadsheet.

Troubleshooting
I don't see a toolbar in my spreadsheet window.
In Works, you can choose to display the toolbar or turn it off. If the toolbar isn't visible in the spreadsheet window, choose the Tool**b**ar option on the **V**iew menu.

The tools listed in figure 10.2 appear on the standard toolbar. If the toolbar has been customized, some of the standard tools might not be shown. To reset the toolbar to the standard tools, choose the Customize Toolbar command on the Tools menu. When the Customize Works Toolbar dialog box appears, choose the **R**eset tool and then choose OK. Works resets the toolbar to its standard tools.

Moving Around the Spreadsheet

To move around in the spreadsheet work area, you can use the mouse, the arrow keys, the scroll bars, or keyboard shortcuts listed in Table 10.3. In the spreadsheet you don't move an insertion point, you move the "highlight," a bold border that outlines a single cell.

To use the mouse to select a cell, simply click the cell you want to be active. If the cell you want isn't visible on-screen, use the scroll bars or other method to display the cell, and then click the cell.

Table 10.3 Keyboard Shortcuts for Moving Around in a Spreadsheet	
Press	**To move**
Arrow keys	Up, down, right, or left one cell at a time
Tab	One cell to the right
Shift+Tab	One cell to the left
Home	To column A in the current row
Ctrl+Home	To cell A1
End	To the last cell in the current row containing data
Ctrl+End	To the last cell in the spreadsheet containing data
Page Up	Up one window
Ctrl+Page Up	Left one window
Page Down	Down one window
Ctrl+Page Down	Right one window

Selecting Cells

Before you can enter or edit data in a worksheet, you must select a cell or cell range. To select a single cell, you simply move the highlight to the cell or click it with the mouse.

A range of cells, or cell range, is any rectangular area of cells. It could be three columns by five rows, or 350 columns by 1000 rows. A cell range also can be an entire column or an entire row. You select a range of cells when you want to take an action that will affect all cells in the range. For example, you might want to apply dollar signs to all cells in a range, or you might want to move the range of cells to a new location in the spreadsheet.

The address for a cell range is designated by a colon. The cell range A1:C3 means "cells A1 through C3" and includes cells A1, A2, A3, B1, B2, B3, C1,

III

Spreadsheets and Charting

C2, and C3. If you begin selecting the range at cell A1, it remains outlined while the other cells in the range are highlighted. An example of a cell range is shown in figure 10.2.

Fig. 10.2
A cell range is a rectangular group of selected cells.

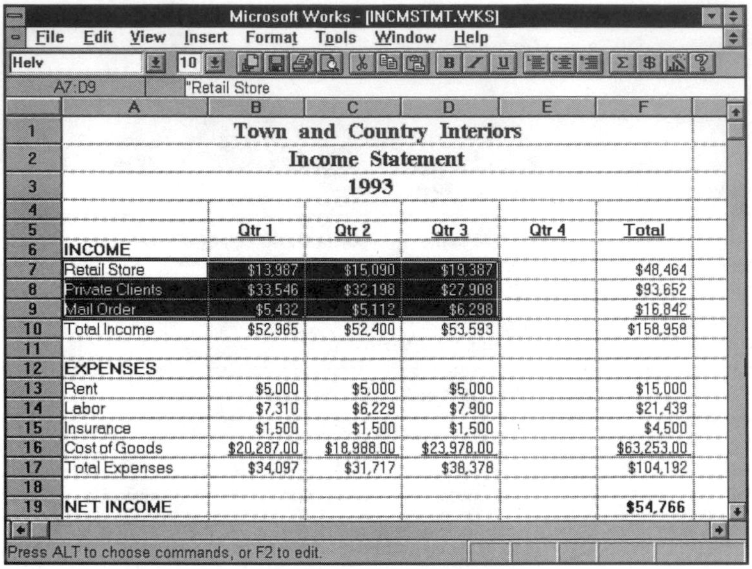

There are several ways to select a cell range, as follows:

- *Dragging the mouse over a range of cells.* To select a cell range with the mouse, point to the first cell in the range, then click and drag the mouse pointer to the cell in the opposite corner of the rectangle—the last cell you want to include in the range. When you release the mouse button, the entire range is highlighted and the first cell you selected in the range is outlined.

- *Clicking a column label or row number.* You can easily select an entire column or row by clicking the column label or row number. To select multiple, consecutive columns or rows, click and drag the mouse pointer across all column labels or row numbers you want to include in the selection. Release the mouse button when the selection is complete.

- *Using menu commands to select a row, column, or all cells in the spreadsheet.* If you prefer to use menu commands, you can select a single row, single column, or all cells in the spreadsheet using the Select Row, Select Column, and Select All commands on the Edit menu. Works selects the row or column in which the highlight is located when you choose a command. If the highlight is in cell C13 when you choose the Select Row command, Works selects row 13; if you choose the Select Column command, Works selects column C. When you choose Select All, Works selects every cell in the spreadsheet.

■ *Using the shift key and arrow or other shortcut keys.* When you press and hold the Shift key, then move the highlight to a new cell, Works highlights all cells in the range from the point of the original active cell to the final cell you select. Release the Shift key when the selection is complete.

■ *Using the F8 key to extend a selection.* Press Ctrl+F8 to select the entire row where the highlight is located. Press Shift+F8 to select the entire column where the highlight is located. When you press Ctrl+Shift+F8, Works highlights the entire spreadsheet. You can also use F8 in combination with any of the arrow keys to extend the selection from the point of the original active cell to the final cell you select.

Using Go To

When you want to move to a specific cell in a spreadsheet, often the fastest way to do so is by using the Go To command on the Edit menu, which displays the Go To dialog box shown in figure 10.3. (The keyboard shortcut for the Go To command is F5, which also displays the Go To dialog box.)

Fig. 10.3
Use the Go To dialog box to quickly move to a specific location in a spreadsheet.

In the **G**o To text box, type the address of the cell you want to highlight, then choose OK. You can type the address of a single cell or a cell range. Works closes the Go To dialog box and immediately highlights the cell or range you specify.

Notice that the Go To dialog box also contains a **N**ames box. In Chapter 12, "Enhancing the Appearance of a Spreadsheet," you learn how to name a range of cells so you can quickly select a named cell range using the **G**o To command.

Entering Information in Cells

Within the cells of a spreadsheet you can enter three types of data: text, numbers, and formulas. The raw data of a spreadsheet is made up of numbers; you use text to label, explain, and describe the numbers. Formulas perform the calculations and display the results.

To enter any type of data in a cell, you select the cell and then type the entry. As you begin typing, an insertion point appears in the formula bar. The characters you type appear in the formula bar as well as in the cell itself. To confirm the entry, press Enter or click the Enter button on the reference bar. You can also confirm an entry and move to another cell in a single step by pressing an arrow key, the Tab key, or by clicking in a new cell.

You also can make entries in cells by *filling* a range of cells, or *copying* information from one cell to a range of cells. In the following sections you learn how to enter text and numbers, how to fill a cell range, and how to copy into a range of cells. Formulas are described later in this chapter.

Entering Text

Any entry that begins with a letter of the alphabet is considered a text entry. You use text in a spreadsheet to label data, add titles to a spreadsheet, and to provide instructions or explanations. *Text* entries are automatically left-aligned with a cell using the *general* alignment format. If the text you type is too long to fit within a cell, it is displayed into the next cell to the right if that cell is empty. If that cell contains data, the cell that contains text displays only the amount of text that fits in the cell. You can still see the complete text entry in the formula bar when the cell is highlighted. To display the entire text entry in the cell, however, you must increase the column width. See the section titled "Adjusting Column Width," later in this chapter.

Because you might want some numeric entries (such as phone numbers and street addresses) to be interpreted as text, you precede these entries with a quotation mark ("). Without this symbol, Works interprets the entry as a number. For example, you might want to precede a zip code with a quotation mark so that Works interprets it as text. When an entry contains both alphabetic characters and numbers (such as a part number like 12-BNC-32) Works interprets it as text. When an entry includes punctuation marks (, . : ; !) and other keyboard symbols (~ ` # $ % ^ & 8 ( ) _ [ ] { }), they also are interpreted as text. The only exceptions to this are entries that begin with the addition symbol (+), the subtraction symbol (–), the equal symbol (=), and the @ symbol and are followed by text. These symbols are used in formulas and functions and are therefore not valid characters to use when followed by text. (Works displays a formula error message if you type + − = or @ followed by text.) To type a text entry such as "@ .49/ea." precede the entry with a quotation mark so that Works interprets the entry as text. Figure 10.4 illustrates valid text entries in a spreadsheet.

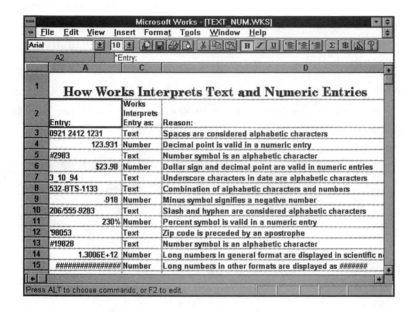

Fig. 10.4
Examples of how Works formats text and numeric entries.

Entering Numbers

In Works, a *number* is defined as an entry where Works can perform calculations. These include numbers, dates, and times. Works automatically right-aligns numbers in a cell using the *general* alignment format. If the entry you type is too long to fit in a cell, Works either displays ##### in the cell or displays the number using scientific notation (refer to fig. 10.4).

Any entry that contains numbers and no alphabetic characters is interpreted as a number. When a number includes commas used as thousands separators, a period used as a decimal point (such as in 1,320.50), or a dollar symbol ($) to signify currency, it is also automatically interpreted as a number. To enter a negative number in a cell, precede the number with a minus symbol. To type a positive number, just type the number. If you type a plus (+) symbol before the number, Works assumes you want a positive number and drops the + from the entry. If you precede a number with an equal symbol (=) or an @ symbol, Works also drops the symbol and enters a positive number. Examples of valid numeric entries are shown in figure 10.4.

Filling Cells

Because numbers are sometimes repeated or occur in a series in spreadsheets, Works offers a way for you to quickly fill cells. Filling cells speeds up your work by eliminating the need to make separate entries in individual cells. You can fill cells with identical entries to the right of the current cell or below the current cell. If your income statement spreadsheet shows the same amount each month in the rent category, for example, you can enter the amount for the first month, and then fill the cells for the remaining months with the same dollar amount.

The Fill Right and Fill Down commands are on the Edit menu. Both commands are very easy to use and do not display a dialog box. Figure 10.5 displays an example of cells that are filled to the right.

Fig. 10.5

Use the Fill Right command to fill a series of cells.

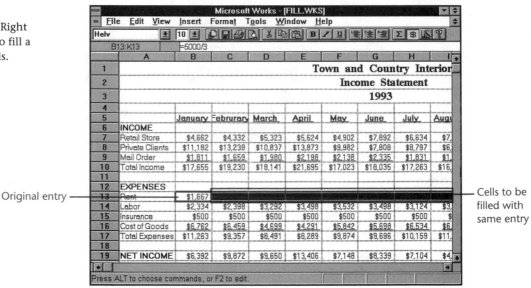

Original entry ——

—— Cells to be filled with same entry

To fill a range of cells to the right of the current cell or below the current cell, follow these steps:

1. In the first cell in the range you want to fill, type the entry that you want to use to fill the other cells.

2. Highlight the first cell and all cells to the right or below the first cell that you want to fill (refer to fig. 10.5).

3. From the Edit menu, choose the Fill Right or Fill Down command. Works fills the range of cells you select with the entry in the first cell.

You also can fill cells with a *series* of data. A series is a set of numbers or dates that are automatically increased or decreased by a specific amount. For example, if your spreadsheet includes item numbers in column B that start at 1 and go through 50, you can fill in the numbers in column B by choosing the Fill Series command on the Edit menu, which displays the Fill Series dialog box (see fig. 10.6). In this example, numbers are incremented by 1. (If you wanted to start with item 50 and count down to item 1, you would increment the numbers by –1.) But, suppose your spreadsheet requires column headings that show the date for every Monday over a 3-month period. Rather than checking a calendar and typing each date individually, you can type the first date in the first column, then fill the remaining columns with a series that is incremented by 7—Works automatically increments each date by 7 days.

Tip
To enter a series of dates, you must enter the first date in one of the following formats: 11/22/94; 11/22; 11/94; 22 November, 94; November, 1994; 22 November; November; or 1994.

> **Note**
>
> If you fill cells frequently, consider adding the Fill Right, Fill Down, and Fill Series buttons to your spreadsheet toolbar. When you click the Fill Right and Fill Down buttons, Works automatically fills the selected range of cells. When you click the Fill Series button, Works displays the Fill Series dialog box.

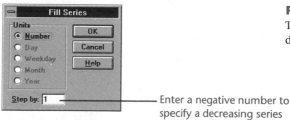

Enter a negative number to specify a decreasing series

Fig. 10.6
The Fill Series dialog box.

In the Fill Series dialog box in figure 10.6, you choose the units (Number, Day, Weekday, Month, or Year) you want to increment, and the step by which you want to increment. In the first cell of the series, you can enter any number or date in a valid date format (see Chapter 13, "Searching, Viewing, and Sorting a Spreadsheet," for information about date formats). If you enter *Monday* in the first cell and increment by 1, for example, Works fills the cell range you select with *Tuesday, Wednesday, Thursday, Friday,* and so on. Or, if you enter *April* in the first cell, Works fills the range with *May, June, July, August,* and so on.

III

Spreadsheets and Charting

To fill a range of cells with a series, follow these steps.

1. In the first cell in the range you want to fill with a series, type the first date, day, or number in the series.

2. Select the first cell and all cells to the right or below the first cell that you want to fill with a series.

3. From the **E**dit menu, choose the F**i**ll Series command. The Fill Series dialog box in figure 10.6 appears.

4. In the Unit box, choose an option.

5. In the **S**tep By box, enter a positive number to increase the series or a negative number to decrease the series.

6. Choose OK. Works fills the selected range of cells with the series you specify.

Copying Cell Entries

While the Fill Do**w**n and Fill Rig**h**t commands allow you to fill an adjacent range of cells with identical data, the copy command lets you copy identical data to a separate range of cells. Copying saves you the trouble of retyping identical entries in a spreadsheet and eliminates the possibility of errors while retyping. You can copy data from one or several cells in the *source* range to a *destination* range. Remember that when you copy data, the data remains unchanged in its source range and is duplicated in the destination range.

In Works, you can copy cell entries using menu commands (**C**opy and **P**aste on the **E**dit menu), the Copy and Paste toolbar buttons, or you can use the drag-and-drop method with the mouse. In either case, you select the source and destination ranges displayed in figure 10.7.

To use menu commands to copy cell data, follow these steps:

1. Select the range of cells you want to copy. Works highlights the selection.

2. From the **E**dit menu, choose the **C**opy command, or click the Copy button on the toolbar.

3. Move the highlight to the first cell in the destination range.

4. From the **E**dit menu, choose the **P**aste command, or click the Paste button on the toolbar. The selection is copied to the destination range of cells.

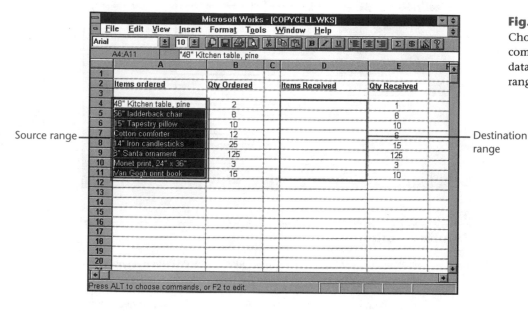

Fig. 10.7
Choose the Copy command to copy data to a separate range.

To use drag-and-drop, first select the cells to copy, then point to the border surrounding the cells until the cross mouse pointer changes to an arrow labeled "Drag." Press and hold the Ctrl key, then click on the border of the selected cells. The mouse pointer is now labeled "Copy." Drag the selection to its new location. As you drag, the data in the cells isn't shown, only a border outlining the shape of the selected range (see fig. 10.8). Position the selection in the correct destination range, then release the mouse button. The selection is copied to the destination range.

Caution

Any data that exists in the destination range is overwritten by the data you copy. This is true whether you use the Copy and Paste menu commands or the drag-and-drop method.

III

Spreadsheets and Charting

Fig. 10.8
Selected cells as they
are dragged to the
destination range to
be copied.

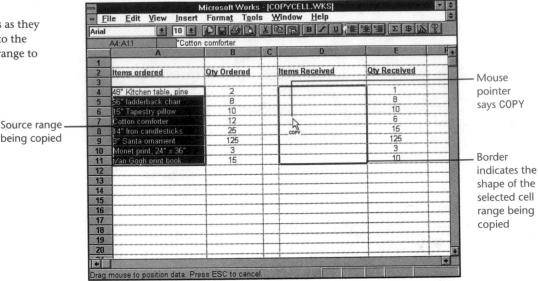

Source range
being copied

Mouse
pointer
says COPY

Border
indicates the
shape of the
selected cell
range being
copied

Troubleshooting

How can I get Works to treat my account number 9843 3498 0021 as a number rather than as text?

The spaces cause Works to interpret the entry as text. The only way to get Works to format this entry as a number is by removing the spaces.

When I select the Fill Right command (or Fill Down), nothing happens in my spreadsheet. What's wrong?

You may have forgotten to select cells, or you may have selected the wrong cells. Before choosing the Fill Right or Fill Down commands, you must select the cells you want to fill, including the cell that contains the data you want to use.

I entered 10–93 as the date in a cell, then chose the Fill Series command. Works displayed an error message instead of the Fill Series dialog box. What's wrong?

To fill a series of cells with a date, the date you enter in the first cell must be typed in a valid date format. 10–93 is not a valid date format, but 10/93 is. See Chapter 13, "Searching, Viewing, and Sorting a Spreadsheet," for more information about formatting dates.

Adjusting Column Width

By default, Works sets the width of all columns in a new spreadsheet to 10. Depending on the font and point size you use, and the data you enter in your spreadsheet, 10 spaces may not be an appropriate width, and a cell may not actually display 10 characters because most fonts are proportionally spaced. (You learned earlier in this chapter that Works displays ###### or scientific notation when a number is too wide to fit in a cell. And you learned that long text entries are not displayed entirely if there is data in the cell immediately to the right.) You might want to increase or decrease the width of all columns in a spreadsheet, or you might want to vary the width of columns on an individual basis.

Works provides several methods for adjusting the width of spreadsheet columns. You can adjust the width of a column by dragging its border, or you can choose the Column **W**idth command on the Forma**t** menu, which displays the Column Width dialog box in figure 10.9. In the dialog box, you can specify an exact column width or you can have Works determine the best width by choosing the **B**est Fit option. If you select a single cell in the column, the **B**est Fit option sizes the column to fit the entry in the selected cell. If you select the entire column, the **B**est Fit option sets the column width to accommodate the widest entry in the column.

Note

Works does not automatically readjust the column width if you change data in a column *after* sizing the column. To adjust the column for the new entry you type, you must select the **B**est Fit option again in the Column Width dialog box.

> **Tip**
> To quickly adjust the column width for the widest entry in the entire column, double-click on the column label.

Fig. 10.9
The Column Width dialog box.

III

Spreadsheets and Charting

To adjust column width using the Column Width dialog box, follow these steps:

1. In the spreadsheet, select any cell in the column you want to adjust. To adjust a column to the widest entry in the column, select the entire column. To adjust multiple columns at once, select multiple columns.

2. From the Format menu, choose the Column **W**idth command. The Column Width dialog box in figure 10.9 appears.

3. In the **W**idth text box, enter a number, or select the **B**est Fit check box to have Works determine an accurate column width.

4. Choose OK. Works automatically adjusts the column width.

When you want to adjust the width of a single column, or several columns individually, using the mouse to drag the column border is the easiest method. Use the mouse pointer to point to the border to the right of the column label. If you want to adjust column B, for example, point to the border between columns B and C. The mouse pointer changes to a left/right arrow labeled "Adjust" (see fig. 10.10). When you see this new pointer, click and drag the column border right or left to adjust the column width. Release the mouse button when the column is the size you want.

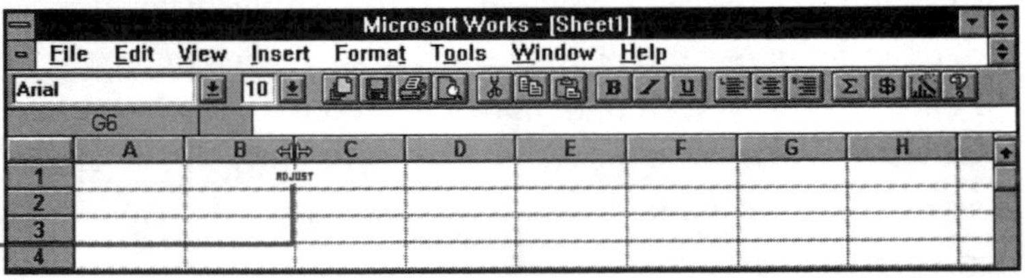

Fig. 10.10
It's easy to adjust column width by dragging the column border.

This mouse pointer lets you adjust column width

Troubleshooting

*I used the **B**est Fit option to size my column, then typed a longer entry in a cell in the same column. Why didn't Works automatically readjust the column width since I chose the **B**est Fit option?*

Works does not automatically readjust the column width if you change data in a column after sizing the column. To adjust the column for the new entry you type, you must select the **B**est Fit option again in the Column Width dialog box, or double-click on the column label.

Because my column wasn't wide enough to display a large number, Works displayed the number exponentially. I widened the column so Works could display the actual number, but it still displays the exponential number. How can I change this?

If the number contains 11 digits or less, Works displays the actual number if the column is wide enough. If the number contains 12 digits or more, it is always displayed exponentially, unless you apply the Fixed format to the cell using the Number command on the Format menu. (Number formats are discussed in Chapter 12, "Enhancing the Appearance of a Spreadsheet.")

Editing a Spreadsheet

As in any file you create—whether it's a word processor document or a database file—you will inevitably want to change, or *edit*, data in a spreadsheet. Editing includes changing, moving, and deleting entries in cells, and inserting, moving, and deleting rows and columns. The following sections discuss each of these topics.

Changing Cell Entries

You can change an entry in a cell as easily as you entered it by simply selecting the cell, and then entering new data. The new entry you type automatically overwrites the original entry. This is the quickest method to use when you want to change an entire entry. But sometimes, particularly when a cell contains a long entry, you might want to make a simple change within an entry itself. For example, if the title of your spreadsheet is "1993 Income Statement for Town and Country Interiors" and you want to change the date to 1994, there is no reason to retype the entire entry, just change 1993 to 1994.

To edit an entry in a cell, select the cell, then press F2 or click anywhere in the formula bar where the cell contents are displayed. The formula bar is now active. If you press F2, an insertion point is visible at the right end of the entry in the formula bar. If you click in the formula bar rather than pressing F2, the insertion point appears wherever you click. Use the right and left arrow keys to position the insertion point, then delete and retype the characters you want to change. If you want to delete a block of text in an entry, select the characters to delete in the formula bar and then press Del. To confirm the change, press Enter or click the Enter button on the reference bar.

Clearing Cells

An alternative to editing or retyping an entry in a cell is to *clear* the cell. Clearing the cell deletes the data in the cell but retains the cell in the spreadsheet. (You can't delete individual cells from a spreadsheet.) You can clear a single cell at a time or a selected range of cells at once. To quickly clear a cell or cell range, select the cells and press Del on the keyboard, or click the Cut button on the toolbar. To clear a single cell or a range of cells using menu commands, use the following steps:

1. Select the cell or cell range you want to clear.

2. Choose the Clear command on the Edit menu. The data in the selected cells is removed.

Inserting Columns and Rows

One of the most common changes you make in a spreadsheet is to insert columns or rows. You may decide to add data to the original spreadsheet, or perhaps you forgot to include some important data when you created the spreadsheet. You also can insert blank columns and rows to improve the appearance and layout of a spreadsheet. When you insert a column, the existing columns are moved to the right; when you insert a row, Works moves the existing rows of data down. Works automatically adjusts any formulas in the moved columns and rows.

Figure 10.11 shows a spreadsheet which includes four rows of expenses. Suppose you want to add a row between the Labor and Insurance rows. Works inserts a row *above* the current row, so you would select the Insurance row, and then insert a new row. Or, suppose that you wanted to insert a column between columns A and B. Works inserts a column *before* the current column, so you would select column B, then insert a column.

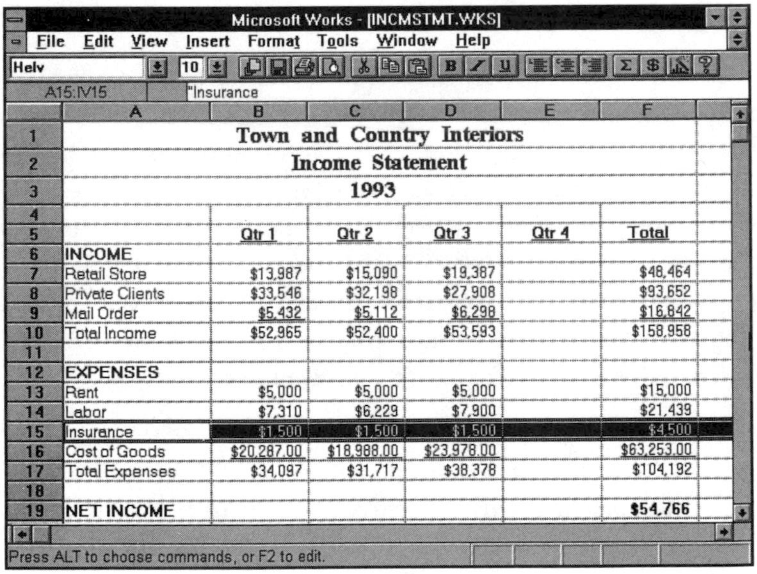

Fig. 10.11
Select any cell in this row to insert a row.

	A	B	C	D	E	F	
		Town and Country Interiors					
1							
2		**Income Statement**					
3		**1993**					
4							
5		Qtr 1	Qtr 2	Qtr 3	Qtr 4	Total	
6	INCOME						
7	Retail Store	$13,987	$15,090	$19,387		$48,464	
8	Private Clients	$33,546	$32,198	$27,908		$93,652	
9	Mail Order	$5,432	$5,112	$6,298		$16,842	
10	Total Income	$52,965	$52,400	$53,593		$158,958	
11							
12	EXPENSES						
13	Rent	$5,000	$5,000	$5,000		$15,000	
14	Labor	$7,310	$6,229	$7,900		$21,439	
15	Insurance	$1,500	$1,500	$1,500		$4,500	
16	Cost of Goods	$20,287.00	$18,988.00	$23,978.00		$63,253.00	
17	Total Expenses	$34,097	$31,717	$38,378		$104,192	
18							
19	NET INCOME					$54,766	

Microsoft Works - [INCMSTMT.WKS]
File Edit View Insert Format Tools Window Help
Helv   10
A15:IV15   "Insurance
Press ALT to choose commands, or F2 to edit.

To insert a row in a worksheet, follow these steps.

1. Select the entire row where you want to insert a new row.

2. From the **I**nsert menu, choose the **R**ow/Column command. Works inserts a new row immediately above the row you selected in step 1.

To insert a new column in a worksheet, follow these steps:

1. Select the entire column where you want to insert a new column.

2. From the **I**nsert menu, choose the **R**ow/Column command. Works inserts a new column immediately before the column you selected in step 1.

If you select a single cell rather than an entire row or column in the above steps, Works doesn't know what you want to insert and displays a dialog box. In the dialog box, select either **R**ow or **C**olumn, and then choose OK. As the steps indicate, you can bypass the dialog box by selecting an entire row or column *before* you choose an insert command.

Deleting Columns and Rows

Deleting columns and rows in a spreadsheet is just as common a task as inserting them. The principle for deleting columns or rows is similar to inserting. If you select an entire row first, Works assumes you want to delete the entire row. But if you select only a single cell, Works displays a dialog box so you can choose the **R**ow or **C**olumn option. When you delete a row or column, existing rows are moved up and existing columns are moved to the left to fill the void. Unlike inserting a column or row, however, you can delete multiple columns or rows at once by selecting more than one.

To delete a single row or multiple rows, follow these steps:

1. In the spreadsheet, click the number of the row to delete. To select more than one row, click and drag the mouse pointer across all row numbers you want to include in the selection.

2. From the **I**nsert menu, choose the **D**elete Row/Column command. Works automatically deletes all selected rows.

To delete a single column or multiple columns, follow these steps:

1. In the spreadsheet, click the label of the column to delete. To select more than one column, click and drag the mouse pointer across all column labels you want to include in the selection.

2. From the **I**nsert menu, choose the **D**elete Row/Column command. Works automatically deletes all selected columns.

Tip

If you insert rows and columns frequently in a spreadsheet, you can add buttons to your toolbar for inserting and deleting rows and columns. These buttons appear in the Insert category in the Customize Works Toolbar dialog box. Refer to Chapter 2, "Getting Started With Works for Windows," for instructions on customizing the toolbar.

III

Spreadsheets and Charting

Moving Columns, Rows, and Cell Entries

In addition to inserting and deleting, you will find that moving columns, rows, and cell entries is a common editing task. Moving is simply "rearranging" to make a worksheet more readable or perhaps to place items in a logical order. You can move a single column, row, or cell entry, or you can move multiple columns, rows, and cell entries at once.

When you move columns or rows in a spreadsheet, Works makes room for the moved data by *inserting* it. If you select column A to move it to column D, for example, Works doesn't overwrite column D, it inserts a new column before column D and places the data from column A in the new column. Therefore, the original column A becomes column C. The original columns B and C are shifted to the left to fill in the void left by column A. Column B becomes column A, and column C becomes column B. This process is illustrated in figures 10.12 and 10.13. Works operates the same way when moving rows: the row you move is inserted above the row you select, and the remaining rows are shifted to fill in the void. While it might seem confusing that Works actually *inserts* columns or rows that you move, inserting is much safer than *overwriting* data in the new location, which might cause you to lose data.

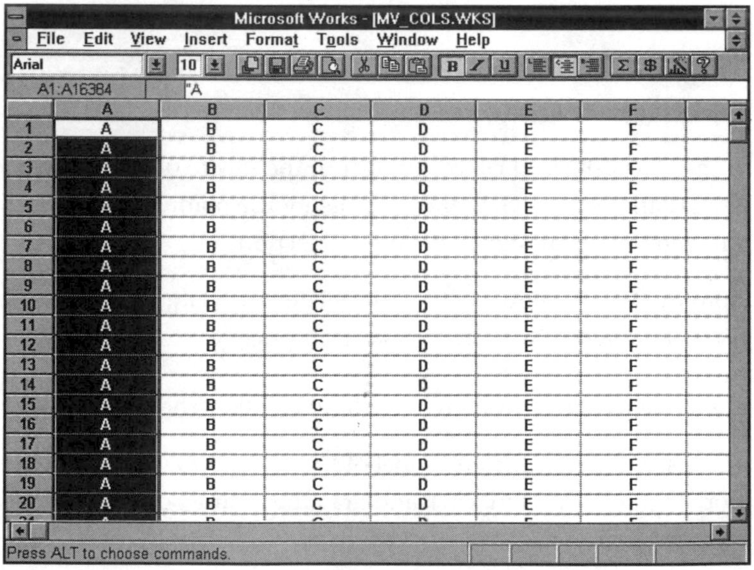

Fig. 10.12
Column A is selected to be moved to column D.

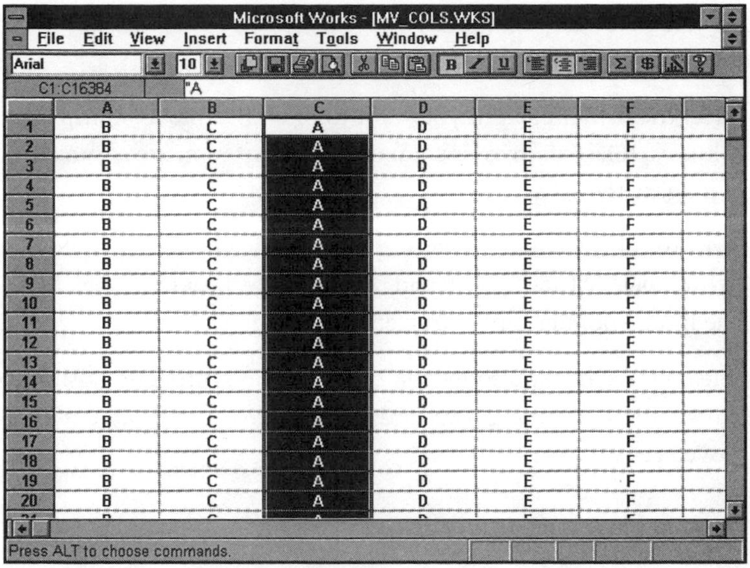

Fig. 10.13
Columns B and C
are shifted to the
left after column
A is moved.

In Works, you can move a row or column using the Cu**t** and **P**aste commands on the Edit menu or using the drag-and-drop method. To move a row or column using menu commands, follow these steps:

1. In the spreadsheet, select the row or column you want to move. To move multiple rows or columns at once, select all rows or columns you want to move. Works highlights the cells.

2. From the **E**dit menu, choose the Cu**t** command, click the Cut button on the toolbar, or press Ctrl+X. Works removes the selected row or column from the spreadsheet and shifts the remaining rows or columns to fill the void.

3. Select the row or column where you want to move the data you cut. If you are moving multiple rows or columns, select the *first* row or column where you want to move the data.

4. Choose the **P**aste command on the **E**dit menu, click the Paste button on the toolbar, or press Ctrl+V. Works inserts a moved row above the row you select; Works inserts a moved column before the column you select.

Using the drag-and-drop method is a quicker, more visual method of moving rows or columns. Follow these steps:

1. Select the row or column you want to move. To move multiple rows or columns, select all rows or columns you want to move at once. Works highlights the cells.

2. Point to the selection border until the mouse pointer changes to an arrow labeled "Drag". Click and drag the selection to its new location. The mouse pointer is now labeled "Move".

3. Release the mouse button when the selection is properly positioned. Works shifts remaining rows and columns to fill the void left by the moved cells.

Troubleshooting

How can I delete a single cell from a spreadsheet?

Because a cell occurs at the intersection of a row and column, you can't delete a single cell from a spreadsheet, you can only delete an entire row or column. You can clear a cell's contents by choosing the Clear command on the **E**dit menu, clicking the Cut key on the toolbar, or by pressing Del.

How can I insert multiple rows or columns in a spreadsheet at once?

To insert more than one row or column at a time, highlight the number of rows or columns you want to insert, then choose the **R**ow/Column command on the **I**nsert menu. Works automatically inserts the number of rows or columns you highlight. For example, to insert 3 rows at row 17, highlight rows 17, 18, and 19, then select the **R**ow/Column command on the **I**nsert menu.

Entering Simple Formulas

Spreadsheets are of little value without their ability to perform mathematical calculations through the use of *formulas*. A formula is an equation that performs a calculation on one or more values and returns a result. In Works, you can use formulas to perform basic arithmetic calculations such as addition, subtraction, multiplication, and division. Or you can perform more complex calculations through the use of *functions*, prepared equations designed to perform a specific task. For example, rather than trying to create a formula yourself, you would use the PMT function to calculate the periodic payment for a loan or an investment. You learn more about functions in Chapter 12, "Enhancing the Appearance of a Spreadsheet." Figure 10.14 shows an example of a simple spreadsheet that doesn't include any formulas. Income and Expenses in columns B, C, and D need to be totaled.

Enter formula here to sum column

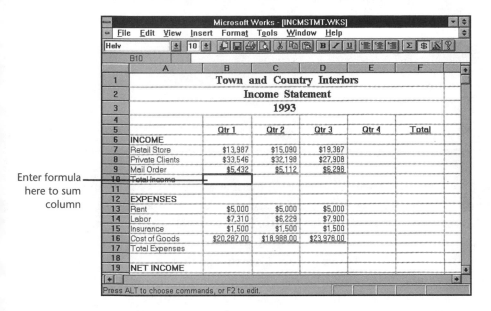

Fig. 10.14
Formulas will be entered in cells B10:D10 and cells B17:D17.

All formulas must begin with an equal symbol. This symbol is followed by a combination of cell references or specific values, and arithmetic operators such as + for addition, – for subtraction, / for division, and * for multiplication. For example, the formula =B8*12 multiplies the value in cell B8 by 12 and places the result in the cell where the formula is located. In figure 10.14, cells B10 through D10 need summation formulas to total the income figures for Q1, Q2, and Q3, so the formula in cell B10 should read =B7+B8+B9.

When a formula contains more than one operator, Works uses standard algebra rules to evaluate the formula, including evaluating values in parentheses first. For example, in the formula =(C13+5)*35/E4, C13+5 is evaluated before the rest of the formula. When parentheses are nested, the innermost set of parentheses is evaluated first. Operators are evaluated in the order shown in Table 10.4.

Table 10.4 Operators and Their Order of Evaluation	
Operator	**Order of Evaluation**
– (negative) and + (positive)	First
^ (exponent)	Second
* (multiplication) and / (division)	Third
+ (addition) and – (subtraction)	Fourth
=, <>, <, >, <=, >=	Fifth
#NOT#	Sixth
#OR#, #AND#	Seventh

There are a number of ways to create even the simplest formula that sums a column of numbers. You can type in the cell references and operators—in this example, type **=B7+B8+B9** in cell B10. However, typing cell references can lead to errors. A faster and more accurate way to create the formula is to "point" to the cells using the arrow keys. Place the highlight in cell B10 and press = (*don't* press Enter yet). Using the up-arrow key, highlight cell B7, then type a plus symbol. The highlight jumps back to cell B10 and the formula now reads =B7+. Use the up-arrow key to highlight cell B8, then press +. Again, the highlight jumps back to cell B10 and the formula now reads =B7+B8. Repeat this process, highlighting cell B9, then press Enter. When you press Enter, the formula is complete and the result of the formula appears in cell B10. The formula itself is displayed in the formula bar rather than the calculated result. If you prefer, you can use the mouse rather than the up arrow to point to the cells you want to include in the formula.

Using the Autosum Button

Because summation is such a common formula in spreadsheets, Works includes a handy toolbar button called Autosum. It uses the SUM function, which automatically sums the values in the specified range of cells. The Autosum button is intelligent; it "reads" the context of the spreadsheet and guesses which cell values you want to sum. An autosum function looks like this:

=SUM(B7:B9)

The equal symbol designates the entry as a formula, the SUM part of the formula is the name of the function being used, and the cells referenced in parentheses are the range of cells whose values will be totaled.

To use the Autosum button, place the highlight in the cell where you want the formula result to appear. Click the Autosum button on the toolbar, or press Ctrl+M, the shortcut key for the Autosum button. Works highlights the range of cells it thinks you want to total and places a formula like the one shown above in the current cell. The cells referenced in the parentheses are the cells Works highlights (see fig. 10.15). If the cell range is correct, press Enter to complete the formula. Works displays the result in the active cell and the formula appears in the formula bar.

The Autosum function first looks above the current cell to find an appropriate range to sum and then looks to the left. If a range is not found, =SUM( ) appears in the cell and the formula bar. Enter the correct cell range in the parentheses to complete the formula.

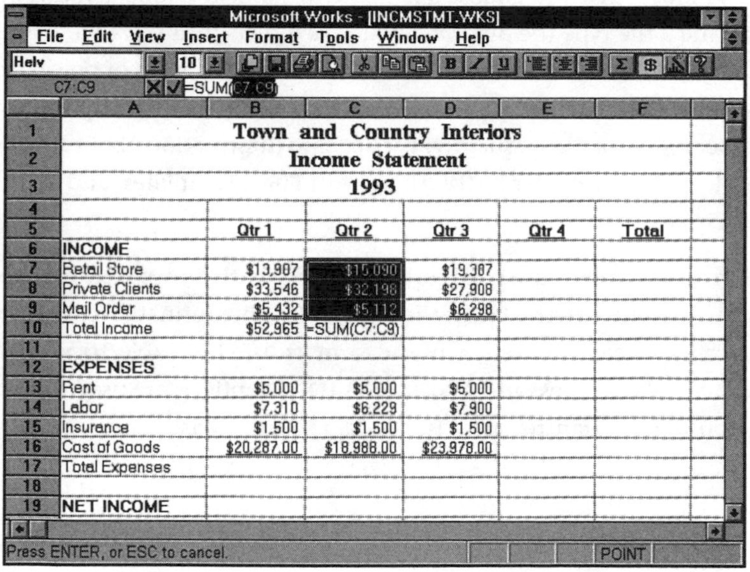

Fig. 10.15
AutoSum highlights cells to sum and displays the formula in the current cell.

Troubleshooting

The cell range that Autosum suggests isn't the range I want to sum.

Sometimes, because of the way the data in your spreadsheet is arranged, Works is not able to accurately guess the range of cells to sum. When this happens, you must type or highlight the correct range to complete the formula.

Works keeps displaying the message "Missing Operand." What's wrong with my formula?

The formula ends with an operator (such as +, –, *, /) instead of an operand. An operand is a number or a cell reference. Remove the final operator from the formula, or add an operand following the operator.

Saving a Spreadsheet

Once you begin creating real spreadsheets, you will want to save your work. You learned in Chapter 3, "Working with Files, Templates, and WorksWizards," that you choose a permanent name for a file, a location to store it, and a file type the first time you save a file. Until you save a spreadsheet, any data that you enter is vulnerable. An interruption of power or an equipment failure will cause an unsaved file to be lost, so it's important to remember to save a file frequently. For specific information about how to save a file, refer to Chapter 3, "Working with Files, Templates, and WorksWizards."

If you think you might use your spreadsheet file with another spreadsheet program, you can save the file in the appropriate file format. Works allows you to save a spreadsheet in any of the formats listed in Table 10.5. The Text & Commas, Text & Tabs, and Text & Tabs (DOS) options are used primarily when you want to transfer spreadsheet data to a database file.

Table 10.5 File Formats Available for Spreadsheet Files
Works SS (Works spreadsheet)
Works for Windows 2.0/Works for DOS SS
Text & Commas
Text & Tabs
Text & Tabs (DOS)
Excel 4.0/5.0 SS
Lotus 1-2-3
Works 3.0 for Macintosh SS

Printing a Spreadsheet

You can print a portion of a spreadsheet or an entire spreadsheet at any time—while you're in the process of creating it or after it's finished. In any case, you should always review page and print settings before printing. Use the Page Setup command on the File menu to display the Page Setup dialog box. In this box you specify the page, header, and footer margins; the source, size, and orientation for the paper you are printing on; page numbering and footnote options, and other standard settings for your particular printer. (You learn how to add headers and footers to a spreadsheet in Chapter 13, "Searching, Viewing, and Sorting a Spreadsheet.") When all page settings are correct, it's a good idea to preview your spreadsheet as a final check before printing. You learn how to specify page settings in the following sections.

Note

The settings you choose in the Page Setup dialog box affect only the current spreadsheet file.

Setting Print Area

Often you don't need to print an entire spreadsheet; you only want to print a portion of it. Printing a selected portion of a spreadsheet is a very useful feature, especially when a spreadsheet becomes rather large.

The portion of a spreadsheet that you print is called the *print area*. Normally the print area includes all cells in the spreadsheet. When you want to print only a portion of a spreadsheet, however, you specify a different print area. To set the print area, use these steps:

1. Select the cells you want to include in the print area.

2. From the Format menu, choose **S**et Print Area. Works displays a dialog box asking you to confirm the current selection as the print area.

3. Choose OK.

Tip
If you frequently print portions of a spreadsheet rather than an entire spreadsheet, you can add the Set Print Area tool to your toolbar. Refer to Chapter 2, "Getting Started with Works for Windows," for instructions on customizing your toolbar.

When you define a print area, Works assigns the range name "Print Area" to the cells you select. (To learn more about naming a range of cells, refer to Chapter 11, "Working with Formulas and Functions.") When you're ready to print the file, Works prints only those cells in the designated print area.

To change the print area back to the entire spreadsheet, use the following steps:

1. Select the Range **N**ame command on the Insert menu. Works displays the Range Name dialog box.

2. In the Names list, select the Print Area and the Dele**t**e button. Works removes the Print Area from the list of range names.

3. Choose the Close command to close the Range Name dialog box.

Setting Margins

Page margins are the white space that surrounds the text on the printed page. To set page margins for your spreadsheet, you use the Page Setup dialog box in figure 10.16. (Notice that Page Setup is a tabbed dialog box. In the figure, the **M**argins tab is selected and the default margin settings are displayed.) Unless you change margin settings, the Page Setup dialog box shows the default margins that Works uses: 1 inch for top and bottom margins, and 1.25 inches for left and right margins. The Sample area of the dialog box displays a graphic representation of these settings.

For some spreadsheets, however, you might want to change the default margin settings in order to fit more data on a page.

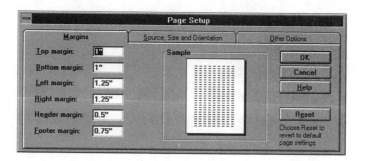

Fig. 10.16
The Page Setup
dialog box
displays margin
settings for the
current spread-
sheet.

To change margin settings, follow these steps:

1. From the **F**ile menu, choose the Pa**g**e Setup command. The Page Setup dialog box is displayed.

2. In the dialog box, choose the **M**argins tab. The dialog box in figure 10.16 appears.

3. In the appropriate margin boxes, type the setting you want to use in inches. Type a decimal fraction for fractions of an inch (such as 1.25 for 1-1/4 inches). The Sample area of the dialog box reflects the settings you choose.

4. When all margin settings are correct, choose OK. Works automatically reformats your spreadsheet using the new margin settings.

> **Note**
>
> If you commonly work with centimeters or another unit of measure rather than inches, you can change the Works default units setting. Choose the **O**ptions command on the **To**ols menu to display the Options dialog box. In the Units box, choose a unit of measure, and then click OK. Notice that the unit of measure you choose applies to *all* tools in Works.

Setting Paper Source, Size, and Orientation

Before printing a spreadsheet, you must specify in Works which paper source to use, the size of the paper you're printing on, and the direction you want the print to appear on the page. To change the paper source, paper size, and print orientation, you use the Page Setup dialog box in figure 10.17. In the figure, the **S**ource, Size, and Orientation tab is selected and the default settings are displayed. The page in the Sample area reflects the current paper size and orientation settings.

Fig. 10.17

The Page Setup dialog box displays paper source, size, and orientation settings for the current spread-sheet.

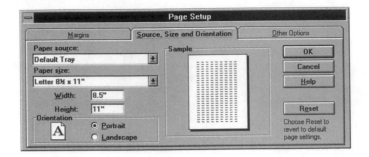

Depending on the type of printer you are using, you can choose the correct paper source (such as the default paper tray, second paper tray, and envelope feeder) from the Paper Source drop-down list. The Paper Size list offers a variety of standard paper and envelope sizes. Choose a size from the list or enter the correct size in the Width and Height boxes.

Paper orientation refers to the direction the print will appear on the paper. Most documents printed on standard 8-1/2 x 11 inch paper are printed in *portrait* orientation, or using the 11 inch dimension as the *height* of the paper. For documents that are printed in landscape orientation, the paper is rotated 90 degrees so that the 8-1/2 dimension is used as the height of the paper. (The paper is not actually rotated in your printer, your printer simply prints the image "sideways.") The default orientation is **P**ortrait; to print in landscape mode, choose the **L**andscape option. The paper in the Sample area of the dialog box is rotated. Notice, also, that for the paper size you specified, the settings in the **W**idth and Hei**g**ht boxes are automatically reversed.

To change source, size, and orientation settings, follow these steps:

1. From the **F**ile menu, choose the Pa**g**e Setup command. The Page Setup dialog box is displayed.

2. In the dialog box, choose the **S**ource, Size, and Orientation tab. The dialog box in figure 10.17 appears.

3. Choose a paper source from the Paper source drop-down list. Choose a paper size from the Paper Size drop-down list, or specify a custom size in the **W**idth and Hei**g**ht boxes. Choose a paper orientation by clicking either the **P**ortrait or **L**andscape option. The Sample area of the dialog box reflects the settings you choose.

4. When all settings are correct, choose OK.

Setting Other Page Options

The third tab in the Page Setup dialog box is Other Options (see fig. 10.18). Use the settings on this tab to print gridlines or to print row and column headers (row numbers and column labels).

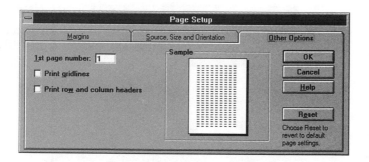

Fig. 10.18
The Page Options dialog box displays miscellaneous page settings.

By default, Works does not print the gridlines that appear on the screen when you print a spreadsheet. However, printing gridlines can sometimes make a spreadsheet easier to read. To print gridlines, check the Print **G**ridlines check box, and then choose OK.

Printing row and column headers also can make a spreadsheet easier to read. This option is helpful when you are still making changes to a spreadsheet and printing draft copies as you work. The row and column headers can help you find the right cell when you go back to the screen to make corrections. To use this option, select the Print Ro**w** and Column Headers check box, then choose OK.

Previewing a Document

One of the most important steps you can take before printing a spreadsheet is to *preview* it. Previewing allows you to see on the screen how your spreadsheet will look on the printed page. When you use the preview screen, Works displays a full-page view, one page at a time, of the spreadsheet. This is your chance to see that margins are the appropriate size, row heights and column widths are acceptable, page separations are correct, header and footer text is positioned correctly, and so on. All of these elements appear on the preview screen.

To preview your spreadsheet, choose the Print Pre**v**iew command on the **F**ile menu. The current document is displayed in a preview screen like the one in figure 10.19.

Fig. 10.19
Previewing a
document shows
you how the
document will
appear when
printed.

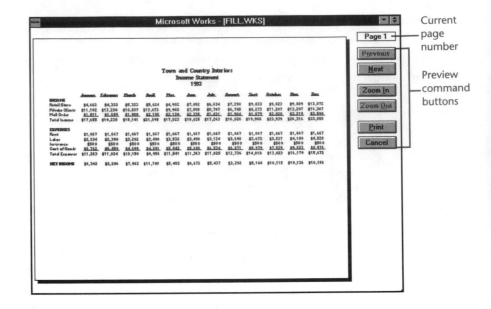

The actual text and numbers displayed in the preview screen can be difficult
to read because it is reduced, but reading the text isn't the important consideration here; checking the layout is. If you think you spot a problem, however, you can zero in on a particular location. Notice that the mouse pointer
changes to a magnifying glass when it is pointing anywhere on the page.
Click the left mouse button once anywhere on the page to zoom on the
spreadsheet, or click the Zoom In button. If you need to magnify the spreadsheet further, click the left mouse button once more anywhere on the page,
or click the Zoom In button again. Use the scroll bars, if necessary, to view a
part of the spreadsheet that isn't visible. To zoom back out, click the mouse
button a third time anywhere on the page, or click the Zoom Out button.

If your spreadsheet is longer than one page, display the page you want to
preview by clicking the Previous or Next button, or use the Page Up and Page
Down keys on the keyboard. When you're ready to print the spreadsheet you
can print directly from the preview screen by clicking the Print button. This
button displays the Print dialog box shown in figure 10.20. You learn how to
use the Print dialog box in the next section.

Printing
If you have access to more than one printer on your computer, you need to
check the settings in the Printer Setup dialog box. This is where you specify
which printer you want to use. To display the Printer Setup dialog box,

choose the **P**rinter Setup command on the **F**ile menu. The printer that is currently selected is highlighted in the Printer Setup dialog box. To choose a different printer, highlight the name, then choose OK.

When you're ready to print your spreadsheet, choose the **P**rint command on the **F**ile menu, which displays the Print dialog box shown in figure 10.20. You use the Print dialog box to specify the number of copies you want to print, the particular pages you want to print, and the quality of printing you want to use. The printer that is currently selected is shown at the top of the dialog box. If the printer shown is not correct, select the correct printer using the **P**rinter Setup command on the **F**ile menu.

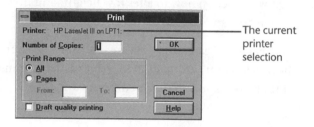

— The current printer selection

Fig. 10.20
The Print dialog box.

To print a spreadsheet, follow these steps:

1. Open the spreadsheet file you want to print.

2. (Optional) From the **F**ile menu, choose the Pa**g**e Setup command to specify print **m**argins, paper **s**ource, size, orientation, and **o**ther print settings.

3. (Optional) From the **F**ile menu, use the Print Pre**v**iew command to preview the spreadsheet.

4. From the **F**ile Menu or from the Print Preview dialog box choose the **P**rint command. The Print dialog box in figure 10.20 appears.

5. Select the appropriate print settings, then choose OK.

III

Spreadsheets and Charting

From Here...

This chapter includes topics that introduce you to working with spreadsheets. For more information about working with spreadsheets, refer to the following chapters:

- Chapter 11, "Working With Formulas and Functions," describes how to work with more complex formulas and functions, and how to name cell ranges so you can use them in your formulas.

- Chapter 12, "Enhancing the Appearance of a Spreadsheet," discusses how to choose character fonts, sizes, colors, and styles; how to align text within cells; how to alter row height; and how to add headers and footers to a spreadsheet.

- Chapter 13, "Searching, Viewing, and Sorting a Spreadsheet," describes how to look for information in a spreadsheet, change your view of a spreadsheet, and sort data in different ways.

Chapter 11

Working with Formulas and Functions

In Chapter 10, "Creating, Saving, and Printing a Spreadsheet," you are introduced to creating simple formulas. By using Works, you can create more complex formulas and use functions in your formulas. You also can name cell ranges and use the range name in your formulas. Using functions and range names simplifies the task of creating formulas in a spreadsheet.

Understanding How Formulas Work

In Chapter 10, "Creating, Saving, and Printing a Spreadsheet," you learn some basic steps for creating a simple formula. You learn that a formula begins with an equal symbol and is followed by a combination of values, cell references, and operators. You also learn that the contents of parentheses are evaluated first in a formula and that operators are evaluated in a specific order. Chapter 10, "Creating, Saving, and Printing a Spreadsheet," also describes how to create a simple formula by typing or pointing to cell references and entering operators, or by using the Autosum button on the spreadsheet toolbar.

The formulas shown in Chapter 10, "Creating, Saving, and Printing a Spreadsheet," are simple summation formulas, but often spreadsheet formulas are more complex than that. Formulas can contain many cell references, constant values, operators, and parentheses, such as in a formula like

This chapter teaches you how to do the following:

- Understand how formulas work

- Understand relative and absolute cell addressing

- Move, copy, and delete formulas

- Use functions in formulas

- Name a range of cells

(3*4^3)–(3*(D18*A4)+(3*E7))+25. Cells may be referenced from locations all over a spreadsheet. Formulas like this are created using the same principles you learn in Chapter 10, "Creating, Saving, and Printing a Spreadsheet,"—that is, point to cells when you want to use a cell reference, and type operators, constants, and parentheses where appropriate—but they require extra care when creating them. Another factor that makes formulas more complex is a concept called relative and absolute cell addressing. In the following section, you see how relative versus absolute cell addressing affects a formula.

Relative and Absolute Cell Addressing

Cell D17 contains the formula =D14–D15, where the value in D15 is subtracted from the value in D14, and the result is displayed in D17. The cell references in such a formula are called *relative* references because Works doesn't interpret them literally. To Works, the formula in D17 means "find the value in the cell 2 rows up and subtract it from the value in the cell 3 rows up, then display the result here." Rather than operating on specific values, a formula that uses relative addresses "follows directions" to find the values on which to calculate a result. If you move or copy the formula =D14–D15 to cell F5, for example, Works automatically changes the formula to =F2–F3 and calculates a result based on the values found in those cells.

When it's important for a formula to calculate on specific values in specific cells, you create a formula with *absolute* references. Figure 11.1 illustrates why you need to use absolute cell references in some formulas. In the figure, the worksheet lists a markup percentage (200%) in cell B4. Column B shows wholesale prices for the items listed in column A, and column C is where the retail price is calculated by multiplying the retail price by a markup percentage. In cell C9, the formula reads =B9*B4, which translates to $350*200%. This formula calculates the correct retail price in cell C9. For this cell, the formula really says: "find the value in the cell one column to the left ($350) and multiply it by the value in the cell one column to the left and five rows up (200%)." Given the location of the formula and the position of the values in the spreadsheet, this formula calculates correctly.

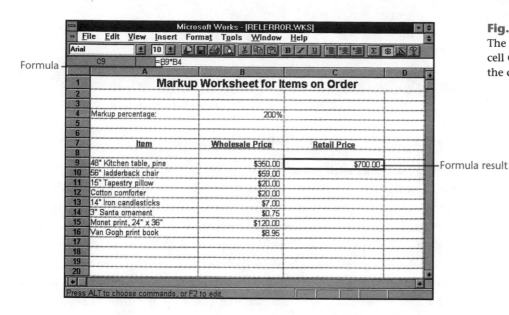

Fig. 11.1
The formula in
cell C9 calculates
the correct result.

But suppose you copy the formula in C9 to C10, thinking it will multiply $59
(in B10) by 200% (in B4). The formula no longer calculates correctly (see fig.
11.2). Because the original formula in C9 contains relative cell addresses, the
formula copied to cell C10 reads =B10*B5, which is incorrect. There is no
value in cell B5, so the formula evaluates to zero.

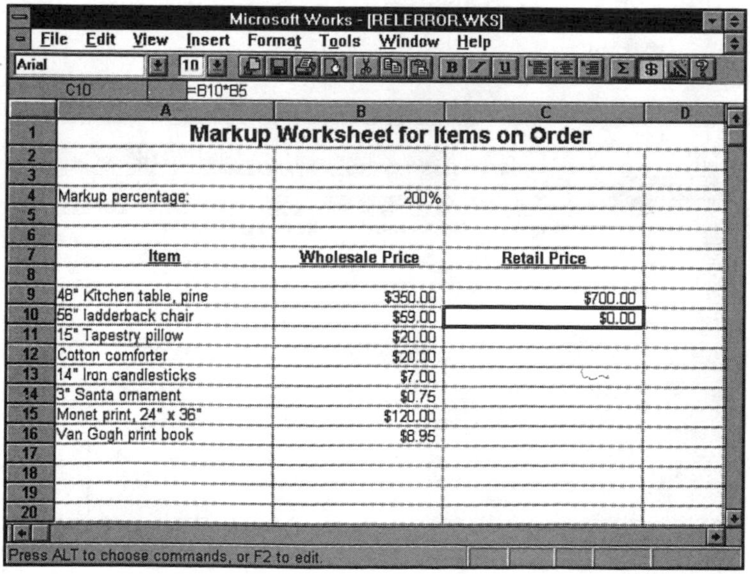

Fig. 11.2
When copied to
C10, the formula
from C9 is
incorrect and
evaluates to zero.

III

Spreadsheets and Charting

If you copy the formula from C9 all the way through cell C16, you find that the formula starts multiplying retail prices by retail prices rather than by the markup percentage because of the location of the cells. Formula errors like these can lead to significant errors in results in a spreadsheet. The way to fix this problem is with an absolute cell reference. That is, you want to multiply *all* of the retail prices in Column B by the markup percentage shown in cell B4, so the cell reference to cell B4 in all formulas should be an absolute reference.

Creating Formulas with Relative and Absolute Addresses

Formulas with relative cell references look like all the formulas you have seen up to this point—they don't contain any special characters, just simple cell references. When you create a formula by pointing to cell references with the mouse or arrow keys, Works automatically inserts relative cell references in the formula. To create a formula with absolute cell references, you insert dollar signs preceding the column and row references. To make the formula =B9*B4 *always* reference cell B4, for example, you write the formula as =B9*B4. The dollar sign preceding the B "locks" the cell reference to column B; the dollar sign preceding the 4 locks the reference to row 4. A "locked" cell reference is what Works refers to as an *absolute* reference. This means that if you copy the formula from cell C9 to cell C10, it now reads =B10*B4, which is exactly how you want it to read. If you copy the formula to C11, it reads =B11*B4. You can now copy this formula to all cells from C10 through C16, and the retail prices will be calculated correctly. Figure 11.3 shows the results.

Fig. 11.3
An absolute cell reference causes all copied formulas to calculate correctly.

Formula contains absolute cell reference

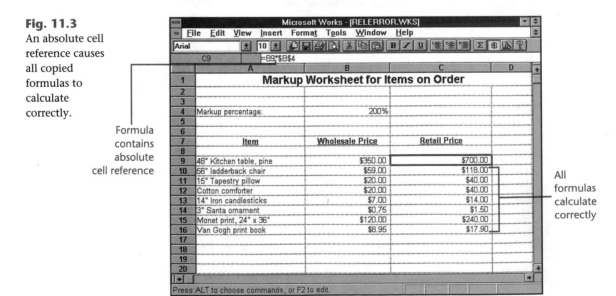

All formulas calculate correctly

To create a formula with absolute cell references, you either type the correct cell reference, including dollar signs, or you create the formula using relative references, and then add the dollar signs by editing the formula. To ensure the accuracy of the cell references, it's often best to create a formula with relative references by pointing to the correct cells, and then add the dollar signs when you edit the formula.

In Works you also can create a *mixed* cell reference, such as $B4 or B$4. In a mixed cell reference, only one reference—either the row or the column—is absolute; the other is not. In the reference $B4, the reference to column B is absolute but the row reference is not. The reference B$4 is just the opposite—the reference to row 4 is absolute but the column reference is not.

You can also quickly insert the dollar signs for absolute references by pressing the F4 key as you create a formula. When you point to a cell, such as C3, the cell reference is highlighted in the formula bar. Press F4 once to make the cell reference absolute. If you press F4 repeatedly, Works cycles through the following list of absolute, mixed, and relative references, creating them automatically for you:

Press F4 once	C3
Press F4 twice	C$3
Press F4 three times	$C3
Press F4 four times	C3

To complete the formula, insert operators and parentheses as you normally would.

Moving Formulas and Cells Referenced by Formulas

When you move a formula in a spreadsheet, Works does not change any of the cell references in the formula. If, for example, you move the formula =B10*B4 from cell C10 to cell K32, the formula still reads =B10*B4. In most cases, you still want the formula to calculate a result on the same values, it's only the *location of the result* that you are changing. Based on the principle that you still want to perform the same calculations regardless of the location of the formula, Works does not change the cell references in a moved formula.

On the other hand, when you change the location of *data* in a spreadsheet, Works changes any formula cell references to that data. Again, Works assumes that you still want to perform the same calculation, but the data is now located in a different cell, so the cell reference in the formula must be changed. For example, if you move the value of 200% in cell B4 to cell B3, Works changes the reference in the formula =B10*B4 to =B10*B3. This change ensures that the same calculation is performed now that the data (200%) is located in a different cell.

Copying Formulas and Cells Referenced by Formulas

When you copy a formula in a spreadsheet, you usually want the formula to perform the same type of calculation but use different data. In figure 11.4, for example, you might copy the formula in cell B10—=SUM(B7:B9)—to cells C10 through M10 to sum total income for the months of February through December. When you copy the formula, you expect it to accurately total the figures in columns C through M, not use the data from column B. To accomplish this, Works must adjust all relative cell references in a formula. So, if you copy =SUM(B7:B9) from B10 to C10, the formula reads =SUM(C7:C9); copied to D10, the formula reads =SUM(D7:D9), and so on.

Fig. 11.4
When copied to
C10 through M10,
the formula in
B10 calculates
accurately.

Formula to
copy

Range to
which
formula
will be
copied

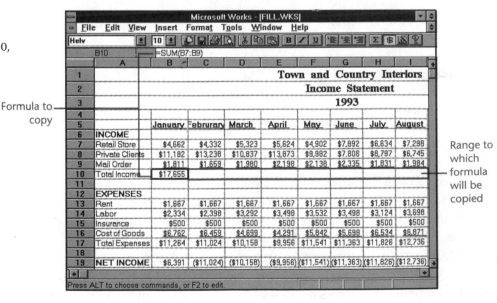

> **Note**
>
> When you copy a formula that contains absolute cell references, such as C9*B4, the relative part of the formula (C9) is automatically adjusted, but the absolute portion of the formula (B4) remains unchanged.

Clearing and Deleting Cells that Are Referenced in a Formula

If you clear a cell that is referenced by a formula, the value of that cell becomes zero, but the cell references in the formula remain unchanged. Suppose the formula cell C14 contains the formula =C10*C11 and you clear the value in C10. The formula now operates on a zero value in C10, but the cell references in the formula are still C10 and C11. This change is no different than if you change the value in C10 to 2 or 1,345,872.93. Zero is a value like any other value, and the formula remains unchanged.

If, however, you *delete* rather than clear a row or column that contains a cell referenced by a formula, the formula displays ERR in the cell where the formula is located. (Recall that you can't delete individual cells.) When you delete a row or column, the referenced cell no longer exists. Because the formula doesn't know where to find the cell, it can't calculate correctly, so Works must display the ERR value. This is your cue to adjust the cell reference in the formula so it can calculate correctly.

Using Functions in Formulas

As you learned in Chapter 10, "Creating, Saving, and Printing a Spreadsheet," functions are prepared equations designed to simplify the task of creating formulas in a spreadsheet. Functions perform such common tasks as finding the sum of a range of numbers (SUM), but also can be as complex as finding the net present value of an investment based on constant future cash flows (NPV). Rather than trying to create a complex formula yourself, you insert a function into a spreadsheet to perform a specific type of calculation. Works contains 76 built-in functions that you select from the Function dialog box (see fig. 11.5), displayed by selecting the **F**unction command on the **I**nsert menu. The functions cover a broad range of categories, including financial, logical, statistical, math, and trigonometry. For a complete summary of all 76 functions included in Works, refer to Appendix B, "Works for Windows Functions."

Functions consist of a function name and one or more *arguments* that represent the values upon which the function operates. An argument can be a constant value, a reference to a cell that contains a value, a reference to a cell that generates a value, a range of cells, or a named range. When you insert a function in a spreadsheet, it begins with an equal symbol, followed by the function name, followed by the arguments enclosed in parentheses. Within the parentheses, arguments are separated by commas and no spaces. For example, the present value function, before cell references or values are entered, looks like this:

    PV(payment,rate,term)

When you use the PV function and substitute the arguments with values or cell references, the formula might look like this:

    =PV(25000,7.75%,4)

Or this:

    =PV(C2,C6,C3)

To insert a function in a spreadsheet, you use the Function dialog box shown in figure 11.5. In the dialog box, functions are listed by category. The Functions box lists function names and their arguments. The Description box briefly describes the purpose of the function that's currently selected.

Fig. 11.5
The Functions list box shows an alphabetized list of functions for the Category selected.

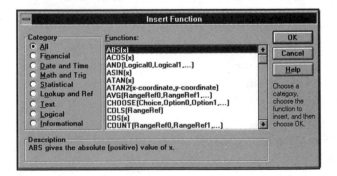

To insert a formula in a spreadsheet, follow these steps:

1. Move the cell selector to the cell where you want the result to be displayed.

2. From the Insert menu, choose the Function command. The Function dialog box in figure 11.5 appears.

3. From the Category box, choose a category.

4. From the Functions list, highlight the function you want to use. Be sure to refer to the Description box for an explanation of the function.

5. When you find the right function, choose OK. Works inserts the function, including all of its arguments, in the current cell. The equal symbol is inserted before the function name to make the entry a formula. In the formula bar, the first argument is highlighted.

6. In the formula bar, replace each argument with the correct value or cell reference, then press Enter or click the Enter button. Works displays the function result in the current cell.

If you make an error as you enter a function, Works displays a dialog box alerting you to the error. When you click OK or press Enter, Works highlights the error in the formula bar so you can correct it.

Using Range Names

A handy feature of Works allows you to assign a *range name* to a cell or range of cells. Using a range name, you can identify cells by a name you recognize rather than a cell reference like C14:F18 or K37. Suppose you have entered the raw data for the spreadsheet shown in figure 11.6 but you haven't entered any formulas yet. You might consider naming cells B7:B9 "Q1 Income" and cells B13:B16 "Q1 Expenses". Or you might name cells B10:E10 "Total Income" and cells B17:E17 "Total Expenses."

Tip
If you use functions frequently, consider adding the Function button to the toolbar, which displays the Function dialog box when you click it. For instructions on customizing a toolbar, refer to Chapter 2, "Getting Started with Works for Windows."

III

Spreadsheets and Charting

Fig. 11.6
Possible cell ranges to name.

Name this range Q1 Income

Name this range Total Income

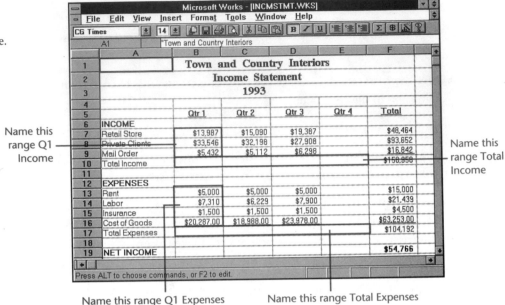

Name this range Q1 Expenses

Name this range Total Expenses

Once you name a range of cells, you can use the name in formulas in place of cell references, and you also can find and highlight a named cell range using the **G**o To command.

Creating, Editing, and Deleting Range Names

You can assign a name to a single cell or any range of cells in a worksheet. Range names can be up to 15 characters and can include any combination of letters, numbers, spaces, and other symbols like *, #, and +. You can use any combination of upper and lowercase letters. To assign a range name to a cell or range of cells, you use the Range Name dialog box (see fig. 11.7), displayed by choosing the Ra**n**ge Name command on the **I**nsert menu. In the dialog box, all existing range names are shown in the Name**s** box along with their respective cell ranges.

Fig. 11.7
Use the Range Name dialog box to list all existing names and create new ones.

Existing range names and their cell references

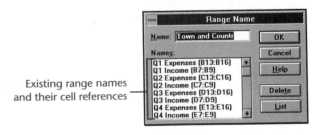

To name a cell range, follow these steps:

1. Select the cell or cell range you want to name.

2. Choose the Range **N**ame command on the **I**nsert menu. The Range Name dialog box in figure 11.7 appears.

3. In the **N**ame box, enter a name for the selected cell or range.

4. Choose OK. Works adds the new name to the Name**s** list and closes the dialog box.

When you change a spreadsheet by inserting or deleting rows and columns, Works automatically adjusts range name cell references. In these cases, you don't need to adjust the cell references in a named range. But suppose you selected the wrong cells when you created the range, or suppose you decide to add more cells to an existing range. You can change the cell reference for a named range by following these steps:

1. Select the new cell or cell range you want to use for an existing named range.

2. From the **I**nsert menu, choose the Range **N**ame command. The Range Name dialog box in figure 11.7 appears.

3. In the Name**s** box, highlight the named range for which you want to change the cell reference.

4. Choose OK. Works changes the cell references for the range you select.

If you make extensive changes in a spreadsheet, you may find that you no longer need some of the named ranges you created. You can delete a range name at any time by opening the Range Name dialog box, highlighting the range to delete in the Name**s** list, and choosing the Dele**t**e button.

Listing Range Names

When a spreadsheet contains many range names, often it's helpful to include them as a list somewhere in a blank area of your spreadsheet. Later you can print that area of the spreadsheet and have a permanent record of the range names and their respective cell references.

To create a list of range names, first choose a blank area of the worksheet where the list will fit without overwriting other data in the spreadsheet. (If the area you choose contains data, Works *will* overwrite it.) Place the cell

Tip

Be careful deleting a range name because you can't use the **U**ndo command on the **E**dit menu to restore a deleted name.

Tip

If you use range names frequently, you can customize your toolbar by adding the Range Name button, which displays the Range Name dialog box when you click it. For instructions on customizing a toolbar, refer to Chapter 2, "Getting Started with Works for Windows."

III

Spreadsheets and Charting

selector in the cell where you want the list to begin, then display the Range Name dialog box. In the dialog box, click the List button. Works inserts a two-column list like the one in figure 11.8.

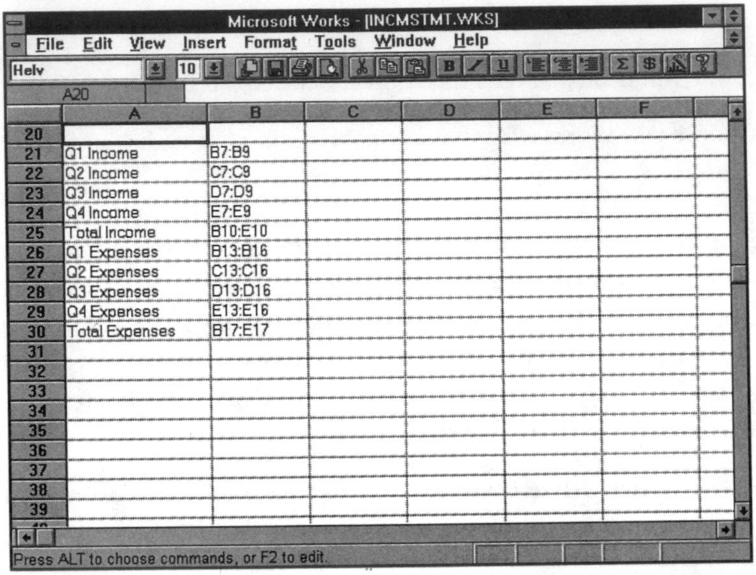

Fig. 11.8

Use the List button in the Range Name dialog box to paste a list of range names into your spreadsheet.

	A	B	C	D	E	F
20						
21	Q1 Income	B7:B9				
22	Q2 Income	C7:C9				
23	Q3 Income	D7:D9				
24	Q4 Income	E7:E9				
25	Total Income	B10:E10				
26	Q1 Expenses	B13:B16				
27	Q2 Expenses	C13:C16				
28	Q3 Expenses	D13:D16				
29	Q4 Expenses	E13:E16				
30	Total Expenses	B17:E17				
31						
32						
33						
34						
35						
36						
37						
38						
39						

Using Range Names in Formulas

Using range names in a formula can make the formula easier to create as well as interpret. The formula =SUM(Q1 expenses) is much more descriptive than the formula =SUM(B7:B9). You use range names in a formula just like you use a constant value or a cell reference. In other words, you can combine range names in a formula with other range names, cell references, operators, and constants. Figure 11.9 illustrates the formulas that were used to complete the totals in the income statement spreadsheet. In cell B17 the formula is =SUM(Q1 Expenses). Net income figures in cells B19:D19 were calculated using the formula =Total Income–Total Expenses.

Using Range Names with the Go To Command

In Chapter 10, "Creating, Saving, and Printing a Spreadsheet," you learned to use the **G**o To command on the **E**dit menu to move the cell selector to a cell or cell range. You also can use the **G**o To command to highlight a named range in a spreadsheet. When you create range names, the names appear in the Go To dialog box as well as the Range Name dialog box. To highlight a named range, choose the **G**o To command on the **E**dit menu or press F5, and then highlight the range name you want to go to and click OK. Works highlights the named range you select.

Range name used in formula

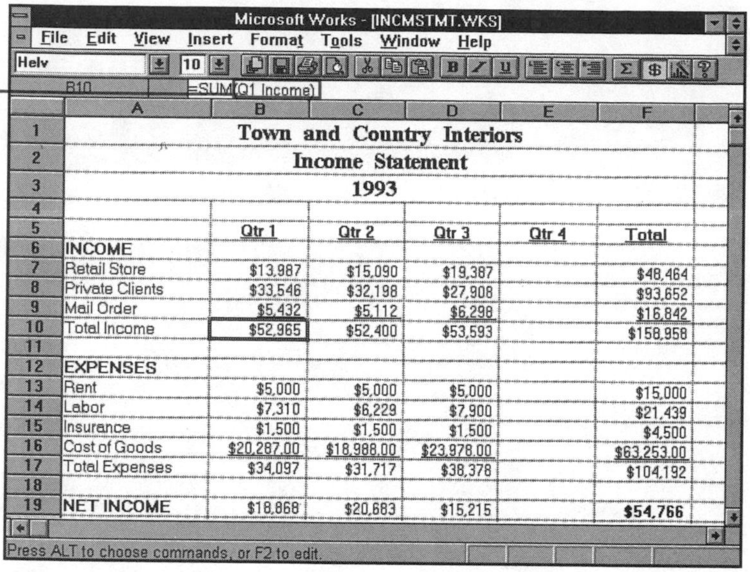
Microsoft Works - [INCMSTMT.WKS]

File Edit View Insert Format Tools Window Help

B10 =SUM(Q1 Income)

	A	B	C	D	E	F
1	Town and Country Interiors					
2	Income Statement					
3	1993					
4						
5		Qtr 1	Qtr 2	Qtr 3	Qtr 4	Total
6	INCOME					
7	Retail Store	$13,987	$15,090	$19,387		$48,464
8	Private Clients	$33,546	$32,198	$27,908		$93,652
9	Mail Order	$5,432	$5,112	$6,298		$16,842
10	Total Income	$52,965	$52,400	$53,593		$158,958
11						
12	EXPENSES					
13	Rent	$5,000	$5,000	$5,000		$15,000
14	Labor	$7,310	$6,229	$7,900		$21,439
15	Insurance	$1,500	$1,500	$1,500		$4,500
16	Cost of Goods	$20,287.00	$18,988.00	$23,978.00		$63,253.00
17	Total Expenses	$34,097	$31,717	$38,378		$104,192
18						
19	NET INCOME	$18,868	$20,683	$15,215		$54,766

Press ALT to choose commands, or F2 to edit.

Fig. 11.9
Formulas that use range names are easier to interpret.

Troubleshooting

What happens to a formula that uses a range name if I delete the name?

The formula still calculates correctly. Works replaces the range name in the formula with the actual cell reference that was used by the name.

I accidentally overwrote some data in my spreadsheet when I created a list of range names. Is there any way to restore my data?

The **U**ndo command isn't available after you insert a list of range names in a spreadsheet. If you overwrote data with the range name list, the only way to restore the data is to close the file without saving changes, but you lose all changes that were made since you last saved the file.

From Here...

In this chapter, you learned about formulas, functions, and range names. For more information on these topics, refer to the following section of this book.

- Appendix B, "Works for Windows Functions," lists a description and examples for all of the 76 built-in functions included in Works.

Chapter 12

Enhancing the Appearance of a Spreadsheet

In Chapter 10, "Creating, Saving, and Printing a Spreadsheet," you learn that enhancing a document makes it more visually appealing and easier to read and comprehend. The same is true of spreadsheets. In fact, an unenhanced spreadsheet can easily look like an incomprehensible sea of numbers. Using different fonts, sizes, borders, patterns, and color to format and define a spreadsheet makes the sea much easier to navigate. This chapter discusses the variety of ways you can make a spreadsheet more attractive and readable.

Applying a Number Format to Selected Cells

When you enter a number in a spreadsheet, Works automatically left-aligns the number in the cell using the General format. Works makes no assumptions about what the number represents, and therefore applies no other notations, such as dollar signs, commas, percent symbols, and so on. These and other notations are called number *formats*. You apply a format to a cell or cell range by choosing the Number command on the Format menu, which displays the Number dialog box (see fig. 12.1). Available formats are displayed in the Format box. Most number formats offer options that you can specify, such as the number of decimal places to display, or a format style, as when choosing a date format. Formats and options are described in Table 12.1.

In this chapter, you learn how to:

- Apply a number format to numeric entries

- Align cell entries

- Choose a font, size, color, and style

- Adjust row heights

- Enhance cells with borders and patterns

- Use headers and footers in a spreadsheet

- Use Auto-Format to format spreadsheets

III

Spreadsheets and Charting

Fig. 12.1
Choose a number
format from the
Number dialog
box.

Available formats

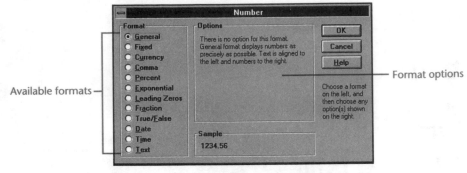

Format options

Table 12.1 Number Formats

Format	Effect
General	Text is left-aligned and numbers are right-aligned. Uses scientific notation when a number is too long to be displayed in a cell.
Fixed	Rounds numbers to the number of decimal places you specify. If you specify 2 places, for example, 34.2391 is displayed as 34.24. Negative numbers are preceded by a minus (–) symbol.
Currency	Numbers are preceded by a dollar symbol ($); large numbers use commas as thousands separators. Use this setting to choose the number of decimal places and to display negative numbers in red.
Comma	Inserts commas as thousands separators. Negative numbers appear in parentheses rather than with a minus (–) symbol. As an option, use this setting to display negative numbers in red.
Percent	Follows a number with a percent symbol (%). Automatically moves decimal points two places to the right. If you enter .081, Works displays 8.1%. You specify the number of decimal places to use.
Exponential	Displays numbers using scientific notation. If you enter 7898.23, Works displays 7.90E+03. You specify the number of decimal places to use.
Leading zeros	Displays the number you enter with leading zeros. You specify the number of digits (up to 8) to display. Use this format when you want to display leading zeros of zip codes, invoice numbers, part numbers, and so on.
Fraction	Displays numbers as fractions, rounded to the fraction you specify (1/2, 1/3, 1/8, 1/10, 1/16, 1/32, 1/100), or choose to display all fractions. If you enter 2.781 and choose the 1/4 setting, works displays 2 3/4.

Format	Effect
True/**F**alse	Displays numbers as logical values, either TRUE or FALSE. All zeros that appear are displayed as FALSE. All non-zero numbers are displayed as TRUE.
Date	Displays entries in the date format you specify. Choose from three numeric formats, such as 3/20/94, or four text formats, such as March 20, 1994.
Ti**m**e	Displays entries in the time format you specify.
Text	Formats the entry as text rather than as a number. This format is useful when you want to sort entries such as phone numbers and postal codes.

You can apply a number format to cells that already contain data, or to cells before you enter data. Select the range of cells to format, then choose the **N**umber command on the Forma**t** menu. Choose a format from the Format box, then specify options for the format, if applicable. When all settings are correct, choose OK.

A Currency button appears on the standard toolbar. When you click this button, Works formats the selected cells with dollar signs, commas (if applicable), and two decimal places. If you don't want two decimal places, use the Number dialog box to specify the number of decimal places for the Currency option.

Aligning Entries Within Cells

As you learned earlier in this chapter, Works automatically applies the **G**eneral format to all entries you make in a spreadsheet. The **G**eneral format causes text to be left-aligned and numbers to be right-aligned in a cell. Often, you may want to change the alignment of entries to improve the overall appearance of a spreadsheet or make data easier to read. For example, it's common to center a spreadsheet title across the columns contained in a worksheet, or to center column labels above columns of data.

In a spreadsheet, you can change the horizontal and vertical alignment of cell entries. You also can choose to wrap text within a cell. To align entries horizontally, you can left-align, right-align, or center an entry in a cell, fill a cell, or center an entry across a selection of columns. These options are available in the Alignment dialog box, displayed when you choose the Alignment command on the Format menu (see fig. 12.2).

Tip
If you work with number formats frequently, you can add Percent and Comma buttons to the toolbar to format numbers quickly. To customize the toolbar, refer to Chapter 2, "Getting Started with Works for Windows."

III

Spreadsheets and Charting

Fig. 12.2
Choose an
alignment style
from the Align-
ment dialog box.

When you choose the **L**eft option, all entries are left-aligned, including numbers. When you choose **R**ight, all entries are right-aligned, including text.
The **C**enter option centers an entry within the width of a cell. If the entry is
too long to be displayed within the borders of the cell, the entry "spills over"
into the cells immediately to the left and right of the current cell, provided
those cells are empty. If the cells to the left and right contain data, the centered entry is cut off on both the right and left edges of the cell. You can view
the entire entry by highlighting the cell and then checking the formula bar.

The **F**ill option duplicates the cell entry as many times as possible until the
cell is filled. For instance, if you type # in a cell and use the **F**ill option,
Works fills the cell with # characters. If you type ABC in a cell formatted with
the **F**ill option, Works displays ABCABC in the cell until the cell is filled.

When you choose the Center **A**cross Selection option, Works centers an entry
across the range of cells you select. Use this option to center a spreadsheet
title across the columns contained in a spreadsheet. If cell A2 contains the
title "1994 Sales Forecast" and you select cells A2:G2, Works centers the title
between the left boundary of cell A2 and the right boundary of cell G2.

To change the horizontal alignment of entries in a cell or cell range, follow
these steps:

1. Select the cell or cell range for which you want to align entries.

2. From the Forma**t** menu choose the **A**lignment command. The Alignment dialog box in figure 12.2 appears.

3. In the Alignment box, choose an alignment style.

4. Click OK.

Left, center, and right alignment buttons are available on the spreadsheet toolbar. To use these buttons rather than the Alignment dialog box, select the cell or cells for which you want to change the alignment, and then click the appropriate toolbar button. If you choose to customize the toolbar, you can add the Center **A**cross Selection button to the toolbar. (Refer to Chapter 2, "Getting Started with Works for Windows," for information on customizing the toolbar.)

Setting Vertical Alignment of Entries

All spreadsheet cells have height as well as width. When you enter data into cells, Works automatically aligns entries along the bottom edge of a cell. This is generally where you want an entry to be aligned because the default row height is appropriate for the height of the default font. However, in some cases, particularly when you are using a large row height or a special font, you might want an entry to be vertically aligned along the top of a cell or through the horizontal center of a cell. Examples of each are shown in figure 12.3. To change the vertical alignment of an entry, choose the **A**lignment command on the Forma**t** menu, then choose the **T**op, C**e**nter, or **B**ottom option in the Alignment dialog box.

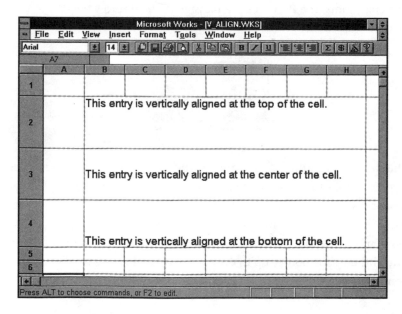

Fig. 12.3
Examples of vertical alignment within a cell.

Adjusting Row Height

When you open a new spreadsheet file, Works uses the Standard row height, which adjusts the height of each row automatically to accommodate the font and point size you choose. The row height throughout a spreadsheet is initially set at 12 points. Because the default font and size for spreadsheets is Arial 10, a row height of 12 adequately accommodates all new entries you type. If you change the font or point size, Works automatically adjusts the row height for the font and size you choose. For example, if you change the font throughout your spreadsheet to CG Times 12, Works automatically sets the row height throughout the sheet to 15. (The three extra points allow for spacing.) If you enter a title on row 1 in Antique Olive 16, Works adjusts the row height of row 1 to 20 points.

You can specify an exact row height by selecting the row or rows you want to adjust and then choosing the Row **H**eight command on the Forma**t** menu. The Row Height dialog box in figure 12.4 appears. In the H**e**ight text box, enter a number in points. (You can enter fractions, such as 131.5, if you like.) If you choose the **B**est Fit check box, Works automatically adjusts the row height for the largest font used in the row. If you select multiple rows that use different fonts, the **B**est Fit option assigns different row heights to each row in the selection.

Fig. 12.4
Use the Row Height dialog box to specify an exact row height or best fit.

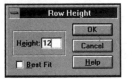

In Chapter 10, "Creating, Saving, and Printing a Spreadsheet," you learned that you can adjust column width by dragging the column border. The same is true for rows. When you point to the bottom border of a row, the standard mouse pointer changes to an up/down arrow labeled "Adjust" (see fig. 12.5). When you see this pointer, click and drag the border down to increase the row height; drag the border up to decrease row height. Release the mouse button when the row is the height you want.

This mouse pointer lets you adjust row height

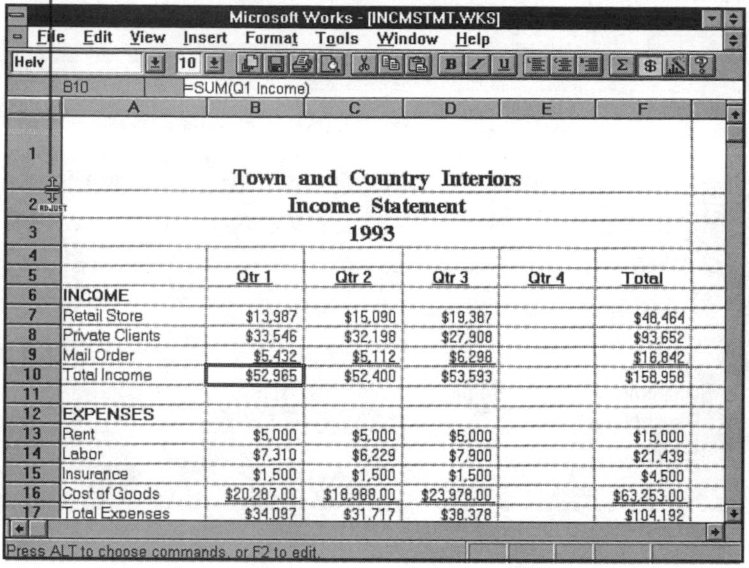

	A	B	C	D	E	F
1						
2		**Town and Country Interiors**				
		Income Statement				
3		**1993**				
4						
5		Qtr 1	Qtr 2	Qtr 3	Qtr 4	Total
6	INCOME					
7	Retail Store	$13,987	$15,090	$19,387		$48,464
8	Private Clients	$33,546	$32,198	$27,908		$93,652
9	Mail Order	$5,432	$5,112	$6,298		$16,842
10	Total Income	$52,965	$52,400	$53,593		$158,958
11						
12	EXPENSES					
13	Rent	$5,000	$5,000	$5,000		$15,000
14	Labor	$7,310	$6,229	$7,900		$21,439
15	Insurance	$1,500	$1,500	$1,500		$4,500
16	Cost of Goods	$20,287.00	$18,988.00	$23,978.00		$63,253.00
17	Total Expenses	$34,097	$31,717	$38,378		$104,192

Microsoft Works - [INCMSTMT.WKS]

File Edit View Insert Format Tools Window Help

Helv   10   B10   =SUM(Q1 Income)

Press ALT to choose commands, or F2 to edit.

Fig. 12.5
Drag the bottom border of a row to adjust row height.

III

Spreadsheets and Charting

Wrapping Text within a Cell

When a cell contains a text entry that's too long to display completely, you can increase the column width to display the entire entry. Often, however, increasing column width isn't a practical solution because the spreadsheet becomes too wide. A more practical solution is to wrap text within the cell, which increases the row height but allows you to maintain a cell's column width. Wrapping text within a cell is commonly used for column headings (see fig. 12.6).

To wrap text with a cell or cell range, select the cells, and then choose the **A**lignment command on the Forma**t** menu. In the Alignment dialog box, choose the **W**rap Text check box, and then click OK. Works automatically wraps existing text within the cell and adjusts row height as appropriate.

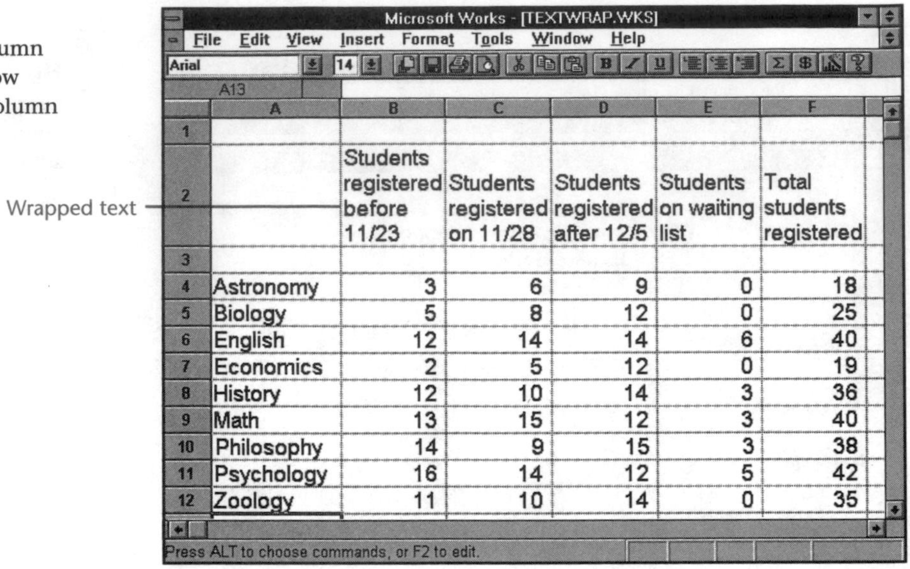

Fig. 12.6
Wrapped column
headings allow
reasonable column
widths in a
spreadsheet.

Wrapped text ──

	Students registered before 11/23	Students registered on 11/28	Students registered after 12/5	Students on waiting list	Total students registered
Astronomy	3	6	9	0	18
Biology	5	8	12	0	25
English	12	14	14	6	40
Economics	2	5	12	0	19
History	12	10	14	3	36
Math	13	15	12	3	40
Philosophy	14	9	15	3	38
Psychology	16	14	12	5	42
Zoology	11	10	14	0	35

Troubleshooting

I typed a spreadsheet title in cell A3 and centered it across columns A through F, but the title is not centered correctly. What's wrong?

Check to see that the title doesn't include any unnecessary spaces before or after the text. Adding spaces to an entry will throw off center alignment across selected cells.

I typed my spreadsheet title in cell C3, then centered it across columns A through G, but the title still isn't centered. What's wrong?

To accurately center an entry across a selection of cells, you must type the entry in the first cell in the range across which you want to center the entry. In this example, if you want to center the title across columns A through G, type your title in cell A3, not C3. When the title appears in cell C3, Works ignores columns A and B when centering because your entry doesn't appear there.

When I wrap text within a cell, Works breaks text in the middle of a word. How do I avoid this error?

Whenever you use the wrap text option, you still need to adjust column width to format the text correctly. To prevent Works from breaking text in the middle of a word, make the column as wide as the longest word in the cell. Notice in figure 12.4 the width of columns B through F was adjusted to fit the longest word, *registered*, in each entry.

Choosing a Character Font, Size, Color, and Style

To emphasize data, draw attention, and make a spreadsheet more visually appealing, you can choose a font, size, color, and style for selected cells or all cells. To apply these characteristics, you can use any of three methods: menu commands, buttons on the toolbar, or keyboard shortcuts. When using menu commands, you use the Font and Style dialog box, shown in figure 12.7, that appears when you choose the **F**ont and Style command on the Forma**t** menu.

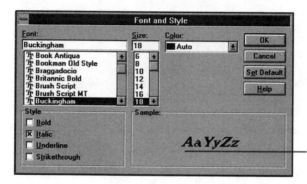

Fig. 12.7
The Font and Style dialog box.

The choices you make are displayed in the Sample box

In the Font and Style dialog box shown in figure 12.7, you see settings for the font, size, color, and style. These attributes are described next:

- *Font.* A font refers to a specific style or design for a set of characters that Works displays on-screen and prints on paper. Each font has a particular shape or other characteristics that distinguish it from other fonts. For example, this sentence appears in the Korinna font.

- *Size.* Most fonts are available in different sizes and are generally measured in *points*. (A point is equal to 1/72 of an inch.) The most common point sizes for use in the body of a spreadsheet are 10 or 12. Other elements in a spreadsheet, such as titles, row and column labels, often appear in larger sizes, such as 14, 16, 18, or 24 points.

- *Color.* If you have a color monitor, you can display selected cells in a variety of colors. If you have a color printer, you also can print the colors that you display in your spreadsheet.

■ *Style.* In Works, a text style refers to bold, italic, underline, or strikethrough. **B**old, **I**talic, and **U**nderline are common styles used to emphasize entries. **St**rikethrough prints a line through an entry, indicating that the entry may be marked for deletion, but the entry itself is still readable.

In the Font and Style dialog box, font, size, and color choices are available from list boxes. Text styles (bold, italic, underline, and strikethrough), however, are represented by check boxes because you can choose more than one style simultaneously. As you make font, size, color, and style choices, the Sample area of the dialog box displays the choices you make. The Sample box is especially helpful for viewing the unique design of a particular font and the relative size of characters.

To apply a character style to cells that contain data or to empty cells, follow these steps:

1. Select the cells to which you want to apply a character style.

2. From the Forma**t** menu, choose the **F**ont and Style command. The Font and Style dialog box in figure 12.7 appears.

3. From the **F**ont, **S**ize, and C**o**lor lists, select one option.

4. From the Style box, choose as many styles as you want to apply to the selected cells.

5. When the text shown in the Sample box appears as you want it, choose OK. Works automatically reformats the selected cells.

If you prefer to use the toolbar to apply a character style, buttons are available for font and size, as well as bold, italic, and underline (see fig. 12.8).

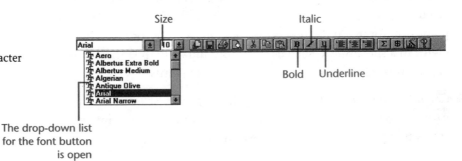

Fig. 12.8
Choose a character style from the spreadsheet toolbar.

The drop-down list for the font button is open

The font and size buttons contain drop-down boxes from which you select a font and point size. To change a font or size, select the cells you want to change, and then select an item from each drop-down list. To add bold, italic, or underline to cell entries, select the cells first, then click the appropriate button. Notice that the bold, italic, and underline buttons toggle on and off, so if you want to remove an attribute, select the affected cells, and then click the appropriate button again.

Works provides keyboard shortcuts for the character styles shown in Table 12.2. To use a keyboard shortcut, select the cells you want to format, and then press the key sequence shown in Table 12.2. Notice that all of the shortcuts listed except Ctrl+Space bar (for plain text) toggle on and off.

Tip

If you choose to customize your spreadsheet toolbar, you can add a button for the Strikethrough style. To customize your toolbar, refer to Chapter 2, "Getting Started with Works for Windows."

Table 12.2 Keyboard Shortcuts for Character Styles

Key Sequence	Character Style
Ctrl+B	Bold
Ctrl+U	Underline
Ctrl+I	Italic
Ctrl+Space bar	Plain text (remove all character styles)

Note

Although the toolbar and keyboard shortcuts for character styles are helpful, they do not replace all menu commands for text character styles. If you want to change the color of text, for example, you still must use the Font and Style dialog box in figure 12.7 because there are no toolbar buttons or keyboard shortcuts for color.

Attributes that you add to text (such as bold, italic, underline, and strikethrough) toggle on and off, whether you choose the setting in the Font and Style dialog box, from the toolbar, or use a keyboard shortcut. To remove any of these character styles individually, select the affected cells, and then select the dialog box option, the toolbar button, or the keyboard shortcut again to remove the attribute.

III

Spreadsheets and Charting

Attributes such as font, size, and color change the *characteristics* of text. Technically, these attributes can be changed but not removed. Select the affected cells, and then choose the **F**ont and Style command on the Forma**t** menu to choose a new font, size, or color.

When cells contain several attributes and you want to remove *all* of them, the quickest way is to select the text, then press Ctrl+Space bar. This keyboard shortcut changes all selected cells back to plain text and saves you the trouble of removing each attribute individually. If you have changed the font used in the selected cells, Works restores the default Arial 10 font.

Adding Borders and Patterns to Cells

In a spreadsheet, you often want to draw attention to a particular cell or cells. In an income statement, for example, you might want to highlight the Net Income/Net Loss row so the reader can instantly focus on "the bottom line." One way to make a cell or cell range stand out is to place a border around it. With Works, you can border cells using a variety of line styles and add a color if you like.

The term *border* is somewhat misleading because it implies that a line completely surrounds a cell. This type of border is called an *outline border*. But in Works, you also can create *partial* borders that fall on the top, bottom, left, or right sides of a cell, or you can use any combination of the four.

To define a border, style, and color, you use the Border dialog box (see fig. 12.9), displayed when you choose the Border command on the Forma**t** menu. To create an outline border, choose the **O**utline check box. To create a partial border, choose any combination of the **T**op, and Botto**m**, **L**eft, and **R**ight check boxes. In the L**i**ne Style box, choose a style. To add color to the style you choose, select a color from the **C**olor list. Note that unless you have a color printer, the color is visible only on-screen.

Fig. 12.9
Use the Border
dialog box to
choose a border,
style, and color.

To add a border to spreadsheet cells, follow these steps:

1. Select the cell or cell range you want to border.

2. From the Format menu, choose the **B**order command. The Border
   dialog box in figure 12.9 appears.

3. Select the **O**utline check box to create an outline border. Or, select any
   combination of the **T**op, Botto**m**, **L**eft, and **R**ight boxes to create a
   partial border.

4. Select a style from the Li**n**e Style box.

5. Select a color from the **C**olor list.

6. Choose OK. Works adds the specified border to the selected cells.

To remove a border, use the steps outlined above, clearing all borders from
the **O**utline, **T**op, Botto**m**, **L**eft, and **R**ight boxes.

Another way to make cells stand out is to add a pattern. A pattern shades the
background of a cell, leaving the entry in the cell readable. You can add a
pattern to individual cells or to a range of cells by choosing a pattern style, a
foreground color, and a background color from the Patterns dialog box (see
fig. 12.10), displayed when you choose the **P**atterns command on the Forma**t**
menu. If you choose a solid pattern, the selected cells display only the foreground color. The Sample box shows an example of the pattern and colors
you choose.

Tip
If you work with
borders frequently,
you can customize
your toolbar by
adding the Border
button, which
displays the Border
dialog box when
you click it. For
instructions on
customizing the
toolbar, refer
to Chapter 2,
"Getting Started
with Works for
Windows."

III

Spreadsheets and Charting

Fig. 12.10
Choose cell pattern and colors in the Patterns dialog box.

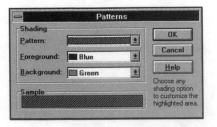

Use the following steps to add a pattern to a cell or cell range. As you make choices in the dialog box, be sure to check the Sample area, which illustrates the choices you make.

1. Select the cell or cells to which you want to apply a pattern.

2. From the Format menu, choose the **P**atterns command. The Patterns dialog box in figure 12.10 appears.

3. From the **P**attern drop-down box, select a pattern style.

4. From the **F**oreground drop-down box, select a color for the pattern foreground.

5. From the **B**ackground drop-down box, select a color for the pattern background.

6. When you create a pattern you like, choose OK.

To switch a pattern back to the colors used in your current color scheme, select the affected cells and then choose the **P**atterns command on the Format menu. In the **F**oreground and **B**ackground boxes, choose the Auto option. To remove a pattern entirely, select the cell or cell range from which you want to remove a pattern, then display the Patterns dialog box and choose None as the option in the Pattern drop-down box. Works removes the pattern from the selected cells.

Adding Headers and Footers to a Spreadsheet

Before you print a spreadsheet, you might want to add a title, page number, date, or other information at the top or bottom of each page. Repetitive text that appears at the top of each page is called a *header*. When the text appears at the bottom of the page, it's called a *footer*. You can add a header, footer, or both to any spreadsheet. (You might want to include a reminder such as "Do Not Copy.") If your spreadsheet is more than one page and you don't want a header or footer on the first page, you can eliminate them from the first page. Headers and footers print within the top and bottom margin areas of your spreadsheet.

In a spreadsheet, a header or footer cannot be longer than one line of text. You can insert special codes that automatically print the current date, current time, page numbers, file name, and so on, but you cannot change the font or add effects such as bold, underline, or italics. You enter the text for a header or footer in the Headers and Footers dialog box, displayed when you choose the **H**eaders and Footers command on the **V**iew menu. When you close the dialog box, the header or footer is visible only on the Print Preview screen (see fig. 12.11).

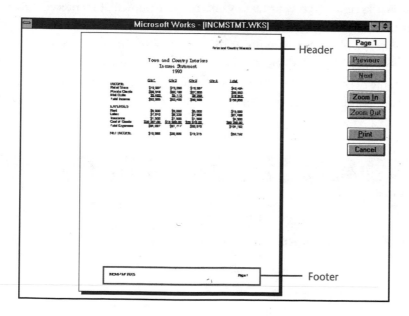

Fig. 12.11
Spreadsheet headers and footers are visible in the Print Preview screen.

To create a standard header, footer, or both, you use the Headers and Footers dialog box (see fig. 12.12). Enter the header text in the **H**eader box; enter the footer text in the **F**ooter box.

Fig. 12.12
Type the text for
a header, footers,
or both in the
Headers and
Footers dialog box.

Selecting these boxes eliminates the header and footer from the first page

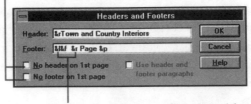

Codes that align text and insert special text

Adding Special Text and Formatting Headers and Footers

Works automatically centers all header and footer text in a spreadsheet. To
align the text differently you insert special codes, as shown in Table 12.3,
into the text itself. Some codes align text while others insert special text such
as a page number, file name, or current date. For codes that align text, you
enter the code immediately preceding the text. For example, you can specify
that Works right-align your text by entering **&r** immediately preceding the
text that you want right-aligned. For codes that insert text, you simply type
the code, such as **&f**, which prints the file name in the header or footer. You
also can combine codes, where appropriate. If you want Works to insert the
file name of the current document and right-align it, type **&r&f**. To make
the codes easier to read, you can separate two different codes with a space if
you like (as in **&r &f**).

Table 12.3 Format and Alignment Codes	
Type	**To**
&l	Left-align the text that follows the code
&r	Right-align the text that follows the code
&c	Center the text that follows the code
&f	Print the file name
&p	Print page numbers
&t	Insert the time at the time of printing
&d	Insert the date at the time of printing (such as 3/2/94)
&n	Insert the long form date at the time of printing (such as 2 March 94)
&&	Print an ampersand (&)

To create a header, footer, or both, follow these steps:

1. From the **V**iew menu, choose the **H**eaders and Footers command. The Headers and Footers dialog box in figure 12.12 appears.

2. In the **H**eader box, enter the text and any codes you want to use for the header.

3. In the **F**ooter box, enter the text and any codes you want to use for the footer.

4. To eliminate a header or footer on the first page of your document, select the **N**o Header on 1st Page or N**o** Footer on 1st Page check boxes.

5. Choose OK.

Changing and Deleting a Header or Footer

You can change the content of a spreadsheet header or footer, as well as the format or any special text you included. To change a header or footer, simply recall the Headers and Footers dialog box and then make the appropriate changes in the Header and Footer text boxes.

Troubleshooting

In my header, I entered the codes &r &f to right-align the document's file name, but when I printed the document, the header reads " & f" at the right margin. What happened?

You typed the &r code correctly, but you typed a space between the & and the f, so Works interpreted the two characters literally. When inserting codes, you can put a space between separate codes to make them easier to read but be careful not to put a space within a code itself.

Using AutoFormat

If you're not inclined to bother with formatting a spreadsheet yourself, you can have Works do it for you. Works includes 14 predefined format styles that are available in the AutoFormat dialog box, displayed when you choose the AutoFormat command on the Format menu (see fig. 12.13). Each format applies a special font, size, and style to text and numbers and adds borders and patterns to make the spreadsheet more attractive. Subtotal and total rows are sometimes formatted in distinctive ways to make these particular numbers stand out. An example of an AutoFormat is shown in figure 12.14.

Fig. 12.13
Choose a spreadsheet format from the AutoFormat dialog box.

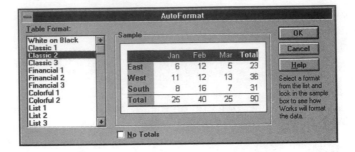

To apply an AutoFormat to a spreadsheet, you use the AutoFormat dialog box (see fig. 12.14). The Table Format box lists all available formats. The Sample area of the dialog box illustrates the format you choose.

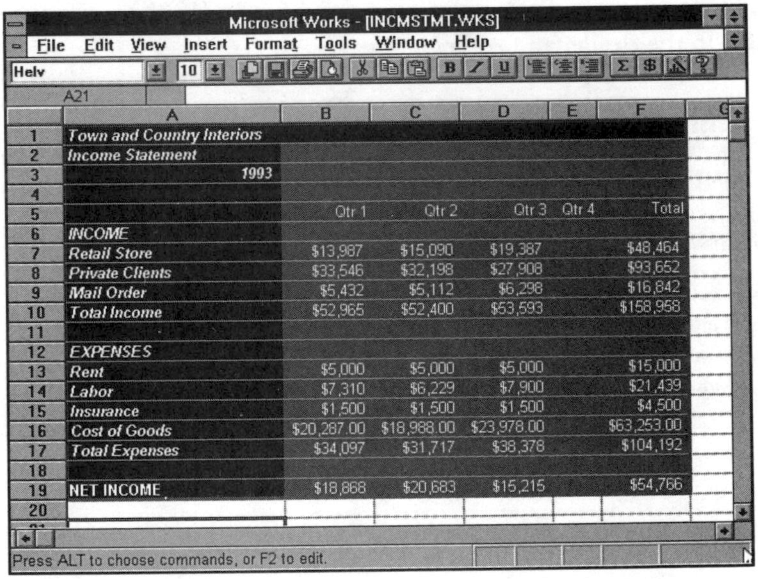

Fig. 12.14
This spreadsheet uses the Colorful1 AutoFormat.

To apply an AutoFormat to a spreadsheet, follow these steps:

1. Select the entire range of cells you want to format.

2. From the Format menu, choose the AutoFormat command. Works displays the AutoFormat dialog box in figure 12.13.

3. In the Table Format box, highlight a format style. The Sample box illustrates the style you choose.

4. To specify that Works not show totals in the formatted table, choose the No Totals check box.

5. When you find a format you want to use, choose OK. Works applies the format to the selected cells in the spreadsheet.

From Here...

This chapter teaches you how to enhance a spreadsheet by using fonts, alignment, row height, borders, and patterns effectively. Refer to the chapters listed below to enhance spreadsheets with charts.

- Chapter 14, "Creating Charts," teaches you how to create charts and graphs using the data in a spreadsheet.

- Chapter 15, "Editing and Enhancing a Chart," discusses methods for changing charts and improving the appearance of charts.

III

Spreadsheets and Charting

Chapter 13

Searching, Viewing, and Sorting a Spreadsheet

After you enter all the numbers, text, and formulas in a spreadsheet, you find there are several ways to work with the data that make your job easier. For instance, when you need to find a specific entry in a spreadsheet—especially a large one—it's easier to have Works search the spreadsheet for you rather than doing it yourself. You can also change your view of a spreadsheet by magnifying or reducing it; hiding gridlines, columns, or rows; freezing row and column headings; splitting the spreadsheet window; or displaying formulas rather than cell values. If you entered information into your spreadsheet in random order, you might find it useful to sort the information alphabetically. These are all features that you can use while working with a spreadsheet.

Searching a Spreadsheet

One of the most useful features in a spreadsheet is its ability to search for and replace characters. You can search a spreadsheet to find specific text or a specific value, or to find cells or cell ranges referenced in a formula. You can search for a partial entry or an entire entry. Once you find the information you're looking for, you can replace it with new information if you wish.

The two commands that enable you to search for and replace text or values are **F**ind and Rep**l**ace, both located on the Edit menu. The **F**ind command enables you to search for text or a value without replacing it. The Rep**l**ace command finds the text or value you specify and replaces all occurrences or selected occurrences with a new entry.

In this chapter, look for the following topics:

- Finding and replacing information in a spreadsheet

- Zooming in on an area of your spreadsheet

- Hiding rows or columns in a spreadsheet

- Hiding gridlines

- Freezing row and column headings

- Displaying formulas rather than cell values

- Sorting spreadsheet data

III

Spreadsheets and Charting

Both the **F**ind and Rep**l**ace commands allow you to specify whether you want Works to search a spreadsheet by rows or by columns. When you choose Rows, Works searches left to right through the spreadsheet one row at a time. If you think the text or value you're looking for is located somewhere near the top of the spreadsheet, choose the **R**ows option to find the information quickly. When you choose **C**olumns, Works searches a spreadsheet from top to bottom one column at a time. If you think the text or value you're looking for is located somewhere within the first few columns of the spreadsheet, choosing the **C**olumns option may help you find the information more quickly.

In both the Find and Replace dialog boxes you also specify whether you want Works to search the values of a spreadsheet or the formulas. When you choose the **V**alues option, Works searches the cells for the text or value you specify. When you choose the **F**ormulas option, Works searches the actual formulas rather than displayed values until it finds the information you are looking for.

Tip
If you use the Find feature frequently, you can add a Find button to the toolbar. Clicking the Find button displays the Find dialog box. Refer to Chapter 2, "Getting Started with Works for Windows," for instructions on customizing the toolbar.

Finding Text

The **F**ind command displays the Find dialog box shown in figure 13.1. Use the **F**ind command to find any text or value in a spreadsheet without replacing it with new information. For instance, suppose you entered the value 10,532 somewhere in your spreadsheet and you want to find the exact location of that entry. Using the Find dialog box, search the values of the spreadsheet to find 10,532. If Works finds the value, it highlights the first cell where the value appears and closes the Find dialog box. If Works doesn't find the value, it displays the message No Match Found.

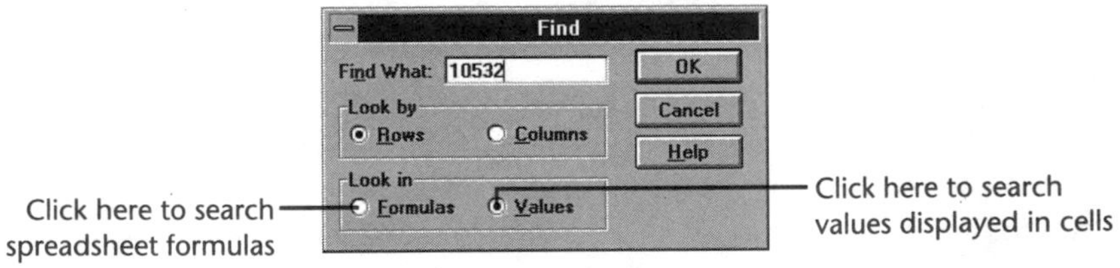

Fig. 13.1
Find any text or value in a spreadsheet's cells or formulas using the Find dialog box.

Click here to search spreadsheet formulas

Click here to search values displayed in cells

If you want to find text or a cell reference in a spreadsheet formula, choose the **F**ormulas option in the **F**ind dialog box. For instance, suppose you entered the formula =Total Income-Total Expenses somewhere in your spreadsheet and you want to check the cells referenced in that formula. You enter the text to search for in the Fi**n**d What text box, then choose the **F**ormulas option in the Find dialog box. If Works finds the formula, it highlights the first cell in which the formula occurs and closes the Find dialog box.

To find text, a value, or a cell reference in a spreadsheet without replacing it, follow these steps:

1. Select the range of cells you want to search (or select no cells to search the entire spreadsheet).

2. From the **E**dit menu, choose the **F**ind command. The Find dialog box shown in figure 13.1 appears.

3. In the Fi**n**d What box, enter the text, value, or cell reference to search for.

4. In the Look By box, choose either **R**ows or **C**olumns.

5. In the Look In box, choose either **V**alues or **F**ormulas.

6. Choose OK. Works finds the first occurrence in the spreadsheet.

Replacing Text

The Rep**l**ace command displays the Replace dialog box shown in figure 13.2. In this dialog box, you specify the text or value you're looking for as well as the replacement text. If Works finds text or a value you specify, it highlights the first occurrence and leaves the Replace dialog box on-screen. You can choose to replace all occurrences of the text you're looking for (using the Replace **A**ll button), you can replace occurrences selectively (using the **Re**place button), or you can skip the occurrence and go on to the next (using the **F**ind Next button).

To replace text or a value in a spreadsheet, follow these steps:

1. Select the range of cells you want to search, or select none to search the entire spreadsheet.

Tip
If you think the spreadsheet contains additional occurrences of the same information you searched for, you can repeat the search by pressing F7. If an additional occurrence is found, Works highlights the cell in the spreadsheet. Pressing F7 repeatedly causes Works to highlight each occurrence found in the spreadsheet.

Fig. 13.2
Use the Replace dialog box to specify the text or value to find as well as the replacement text or value.

III

Spreadsheets and Charting

2. From the **E**dit menu, choose the Rep**l**ace command. The Replace dialog box shown in figure 13.2 appears.

3. In the Fi**n**d What box, enter the text, value, or cell reference to search for.

4. In the Re**p**lace With box, enter the replacement information.

5. In the Look By box, choose either **R**ows or **C**olumns.

6. Choose the **F**ind Next button. Works finds the first occurrence.

7. If you want to replace all occurrences in the spreadsheet, click the Re-place **A**ll button. If you want to replace only the current occurrence, click the **R**eplace button. If you want to find the next occurrence with-out replacing the current one, click the **F**ind Next button.

8. Repeat step 8 until you are finished searching and replacing.

9. Close the Replace dialog box by choosing the Clos**e** button. (The Cancel button changes to Clos**e** when Works is finished replacing.)

Using Wild Cards in a Search

When you're uncertain of the exact text or value to search for in a spread-sheet, you can use a wild card to represent any single character. For instance, if you search for *?00*, Works finds *100*, *300*, and *500*. If you enter **1???3**, Works finds all five-digit values that begin with 1 and end with 3. Wild cards can be very useful for finding text or values when you're not sure of the spell-ing or the exact amount of a number. To use a wild card in either the Find or Replace dialog box, type a question mark for each unknown character you are searching for in the Find What text box.

Troubleshooting

I know I typed the number 10,550 in my spreadsheet, but when I used the Find com-mand to search for it, nothing was found. Why?

There could be several reasons. If you select only a portion of the spreadsheet before you choose the Find command, Works searches only the selection. If the number is located somewhere outside of the selected range of cells, Works will not find it. Or, you might have entered the number incorrectly, in which case Works would not find it. You might try using one or more wild cards to search for the value, such as 1???0.

I used the range name Total Sales in my spreadsheet, but when I searched for this text, Works didn't find it.

If Works didn't find the range name you entered, you probably specified **V**alues rather than **F**ormulas in the Find dialog box. Remember that range names are used in formulas only, so you must search the formulas of your spreadsheet. Be sure you check the **F**ormulas option in the dialog box. If Works still doesn't find the range name, perhaps you misspelled it. Try finding it using a wild card.

Viewing a Spreadsheet in Different Ways

Although the standard view of a spreadsheet on-screen is adequate for many of the editing tasks you perform, for some tasks it's nice to be able to change your view of a spreadsheet. For instance, you might want to reduce your view of a large spreadsheet so you can see more of the cells on-screen at once. Or, you might want to include sensitive information (such as employees' salaries) in the calculations in a spreadsheet but hide that information from other viewers. In the following sections, you learn these and other techniques for altering your view of a spreadsheet.

Using Zoom

One way to change your view of a spreadsheet is to magnify or reduce a particular area. This feature is called Zoom and is particularly helpful with a large spreadsheet if you want to display more cells on-screen at one time. When you choose the **Z**oom command on the **V**iew menu, Works displays the Zoom dialog box shown in figure 13.3. The dialog box contains five preset magnification and reduction levels: **4**00%, **2**00%, **1**00%, **7**5%, and **5**0%. You can also use the **C**ustom text box to specify a custom magnification level. In the custom box, you can enter any number from 25 to 1000.

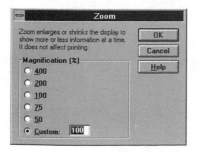

Fig. 13.3
The Zoom dialog box displays magnification levels of 400, 200, 100, 75, and 50.

III

Spreadsheets and Charting

Use the following steps to use the Zoom feature on a spreadsheet.

1. From the **V**iew menu, choose the **Z**oom command. Works displays the **Z**oom dialog box (refer to fig. 13.3).

2. Choose a magnification level, or enter a number from 25 to 1000 in the **C**ustom text box.

3. Choose OK. Works displays the current spreadsheet at the magnification level you choose.

To return to normal magnification, use the steps above, choosing the **1**00% option. An example of a reduced spreadsheet is shown in figure 13.4.

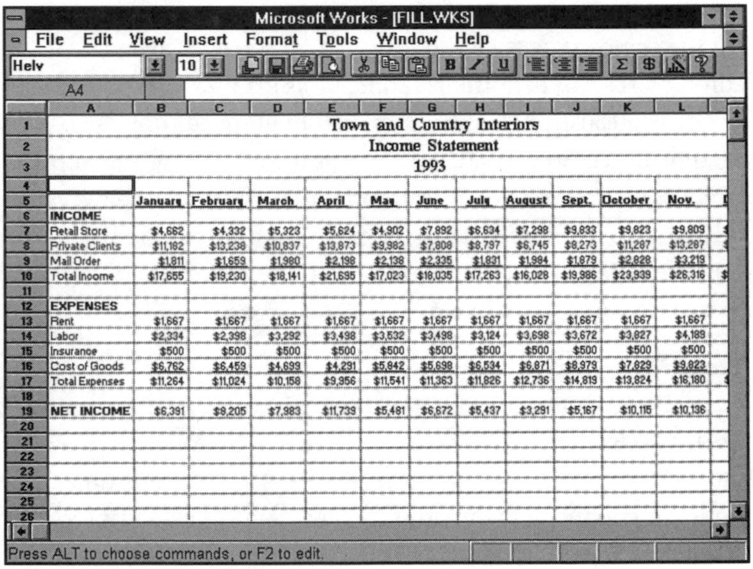

Fig. 13.4
This spreadsheet is displayed at 75%.

Hiding and Redisplaying Columns and Rows

When a spreadsheet contains data that you don't want or need to display on-screen, you can hide entire rows or columns of data. This feature is often used in spreadsheets that contain employee information such as salaries and wages, job classifications, and other personal data that you don't want displayed on-screen. When you hide a row or column in a spreadsheet, the spreadsheet continues to calculate correctly. The row or column is not removed from the spreadsheet, it is simply hidden from view. If you print the spreadsheet, the hidden row or column is not printed.

You hide a row or column by setting the row height or column width to zero. To do so, you can use the Row **H**eight or Column **W**idth commands on the Forma**t** menu, or you can use the mouse to drag the row or column border to zero.

Use the following steps to hide a row or column in a spreadsheet using the menu commands:

1. Highlight a cell anywhere within the row or column you want to hide.

2. From the Forma**t** menu, choose the Row **H**eight or Column **W**idth command. The appropriate dialog box appears.

3. In the **H**eight or **W**idth text box, enter the number zero, then choose OK.

You can also use the mouse to change the width of columns and the height of rows. When you point to a column or row border, the mouse pointer changes to a two-headed arrow named "Adjust." When you see this pointer, click and drag the mouse to adjust the width of a column or the height of a row. You can use this same technique to hide a column or row in a spreadsheet. Drag a column border to the left until the column disappears; drag a row border up until the row disappears.

On the screen, you can tell when a row or column is hidden because the row numbers and column labels do not appear in sequence. For instance, if you hide column D, the column labels across the top of the spreadsheet read A, B, C, E, F, G, and so on. If you hide row 4, row numbers read 1, 2, 3, 5, 6, 7, and so on. An example is shown in figure 13.5. In the figure, the columns showing employees' hourly rate and hours worked are hidden.

The only way to view the data in a hidden row or column is to restore the row height or column width to a size large enough to display the entries. You can select a hidden row or column only by using the **G**o To command on the **E**dit menu; you can't scroll to a hidden row or column by using the arrow keys.

To restore a hidden row or column, follow these steps:

1. From the **E**dit menu choose the **G**o To command. The Go To dialog box appears.

Tip

If you use the Go To command frequently, you can customize your toolbar by adding a Go To button, which displays the Go To dialog box when you click it. For instructions on customizing the toolbar, refer to Chapter 2, "Getting Started with Works for Windows."

III

Spreadsheets and Charting

2. In the **G**o To box, type any cell reference in the hidden row or column. For example, to restore row 9, type any cell reference to the row such as C9. Works highlights the row or column but doesn't display it yet.

3. From the Format menu, choose the Row Height command to restore a hidden row or the Column Width command to restore a hidden column. Works displays the appropriate dialog box.

4. In the **H**eight or **W**idth box, type a number adequate to display the entries in the hidden row or column (you might check the height or width of other rows or columns first), or use the Best Fit option.

5. Choose OK. Works restores the hidden row or column to the spreadsheet.

Columns D and E are hidden

Fig. 13.5
A hidden row or column does not appear in a spreadsheet on-screen or when printed.

	A	B	C	F	G
1	Last Name	First Name	Department	Total	
2	Anderson	Sam	Finance	$370.72	
3	Armond	Allen	Marketing	$276.90	
4	Curtis	Jenny	Accounting	$538.00	
5	Evans	Pam	Sales	$336.26	
6	Green	Michael	Accounting	$553.28	
7	Harrison	Tom	Marketing	$962.34	
8	Lamont	Henry	Sales	$727.74	
9	Larson	Jenny	Finance	$513.24	
10	Lindsay	Linda	Sales	$790.44	
11	Mitchell	Chris	Finance	$640.35	
12	Morris	Thomas	Finance	$773.67	
13	Patterson	Fred	Marketing	$236.10	
14	Phillips	Leonard	Marketing	$643.52	
15	Reed	Katie	Marketing	$538.86	
16	Roberts	Jeff	Purchasing	$390.64	
17	Schmitz	Denise	Accounting	$498.00	

Microsoft Works - [HIDDEN.WKS]
File Edit View Insert Format Tools Window Help
Arial 12 A17 "Schmitz
Press ALT to choose commands, or F2 to edit.

Tip
If you turn gridlines on and off frequently, consider adding the Gridlines button to your toolbar. The Gridlines button is found in the View category in the Customize Works Toolbar dialog box. For information on customizing your toolbar, refer to Chapter 2, "Getting Started with Works for Windows."

Hiding Gridlines

Gridlines are the vertical and horizontal lines on a spreadsheet that define the boundaries of cells. Works automatically displays gridlines whenever you create a new spreadsheet file. If you prefer not to display the gridlines in a spreadsheet, select the Gridlines command on the View menu. This command toggles the Gridlines feature on and off; to display gridlines again, choose the Gridlines command again to turn this feature back on.

Freezing Row and Column Headings

When you work with "average" column widths, row heights, and font sizes, your screen can display approximately 6 to 10 columns and 20 to 30 rows at a time. If your spreadsheet is large (more than 10 columns or 30 rows) and requires a lot of scrolling down or to the right, you will inevitably experience the column and row headings disappearing off the screen due to scrolling. Even if you reduce the view of the spreadsheet, the screen can display only a limited number of columns and rows at one time. So if you scroll far enough down or to the right, the column or row headings eventually scroll out of your view, making it difficult to identify the data in your spreadsheet.

To avoid this problem, Works enables you to *freeze* row headings, column headings, or both by using the Freeze **T**itles command on the Forma**t** menu. When you freeze row headings that appear, for example, in column A, and then scroll the spreadsheet to the right, the row headings in column A remain stationary while column B and the following columns scroll to the right. Likewise, when you freeze column headings that appear, for example, in row 5, and then scroll the spreadsheet down, the column headings in row 5 remain stationary while rows 6 and those following scroll downward. Works inserts a bold line in the spreadsheet beneath the row or to the right of the column that is frozen. In figure 13.6, row and column headings are frozen.

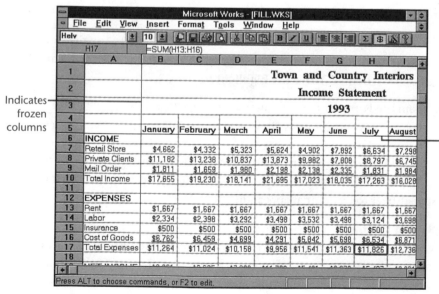

Fig. 13.6

When row and column headings are frozen, you can identify remote rows and columns in a spreadsheet.

Indicates frozen columns

Indicates frozen rows

III

Spreadsheets and Charting

When you choose the Freeze **T**itles command on the Forma**t** menu, Works freezes headings *above and to the left of* the location of the highlighted cell. So, for example, if cell C3 is highlighted, Works freezes columns A and B (above the highlighted cell) and rows 1 and 2 (to the left of the highlighted cell). If Cell C1 is highlighted, Works freezes only columns A and B. If cell A3 is highlighted, Works freezes only rows 1 and 2.

To freeze rows only in a spreadsheet, follow these steps:

1. Move the highlight to the leftmost column and the row *below* the last row you want to freeze. For example, to freeze rows 1 and 2, move the highlight to cell A3.

2. From the Forma**t** menu, choose the Freeze **T**itles command. Works freezes the rows above the row you select.

To freeze columns only in a spreadsheet, follow these steps:

1. Move the highlight to the topmost cell in the column *to the right of* the last column you want to freeze. To freeze columns A and B, for example, move the highlight to cell C1.

2. From the Forma**t** menu, choose the Freeze **T**itles command. Works freezes the columns to the left of the column you select.

Tip
You can add a Freeze Titles button to the toolbar if you use this feature frequently. Refer to Chapter 2, "Getting Started with Works for Windows," for instructions on customizing the toolbar.

To freeze rows *and* columns in a spreadsheet, follow these steps:

1. Move the highlight to the cell below the last row and to the right of the last column you want to freeze. For example, to freeze columns A and B and rows 1 and 2, move the highlight to cell C3.

2. From the Forma**t** menu choose the Freeze **T**itles command. Works freezes rows and columns above and to the left of the cell you select.

The Freeze **T**itles command on the Forma**t** menu toggles on and off. To remove frozen titles, choose the Freeze **T**itles command again. Works restores the spreadsheet to its original appearance.

Displaying Formulas

Most of the time when you work with a spreadsheet, you display actual values in the cells. To check on the content or structure of a particular formula, you select the cell where the formula appears, and then look in the formula bar for the exact formula. Sometimes, however, you might find it useful to display *all* formulas in a spreadsheet at once. This feature is useful when you want to check the accuracy of all formulas in a spreadsheet.

To display all formulas in a spreadsheet at once, choose the **F**ormulas command on the **V**iew menu. When you choose this command, Works displays formulas in all cells that contain formulas rather than displaying their calculated results. All other cells in the worksheet are displayed normally. That is, cells that contain text or values are displayed in the spreadsheet as well. An example of a spreadsheet that displays formulas is shown in figure 13.7.

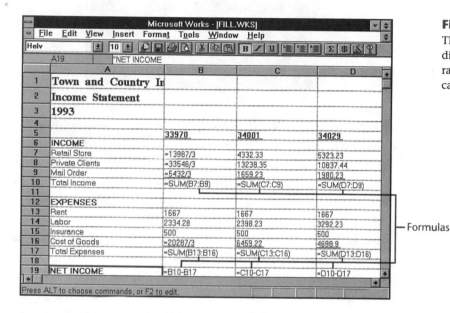

Fig. 13.7
The spreadsheet displays formulas rather than calculated values.

To restore the spreadsheet to its normal appearance, open the **V**iew menu and again choose the **F**ormulas command, which toggles on and off. Works restores the calculated values to the spreadsheet and formulas appear in the formula bar when a formula cell is highlighted.

Sorting a Spreadsheet

When you enter new information into a spreadsheet, you often enter it in random order. A spreadsheet can be easier to work with when you sort the information in different ways. You can rearrange entries in a spreadsheet either alphabetically or numerically in ascending or descending order. Works sorts text as well as numbers, whether they are dates, times, part numbers, dollars, or other types of values. When you sort in ascending order on entries that contain both text and numbers, Works lists text entries first, then numbers. When you sort in descending order, numeric entries appear first and text entries follow.

To sort information in a spreadsheet, you choose the Sort Rows command on the Tools menu, which displays the Sort Rows dialog box shown in figure 13.8.

Fig. 13.8
In the Sort Rows dialog box, sort on one, two, or three columns.

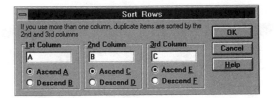

Tip
To create a column of sequential numbers, insert a new column before column A. Type the number 1 in the cell to the left of the first item in the spreadsheet. Select that cell and all cells in the column where you want a number to appear. Now choose the Fill Series command on the Edit menu. In the Fill Series dialog box, choose the Number option, and then select OK.

You can sort information on one, two, or three columns in ascending or descending order. When items in the first column match, Works sorts items based on the second column. When items in the first and second column match, Works sorts items based on the third column. This concept is illustrated in figure 13.9. In the figure, a payroll spreadsheet lists employees by last name, first name, department, hourly rate, hours worked, and total. The spreadsheet is sorted by last name, first name, and department. To sort the list by last name, which appears in column A, you type **A** in the **1**st Column box of the Sort Rows dialog box (refer to figure 13.8). To sort the list by last name, then first name, you type **B** in the **2**nd Column box. In this example, there are two employees named Joe Smith. Since their last and first names match, a third column must be used to determine the order in which these two names are sorted. To sort by department, you type **C** in the **3**rd Column box. This final sort by department ensures that Joe Smith in Accounting appears in the list before Joe Smith in Purchasing.

To sort a spreadsheet, follow these steps:

1. Select the rows you want to include in the sort. For example, don't include rows that contain column headings or blank rows.

2. From the Tools menu choose the Sort Rows command. The Sort Rows dialog box shown in figure 13.8 appears.

3. To sort on one column, enter the column label (A, B, C, or other column) you want to sort on in the **1**st Column box. Select either Ascend or Descend for the first column.

4. To sort on two columns, repeat step 3 for the **2**nd Column box.

5. To sort on three columns, repeat step 3 for the **3**rd Column box.

6. Choose OK. Works automatically sorts the spreadsheet in the order you specify.

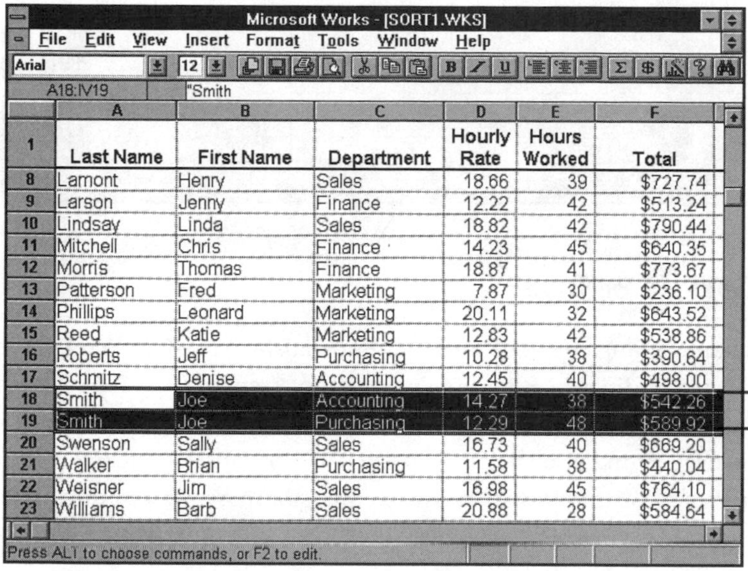

	A	B	C	D	E	F
1	Last Name	First Name	Department	Hourly Rate	Hours Worked	Total
8	Lamont	Henry	Sales	18.66	39	$727.74
9	Larson	Jenny	Finance	12.22	42	$513.24
10	Lindsay	Linda	Sales	18.82	42	$790.44
11	Mitchell	Chris	Finance	14.23	45	$640.35
12	Morris	Thomas	Finance	18.87	41	$773.67
13	Patterson	Fred	Marketing	7.87	30	$236.10
14	Phillips	Leonard	Marketing	20.11	32	$643.52
15	Reed	Katie	Marketing	12.83	42	$538.86
16	Roberts	Jeff	Purchasing	10.28	38	$390.64
17	Schmitz	Denise	Accounting	12.45	40	$498.00
18	Smith	Joe	Accounting	14.27	38	$542.26
19	Smith	Joe	Purchasing	12.29	48	$589.92
20	Swenson	Sally	Sales	16.73	40	$669.20
21	Walker	Brian	Purchasing	11.58	38	$440.04
22	Weisner	Jim	Sales	16.98	45	$764.10
23	Williams	Barb	Sales	20.88	28	$584.64

Sorting by department determines which Joe Smith appears first

Fig. 13.9
Sorting on three columns sorts two Joe Smiths correctly.

Sometimes when spreadsheet data is entered in random order, you want to preserve that spreadsheet before you sort it. You could keep a backup copy of the spreadsheet, or a duplicate copy under a different name. But another way to preserve the original random order of items in a spreadsheet is to add a column that sequentially numbers items in the spreadsheet as they were originally entered. For example, figure 13.10 illustrates the payroll spreadsheet showing data as it was originally entered (in random order). Column A was inserted to number each entry sequentially. If you sort a spreadsheet incorrectly or by mistake, this column of sequential numbers enables you to re-sort the list into its original order if necessary. Just select the rows to sort, then sort on column A in ascending order. Works re-sorts the spreadsheet in its original order.

Fig. 13.10
A column that sequentially numbers entries enables you to re-sort in the original order.

Column of sequential numbers

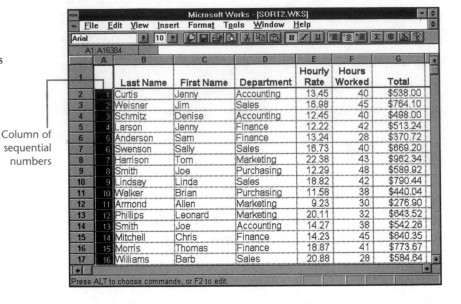

From Here...

This chapter completes your tour of the spreadsheet itself. In this chapter and the three preceding chapters, you learned the essential skills for creating, saving, printing, changing, enhancing, searching, viewing, and sorting a spreadsheet. Works also enables you to chart the data you include in your spreadsheets. Refer to the following chapters for more information about charts.

■ Chapter 14, "Creating Charts," introduces you to the concept of charting spreadsheet data and describes how to create, name, display, and print a chart.

■ Chapter 15, "Editing and Enhancing a Chart," discusses how to make changes to a chart to correct errors or to make a chart more attractive.

Creating Charts

Without a doubt, spreadsheets are excellent tools for compiling, summarizing, calculating, and analyzing data. But all the data in a spreadsheet is of little value if it cannot be readily understood. When data is presented in a graphical form, however, it is often much easier to interpret, even at a glance. Charts provide the means for depicting spreadsheet data in a graphical form. Charts can help you recognize trends, compare data, identify percentages of a whole, and spot relationships between two or more items.

In Works, charts are tied to data in a spreadsheet. You tell Works which data to use to create the chart and then Works creates the chart for you. If you change the data in your spreadsheet, Works automatically updates the data in the chart. You can create up to eight charts for each Works spreadsheet.

Understanding Charts

Before you begin creating charts in Works, it's helpful to have a basic understanding of the chart types available in Works, the standard elements of a chart, and how Works goes about plotting data in a chart. This section includes a discussion of these topics.

Reviewing the Basic Chart Types

Works includes 12 basic chart types: area, bar, line, pie, stacked line, X-Y scatter, radar, combination, 3-D area, 3-D bar, 3-D line, and 3-D pie charts. Each chart type has a unique purpose and characteristics. For each of the 12 chart types, you can choose from a variety of style variations. The 12 chart types are described and illustrated next. Review the illustrations and descriptions to choose the chart type that best illustrates your particular data.

In this chapter, you learn about:

- The basic chart types and their characteristics

- The elements of a typical chart

- How Works plots charts

- Creating a new chart

- Naming, deleting, and duplicating a chart

- Printing a chart

Area charts emphasize the relative contribution of each item in a category of data. Rather than emphasizing the time period itself, an area chart emphasizes the change in data over a period of time. In figure 14.1, the area chart shows how each category of income contributed to total income throughout the year.

Fig. 14.1

Area charts emphasize the relative contribution of items in a category.

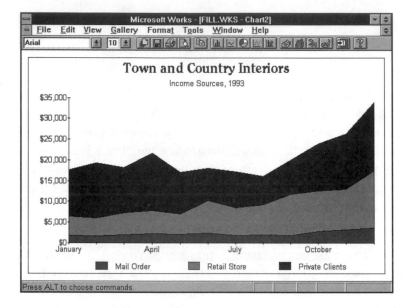

Bar charts enable you to compare distinct items or emphasize the relationship of items to one another over a period of time. Bar charts emphasize comparisons and relationships among items more than the flow of time. Positive values appear above the horizontal axis (the x-axis); negative values appear below. Figure 14.2 illustrates 1993 expenses for Town and Country Interiors. Bar chart variations include stacked bar charts, which depict each data item as a percentage of the entire category (100%).

Line charts are best used for illustrating trends among data items, so the x-axis usually represents time, whether days, months, quarters, or years. Each line in the chart represents a distinct data item; markers on the line pinpoint the exact values charted. In figure 14.3, retail store, private clients, and mail order are the three sources of income (data items) depicted using a line chart.

Pie charts emphasize how individual parts contribute to a whole. Pie slices correspond to individual values in the spreadsheet; the entire pie corresponds to the sum of those values. Unlike area, line, and bar charts, pie charts can depict data at only one specific point in time. Pie chart variations let you explode one or all slices. In figure 14.4, total income for 1993 is depicted using a pie chart. The Retail Store slice is exploded.

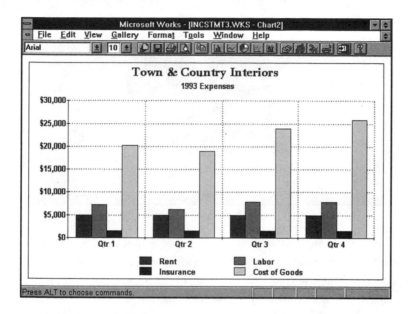

Fig. 14.2
A bar chart compares distinct items over a period of time.

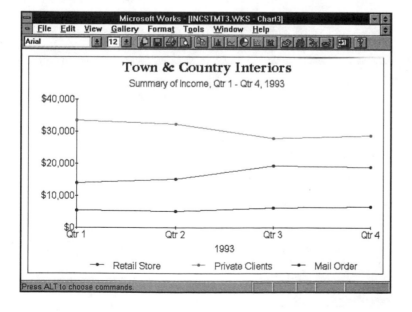

Fig. 14.3
Line charts illustrate trends among data items.

III

Spreadsheets and Charting

Fig. 14.4
The pie chart illustrates how parts contribute to the whole.

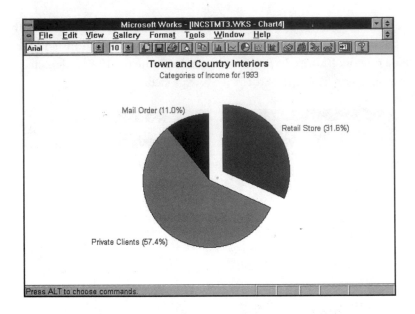

Stacked line charts are similar to line charts except that the lines are stacked to show the total of all items shown. Works adds the values of the first line to the second line, the second line to the third line, and so on. In figure 14.5, three categories of income for the year 1993 are shown in a stacked line chart.

Fig. 14.5
A stacked line chart depicts the total of all items shown.

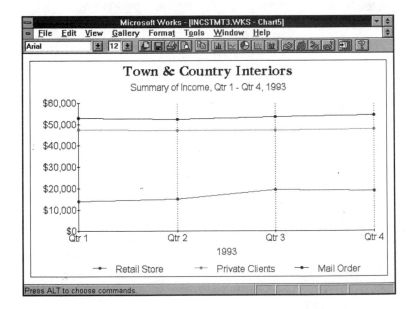

An *X-Y chart* (also called a scatter chart) shows the correlation between two related values (such as productivity and number of hours worked, or temperature and relative humidity). It illustrates how a change in one value affects the other. In figure 14.6, the x-y scatter chart shows how the number of consecutive hours worked affects employees' productivity.

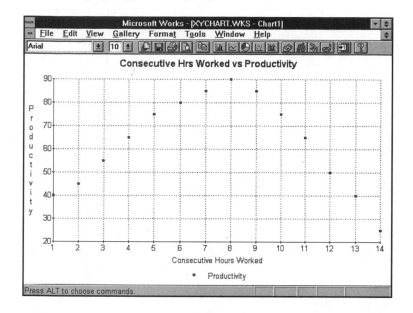

Fig. 14.6
An x-y scatter chart shows the correlation between two related values.

Use a *radar chart* to compare two sets of data relative to a center point. For example, suppose that you want to make a purchasing decision between two cars. You rank the cars on a scale of 1 to 10 based on purchase price, options, horsepower, reliability, and cost of maintenance. The center point of the chart represents the fact that the cars are equally matched for comparison. The radar chart depicting this comparison is shown in figure 14.7.

Combination charts mix bars and lines in the same chart. They are also referred to as mixed charts. The chart in figure 14.8 displays total income as bars and total expenses as a line.

3-D area, bar, line, and pie charts are similar to their 2-D counterparts (shown earlier) except that they add depth to the areas, bars, lines, and pie slices used in the charts. The 3-D variation adds interest and can sometimes help emphasize data better than a 2-D chart. In addition, 3-D area and bar charts enable you to show each data item on its own rather than stacked. For instance,

III

Spreadsheets and Charting

rather than stacking three types of income on top of one another, as shown in the area chart in figure 14.1, a 3-D area chart enables you to depict each type of income as its own 3-D area, as illustrated in figure 14.9.

Fig. 14.7
A radar chart compares two sets of data relative to a center point.

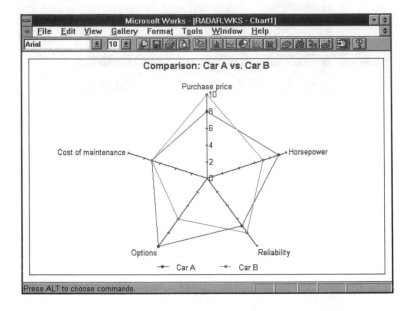

Fig. 14.8
In a combination chart, a line overlays bars.

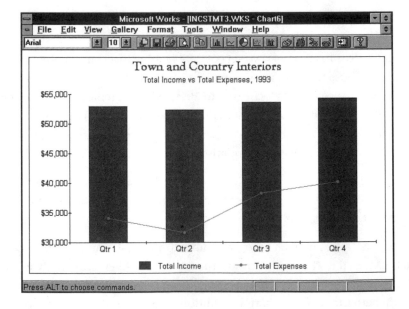

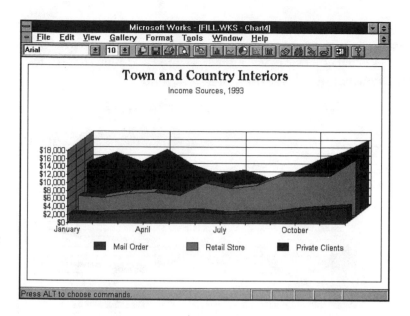

Fig. 14.9
This 3-D variation
shows each data
item separately.

A *3-D bar chart* can also depict distinct data items separately rather than side-by-side or stacked. In figure 14.10, 1993 expenses for Town and Country Interiors are depicted in a 3-D bar chart. The same data is charted using a 2-D bar chart in figure 14.2.

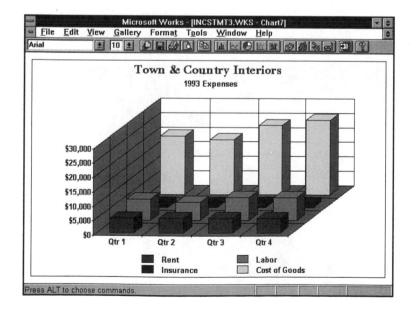

Fig. 14.10
A 3-D bar chart
depicts distinct
data items
separately.

III

Spreadsheets and Charting

3-D line charts are essentially the same as 2-D line charts except that they represent lines of data as ribbons. This style is especially effective for displaying lines of data that cross one another. Figure 14.11 illustrates the test scores of two different students across a nine-week period.

Fig. 14.11
In a 3-D line chart, individual data items are represented by ribbons.

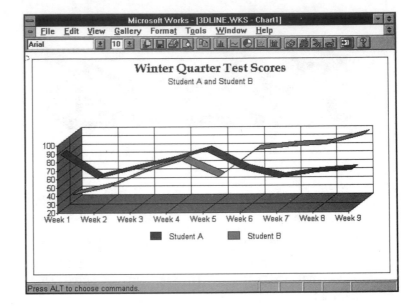

3-D pie charts are essentially the same as 2-D pie charts. Figure 14.12 shows the same data from figure 14.4 charted as a 3-D pie with slices exploded.

Fig. 14.12
A 3-D pie chart illustrates how parts contribute to a whole.

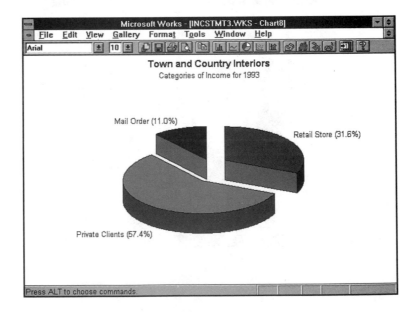

Learning the Elements of a Chart

Before you begin creating charts, it's important to know and recognize the elements that make up a chart. Figure 14.13 shows a bar chart that includes many of the common chart elements. Most of the chart elements are optional features that you can add or remove to suit your particular needs. The charts you create may contain any or all of the elements described in the text that follows.

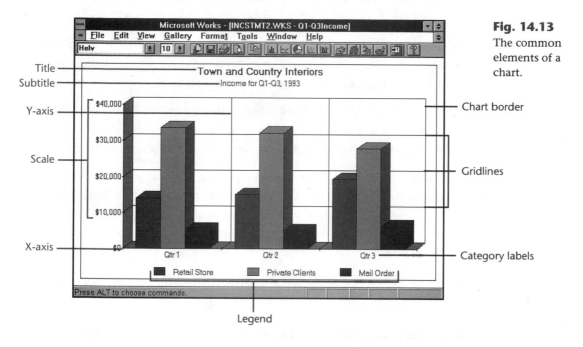

Fig. 14.13
The common elements of a chart.

- *Axes.* Except for pie charts, all charts have two axes. The horizontal axis, or *x-axis*, along the bottom of a chart often represents dates. The vertical axis, or *y-axis*, often represents percentages or a quantity such as dollars. *Tick marks* mark the intervals along an axis. With some chart types, you can choose a style variation that adds a right y-axis. A right y-axis makes it easier to interpret bars or lines located on the far right side of a chart.

- *Scale.* A scale depicts units of measurement (such as dollars) along an axis. Based on the data you select to chart, Works automatically determines the maximum number, the minimum number, and the interval used in the scale.

■ *Chart Titles.* The chart title identifies the content of a chart. You can enter a title by itself or include a subtitle. You can format a chart title individually using any font or point size. When you choose a font or size for a chart subtitle, the font and size are applied to all other text in a chart. In addition to chart titles, you can also add titles to the horizontal and vertical axes of a chart.

■ *Legend.* A legend appears at the bottom of a chart and identifies the bars, lines, pie slices, or other markers that represent data.

■ *Gridlines.* Gridlines can make a chart easier to read, especially when data points are close in value. Horizontal gridlines mark the intervals along the x-axis; vertical gridlines mark the intervals along the y-axis.

■ *Category labels.* Category labels identify the specific categories of data represented in a graph. For example, in figure 14.13, the categories are quarters; the bars within each category are individual data items.

■ *Data labels.* Data labels are used to mark the exact value or percentage represented by a data point. When a chart contains a lot of data, data labels can make the chart look very cluttered, so use them with care. (Data labels identify exact percentages of the pie slices shown in fig. 14.12.)

■ *Border.* To give a chart a more finished appearance, add a border, which surrounds the chart data, title, and legend.

Knowing How Charts Are Plotted

Creating a chart in Works is a relatively straightforward task that involves selecting the range of cells to be charted. Since Works creates a bar chart automatically from the cell range you select, it is helpful to understand how Works interprets the content of the selected cell range. The example shown in figure 14.14 helps to illustrate the process.

Works determines how to create a chart based on the shape of the cell range you select and the data contained within the range. When your selection contains more columns than rows—which is most often the case—Works translates the columns into categories and places them along the x-axis (refer to fig. 14.14). This data from the selected columns is referred to as the *x series*. In figure 14.14, the entire cell range selected is A2 through E5. The x-series categories are Qtr 1, Qtr 2, Qtr 3, and Qtr 4, taken from cells B2 through E2.

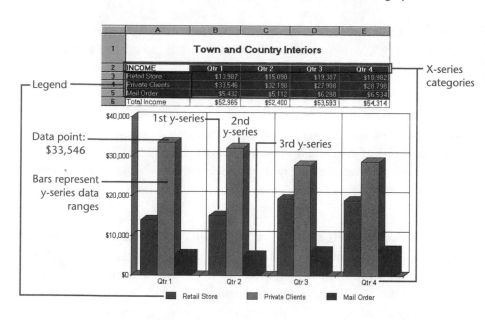

Fig. 14.14
Works translates a
selection of cells
into a chart.

The individual rows of data you select represent distinct *data items* (such as
Retail Store, Mail Order, and Private Clients). Works plots the *data points*, or
values, for each data item along the y axis. A row of cells that represents a
data item is referred to as a *y series*. You can include up to six y-series data
ranges in a chart. The chart in figure 14.14 includes three y-series ranges:
Retail Store, Mail Order, and Private Clients, taken from rows 3, 4, and 5.

If you include both row and column headings in your cell selection, Works
translates row headings into the chart *legend* and column headings into the
x-axis *category labels*. In figure 14.14, the row headings in cells A3:A5 make up
the chart legend. The category labels, as described earlier, are taken from cells
B2:E2. (The "Income" label in cell A2 is ignored.)

Selecting Spreadsheet Data to Chart

As illustrated in figure 14.14, when the cell range you select for your chart
contains more columns than rows, Works translates columns into categories
along the x-axis and translates the values in each row into data points on
the y-axis represented by bars. If the range you select contains more rows
than columns, Works interprets and transfers the data to the chart in exactly
the opposite order: row headings are transferred to the x-axis as categories
and values in columns are used to plot data points on the y-axis as bars.

Regardless of the shape of the range, when the selection contains row and column headings, Works automatically creates a chart legend and adds category labels to the chart.

Recall that pie charts can only show one data item at a time, so be sure to select the correct y-series cell range if you are creating a pie chart. For instance, to use the data shown in figure 14.14 to create a pie chart, you must choose only one of the three income sources (B3:E3, B4:E4, or B5:E5), or choose the total income (B5:E6) as the y-series range. If you select more than one y-series range, Works charts the first range and ignores the remaining ranges.

Because Works interprets data automatically based on the shape of the cell range you select, it is important to remove any unnecessary blank rows or columns from the body of a spreadsheet before you create a chart. Notice in figure 14.14 that the selection does not include any blank rows or columns. Blank rows and columns within the spreadsheet cause blank categories and bars in a chart. For the same reason, do not select entire rows or entire columns when you select a cell range to be charted because they invariably contain blank cells.

Note

If it isn't possible to remove blank rows or columns from a spreadsheet, you can still plot a chart. Refer to the section "Changing X- and Y-Series Cell Ranges" in Chapter 15, "Editing and Enhancing a Chart."

Creating and Viewing a Chart

To create a new chart, first select the range of cells to be charted, and then choose the Create New Chart command on the Tools menu or click the New Chart button on the toolbar. The New Chart dialog box shown in figure 14.15 appears. In the What type of chart do you want? box, Works highlights the Bar option by default, so a sample bar chart showing the data you selected in your spreadsheet appears on the right side of the dialog box. If you included column and row headings in your selection, a legend is displayed under the sample chart.

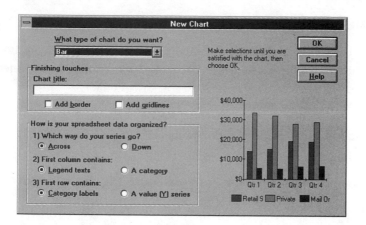

Fig. 14.15
The New Chart
dialog box.

Based on the cell range you select, Works fills in the options in the How is your spreadsheet data organized? section of the dialog box. In this box are three items. The first, Which way do your series go?, **A**cross or **D**own, refers to the y-series data ranges. If your data items appear in rows, Works chooses the Across option. If your data items appear in columns, Works chooses the Down option. The second statement, First column contains, **L**egend texts or A catego**r**y, refers to the purpose of the entries in the first column. If the first column describes data items, Works creates a legend from the entries. If the first column describes categories of data, Works creates category names from the entries. The final statement, First row contains, **C**ategory labels or A value (**Y**) series, refers to the purpose of the entries in the first row. If the first row describes categories of data, Works creates category names from the entries. If the first row describes data items, Works creates a legend from the entries.

If Works misinterprets the cell range you selected (that is, confuses the x-series range with y-series ranges), you can change any of the settings in the How is your spreadsheet data organized? section of the dialog box. Always check the sample chart display to determine whether Works is interpreting the selected data correctly.

The Finishing Touches box enables you to enter a chart title, as well as add a border and gridlines to your chart. If you don't select these options now, you can add a title, border, and gridlines to a chart later, as described in Chapter 15, "Editing and Enhancing a Chart."

To create a new chart, follow these steps:

1. In the spreadsheet, select the range of cells you want to chart. If you want Works to create category labels and a legend, be sure to select row and column headings along with spreadsheet data.

2. From the T**o**ols menu, choose the **C**reate New Chart command; or click the New Chart button on the toolbar. The New Chart dialog box shown in figure 14.15 appears.

3. From the **W**hat type of chart do you want? list, choose a chart type.

4. To add a title to your chart, type the title text in the Chart **T**itle text box.

5. To add a border or gridlines to a chart, choose the Add **B**order or Add **G**ridlines check boxes.

6. To change the way Works interprets and charts the selected data, choose any of the options in the How is your spreadsheet data organized? box.

7. Check the sample chart to make sure that the chart is correct, then click OK. Works displays your chart in a separate window on-screen. Your spreadsheet window, still open, is located under the chart window.

Using the Charting Toolbar

As you learned in Chapter 1, "Introducing Works for Windows," each of the Works tools has a unique toolbar. Once you create a chart using spreadsheet data and the chart window is active, the spreadsheet toolbar changes to the charting toolbar shown in figure 14.16.

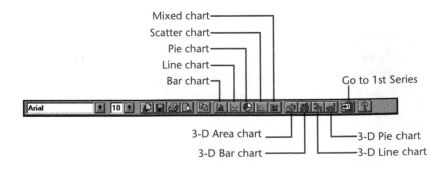

Fig. 14.16
Use buttons on the charting toolbar to speed up your work.

The first seven buttons and the last button on the toolbar are familiar: font, point size, save, print, help, and so on. The remaining 10 buttons let you choose a 2-D or 3-D chart type, or switch you back to the first series in the spreadsheet window. Clicking a chart type button displays a dialog box that displays all the variations for a particular chart type. When you select a variation from the dialog box, Works switches the current chart to the chart type you select.

To switch quickly back to the spreadsheet window and highlight the cells that represent the first series, click the Go to 1st Series button on the toolbar. You learn more about changing chart types in Chapter 15, "Editing and Enhancing a Chart."

Tip
You can also add buttons to the chart toolbar for area, stacked line, and radar charts. To customize the toolbar, refer to Chapter 2, "Getting Started with Works for Windows."

Managing Charts

After you create one or more charts, you need to know how to name and save the charts you want to keep, delete the charts you don't want, and recall a chart when you want to use it again. These topics are described in the following sections. You also learn how to duplicate a chart.

Troubleshooting

Category labels weren't included in my chart when I created it. What did I do wrong?

When you select the range of cells to chart, you must include the cells that contain category labels in order for them to be included in the chart. In a cell range that contains more columns than rows, category labels usually appear in the first row. To add category labels to an existing chart, refer to the section "Changing X and Y Series Cell Ranges" in Chapter 15, "Editing and Enhancing a Chart."

The x and y ranges in my chart were plotted exactly the opposite of what I expected; row headings were translated to x-axis categories and values in columns were used to plot data points. What did I do wrong?

You didn't do anything "wrong"; the range of cells you selected had more rows than columns, so Works placed the row headings on the x-axis. You can reverse the way Works plots the chart without re-creating it by changing the cell ranges that define the x series and y series. Refer to the section "Changing X and Y Series Cell Ranges" in Chapter 15, "Editing and Enhancing a Chart."

III

Spreadsheets and Charting

Saving a Chart

Because charts are tied to spreadsheet data, charts are saved with the spreadsheet to which they belong; they are not saved as separate files. Once you create a chart, it is treated just like new or edited data within the spreadsheet. When you choose the **S**ave or Save **A**s command from the **F**ile menu, Works saves the chart along with any changes to the spreadsheet itself.

Naming a Chart

As you learned earlier in this chapter, you can create up to eight charts per spreadsheet in Works. The first chart you create is assigned the name Chart1. Subsequent charts you create are named Chart2, Chart3, and so on, through Chart8. You can use these chart names that Works assigns, or you can assign more meaningful names to your charts, such as 1993 Income Sources. Works displays chart names in the title bar of a chart window, on the Window menu when a chart is open, and in the Charts dialog box when you select the Chart command on the View menu.

Follow these steps to rename a chart:

1. From either the spreadsheet or chart window, choose the **N**ame Chart command from the T**o**ols menu. The Name Chart dialog box appears. All existing charts for the current spreadsheet are shown in the **C**harts list.

2. In the **C**harts list, highlight the name of the chart you want to rename.

3. In the **N**ame text box, type a new name of no more than 16 characters. The name can include spaces if you like.

4. Click the **R**ename button.

5. Repeat steps 2 through 4 to rename additional charts.

6. When you are finished renaming charts, click OK.

Deleting a Chart

Because you can create only eight charts per spreadsheet, it's important to delete charts that you no longer use or need. To delete a chart, follow these steps:

1. From either the spreadsheet or chart window, choose the De**l**ete Chart command from the T**o**ols menu. The Delete Chart dialog box appears. All existing charts for the current spreadsheet are shown in the **C**harts list.

2. In the **C**harts list, highlight the name of the chart you want to delete.

3. Click the **D**elete button.

4. Repeat steps 2 and 3 to delete additional charts.

5. When you are finished deleting charts, click OK.

Duplicating a Chart

When you are creating a variety of charts using the same or similar data, it's often easier to duplicate an existing chart rather than to create a new chart from scratch. For instance, suppose you want to create a chart that depicts expenses for 1993, but you want a bar chart as well as a line chart. The data series, titles, and legend are the same for both charts, so it's quicker to duplicate the first chart and then change the chart type.

After a chart is duplicated, you can change any of the data, titles, or other features, if necessary. When you duplicate a chart, Works assigns the new chart the next available chart name. So, if you have already created three charts, and then you duplicate one of them, Works automatically names the new chart Chart4.

Use the following steps to duplicate a chart:

1. From either the spreadsheet or chart window, choose the Duplicate Chart command from the **T**ools menu. The Duplicate Chart dialog box appears. All existing charts for the current spreadsheet are shown in the **C**harts list.

2. In the **C**harts list, highlight the name of the chart you want to duplicate.

3. In the **N**ame text box, type a name of no more than 16 characters for the duplicate chart. The name can include spaces if you like.

4. Click the **D**uplicate button.

5. Repeat steps 2 through 4 to duplicate additional charts.

6. When you are finished duplicating charts, click OK.

Recalling a Saved Chart

To recall a saved chart, the spreadsheet to which the chart belongs must be open and displayed in the active window. Then choose the **C**hart command from the **V**iew menu, which displays the Charts dialog box. All saved charts that belong to the current spreadsheet are shown in the **C**harts list. Highlight the chart you want to recall, and then choose OK. Works opens the chart in its own window on top of the spreadsheet window.

Switching Between a Spreadsheet and a Chart

As you are working with your spreadsheet and creating new charts, you may find it helpful to switch back and forth between the chart window and the spreadsheet window. If the two windows are not maximized, you should be able to see at least a portion of each window on-screen and click the window you want. If you are not able to see the window you want on-screen, and therefore cannot click it, you use either the **V**iew menu or the **W**indow menu to choose a new active window.

To switch back to the spreadsheet window from a chart window, choose the **S**preadsheet command from the **V**iew menu. Or, open the **W**indow menu, highlight the spreadsheet's file name in the list at the bottom of the menu, and press Enter. If you want to return to the first y-series in the spreadsheet, you can click the Go to 1st Series button on the toolbar (refer to fig. 14.16).

To switch back to a chart window from a spreadsheet window, open the **W**indow menu, and then highlight the chart name at the bottom of the menu, and press Enter. On the **W**indow menu, all open charts are listed with the spreadsheet name first, followed by the chart name, as in INCMSTMT.WKS - Chart1. To switch to a different chart window (one that is not currently open), choose the **C**hart command from the **V**iew menu, or click the New Chart button on the toolbar. When the New Chart dialog box appears, highlight the chart you want and press Enter. All additional chart windows you open are added to the list at the bottom of the **W**indow menu.

Setting a Preferred Chart Type

If you don't select a chart type in the New Chart dialog box, Works always defaults to creating a bar chart. If you seldom use bar charts, or most often create a different type of chart, you can change the default, or *preferred*, chart type by following these steps:

1. Create a new chart of the type you want to use as a default.

2. When the new chart appears on-screen in its own window, open the **G**allery menu. A check mark appears next to the current chart type on the menu.

3. From the **G**allery menu, choose the Se**t** Preferred Chart command. Works sets the current chart type as the preferred chart type.

The next time you create a new chart, the chart type you specified as the preferred chart is highlighted in the New Chart dialog box. You can redefine the preferred chart type at any time using the preceding steps.

Printing a Chart

Before printing a chart, you should review the current page and print settings shown in the Page Setup dialog box. (Use the Pa**g**e Setup command from the **F**ile menu to display the Page Setup dialog box.) In this dialog box, you specify the page, header, and footer margins; the source, size, and orientation for the paper you are printing on; page numbering and footnote options; and other standard settings for your particular printer. When all page settings are correct, it's a good idea to preview a chart as a final check before printing. In the following sections, you learn how to specify page settings in the Page Setup dialog box.

Setting Margins

Page margins are the white space that surrounds the text on the printed page. To set page margins for a chart, you use the Page Setup dialog box shown in figure 14.17. (Notice that Page Setup is a tabbed dialog box. In the figure, the Margins tab is selected and the default margin settings are displayed.) Unless you change margin settings, the Page Setup dialog box shows the default margins that Works uses: 1 inch for top and bottom margins, and 1.25 inches for left and right margins. The Sample area of the dialog box displays a graphic representation of these settings. For some charts, you might want to change the default margin settings in order to fit a larger chart on a page.

To change margin settings, follow these steps:

1. From the **F**ile menu, choose the Pa**g**e Setup command. The Page Setup dialog box appears.

2. In the dialog box, choose the **M**argins tab. The dialog box shown in figure 14.17 appears.

3. In the appropriate margin boxes, type the settings you want to use in inches. Type a decimal fraction for fractions of an inch (such as **1.25** for 1 1/4 inches). The Sample area of the dialog box reflects the settings you choose.

4. When all margin settings are correct, choose OK.

> ### Note
>
> If you commonly work with centimeters or another unit of measure rather than inches, you can change the Works default units setting. Choose the **O**ptions command from the **T**ools menu to display the Options dialog box. In the Units box, choose a unit of measure, and then choose OK. Notice that the unit of measure you choose applies to *all* tools in Works.

Fig. 14.17
The Page Setup dialog box displays margin settings for the current chart.

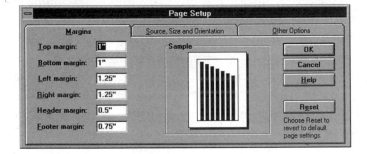

Setting Paper Source, Size, and Orientation

Before printing a chart, you must specify in Works which paper source to use, the size of the paper you're printing on, and the direction you want the print to appear on the page. To change the paper source, paper size, and print orientation, you use the Page Setup dialog box (see fig. 14.18). In the figure, the **S**ource, Size, and Orientation tab is selected, and the default settings are displayed. The page in the Sample area reflects the current paper size and orientation settings.

Depending on the type of printer you are using, you can choose the correct paper source (such as the default paper tray, second paper tray, envelope feeder) from the Paper Source drop-down list.

The Paper **Si**ze drop-down list offers a variety of standard paper and envelope sizes. Choose a size from the list or enter the correct size in the **W**idth and Hei**g**ht boxes.

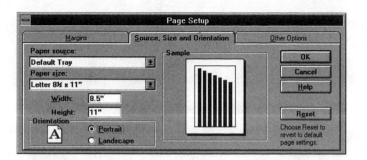

Fig. 14.18
The Page Setup dialog box displays paper source, size, and orientation settings for the current chart.

Paper orientation refers to the direction the paper is facing before it is printed on. Most documents printed on standard 8 1/2-x-11-inch paper are printed in *portrait* orientation, using the 11-inch dimension as the *height* of the paper. For documents that are printed in landscape orientation, the paper is rotated 90 degrees so that the 8 1/2-inch dimension is used as the height of the paper. (The paper is not actually rotated in your printer; your printer simply prints the image "sideways.")

The default orientation is **P**ortrait; to print in landscape mode, choose the **L**andscape option button. For many charts, you will prefer to use landscape orientation. The illustration of the paper in the Sample area of the dialog box is rotated. Notice, also, that for the paper size you specify, the settings in the **W**idth and Hei**g**ht boxes are automatically reversed.

To change source, size, and orientation settings, follow these steps:

1. From the **F**ile menu, choose the Pa**g**e Setup command. The Page Setup dialog box appears.

2. In the dialog box, choose the **S**ource, Size, and Orientation tab. The dialog box shown in figure 14.18 appears.

3. Choose a paper source from the Paper Source drop-down list.

4. Choose a paper size from the Paper Size drop-down list, or specify a custom size in the **W**idth and Hei**g**ht boxes.

5. Choose a paper orientation by clicking either the **P**ortrait or **L**andscape option button.

   The Sample area of the dialog box reflects the settings you choose.

6. When all settings are correct, click OK.

III

Spreadsheets and Charting

Setting Other Page Options

The third tab in the Page Setup dialog box is **O**ther Options (see fig. 14.19). Use the settings on this tab to specify the first page number and how you want a chart to be printed—that is, screen size or full page size.

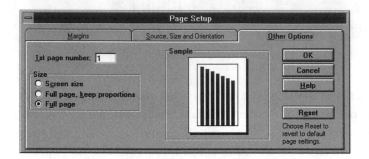

When you choose the **Sc**reen Size option, Works prints a chart as closely as possible to the size that is displayed on-screen. You can also choose to print a chart using the full page, and maintain the correct proportions. Or, you can print a chart using the full page but ignoring the correct proportions. When you choose this last option, Works stretches the chart to fill as much of the page as possible.

Previewing a Chart

One of the most important steps you can take before printing any document is to *preview* it. Previewing enables you to see on-screen how your chart will look on the printed page. When you use the preview screen, Works displays a full-page view of your chart. This gives you a chance to see how the chart fills the page, how the proportions look, and to check the page orientation.

To preview a chart, choose the Print Pre**v**iew command from the **F**ile menu, or click the Preview button on the toolbar. The current chart appears in a preview screen like the one shown in figure 14.20.

The actual text and numbers displayed in the preview screen can be difficult to read because it is reduced, but reading the text isn't the important consideration here; checking the layout is. If you think you spot a problem, however, you can zero in on a particular location. Notice that the mouse pointer changes to a magnifying glass when it is pointing anywhere on the page. Click the left mouse button once anywhere on the page to zoom on the spreadsheet, or click the Zoom **I**n button. If you need to magnify the spreadsheet further, click the left mouse button once more anywhere on the page, or click the Zoom **I**n button again. Use the scroll bars, if necessary, to view a part of the spreadsheet that isn't visible. To zoom back out, click the mouse button a third time anywhere on the page, or click the Zoom **O**ut button.

When you're ready to print a chart, you can print directly from the preview screen by clicking the **P**rint button. This button displays the Print dialog box, described in the next section.

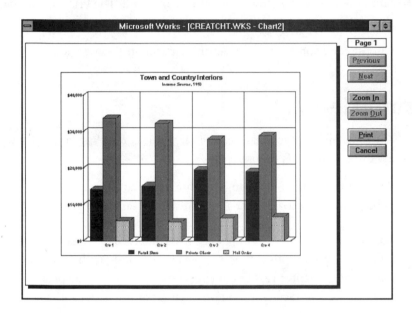

Fig. 14.20
Previewing a chart shows you how it will appear when printed.

Sending the Chart to the Printer

You use the Print dialog box shown in figure 14.21 to specify the number of copies you want to print. The printer that is currently selected is shown at the top of the dialog box. If the printer shown is not correct, select the correct printer using the P**r**inter Setup command from the **F**ile menu.

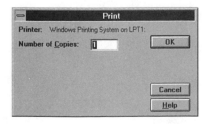

Fig. 14.21
The Print dialog box.

III

Spreadsheets and Charting

Tip
From the Preview
screen, you can
just click Print to
print the chart.

To print a chart, follow these steps:

1. Open the chart you want to print.

2. From the **F**ile menu, choose the Pa**g**e Setup command to specify print margins, paper source, size, orientation, and other print settings.

3. To preview the chart, choose the Print Pre**v**iew command from the **F**ile menu; or click the Preview button on the toolbar.

4. From the **F**ile menu, choose the **P**rint command. The Print dialog box shown in figure 14.21 appears.

5. Choose the appropriate print settings, and then choose OK.

From Here...

The basic steps involved in creating, saving, naming, recalling, and printing a chart are discussed in this chapter.

■ To learn more about changing the data in a chart or improving a chart's appearance, refer to Chapter 15, "Editing and Enhancing a Chart."

■ To review spreadsheet concepts, refer to Chapter 10, "Creating, Saving, and Printing a Spreadsheet," Chapter 11, "Working with Formulas and Functions," Chapter 12, "Enhancing the Appearance of a Spreadsheet," and Chapter 13, "Searching, Viewing, and Sorting a Spreadsheet."

Chapter 15

Editing and Enhancing a Chart

After you have created a basic chart, you may want to change the data the chart represents or switch to a different chart type. You also may want to make a chart more attractive by experimenting with different fonts and colors, adding titles, a legend, borders, gridlines, patterns, and so on. You can make these kinds of changes at any time and as often as you like.

Editing a Chart

After you have created a chart, you sometimes realize you selected the wrong cell range to chart or you want to change some of the data in the spreadsheet. Or perhaps you want to experiment with a different chart type. These changes all are considered editing changes you can do at any time. The following sections describe these tasks in more detail.

Changing the Chart Type

When you first begin working with charts, experimenting with different chart types is a good idea. The more you work with charts, the more familiar you become with the unique features of each chart type. You also want to find the chart type that best conveys the message of the numbers you're charting. Obviously, some chart types are more appropriate than others depending on the data you're charting and the data you want to emphasize.

You learn in Chapter 14, "Creating Charts," that Works automatically creates a bar chart unless you specify a different chart type in the New Chart dialog box. You also learn that every chart type offers several chart variations from which to choose. After you create a standard bar chart, you may decide to use a variation of the bar chart or a different type of chart altogether.

Look for a discussion of these topics in this chapter:

- Choosing a different chart type

- Adding titles, subtitles, and axis titles

- Adding borders and gridlines

- Choosing a font, size, color, and style for text

- Creating a chart legend

- Specifying various x- and y-axis settings

III

Spreadsheets and Charting

To see a sample of the chart variations, you select a chart type from the **G**allery menu or click one of the chart buttons on the charting toolbar. (Note that the **G**allery menu appears on the menu bar only when the active window contains a chart.) The Bar dialog box shows examples of the bar chart variations (see fig. 15.1).

Fig. 15.1
Works offers
six bar chart
variations in the
Bar dialog box.

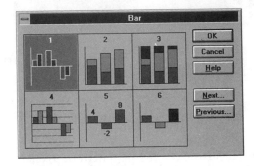

Each of the six bar chart variations is slightly different. For example, the first variation is the standard bar chart that Works creates automatically. The second variation stacks the bars on top of one another, illustrating the combined total of data items. The third variation also stacks the bars but shows each value as a percentage of the whole. The fourth variation is identical to the first except with horizontal gridlines. The fifth variation adds data labels to each bar. And finally, the sixth bar chart variation displays a single y-series (rather than multiple y-series), varying the color of each bar.

Each type of chart offers variations similar to those just described for the bar chart. Most charts offer variations that add data labels and gridlines. Some variations are unique, appropriate to the particular chart type. For instance, pie chart variations include exploded slices, and 3-D area and bar charts enable you to show each data series as an independent area.

To change the chart type of an existing chart, you display the chart in the active window then select a new variation or chart type from the chart type dialog box. In most cases, the new chart type does not affect the x- and y-series cell ranges you originally selected. The exception to this rule is when you change from a chart that depicts multiple y-series ranges (such as a bar chart) to a chart that depicts only one y-series range (such as a pie). In this case, Works charts only the first y-series you selected. To adjust x- or y-series cell ranges, refer to the "Changing X and Y Series Cell Ranges" section in this chapter.

To select a new chart type or a variation of the same chart, follow these steps:

1. In the active window, display the chart you want to change.

2. From the **G**allery menu, select the type of chart you want to switch to; or click the appropriate toolbar button. Works displays a dialog box showing the available chart variations.

3. Click the variation you want to use then choose OK. Works redisplays your chart using the new variation or chart type you selected.

Changing the Spreadsheet Data

After you create a chart, you can make changes to the data in the spreadsheet at any time. The changes you make in individual cells are automatically reflected in the chart. For instance, if you change one value from $2,345 to $2,298, Works automatically adjusts the markers in the chart to reflect the changed entry. Or if you change a row heading from *Mail Order* to *Catalog*, Works changes the reference in the chart legend. If, however, you change the *type* of entry in a cell, for example, from a value to a row heading, you must adjust the x- and y-series ranges the chart uses because Works no longer charts the ranges the same way.

Recall from Chapter 14, "Creating Charts," that Works determines x- and y-series ranges based on the shape of the cell range you select. If the range includes more columns than rows, columns become x-series ranges (categories) and rows become y-series ranges (data items). If you insert a new row or column in a spreadsheet that would add a category to a chart, Works automatically includes the new cells in the x-series range and adds the new category to all the spreadsheet's existing charts. Likewise, if you delete a row or column that represents a category in a chart, Works automatically deletes the category from the chart.

The rule is not the same, however, for data items. If you insert a new row or column that would add a data item to a chart, Works *does not* automatically add the new data as a y-series; you must add the new y-series range and adjust the existing y-series ranges, if necessary. The reason Works does not automatically add new y-series ranges is so you can control the order in which y-series ranges appear in a chart.

Changing X- and Y-Series Cell Ranges

As discussed in the previous section, because Works automatically determines x- and y-series ranges from the shape of the cells you select, you sometimes

Tip

You can add buttons to the charting toolbar for area, stacked line, and radar charts. To customize the toolbar, refer to Chapter 2, "Getting Started with Works for Windows."

may need to adjust the x-, y-, or both series ranges. In addition to the case mentioned earlier where you add data to a spreadsheet, perhaps in another case you originally selected the wrong cell range. This situation also requires you to alter series ranges.

Before you change a range reference, check your spreadsheet and make note of the new ranges you want to define. Then define a new range by choosing **E**dit, **S**eries, which displays the Series dialog box shown in figure 15.2.

Fig. 15.2

The Series dialog box displays existing x- and y-cell ranges.

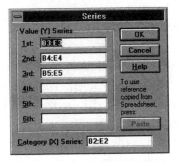

Use the following steps to add or change existing series ranges:

1. In the active window, display the chart for which you want to change series ranges.

2. From the **E**dit menu, choose the **S**eries command to display the Series dialog box shown in figure 15.2. The Value (Y) Series box lists y-series cell ranges from 1st to 6th. The **C**ategory (X) Series box lists the x-series cell range.

3. To add a range or adjust existing y-series ranges, enter the correct cell range in the **1**st, **2**nd, **3**rd, **4**th, **5**th, or **6**th boxes.

4. To adjust the x-series range, enter the correct cell reference in the **C**ategory (X) Series box.

5. When you have entered the new ranges correctly, choose OK. Works redisplays your chart reflecting the new series ranges you specify.

Troubleshooting

When I switched my chart type from a bar chart to a line chart, the data labels, colors, and patterns I added to my bar chart disappeared. Why?

When switching from one chart type to another, try to make the switch before enhancing the chart. When you switch to a new chart type, Works erases all previous enhancements such as colors, patterns, gridlines, data labels, and so on.

When I switched my bar chart to a pie chart, Works charted the wrong data series in the pie chart. Why does this happen, and how can I solve this problem?

When you switch from a chart that displays multiple y-series ranges (such as a bar) to a chart that displays only one y-series range (such as a pie), Works charts the first y-series in the new chart and ignores the remaining y-series ranges. If the new chart doesn't show the correct data, the correct data is not defined as the first y-series range. In the Series dialog box, enter the correct range reference in the **1**st box then choose OK.

Enhancing a Chart

Chapter 14, "Creating Charts," introduces you to the wide variety of chart types Works offers. Figures 14.1 through 14.12 show many of the enhancements you can add to a chart, such as titles, borders, gridlines, colors, patterns, and so on. Enhancements constitute anything you can add or remove from a chart to improve its appearance or make a chart more readable. The following sections describe in detail how to add and remove enhancements.

Adding a Title, Subtitle, and Axis Titles

When you create a new chart using the New Chart dialog box, you can specify a chart title at that time. If you don't specify a title when you create a new chart, you can add a title to an existing chart by choosing **E**dit, **T**itles, which displays the Titles dialog box shown in figure 15.3. You also use this dialog box to specify a chart subtitle and horizontal and vertical axis titles.

Fig. 15.3

Use the Titles dialog box to add a title, subtitle, and axis titles to a chart.

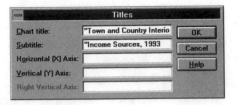

Works centers a chart title at the top of a chart. If you add a subtitle, Works centers it just beneath the chart title. When you add a title such as *Dollars* to the vertical axis, the title appears alongside the scale. A title for the horizontal axis appears just below the axis and above the legend, if the chart includes one. Some chart types enable you to add a right vertical axis to a chart. When you use a chart of this type, you can add a title to the right vertical axis as well.

To add titles to a chart, use the following steps:

1. In the active window, display the chart to which you want to add titles.

2. From the **E**dit menu, choose the **T**itles command. The Titles dialog box shown in figure 15.3 opens.

3. Enter text for the titles in the appropriate text boxes.

4. Choose OK. Works returns to your chart and inserts the titles you specify.

To remove a title from a chart, open the Titles dialog box and clear the text box that contains the title you want to remove. When you return to the chart, the title is gone.

Adding a Border, Gridlines, Droplines, and 3-D Effect

The New Chart dialog box you first saw in Chapter 14, "Creating Charts," enables you to add a border to a chart when you create it. If you choose not to add a border at the time you create a new chart, you can add a border later to an existing chart. First, display the chart in the active window then choose the Add **B**order command from the Format menu. Works shrinks the chart slightly and adds a border that surrounds all chart elements. A check mark appears next to the Add **B**order command on the Format menu. To remove a chart's border, choose the Add **B**order command from the Format menu again to remove the check mark.

Gridlines help your eye follow the scale across a chart or the category markings on the x-axis of a chart. Gridlines also help you pinpoint exact values depicted in a chart. If you add gridlines to a new chart using the New Chart dialog box, Works automatically adds both horizontal and vertical gridlines. However, if you wait until after you create a chart to add gridlines, you have the freedom to add horizontal or vertical gridlines separately.

To add gridlines to an existing chart, use the following steps:

1. In the active window, display the chart to which you want to add gridlines.

2. To add horizontal gridlines, choose the **H**orizontal (X) Axis command from the Forma**t** menu.

3. Select the Show **G**ridlines check box, then choose OK.

4. To add vertical gridlines, repeat steps 2 and 3, choosing the **V**ertical (Y) Axis command rather than the **H**orizontal (X) Axis command.

When you create a 2-D area or 3-D area chart, consider adding droplines to the chart. *Droplines* are vertical lines that extend from data markers to the x-axis to help emphasize the data points along the x-axis for each of the data items in the chart. In figure 15.4, droplines make the data points for each of the income sources much easier to distinguish from month to month.

Tip
If you use chart borders frequently, you can add a Borders tool to the charting toolbar. Refer to Chapter 2, "Getting Started with Works for Windows," for instructions on customizing the toolbar.

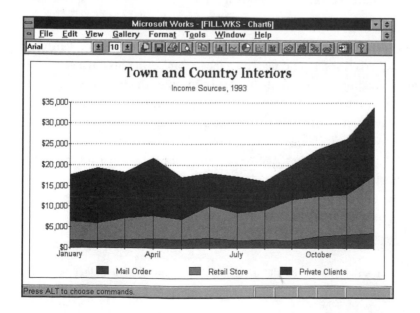

Fig. 15.4
In area charts, droplines extend from data markers to the x-axis.

III

Spreadsheets and Charting

To add droplines to an area or 3-D area chart, display the chart in the active window then choose the **H**orizontal (X) Axis command from the Forma**t** menu. In the dialog box, select the Show **D**roplines check box then choose OK. To remove droplines from a chart, remove the check mark from the Show **D**roplines check box in the Horizontal Axis dialog box.

Tip
You can rotate a 3-D chart 5 degrees at a time by pressing Ctrl and any arrow key. Press Ctrl+Home to return the chart to its original position.

The Forma**t** menu includes a handy command, Make **3**-D, that enables you to change a 2-D chart into a 3-D chart instantly. When you choose this command, Works switches the area, bar, line, or pie chart displayed in the current window to a 3-D version of the same chart and retains the current chart variation. The Make **3**-D command saves you the trouble of choosing the correct variation of a 3-D chart from a dialog box. To switch back to a 2-D version of the same chart variation, select the Make **3**-D command again from the Forma**t** menu to remove the check mark.

Choosing a Character Font, Size, Color, and Style

In the word processor and spreadsheet sections of this book, you learned how to use the Font and Style dialog box to change the font, size, color, and style of text. Recall that *font* refers to the unique design of characters, *size* refers to the point size of characters, *color* refers to the color of text displayed on-screen, and *style* refers to special features such as bold, underline, italic, and strikethrough. These characteristics collectively are called *text format*. To change the text format for a chart, you use the same Font and Style dialog box you have worked with before in the word processor and spreadsheet tools.

In a chart, you can change the text format of the title independently of the subtitle, axis titles, legend text, data labels, and other text in a chart. However, changing the format of any text other than the title affects *all* other text. The Font and Style dialog box for a chart title is shown in figure 15.5. Notice the name in the dialog box specifically states Font and Style for Title. When you change the text format for other text in a chart, the title in the dialog box reads Font and Style for Subtitle and Labels but the options in the dialog box are identical. The Sample area of the dialog box displays sample text using the settings you choose. Remember to look at this box to preview your choices before closing the dialog box.

To change the text format of a chart's title, use the following steps:

1. Click on the chart title, press Ctrl+T, or choose the Select Title Te**xt** command from the **E**dit menu. Works highlights the title.

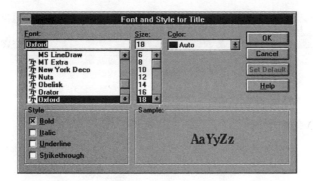

Fig. 15.5
Use the Font and
Style dialog box to
change font, size,
color, and style of
text in a chart.

2. From the Forma**t** menu, choose the **F**ont and Style command. The Font
   and Style for Title dialog box opens.

3. In the **F**ont box, select a font for the title.

4. In the **S**ize box, select a point size for the title.

5. In the C**o**lor box, select a screen-display color for the title text.

6. In the Style box, choose the **B**old, **I**talic, **U**nderline, or **St**rikethrough
   options to add these features to the title.

7. When all settings are correct, choose OK. Works reformats the title
   using the settings you specify.

To change the format of all text other than the chart title, click anywhere
in the chart to make sure the title text is not selected then follow steps 2
through 7. Works displays the Font and Style dialog box for Subtitle and
Labels, which includes identical settings to the Font and Style dialog box
for Title.

Choosing Colors, Patterns, and Markers

When you create a new chart, Works automatically assigns colors to the bars,
lines, areas, and pie slices that depict spreadsheet data. *Color* refers to the
color used to create the lines, bars, areas, and slices. For the y-series data
ranges 1 through 6, Works uses red, green, blue, yellow, cyan, and magenta
as the default colors. *Patterns* are designs that appear inside bars, areas, and
slices of a pie, or the line style used in a line chart. By default, Works does not
use patterns in the charts it creates, but you can assign patterns to selected
y-series ranges in a chart if you want. Figure 15.6 shows an example of
pattern style used in a pie chart.

III

Spreadsheets and Charting

Fig. 15.6
Various pattern styles appear in the slices of this pie chart.

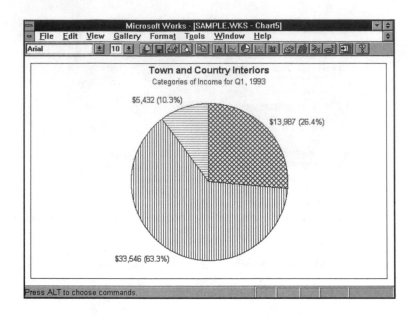

When you create a line chart or an x-y scatter chart, Works uses data markers for each data item. *Data markers* pinpoint the locations in the chart that represent actual values from the spreadsheet. The default data marker is a filled circle, but you can change the style of the data markers for each y-series range, just as you can change colors and patterns used in the bars, lines, areas, and pie slices. Data marker styles include a filled circle, filled box, filled diamond, asterisk, hollow circle, hollow box, hollow diamond, dot, or dash.

Tip
If you change patterns and colors in a chart frequently, you can add a Patterns and Colors button to the charting toolbar. Refer to Chapter 2, "Getting Started with Works for Windows," for instructions on customizing the toolbar.

To change the color, pattern, or data markers used in a chart, you choose Forma**t**, **P**atterns and Colors, which displays the Patterns and Colors dialog box shown in figure 15.7. In the Series area, you choose the y-series for which you want to make changes then scroll through the lists in each of the C**o**lors, **P**atterns, and **M**arkers boxes to make specific choices. (Note that the **M**arkers box is available only for line and x-y scatter charts.) The patterns available in the **P**atterns box vary depending on the type of chart you are using.

The **F**ormat command button changes the color, pattern, and marker for the y-series currently selected. The Format **A**ll button changes *all* y-series ranges to the current color, pattern, and marker choices.

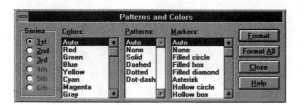

Fig. 15.7
Use this dialog box
to customize the
colors, patterns,
and markers in
your charts.

To change colors, patterns, or markers in an existing chart, use the following steps:

1. In the active window, display the chart you want to change.

2. From the Forma**t** menu, choose the **P**atterns and Colors command to display the dialog box shown in figure 15.7.

3. In the Series box, select one y-series range.

4. In the C**o**lors, **P**atterns, and **M**arkers list boxes, highlight the option you want to use.

5. To assign the current choices to the selected y-series range, click the **F**ormat button. Or to assign the current choices to all y-series ranges, choose the Format **A**ll button.

6. Repeat steps 3, 4, and 5 to select a color, pattern, or marker for other y-series ranges.

7. When all settings are correct, choose the **C**lose button. Works returns to your chart and assigns the colors, patterns, and markers you specify.

Adding a Chart Legend

When you create a new chart using the New Chart dialog box, Works automatically creates a chart legend for you if your cell selection includes row and column headings. If you don't include row and column headings in your original cell selection, you can add a legend to an existing chart later.

To add a legend, choose **E**dit, **L**egend/Series Labels, which displays the dialog box shown in figure 15.8. Use this box to specify which cells contain the data for the legend. In the Series Labels section, you enter the cell address for the label of each y-series data range. For instance, suppose that your first y-series range in cells A3:E3 is mail order income and cell A3 contains the entry *Mail Order*. To use this entry in the chart legend, you enter **A3** in the **1**st Value Series box.

Tip
You can display the Legend/Series Labels dialog box instantly if you add the Legend/ Series Labels button to the charting toolbar. For instructions on customizing the toolbar, refer to Chapter 2, "Getting Started with Works for Windows."

Fig. 15.8

Use the Legend/
Series Labels
dialog box to add
a legend to an
existing chart.

Follow these steps to add a legend to an existing chart:

1. In the spreadsheet, note the cell range that contains the descriptions for each y-series range.

2. Display the chart for which you want to add a legend.

3. From the **E**dit menu, choose the **L**egend/Series Labels command. The Legend/Series Labels dialog box shown in figure 15.8 opens.

4. In the **1**st Value Series box, enter the cell reference for the description of the first y-series data range.

5. Repeat step 4 for all y-series ranges, entering references in the **2**nd and **3**rd Value Series box, and so on.

6. Choose the Use as **L**egend option button, then choose OK. Works adds a legend to your chart.

> **Note**
>
> If you select the **A**uto Series Labels check box in the Legend/Series Labels dialog box, Works creates a legend using *Series 1*, *Series 2*, *Series 3*, and so on as the legend text for the y-series ranges in your chart. Use this option only when you did not include y-series cells in the original selection for your chart.

After you add a legend to a chart, you can turn the legend on and off easily without deleting the cell references in the Legend/Series Label dialog box. When the legend appears in a chart, the Add **L**egend command at the bottom of the Forma**t** menu has a check mark next to it. To remove the legend from the current chart, choose this command to remove the check mark. Works automatically removes the legend for your chart but doesn't delete the cell references. To bring the legend back, choose the Add **L**egend command again on the Forma**t** menu.

Adding Data Labels

If showing precise values is important, you may want to enhance your chart with *data labels*. Data labels show the exact values used to plot a y-series range in a chart. Works inserts the labels at the top of each bar in a bar chart, next to the points plotted in a line or area chart, or to the side of each slice in a pie chart.

An example is shown in figure 15.9. In the figure, you clearly can see that expenses for Q1, Q2, Q3, and Q4, respectively, are *$34,097*, *$31,717*, *$38,378*, and *$40,203*, but the exact values may be difficult to determine without the use of data labels.

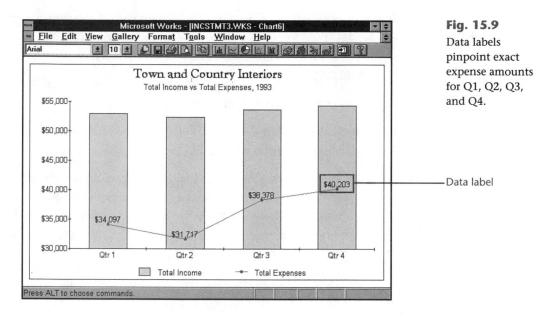

Fig. 15.9
Data labels pinpoint exact expense amounts for Q1, Q2, Q3, and Q4.

You can add data labels for all y-series ranges in a chart or just to selected y-series ranges. Notice in figure 15.9 that data labels were added to the expense data points but not the income bars. Use data labels sparingly as they can make a dense chart look cluttered. Data labels are not available for 3-D charts.

To add data labels to a chart, you choose **E**dit, **D**ata Labels, which displays the dialog box shown in figure 15.10. In each of the Value (Y) Series boxes, you enter the cell range from the spreadsheet containing the values. If you are adding data labels for only one y-series range, you can select and copy (using the **C**opy command on the **E**dit menu) the correct cell range in the spreadsheet, then choose the **P**aste button in the Data Labels dialog box. When you choose the **P**aste button, Works automatically inserts the cell reference you copied from the spreadsheet.

III

Spreadsheets and Charting

Fig. 15.10
Use the Data
Labels dialog box
to add data labels
to a chart.

To add data labels to selected y-series ranges in a chart, use the following steps:

Tip
To add data labels
to all y-series
ranges, select Use
Series Data in the
Data Labels dialog
box. Works reads
the correct cell
ranges from the
select cells and
inserts the correct
data labels.

1. In the spreadsheet, note the cells that contain the values you want to use as data labels for y-series ranges. If you are adding data labels to a single y-series range, you can select the cell range then choose the **C**opy command on the **E**dit menu.

2. Display the chart for which you want to add data labels.

3. From the **E**dit menu, choose the **D**ata Labels command. The Data Labels dialog box shown in figure 15.10 opens.

4. Click the Value (Y) Series box (**1**st, **2**nd, **3**rd, and so on) for which you want to add data labels. If you copied a cell range from the spreadsheet in step 1, choose the **P**aste button to automatically insert the correct range. Otherwise, type the correct cell range in the Value (Y) Series box, or select the **U**se Series Data check box.

5. Type the correct cell range in all other Value (Y) Series boxes for which you want to add data labels.

6. When you have entered all ranges correctly, choose the OK button. Works returns to your chart and adds data labels.

Troubleshooting

I changed the colors, patterns, and markers used in my chart, and now I want to change them back to the default settings Works uses. I can't undo the changes I made, because the charting Edit menu doesn't have an Undo command.

Display your chart again then recall the Patterns and Colors dialog box by choosing Forma**t**, **P**atterns and Colors. In the **C**olors, **P**atterns, and **M**arkers boxes, select the Auto setting then choose the Format **A**ll button. Works restores the default colors, patterns, and markers to your chart.

When I checked the Auto Series Labels in the Legend/Series Labels dialog box, Works used Series 1, Series 2, Series 3, and so on, as data labels in my chart. Why didn't it use the actual labels from the spreadsheet?

To use the actual labels, you must include the cells that contain the labels in your original range of cells to chart. If labels aren't included in that range, Works doesn't know what they are and uses Series 1, Series 2, and Series 3 instead. You can change these to the actual labels by entering the correct cell addresses in the Value Series areas of the Legend/Series Labels dialog box.

Specifying Various X- and Y-Axis Settings

Earlier in this chapter you learned how to add gridlines to a chart's axes. Works lets you control other aspects of a chart's axes as well. These options are described in the following sections.

Specifying Horizontal X-Axis Settings

Works also enables you to control the label frequency used on the x-axis or remove the x-axis entirely from a chart. *Label frequency* refers to the intervals along the x-axis where labels appear. In figure 15.11, some of the month labels are so long that they overlap and cause the x-axis to look cluttered. This chart uses a label frequency of 1; that is, Works labels each month.

To improve the appearance of this chart and still print category labels, you should change the label frequency so a label prints for every other month or every third month. A small number creates more frequent labels; a large number creates less frequent labels. For example, a label frequency of 2 prints a label every other month; a label frequency of 6 prints a label every sixth month. In figure 15.12, the label frequency is 3, so January, April, July, and October labels are well-spaced. Each label is quite readable, and the x-axis displays tick marks for the intermediate months.

To control horizontal axis settings, you use the Horizontal Axis dialog box shown in figure 15.13. This dialog box is the same box you use to add gridlines and droplines to a chart. Notice the third setting in this dialog box enables you to remove the x-axis entirely from a chart.

Fig. 15.11
Category labels
that overlap clutter
the x-axis.

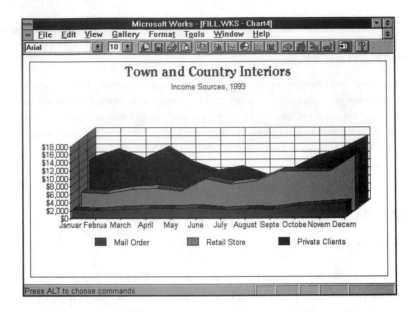

Fig. 15.12
A label frequency
of 3 prints labels
every third month.

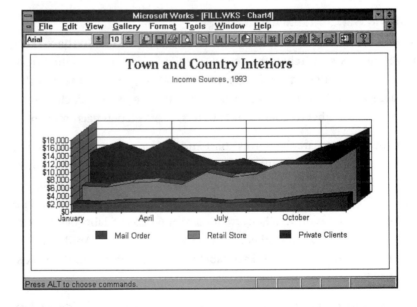

To specify horizontal axis settings, use these steps:

1. In the active window, display the chart you want to change.

2. From the Format menu, choose the **H**orizontal (X) Axis command,
   which displays the Horizontal Axis dialog box shown in figure 15.13.

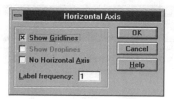

Fig. 15.13
Use the Horizontal
Axis dialog box to
specify x-axis
settings.

3. To remove the horizontal axis for the displayed chart, select the No
   Horizontal **A**xis check box.

4. To change the label frequency of the x-axis, enter a number in the
   Label Frequency text box.

5. Choose OK.

Specifying Vertical Y-Axis Settings

Just as you can specify horizontal axis settings, you can specify vertical axis
settings. From the Forma**t** menu, choose **V**ertical (Y) Axis, which displays the
dialog box shown in figure 15.14. On the left side of the dialog box, you
specify the markings and measurements to use on the y-axis scale (**M**inimum,
Ma**x**imum, and **I**nterval).

Figures 15.15 and 15.16 illustrate how you can change the y-axis scale. In
figure 15.15, Works uses Auto as the setting in the **M**inimum, Ma**x**imum, and
Interval boxes. Auto means that Works determines the best scale to use based
on the data you selected to chart. For this chart, Works uses 0 as the minimum, 100 as the maximum, and 10 as the interval.

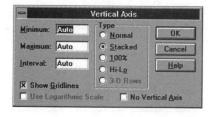

Fig. 15.14
Use the Vertical
Axis dialog box to
specify y-axis
settings.

If you examine the spreadsheet for this chart, you find that Student A's test
scores range from 59 to 91, and Student B's test scores range from 28 to 95.
If you wanted the chart to show scores more precisely, you could change the
minimum to 25, the maximum to 95, and the interval to 5. An example of
this scale is shown in figure 15.16.

III

Spreadsheets and Charting

Fig. 15.15
Works determines
the y-axis scale
when you use the
Auto setting.

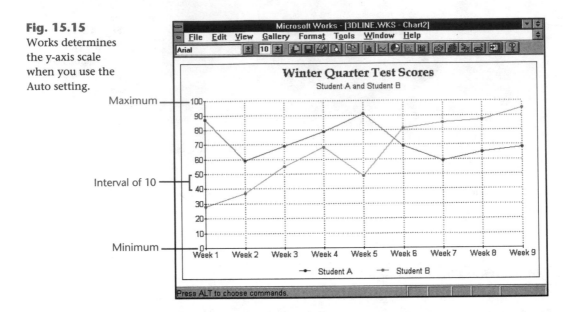

Fig. 15.16
Customized
maximum,
minimum, and
interval settings
on the y-axis.

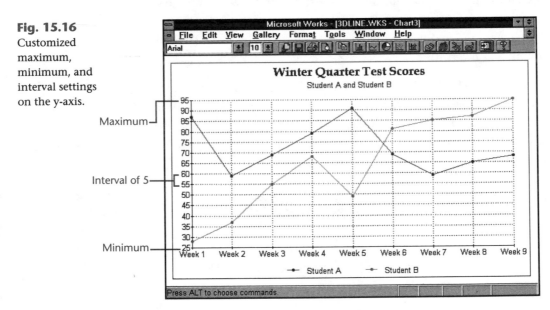

The Vertical Axis dialog box also enables you to choose the type of axis to use in a chart. Normal is the setting Works chooses by default. For a line chart, you could use a scale that stacks y-series ranges, a 100% scale, or a Hi-Lo scale (commonly used for charting stock performance). (Note that the options in the Type box are different depending on the type of chart you are using.)

Suppose that the data shown in figures 15.15 and 15.16 reflected Student C's test scores on quizzes and exams rather than the test scores for Student A and Student B. To chart Student C's cumulative performance over the nine-week period, you would choose the **S**tacked option from the Type box. A stacked scale produces a very different type of chart, as shown in figure 15.17.

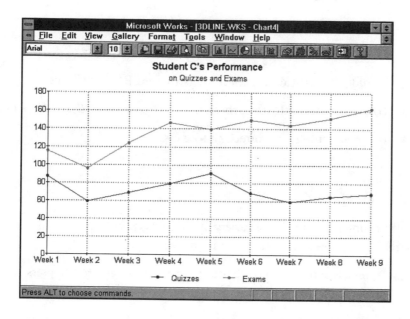

Fig. 15.17
A stacked scale stacks y-series ranges to show cumulative values.

The check boxes in the Vertical Axis dialog box enable you to show or hide gridlines, show or hide the y-axis, or use a logarithmic scale.

> **Note**
>
> When you use a logarithmic scale, the interval you specify in the **I**nterval box is the factor by which numbers are multiplied to determine the scale for the y-axis. For example, if you specify 10 as the interval, the y-axis scale is 10, 100, 1000, 10000, and so on. Using a logarithmic scale works best when the values you are plotting are very large.

To change any of the vertical axis settings in the Vertical Axis dialog box, use the following steps:

1. In the active window, display the chart for which you want to change axis settings.

2. From the Format menu, choose the **V**ertical (Y) Axis command to open the Vertical Axis dialog box shown in figure 15.14.

3. To change the y-axis scale, enter values in the **M**inimum, Maximum, and **I**nterval boxes.

4. To use a scale type other than **N**ormal, choose an option in the Type box.

5. To show gridlines, select the Show **G**ridlines check box.

6. To hide the vertical axis, select the No Vertical **A**xis check box.

7. To use a logarithmic scale, check the Use **L**ogarithmic Scale check box.

8. When all settings are correct, choose OK.

From Here...

In this chapter, you learned a variety of methods for editing and enhancing charts. This chapter completes your study of charting spreadsheets.

■ To review spreadsheet or charting instructions, refer to Chapters 10 through 14.

■ To begin learning about the database tool in Works, refer to Chapter 16, "Creating and Saving a Database File."

Part IV

Databases

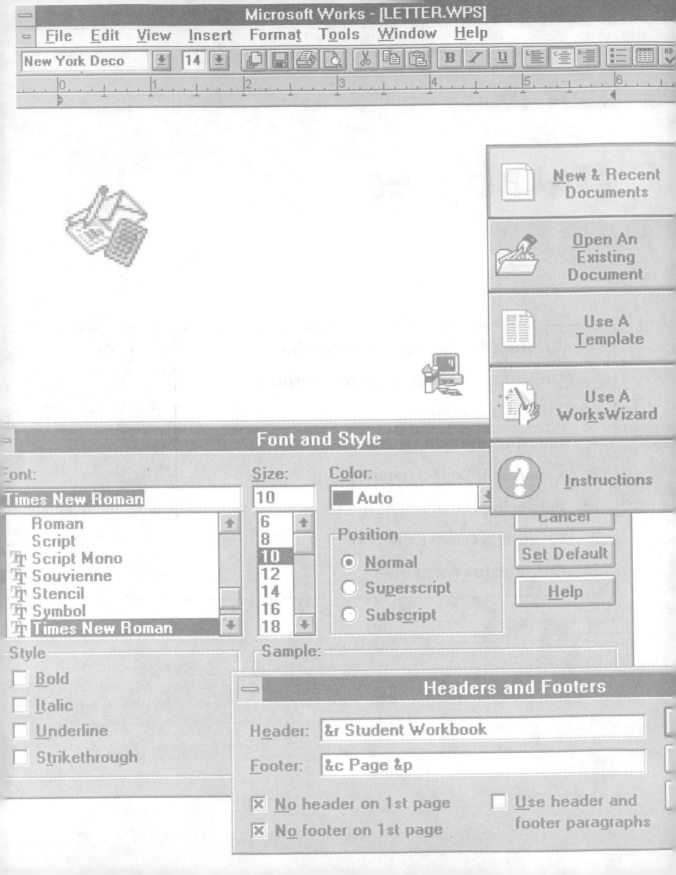

Creating and Saving a Database File

With the Microsoft Works for Windows Database module, you can store many common types of information, such as mailing lists, inventories, employee data, sales contact information, and fundraising records. You even can store spreadsheets and graphic images.

Works makes creating a database easy. Unlike many other programs, Works performs most of the chores involved in designing a database form and printing reports. With the supplied database *WorksWizards*, you even can select a predesigned database application and choose a variety of appearance and design options.

After you store information in a database, Works enables you to retrieve the information in flexible ways. For example, you can sort records and use the Query command to retrieve data according to simple or complex selection criteria. You can print your stored data in the form of simple lists or complex reports, and you can use the stored data to print labels or mail-merge letters with the help of the word processor.

Works enables you to give your databases an attractive appearance with drawings, lines, fonts, colors, and patterns. You even can add pop-up Note-It messages to display important information for the user.

In this chapter, you learn:

- Planning a new database

- Creating a database file

- Naming and saving database files

- Understanding the Database window and toolbar

- Using Form and List views

Understanding a Database

In its simplest form, a *database* is like a traditional file card system. In a file card drawer, you store file cards, each of which contains the same type of information: names and addresses, for example, or a videotape collection, or business equipment records, or pledge information for a school jogathon. In the Works Database, each file card is called a *record*.

Each record (card) in the database (file drawer) holds information about just one item: one name and address, one videotape, one item of business equipment, etc.

In each record, you list relevant information about the item. For example, a personnel record might list an employee's name, address, city, state, ZIP code, and birth date. A videotape record might list the videotape title, category (action, adventure, comedy, etc.), length, cost, purchase date, and so on.

Each type of information in a record is called a *field*. Figure 16.1 shows a sample record from a Works database that contains information about business clients.

Fig. 16.1
A sample record from a Works client database, displayed in Form view.

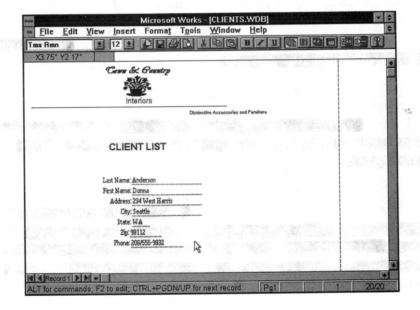

Figure 16.1 shows one record in the Client List database. Notice the fields in the record: Last Name, First Name, Address, City, State, ZIP, and Phone.

The blank data input screen, corresponding to a blank card in a file card drawer, is called a database *form*. Laying out a database form is very much like typing in the Works word processor. Creating database forms is discussed in Chapter 17, "Creating and Editing a Database Form," and Chapter 18,

"Enhancing a Database Form." You can change a form at any time, even after you add records to the database. Notice in figure 16.1 that Works enables you to add graphic images, fonts, and lines to make your database forms visually attractive.

Planning a Database

In Works, you can change your database forms at any time, even after you add information to a database. For example, you may discover that a better arrangement of fields would enable you to enter data more efficiently. However, adding or combining fields may require hours of retyping or reformatting. For example, imagine that you have created a database of names and addresses. The database form contains the following fields:

> Last Name:
> First Name:
> Address 1:
> Address 2:

A sample record looks like this:

> Last Name: Anderson
> First Name: Donna
>   Address 1: 234 West Harris
>   City: Seattle, WA 98112

After creating your database form, you enter 250 records. Then you decide to do a bulk mailing. The U.S. Postal Service may require you to sort your labels in ZIP order. But Works is unable to sort your records because the Address 2 field combines the city, state, and ZIP code. With separate fields, you can sort records based on the city, state, or ZIP code.

You're faced with a real dilemma. The brochure needs to be mailed immediately, but before you can print labels, you need to create new fields for the city, state, and ZIP information, and retype that information for all 250 records.

Clearly, you would have been ahead to create separate fields initially:

Last Name:
First Name:
Address:
City:
State:
ZIP:

Works cannot design your database forms for you—unless, of course, you use a Database WorksWizard. To find out how to use WorksWizards, see Chapter 3, "Working with Files, Templates, and WorksWizards." Briefly, follow these steps:

1. From the Startup dialog box, choose Use A WorksWizard.

   or

   From the Database, choose File, WorksWizards.

2. Choose a Database WorksWizard from the list, and then choose OK.

3. Follow the directions in the WorksWizard screens to create the type of database you want.

Therefore, planning your database form on paper is highly advisable before sitting down at the computer to create the Works version of the form. When planning database forms, consider the following factors:

- Which fields are always filled, and which fields are seldom filled? Entering data goes more efficiently if you don't have to press the Tab key to skip over seldom-used fields. You may want to group the most often-used fields together, at the top of the form.

- Will you use the database to print mail-merge letters? If so, you may want to include Greeting and Title fields. For example, you may want to address Donna Anderson as *Mrs. Anderson*, Susan Caran as *Ms. Caran*, Don Ritchie as *Don*, and Dr. Carl Ekman as *Dr. Ekman*. Including a

Greeting field allows you to format mail-merged letters appropriately. And a Title field enables you to include the addressee's title: *Vice-President*, *Chairman of the Board*, and so on.

- Do you have fields you're not sure you will ever use? Include them! Typing the information now may be somewhat inconvenient, but it's much less frustrating than adding later.

- Will other people use the database to add and retrieve information? Be sure to include labels or Note-Its to guide the user through the database form. For example, you may add a Note-It that advises: Fill in the part number only if the part is in stock! To learn about Note-Its, see Chapter 25, "Using WordArt and Note-It."

Starting a New Database File

This section shows you the basic steps for designing a new Works Database. For detailed instructions on designing database forms, see Chapter 17, "Creating and Editing a Database Form."

The easiest way to create a new database is with a Database WorksWizard or an AutoStart template. WorksWizards and AutoStart templates are explained in Chapter 3, "Working with Files, Templates, and WorksWizards."

To create a new database from scratch, you first should design the database form on paper, as discussed in the preceding section. Then from the Startup dialog box, choose **D**atabase. Or if you already are in the Works Database, choose the Create **N**ew File command from the **F**ile menu. Then from the Startup dialog box, choose **D**atabase.

Works opens a new database in Form view and names the file DATA1 (see fig. 16.2).

You now can begin laying out the database form on-screen. To learn the actual steps to create database forms, see Chapter 17, "Creating and Editing a Database Form."

Fig. 16.2
Works opens a
new database in
Form view.

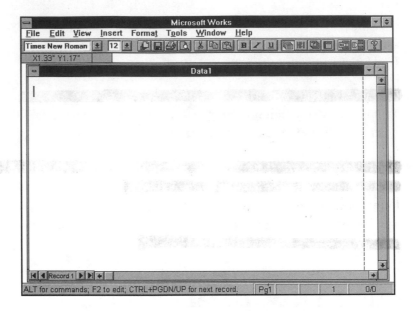

Opening an Existing Database File

After you create a database form, you need to save it on your computer's hard disk, just as you would save a Works word processor document. To learn how to save a file, see the next section, "Saving a Database File."

To open a database file that you have saved on disk, choose the Open Existing File command from the File menu. Works displays the Open dialog box (see fig. 16.3). In the Open dialog box, select a file from the File Name list box, or type a file name in the text box and then choose OK.

Fig. 16.3
The Open dialog
box showing
Works files.

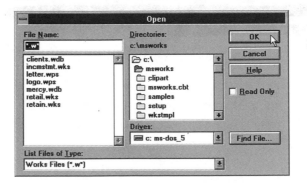

If you select **O**pen An Existing Document from the Startup dialog box, Works displays the Open dialog box (see fig. 16.4).

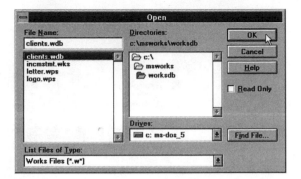

Fig. 16.4
The Open dialog
box.

To open a database with the Open dialog box, you can double-click the
name of the database in the File **N**ame list or highlight the file name and
choose OK.

Note

If a database file does not appear in the Open dialog box, it may be located on
another drive or in another directory. Use the **D**irectories and Dri**v**es list boxes to
select the drive or directory that contains the file. Using dialog boxes and opening
files is described in Chapter 2, "Getting Started with Works for Windows."

Saving a Database File

After entering or editing records in a database file, you need to save the new
information on disk. Until you save your changes, they are held in your
computer's memory and can be lost if power is interrupted or if you accidentally turn the computer off.

When you create a new database, as described in an earlier section, "Starting
a New Database File," Works names the new file DATA1 (or DATA2, DATA3, etc.,
if you have already created other databases in the current Works session). To
save the database and give it a new name, choose the **S**ave command from
the **F**ile menu; press Ctrl+S; or click the Save toolbar button. Works displays
the Save As dialog box (see fig. 16.5).

In the Save As dialog box, type a new name for the database in the File **N**ame
text box. A database name can be up to eight characters long. Then choose
OK. Works saves the database and automatically assigns the file name extension .WDB (for *Works Database*).

Tip
You also can dis-
play the Save As
dialog box by
clicking the Save
button on the
Database toolbar.
For more informa-
tion, see "The
Database Toolbar,"
later in this
chapter.

Fig. 16.5
The Save As dialog
box.

Reviewing the Database Window

Figure 16.6 shows the Works Database window, with each element labeled.

Fig. 16.6
The Works Data-
base window, with
a database dis-
played in List view.

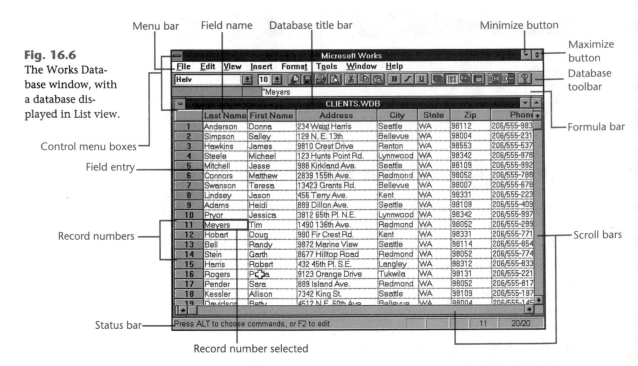

Notice in figure 16.5 that the formula bar displays the contents of the selected field, preceded by double quotation marks: "Meyers. If you select more
than one field, the formula bar displays the contents of the first field in the
selection. To select multiple fields, hold down the Ctrl key and click each
field.

> **Note**
>
> In the illustrations for this book, the database window is maximized and the database title bar is hidden. Maximizing the database window allows you to display more database records in List view or more of a record in Form view.

Notice also in figure 16.6 that the status bar in List view displays the number of the currently selected record: 11. The status bar also shows the total number of records in the database and the number of records currently displayed: 20/20. If you use the Query function to display just five database records, as described in Chapter 21, "Retrieving Database Information," the status line indicates 5/20, meaning that five records of 20 total records are displayed.

To learn how to move around in the Works Database window and use windows, toolbars, dialog boxes, menus, and commands, see Chapter 2, "Getting Started with Works for Windows."

Using the Database Toolbar

With the Database *toolbar*, you can perform common procedures with a simple mouse click. Toolbar buttons can format text, insert new fields and records, and cut, copy, or move data, for example. You can customize the toolbar to add buttons for the commands you use most frequently.

> **Note**
>
> You cannot use the toolbar with the keyboard.

To learn what each toolbar button does, move the mouse pointer onto the button and read the message that Works displays (see fig. 16.7). When you move the mouse cursor onto a button to find out what it does, be sure not to click the button! Just move the mouse pointer onto the button and wait briefly until the explanation appears.

When you press a key or move the mouse cursor away from the button, the message disappears. To turn off display of toolbar button messages, choose Customize Tools from the Tools menu and deselect the Enable Tool Tips check box.

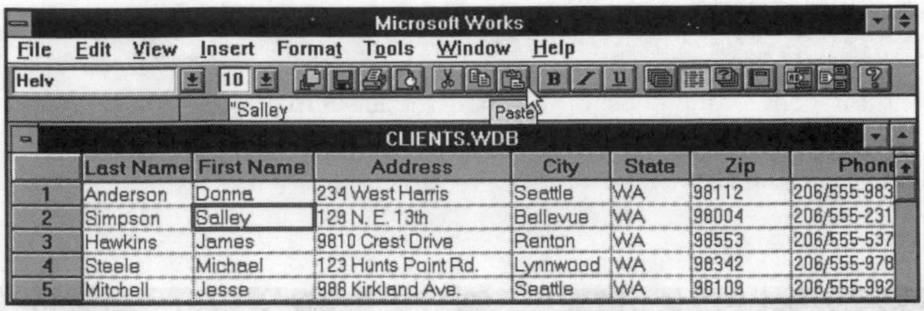

Fig. 16.7
Pointing to a toolbar button displays a message that tells what the button does.

Note

If you turn off display of button messages, Works still displays a button description in the status bar when you place the mouse cursor on a toolbar button.

Table 16.1 shows the buttons on the default toolbar and their functions.

Table 16.1 The Default Toolbar Buttons

Button	Function
 Helv	Clicking the down arrow displays a list of available fonts. (See "Using Fonts" in Chapter 18, "Enhancing a Database Form.")
 10	Clicking the down arrow displays a list of standard font sizes available for the currently selected font. If the font is proportionally spaced, you can specify a different size by typing it in the Font Size box.
	Displays the Startup dialog box.
	Saves the file displayed in the active Database window. When you save a file for the first time, clicking the Save button displays the Save As dialog box.
	Prints the file displayed in the active Database window. (See "Printing Database Records" in Chapter 20, "Expanding Your Database Skills.")
	Displays the Print Preview screen. (See "Printing Database Records" in Chapter 20, "Expanding Your Database Skills.")
	Cuts selected text. (See "Editing Database Information" in Chapter 19, "Entering and Editing Data.")
	Copies selected text. (See "Editing Database Information" in Chapter 19, "Entering and Editing Data.")
	Pastes selected text. (See "Editing Database Information" in Chapter 19, "Entering and Editing Data.")

Table 16.1 The Default Toolbar Buttons

B	Boldfaces selected text. (See "Using Fonts" in Chapter 18, "Enhancing a Database Form.")
I	Italicizes selected text. (See "Using Fonts" in Chapter 18, "Enhancing a Database Form.")
U	Underlines selected text. (See "Using Fonts" in Chapter 18, "Enhancing a Database Form.")
	Switches to Form view. (See "Database Views" later in this chapter.)
	Switches to List view. (See "Database Views" later in this chapter.)
	Switches to Query view. (See "Database Views" later in this chapter.)
	Switches to Report view. (See "Database Views" later in this chapter.)
	Inserts a new field. (See "Adding a New Field" in Chapter 17, "Creating and Editing a Database form.")
	Inserts a new record. (See "Entering Data in a Works Database" in Chapter 19, "Entering and Editing Data.")
	Runs the Works Tutorial.

Turning the Toolbar On and Off

If you prefer not to use the toolbar, you can turn it off. Choose the Tool**bar** command from the **V**iew menu. Turning the toolbar off lets you see more information in the Database window.

Customizing the Toolbar

You can customize the toolbar so it works more efficiently for tasks you routinely perform. For example, you can rearrange the toolbar buttons, placing the most frequently used buttons together at the left end of the toolbar. Or you can simplify the toolbar by removing seldom-used buttons.

To add a button to the toolbar, refer to the steps in Chapter 2, "Getting Started with Works for Windows." To return the toolbar to its original default configuration, choose C**u**stomize Toolbar from the T**o**ols menu, then choose R**e**set.

Tip
When designing a database form, you want to be able to see as many fields as possible to avoid scrolling back and forth. You can accomplish this by turning off the toolbar and by maximizing the Database window.

IV

Databases

You can install several useful toolbar buttons that perform Database functions. The following list shows the toolbar buttons and describes what they do.

Edit Menu Toolbar Buttons

	Copies values, formats, formula to the right.
	Copies values, formats, formula down.
	Fills selected cells with numbers or date series.

View Menu Toolbar Buttons

	Applies predefined query.
	Displays all records.
	Displays hidden records and hides visible records.
	Hides selected records.
	Displays field lines.
	Displays gridlines.

Insert Menu Toolbar Buttons

	Inserts a page break.
	Deletes selected records.
	Inserts a Microsoft Draw object.
	Inserts a Microsoft Note-It object.
	Inserts a Microsoft ClipArt objet.
	Inserts a Microsoft WordArt object.

Format Menu Toolbar Buttons

	Left aligns text.
	Centers text.
	Right aligns text.
	Positions field on grid.

Format Menu Toolbar Buttons

[icon]	Protects form from accidental changes.
[icon]	Protects data from accidental changes.
[icon]	Shows field name (toggle).

Tools Menu Toolbar Buttons

[icon]	Sorts records in ascending order (A to Z).
[icon]	Sorts records in descending order (Z to A).

Your customized Database toolbar settings take effect in all database views. To learn how to display database views, see the section that follows.

Selecting the Database View

The Works Database gives you four ways to view or print your data:

- Form view and List view display information on your computer's screen. Form view displays just one record at a time. List view displays 20 records in the Database window, with the window maximized and the toolbar displayed.

- You use Query view to select records from a database for printing or for viewing on-screen.

- You use Report view to format data for printing or for viewing with the Print Preview command.

To switch between Form view and List view, press F9; or choose the **Form** or **List** command from the **View** menu; or click the Form View or List view toolbar button. (To learn how to move around in form and List views, see "Entering Data" in Chapter 17, "Creating and Editing a Database Form.")

Figure 16.8 shows an example of a record in Form view.

In List view, you see several database records at one time (see fig. 16.9).

In Query view, you see a single form in which you can enter query formulas (see fig. 16.10). To learn how to use Query view, see "Creating a Simple Query" in Chapter 21, "Retrieving Database Information."

Tip

To free toolbar space for up to five more buttons, open the Customize Works Toolbar dialog box and select Remove **F**ont Name and Point Size from the toolbar.

IV

Databases

Fig. 16.8
A database record
in Form view.

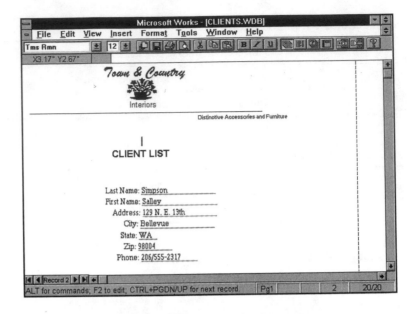

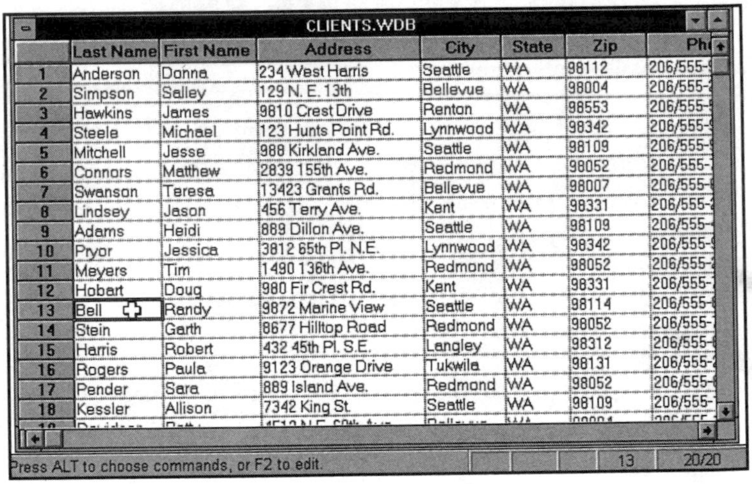

Fig. 16.9
A database in List
view.

In Report view, you see a screen in which you can format data with report commands (see fig. 16.11). To learn how to use Report view, see "Using Report View" in Chapter 22, "Creating a Database Report."

IV

Databases

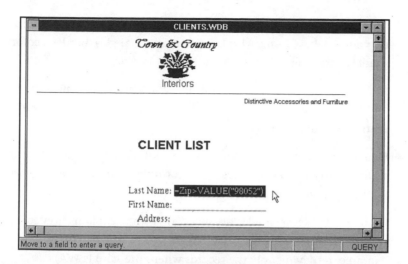

Fig. 16.10
A database form in Query view.

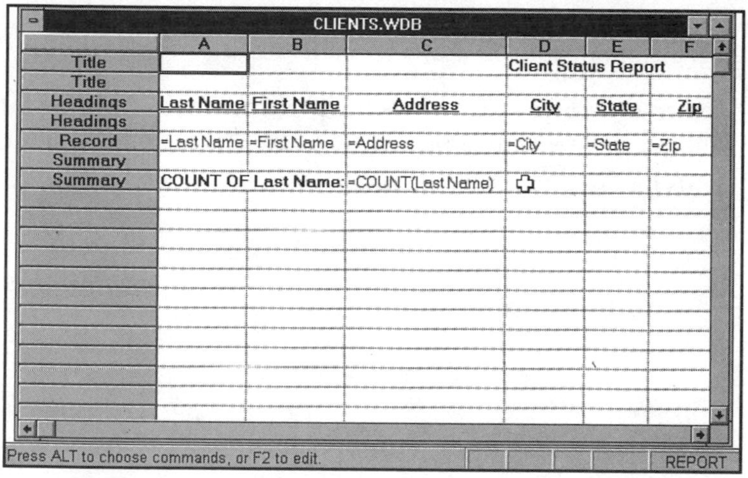

Fig. 16.11
The Report view screen.

From Here...

In this chapter you learned basic skills for creating and saving a database file, using and customizing the Database toolbar, and switching between database views. To expand your knowledge of the Works Database, see the following chapters:

■ Chapter 17, "Creating and Editing a Database Form," tells you how to lay out a database form and create data entry fields.

- Chapter 18, "Enhancing a Database Form," shows you how to spruce up your database forms with labels, fonts, rectangles, borders, colors, shading, drawings, pictures, Note-Its, and WordArt.

- In Chapter 19, "Entering and Editing Data," you learn how to type data and save records. In addition, you learn how to copy and move information and hide records.

- Chapter 20, "Expanding Your Database Skills," explains how to sort and print records, use dates, times, math formulas and functions, protect your data, and format data in fields.

- Chapter 21, "Retrieving Database Information," explains how to retrieve information from a database by using specific criteria (for example, retrieving only the records where the state is *WA*).

- Chapter 22, "Creating a Database Report," tells you how to print database information in neatly formatted lists.

- Chapter 23, "Customizing a Report," explains how to create reports that require customized formatting and data selection and how to print reports for use with other applications.

Chapter 17

Creating and Editing a Database Form

IV

Databases

Before you can save information in a Works Database, you must create a database *form*. In Chapter 16, "Creating and Saving a Database File," you learned about opening and saving database files. You also learned about database records, forms, and fields. Remember that a database consists of *records*. Each record contains information about one database entry, such as a sales person, employee, or inventory item. The information in the record is laid out in *fields*. For example, the record might include fields for Name, Address, City, State, ZIP, Phone, and Employee Identification Number.

In this chapter, you learn how to create a new database form and place data input fields on the form. If you need to review the basic steps to designing a database, see the section on "Planning a Database" in Chapter 16, "Creating and Saving a Database File."

Chapter 16, "Creating and Saving a Database File," gives the theory of database design. In this chapter you learn the actual steps of laying out Works Database forms.

In this chapter, you learn how to do the following:

■ Open a new database form

■ Create data input fields on a database form

■ Move, edit, and delete fields

■ Format data in fields

Creating a Database Form

When you enter information in a Works database form, you must type the information in fields, as described in Chapter 16, "Creating and Saving a Database File." Figure 17.1 shows the terms used to describe the various parts of a Works database form.

Fig. 17.1

The parts of a
Works database
form.

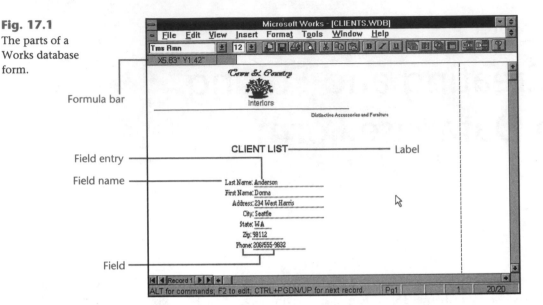

Formula bar

Field entry

Field name

Field

Label

Figure 17.1 shows a record in a database called CLIENTS.WDB. Notice that
the database file name appears in the Works title bar. The figure shows the
record for Donna Anderson, consisting of data entry fields for Last Name,
First Name, Address, City, State, ZIP, and Phone. You can create very simple
Works database forms that contain only data entry fields, or you can customize your forms with clip art, lines, fonts, and labels, as shown in figure 17.1.

Creating a Form Using a WorksWizard

You can create a Works database quickly with a WorksWizard. You can
choose from WorksWizards that create databases for addresses, business contacts, business inventory, and so on. To use a WorksWizard, from the Startup
dialog box, choose Use A WorksWizard; or from the Works Database window,
choose File, WorksWizards. Choose the type of database you want in the list,
and then choose OK and answer the prompts as Works guides you through
the steps to create the database.

Creating a Form in the Database Window

To begin creating a database, you first must open a new database file. This
process was described in Chapter 16, "Creating and Saving a Database File."
The following step reviews the process:

From the Works Startup dialog box, choose **D**atabase

or

From the Database window, choose Create **N**ew File from the **F**ile menu, then choose **D**atabase

or

Click the Startup Dialog toolbar button then choose Database.

Works opens a new database in Form view. Works names the database DATA1 (or DATA2, DATA3, etc., depending on whether you have created other forms during the current Works session). To learn about database views, see "Database Views" in Chapter 16, "Creating and Saving a Database File."

Creating a New Field

You can find useful tips for designing a database form in the section "Planning a Database" of Chapter 16, "Creating and Saving a Database File." You probably want to plan your database form first on paper before creating the fields in the Works Database window. If you plan carefully, you may not have to move fields on the form or create new fields later.

> **Note**
>
> If you later discover that you need to change, move, or delete fields, or add new fields, you can do so. See the following sections in this chapter: "Deleting a Field," "Changing Field Size," "Changing a Field Name," and "Changing Field Position."

Follow these steps to create a database field:

1. With the mouse or arrow keys, move the cursor anywhere on the form and type the field label, followed by a colon. For example:

    Last Name:

    When typing fields, you must follow these rules:

    ■ Each field name can contain up to 15 characters.

    ■ Each field name must be followed by a colon.

    ■ You cannot use field names that begin with a single quotation mark (').

    ■ A field can contain up to 254 characters. (To create multiple-line fields, see step 4.)

2. Press Enter.

Works displays the Field Size dialog box (see fig. 17.2).

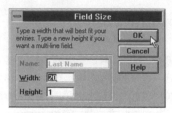

3. In the **W**idth box, accept the default field size (20) or type the size of the field (up to 254 characters).

4. In the H**e**ight box, accept the default field height (1) or type the number of lines for the field.

For example, to create a field with three 50-character lines, type **50** in the **W**idth box and **3** in the H**e**ight box (see fig. 17.3).

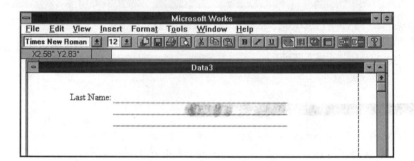

5. Choose OK to return to the Database window and insert the new field.

Repeat the preceding steps for each field in the database.

You can use a shorter process to insert a new field and specify the width and height. Follow these steps:

1. Click the Insert Field toolbar button or choose **F**ield from the **I**nsert menu.

Works displays the Insert Field dialog box (see fig. 17.4).

2. Type a **N**ame, **W**idth, and H**e**ight for the field, then choose OK to return to the Database window and insert the new field.

IV

Databases

Caution

When you create new fields, be careful to move the cursor after inserting each new field; otherwise, Works places the next new field on top of the previous one.

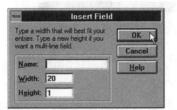

Fig. 17.4
The Insert Field dialog box.

Note

When you first insert a new field, it is unlikely that Works will align the field colons exactly as you want them. You will almost certainly need to reposition the fields. To do so, use the procedures described in the sections "Using Field Lines and Grid Lines" and "Moving a Field in Form View" in this chapter.

Using Field Lines and Grid Lines

When you create a new field in Form view, Works displays a line under the field's data entry area (refer to fig. 17.1). You can turn off display of field lines. For example, you may want to turn off field lines to print forms you have designed as formal invitations. To turn off field lines, choose Field Lines from the View menu.

In List view, Works separates fields and records with gridlines. Turning gridlines off may make reading records across the screen more difficult; but if you prefer this effect, you can turn off gridlines by choosing **G**ridlines from the **V**iew menu.

Moving a Field in Form View

After creating a database form, you may discover that the fields are positioned inconveniently for fast data entry. You can move fields at any time in Form view or List view. For example, you may prefer to group often-used fields together in List view.

Tip
If you plan to work with a database mostly in List view, you should know that Works places fields from left to right in List view in the order you create them in Form view, regardless of their position in Form view. Creating fields in the desired order saves you the step of repositioning fields in List view.

> **Note**
>
> Moving a field in one view has no effect on the field's position in the other view.

You can move a field in Form view easily by clicking and dragging the field to the new position. Or you can follow these steps:

1. Highlight the field you want to move.

   To highlight a field, click it or use the arrow keys to move the highlight onto the field name.

2. Choose Position Selection from the Edit menu.

   The mouse pointer becomes an arrow with the DRAG under it.

3. Use the arrow keys to move the field to the new position.

4. Press Enter.

Works drops the field into the new position.

Using Snap to Grid

The Snap to Grid feature enables you to easily align field names and other elements on a form, such as drawings and labels.

> **Note**
>
> Snap to Grid is available only in Form view.

Tip

With **S**nap to Grid turned off, Works positions elements in increments of .01". For very accurate placement of elements, turn Snap to Grid off.

When you move an element such as a field name and drop the element in place by pressing Enter or releasing the mouse button, Works aligns the element with the nearest invisible vertical and horizontal gridlines. The invisible gridlines are positioned .08" apart horizontally and vertically. You cannot display the gridlines on-screen.

Snap to Grid is a toggle command. To turn the feature on or off, choose **S**nap to Grid from the Forma**t** menu.

Moving a Field in List View

In List view, fields appear in columns. This format makes moving fields much easier in List view, because you don't need to worry about aligning the field labels precisely. Works automatically aligns the columns.

To move a field in List view:

1. Select the field.

2. From the **E**dit menu, choose Cu**t**; or press Ctrl+X.

3. Highlight the field to the right of the position where you want to insert the cut field.

4. From the **E**dit menu, choose **P**aste; or press Ctrl+V.

Works realigns the remaining fields to accommodate the pasted data.

Works inserts the field to the left of the highlighted field.

Saving Your Form Design

After you finish creating new fields, you should save the new database form so you can later retrieve it and use it to enter information in the database. Saving a form was discussed in the section "Naming and Saving a Database File" in Chapter 16, "Creating and Saving a Database File." The following steps review this procedure:

1. Choose Save **A**s from the **F**ile menu; or click the Save toolbar button; or press Ctrl+S.

Works opens the Save As dialog box.

2. Type a new name of up to eight characters for your database file and choose OK.

Works saves the file under the new name, adding a .WDB file name extension.

Adding a Field to an Existing Database

After working with a database form, you may discover that you need to add a new field. You can add new fields in Form view or List view. Database views are discussed in the section "Database Views" in Chapter 16, "Creating and Saving a Database File." Opening an existing file is described in the section "Opening an Existing Database File" in Chapter 16, "Creating and Saving a Database File."

In Form view, you can add new fields by following the steps given in "Creating a New Field" earlier in this chapter.

Tip

To switch to List
view, click the List
View toolbar
button; or press
F9; or choose **List**
from the **View**
menu.

To add a new field in List view, follow these steps:

1. Highlight the entire field to the right of where you want the new field inserted.

To highlight an entire field, click the field name; or move the highlight into the field with the arrow keys and press Shift+F8.

2. Choose **R**ecord/Field from the **I**nsert menu; or click the Insert Field toolbar button.

Works inserts a new field to the left of the highlighted column (see fig. 17.5).

3. To name the new field, choose Field **N**ame from the **E**dit menu and type a new field name of up to 15 characters. Then choose OK.

Fig. 17.5
Works inserts a
new field.

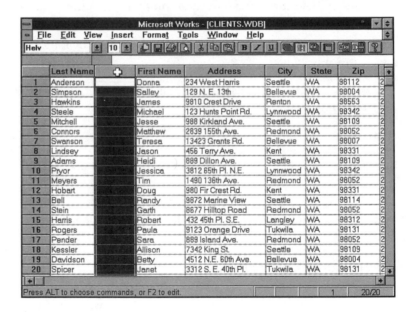

Works inserts the new field name in the header row at the top of the column.

Deleting a Field

In Works, you can *clear* a field or you can *delete* a field. Clearing a field removes only the data in the field. Deleting removes the field, the field's name, and all the data and formatting.

> ### Caution
>
> Clearing a field removes the field's contents permanently. Clearing a field with the field's column selected in List view removes the contents of the field from each record in the database. Deleting a field permanently removes the field, as well as all data saved in the field, from the entire database. You can undo a clear (see accompanying tip), but you cannot undo a deletion.

Tip

To reverse a clear, before you perform any other actions, choose **U**ndo Clear from the **E**dit menu.

IV

Databases

Deleting a Field in Form View. To delete a field in Form view:

1. Click the field name; or move the highlight to the field name.

2. From the **I**nsert menu, choose **D**elete Selection.

   Works prompts you to confirm the deletion and warns that you cannot undo this operation.

   > ### Note
   >
   > Although you cannot undo a deletion in Form view, you *can* undo a deletion in List view. See following section, "Deleting a Field in List View."

3. Choose OK to confirm the deletion.

   Works deletes the field and all its data immediately.

> ### Troubleshooting
>
> *When I try to delete a field, I can't.*
>
> If Works won't delete a field, make sure the field is not protected. For example, databases that you create with WorksWizards contain protected fields. To unprotect a field, choose Format, Protection, and then deselect the Protect Form check box and choose OK.

Deleting a Field in List View. Follow these steps to delete a field in List view:

1. Highlight the field you want to delete by clicking its name; or move the highlight into the field and press Shift+F8; or move the highlight to the field and choose Select Field from the **E**dit menu.

2. Choose **D**elete Record/Field from the **I**nsert menu.

Works deletes the field and all its data immediately, without asking you to confirm the action.

Troubleshooting

How can I undo a deletion in List view?

To undo the deletion, choose **U**ndo Delete Field from the **E**dit menu; or press Ctrl+Z. You must undo the deletion before you choose another command or delete another field, record, or data.

In List view, you can delete several adjacent fields at one time. To select the fields, click the first field and drag to the last field name in the series; or hold down the Shift key and click the first and last fields in the series. Then choose **I**nsert, **D**elete Record/Field.

To find out how to delete data from a field, see "Removing Information and Objects" in Chapter 19, "Entering and Editing Data."

Changing Field Size in Form View

You can type up to 254 characters in a Works Database field, regardless of the field's length on the database form. Works enables you to type data in a field even if the data is longer than the field. If the field is a text field, the long text scrolls past the right end of the field and becomes invisible. If the field is a number or date field, Works replaces the long number or date with number symbols: #####. (To find out how to format number and date fields, see "Formatting Numbers in Fields" later in this chapter.

Tip

You can view and edit long data in the formula bar. For details, See "Entering Data in a Works Database" in Chapter 19, "Entering and Editing Data."

Note

Field sizes are set separately in Form and List views—for example, a field can be 10 characters wide in Form view and 125 characters wide and 3 lines long in List view.

If you need to see long data on-screen, you can change the size of a field. You use different commands to change field size in Form and List views. To learn how to change a field's size in List view, see "Changing Field Size in List View" later in this chapter.

Follow these steps to change the size of a field in Form view:

1. Select the field you want to change.

2. To resize the field with the mouse, move the mouse pointer onto one of the field sizing boxes at the right edge of the field until the pointer changes to a box with a diagonal arrow labeled RESIZE. Then drag the field to the size you want.

   or

   To resize the field with the keyboard, choose Field Size from the Format menu.

   Works displays the Field Size dialog box, which is the same as the Insert Field dialog box (refer to fig. 17.4).

3. Type a **W**idth between 1 and 325 characters.

4. Type a **H**eight between 1 and 325 lines.

5. Choose OK to return to the Database window.

   Works resizes the field.

Changing Field Size in List View

In List view, Works displays fields in columns. By default, Works sets the column width to the field width you specified when you created the field in List view.

Field size is set separately in Form and List views. For example, if you create a field in Form view, Works automatically sets the field's width in List view to the size you specified. But if you later resize the field in Form view, Works does not change the field size in List view. To change the field size in List view, follow the directions given in this section.

You can set the field width easily in List view by dragging the right field border to the width you want. Or you can follow these steps:

1. Move the highlight into the field whose width you want to change.

2. From the Format menu, choose Field **W**idth and type the width you want.

> **Note**
>
> Field width in List view can be 0 to 79 characters, and record height can be 0 to 409 lines. If you choose 0 for either setting, the field or record will be hidden. For further information about hiding fields and records, see "Hiding Fields and Records" in Chapter 19, "Entering and Editing Data."

3. To create a field wide enough to display the longest data in the field, choose **B**est Fit.

> **Note**
>
> If you plan to choose the Best Fit option, you must highlight the entire field in step 1 above. To highlight the field, click its name; or move the highlight into the field and press Shift+F8.

4. Choose OK.

Figure 17.6 shows a field that contains information wider than the field, and figure 17.7 shows the field after choosing the **B**est Fit option.

Fig. 17.6
A field with contents wider than the field.

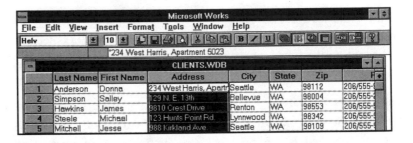

Fig. 17.7
The same field after choosing the Best Fit option.

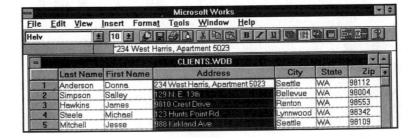

Note

Long field contents appear on a single line in List view. With the **B**est Fit option selected, a field with very long data can take up most of the screen. Don't choose **B**est Fit unless you can live with this effect. To make text wrap within a field in List view, click the field's name to highlight the field. Then choose Field **W**idth from the Forma**t** menu. Type the field width in the **W**idth box and choose OK. Figures 17.8 and 17.9 show the same field, one formatted with **B**est Fit and the other with a 25-character width.

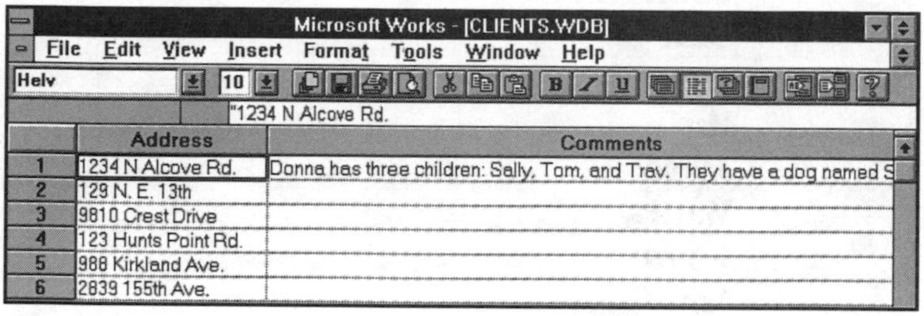

Fig. 17.8
The Best Fit option displays long data in a single line.

To see more fields on-screen, turn off **B**est Fit or specify a set width as shown in figure 17.9.

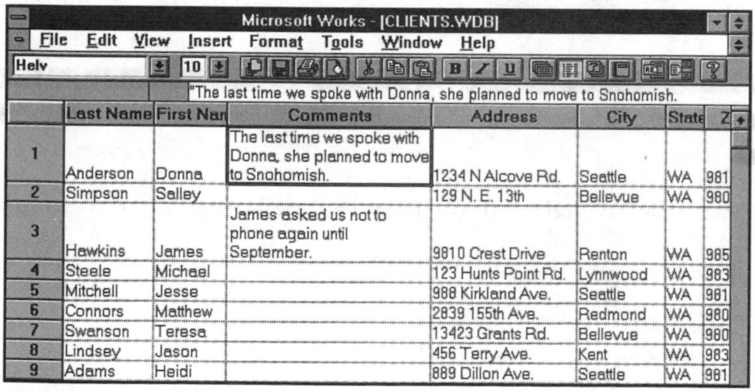

Fig. 17.9
A multiple-line field displayed in List view and formatted with a 25-character width.

Note

Best Fit does not work with objects. (To learn how to work with objects, see "Linking and Embedding" in Chapter 19, "Entering and Editing Data.") If you apply **B**est Fit to a field that contains an object such as a drawing, the field width may not be wide enough to display the entire name of the object.

Changing Record Height in List View

In List view, Works displays records in rows. Works sets record height to one line at the size of the largest font used in the line. For example, if the largest font size used in the record is 24 points, the record height is made tall enough in List view to accommodate the 24-point font (see fig. 17.10)

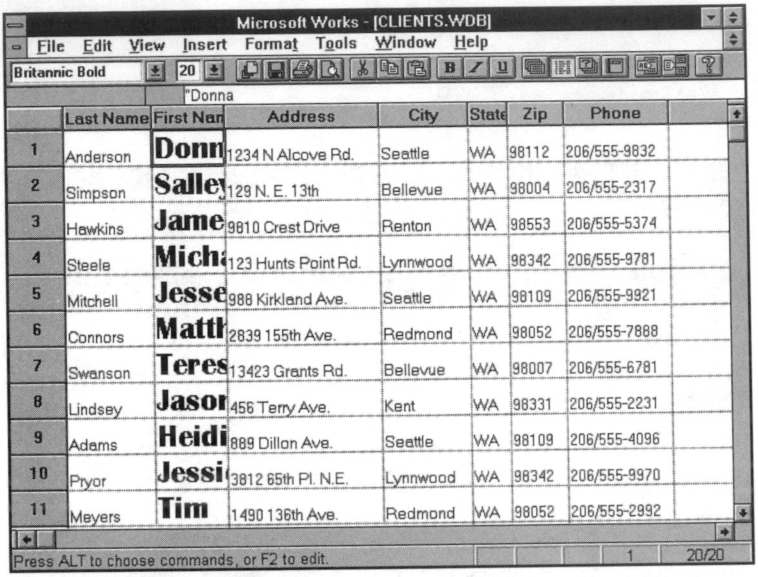

Fig. 17.10

In List view, Works formats record height to accommodate the largest font in a record.

You can set record height easily in List view by dragging the bottom edge of the record number box to the height you want. Or you can follow these steps:

1. Move the highlight into the record whose height you want to adjust.

2. Choose Record **H**eight from the Forma**t** menu.

3. Type a new H**e**ight.

4. Choose OK.

As mentioned earlier, Works automatically formats records to accommodate the largest font in the record. However, typing a height in the H**e**ight text box overrides the automatic line height option. For example, if you type **10** in the H**e**ight text box and the record contains a 24-point font, the large font is truncated in List view. To turn the automatic line height feature back on, choose **B**est Fit in the Record Height dialog box.

Changing a Field Name in Form View or List View

You can change a field name at any time. For example, you may want to change a field's name if you discover that it doesn't accurately describe the field's contents and creates confusion for other users.

To change a field name in Form view:

1. Select the field name by clicking it or moving the highlight onto the name with the arrow keys.

2. Type the new field name.

Remember, field names may contain up to 15 characters, may not begin with a single quotation mark ('), and must be followed by a colon.

3. Press Enter.

To change a field name in List view:

1. Move the highlight into the field whose name you want to change.

2. Choose Field **N**ame from the **E**dit command.

3. Type a new name then choose OK.

Field names may contain up to 15 characters, may not begin with a single quotation mark ('), and must be followed by a colon.

Aligning Data in Text Fields

So far in this chapter, you have learned to create standard text fields. Works automatically formats standard text fields with flush-left alignment for text and flush-right alignment for dates and numbers. (Inserting dates and numbers in fields is discussed in the section "Using Dates and Times" in Chapter 20, "Expanding Your Database Skills.")

The default formatting works well for most text data, such as names and addresses, comments, descriptions, etc. But certain types of information may require customized formatting. For example, you may want to center text in a field in List view. Or you may want to format text flush-right in a field in Form view. The following sections show you how to format text fields in Form and List views. Later in this chapter, you learn how to create and format numeric fields.

Aligning Data in Form View

In Form view, you can tell Works to align entries in a field flush left, flush right, or centered. Figure 17.11 shows fields in Form view formatted with the default flush-left alignment.

Fig. 17.11
A database record showing fields formatted with flush-left alignment.

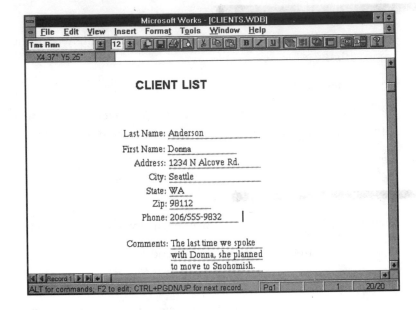

To change field alignment, follow these steps:

1. Select the field or fields you want to align.

2. Choose **Alignment** from the Forma**t** menu.

   Works displays the Alignment dialog box (see fig. 17.12).

Fig. 17.12
Use the Alignment dialog box to align entries in a field.

3. Choose **G**eneral, **L**eft, **R**ight, **C**enter, or **S**lide to Left, then choose OK.

Works aligns the entries in the selected fields.

The following list describes each alignment option:

- *General*. Aligns text entries to the left and numbers and dates to the right.

- *Left*. Aligns all entries to the left, including numbers and dates.

- *Right*. Aligns all entries to the right, including numbers and dates.

- *Center*. Places entries in the center of the field, including numbers and dates.

- *Slide to Left*. Aligns entries in a field to the left when you print the form. Slide to Left has no effect in the on-screen form. Printing forms is described under "Printing Database Records" in Chapter 20, "Expanding Your Database Skills."

Aligning Data in List View

You can align entries in fields in List view. Changing the alignment in List view does not affect the alignment in Form view, and vice versa. Follow these steps:

1. Select the field name.

2. From the Format menu choose Alignment.

   Works displays the Alignment dialog box (refer to fig. 17.12).

3. Select an alignment option then choose OK.

Works aligns all the entries in the field.

Alignment options are described in the preceding section, "Aligning Data in Form View."

Figure 17.13 shows entries centered in the First Name field. To center field contents in List view, choose the Center option in the Alignment dialog box.

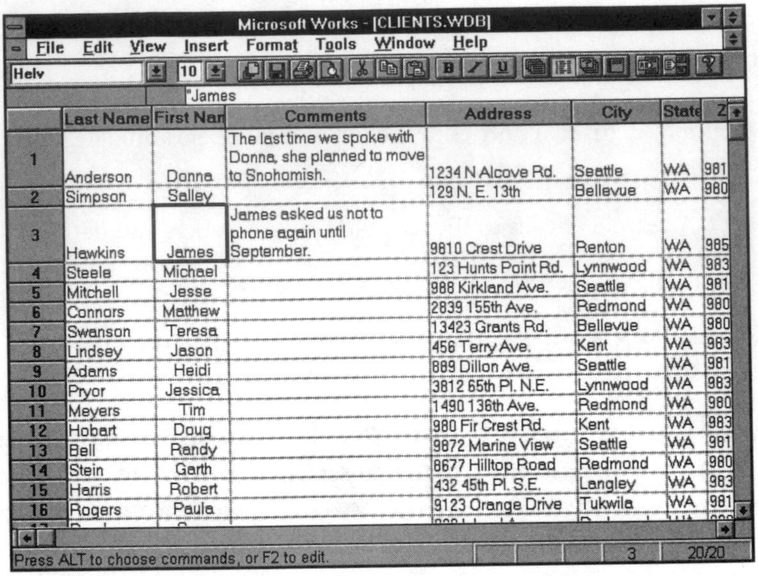

Fig. 17.13
A centered name
in the first name
field.

Wrapping Entries in List View

In figure 17.13, notice that text in the Comments field is wrapped and the
record height is automatically set so you can read the entire field contents.

> **Note**
>
> Works can wrap text fields but does not wrap dates, times, numbers, or other values.

To turn the field wrapping feature on or off, follow these steps:

1. Select the field name.

2. Choose **Alignment** from the Forma**t** menu.

   Works displays the Alignment dialog box (see fig. 17.14). Notice that in
   List view, the dialog box contains several options not available in Form
   view (compare to fig. 17.12).

3. Select alignment options then choose OK.

   Works aligns the text in the field.

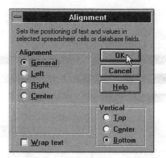

Fig. 17.14
The Alignment
dialog box in List
view includes
Wrap Text and
Vertical options.

The **W**rap Text and **V**ertical options aren't available in Form view. The Vertical options are described in the next section, "Changing Vertical Alignment in List View."

Figure 17.15 shows the Comments field with **W**rap Text turned off. Notice that the field is formatted in a single line and most of the field contents are hidden past the right field border.

	Last Name	First Nan	Comments	Address	City	State	Z
1	Anderson	Donna	The last time we spoke with D	1234 N Alcove Rd.	Seattle	WA	981
2	Simpson	Salley		129 N. E. 13th	Bellevue	WA	980
3	Hawkins	James	James asked us not to phone	9810 Crest Drive	Renton	WA	985
4	Steele	Michael		123 Hunts Point Rd.	Lynnwood	WA	983
5	Mitchell	Jesse		988 Kirkland Ave.	Seattle	WA	981
6	Connors	Matthew		2839 155th Ave.	Redmond	WA	980
7	Swanson	Teresa		13423 Grants Rd.	Bellevue	WA	980
8	Lindsey	Jason		456 Terry Ave.	Kent	WA	983
9	Adams	Heidi		889 Dillon Ave.	Seattle	WA	981
10	Pryor	Jessica		3812 65th Pl. N.E.	Lynnwood	WA	983
11	Meyers	Tim		1490 136th Ave.	Redmond	WA	980
12	Hobart	Doug		980 Fir Crest Rd.	Kent	WA	983
13	Bell	Randy		9872 Marine View	Seattle	WA	981
14	Stein	Garth		8677 Hilltop Road	Redmond	WA	980
15	Harris	Robert		432 45th Pl. S.E.	Langley	WA	983
16	Rogers	Paula		9123 Orange Drive	Tukwila	WA	981
17	Pender	Sara		889 Island Ave.	Redmond	WA	980
18	Kessler	Allison		7342 King St.	Seattle	WA	981
19	Davidson	Betty		4512 N.E. 60th Ave.	Bellevue	WA	980
20	Spicer	Janet		3312 S. E. 40th Pl.	Tukwila	WA	981

Microsoft Works - [CLIENTS.WDB]
File Edit View Insert Format Tools Window Help
Helv   10   "James asked us not to phone again until September.
Press ALT to choose commands, or F2 to edit.   3   20/20

Fig. 17.15
Turning off Wrap
Text hides long
field contents that
extend beyond the
right field border.

Changing Vertical Alignment in List View

In List view, you can align field entries vertically as well as horizontally. You can tell Works to position field contents at the top, bottom, or center of the field. Notice in figure 17.13 that with **W**rap Text turned on for the

Comments field, the other field entries are formatted with bottom vertical alignment. Works aligns field entries at the bottom of the data cell by default.

Figure 17.16 shows the result of choosing the **T**op alignment option for the Address field. Notice that the addresses of Donna Anderson and James Hawkins are now aligned at the top of the field.

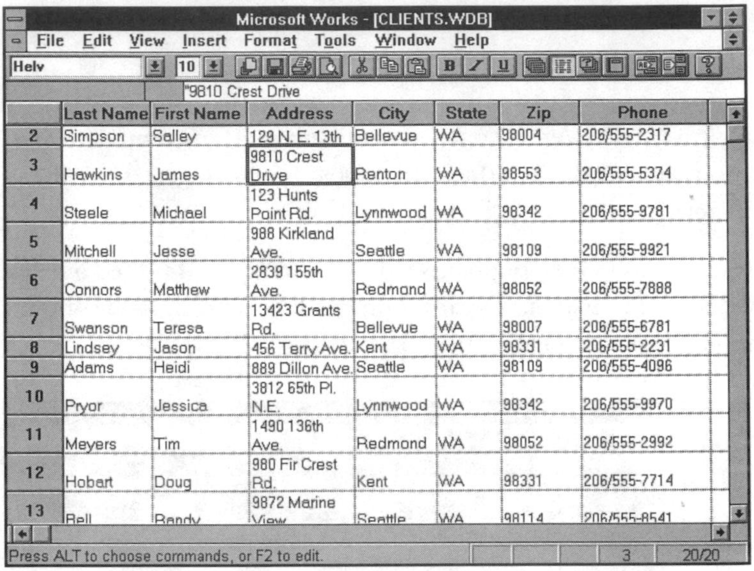

Fig. 17.16
This figure shows the result of formatting the Address field with the Top vertical alignment and the Wrap Text options from the Alignment dialog box.

Follow these steps to change vertical field alignment in List view:

1. Select the field name.

2. From the Forma**t** menu, choose **A**lignment.

Works displays the Alignment dialog box.

3. Select **T**op, **C**enter, or **B**ottom.

4. Choose OK.

Works aligns the field's entries.

Formatting Numbers in Fields

Works can display numbers in a wide variety of formatting options. For example, you can tell Works to format currency amounts with zero or two decimal places, and you can have negative amounts displayed on-screen in red. Works offers formatting options for percentages, fractions, true/false fields, and many other field types. Depending on the type of data you enter in a field, formatting the field appropriately may be important. For example, if you type a percentage amount such as 75% in a field that has the default number format, works formats the percentage as 0.75, which may not be the effect you want.

Choosing a Number Format

When you first create a field, Works automatically formats it as a text field and applies the **G**eneral alignment format, described earlier in this chapter in "Aligning Data in Form View." If you type text in the field, Works formats the text flush left. If you type a number or date in the field, Works automatically formats the number or date flush right. Works applies the **G**eneral number format to any numbers you type in the field. The **G**eneral format is described later in this section.

Follow these steps to change the way Works formats field numbers in Form or List view:

1. Move the highlight into the field. In List view, you also can click the field name.

2. From the Forma**t** menu, choose **N**umber.

    Works displays the Number dialog box (see fig. 17.17).

3. Select a format then choose OK.

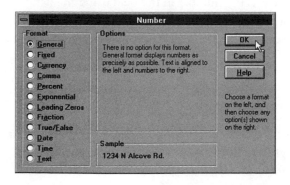

Fig. 17.17
The Number dialog box with available options for selected format.

When you select a format, Works displays any available options for that format. For example, if you choose C**u**rrency, Works displays a text box where you can type the number of decimal places for currency amounts. In an option box, you can tell Works whether to format negative numbers in red.

The following list includes the Format options and their descriptions.

- *General*. The default format. Works aligns text to the left and numbers and dates to the right.

- *Fixed*. Works rounds numbers to the number of decimal places you specify.

- *Currency*. Works formats numbers with a currency symbol. You can specify decimal places and have Works display negative numbers in red.

- *Comma*. Numbers appear with a comma inserted every three places. You can specify decimal places and have Works display negative numbers in red.

- *Percent*. Numbers appear as percentages. For example, if you type .252, Works displays 25.2%. You can specify decimal places.

- *Exponential*. Works displays numbers in scientific notation. For example, 743998 displays as 7.43E+05. You can specify decimal places.

- *Leading Zeros*. Numbers appear with a zero as the first digit. You can specify the number of digits, up to eight. For example, if you specify four digits, Works displays 769 as 0769. If you don't specify Leading Zeros, Works deletes zeros from the start of numbers.

- *Fraction*. Works displays numbers as fractions. The All Fractions option converts a number to its precise fractional value. For example, Works converts .75 to 3/4. If you select a specific fraction from the list box, Works converts the number in the field using the denominator you select. For example, if you select 1/4 and select the Do not reduce check box, Works converts .75 to 3/4; but if you select 1/8, Works converts .75 to 6/8.

- *True/False*. Any number except zero (0) appears as TRUE. A field containing a zero appears as FALSE.

- *Date*. Works enables you to select a date format and display dates accordingly. For details, see "Using Dates and Times" in Chapter 20, "Expanding Your Database Skills."

■ *Time.* Works enables you to select a time format and display times accordingly. For details, see "Using Dates and Times" in Chapter 20, "Expanding Your Database Skills."

■ *Text.* Works enables you to display numbers as text so that leading zeros are not automatically deleted. This choice is good for fields that contain telephone numbers and ZIP codes or other fields containing numbers that may begin with zeros, to prevent Works from deleting the leading zeros.

Changing Default Decimal Places

You can change the default that Works proposes for the number of decimal places when you display format options in the Number dialog box. For example, when you choose **P**ercent, **C**omma, or **C**urrency, Works proposes two decimal places.

To change the default decimal places, follow these steps:

1. From the T**o**ols menu, choose **O**ptions.

Works displays the Options dialog box (see fig. 17.18).

2. Select Default num**b**er of decimals and type the new number of decimals.

3. Choose OK.

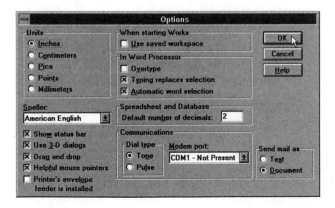

Fig. 17.18
The Options dialog box enables you to change the number of default decimals and other Works Database defaults.

Works proposes the new number of decimals in any text box where a decimal place option is available.

Note

When you change the default decimal place setting, Works does not automatically reformat any fields that you created before you changed the default. To reformat existing fields, you must repeat the steps described earlier in this chapter in the section "Formatting Numbers in Fields."

From Here...

In this chapter, you learned how to create and work with fields to develop a simple Works Database form. To learn more about the Works Database, see the following chapters:

- Chapter 18, "Enhancing a Database Form," shows you how to spruce up your database forms with labels, fonts, rectangles, borders, colors, shading, drawings, pictures, Note-Its, and WordArt.

- Chapter 19, "Entering and Editing Data," teaches you how to type data and save records. You also learn how to copy and move information and hide records.

- Chapter 20, "Expanding Your Database Skills," shows you how to sort and print records, use dates, times, math formulas and functions, protect your data, and format data in fields.

- In Chapter 21, "Retrieving Database Information," you learn how to retrieve information from a database by using specific criteria (for example, retrieving only the records where the state is *WA*).

- Chapter 22, "Creating a Database Report," tells you how to print database information in neatly formatted lists.

- In Chapter 23, "Customizing a Report," you learn how to create reports that require customized formatting and data selection, and how to print reports for use with other applications.

Chapter 18

Enhancing a Database Form

In Chapter 17, "Creating and Editing a Database Form," you learn how to create a simple database form. In this chapter, you learn how to make your forms more visually attractive.

Creating Field Labels and Text

In the Works Database form view, you can insert descriptive text and labels to guide the user around a form and provide other useful information.

For example, if you have two databases that use identical name-and-address forms, you easily may forget which database you are working in. Placing a descriptive label at the top of each form saves the user from checking the Works or Database title bar to find out which database is active. Alternatively, you can use labels to provide useful information, such as how to format phone numbers (see fig. 18.1).

To create a label in a database form:

1. Move the cursor to the position where you want to place the label.

2. Type the label's text, using any fonts and character enhancements (see "Using Fonts" later in this chapter).

3. Press Enter.

This chapter shows you how to perform the following tasks:

■ Enhance a database form with labels and descriptive text

■ Use rectangles, borders, colors, and shading to set off areas of a form

■ Add drawings and pictures to lend visual appeal and guide users

Fig. 18.1

Labels can identify the database and tell other users how to format data.

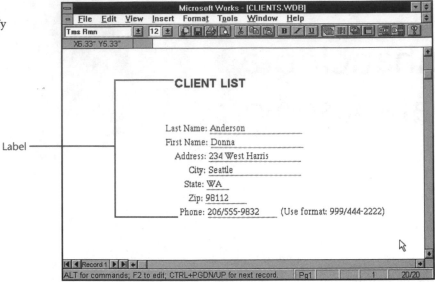

Label

Works inserts the label in the form. If the label is not positioned exactly where you want it, you can move the label. See the next section "Moving a Label."

Unlike field names, labels don't end with a colon. If you want to create a label that ends with a colon, begin the label with a double-quotation mark (") and end with a colon; if you don't type the double-quotation mark, Works interprets the label as a field name.

Moving a Label

To move a label with the mouse, click and drag the label to the new position on the form. For information about moving fields on a form, including using gridlines to position fields and labels, see "Moving a Field in Form View," "Using Snap to Grid," and "Moving a Field in List View," in Chapter 17, "Creating and Editing a Database Form."

To move a label with the keyboard, follow these steps:

1. Highlight the label.

   To highlight a label, click it; or move the highlight onto the label with the arrow keys.

2. From the **E**dit menu, choose Postion Selection.

3. Move the label with the arrow keys.

4. Press Enter.

Works places the label in the new position.

Deleting a Label

You may need to remove labels when you redesign a form or you discover that you don't need the label. Follow these steps:

1. Highlight the label.

2. Press Delete; or choose Delete **S**election from the **I**nsert menu.

Works removes the label immediately. To undo a deletion, before you make another deletion, choose **U**ndo Delete Selection from the **E**dit menu; or press Ctrl+Z.

Using Fonts

You can use *fonts* in the Works Database form and list views to create a decorative effect, to make text stand out on the page, or to fit more information on-screen. On a database form, you can type labels, field names, and field contents in different fonts. You even can use the Works WordArt utility to create special effects with text. (See "Using Microsoft Draw, WordArt, and Note-It" later in this chapter.)

> **Note**
>
> What is the difference between a font and a typeface? A *typeface* is a family of similar-looking fonts. For example, Microsoft Windows includes a TrueType typeface called Century, with two font variations: Century Gothic and Century-WP. A typeface may have dozens of fonts. The Works font list on the toolbar lists the fonts available with your printer.

Selecting a Font with the Mouse

Before you can type text with a new font, you must select the font from the Works font list.

Follow these steps to select a font:

1. Select the field names or labels you want to change. To highlight multiple names, hold down Ctrl and click each name or label.

or

Position the cursor where you want to begin typing with the new font.

2. Click the Font Name toolbar arrow to drop down the Font Name list box (see fig. 18.2).

Fig. 18.2

A database form with field names highlighted and the Font Name list box displayed.

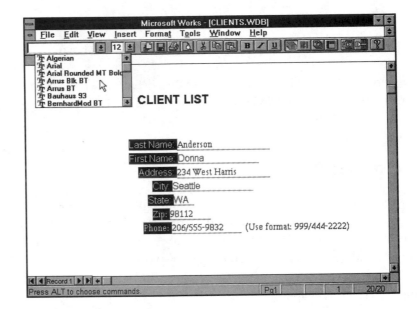

3. Click the font you want to apply.

Works changes the highlighted text to the font you selected or enables you to begin typing with the new font.

4. To change the font size, click the Font Size toolbar arrow. Then type a new size or click a size on the drop-down list.

Works adjusts the highlighted text to the selected font size or enables you to begin typing in the new size.

To reverse your changes, before choosing another format command or deleting text, choose **U**ndo Format from the **E**dit menu; or press Ctrl+Z.

Selecting a Font with the Keyboard

You can select a font with the keyboard. Follow these steps:

1. Highlight the field names or labels you want to change

   or

   Position the cursor where you want to begin typing with the new font.

2. From the Forma**t** menu, choose **F**ont and Style.

   Works displays the Font and Style dialog box (see fig. 18.3)

3. In the Font and Style dialog box, choose **F**ont and select a font from the list box.

4. To change the font size, click a number in the **S**ize list; or type a number in the **S**ize text box.

5. Choose OK.

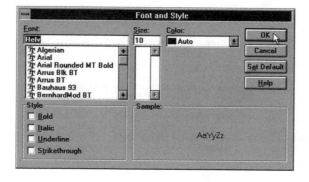

Fig. 18.3
Use the Font and Style dialog box to select fonts with the keyboard.

Works converts the highlighted text to the selected font or enables you to begin typing with the new font.

Choosing a Font Color

Works can display fonts in color on color monitors. Using color is a good way to set off labels and field names on-screen. With a supported color printer, color fonts also print in color. If your printer doesn't support color, these fonts print in black.

To change the color of a field, label, or field name:

1. Highlight the text you want to change

   or

   Position the cursor where you want to begin typing in color.

2. Choose Forma**t**, **F**ont and Style.

   Works displays the Font and Style dialog box (again see fig. 18.3.)

3. Choose C**o**lor to drop down the list box.

4. Select a color from the list then choose OK. Works returns to the Database window and applies the color to the highlighted text.

Choosing Character Enhancements

You can make text bold, italic, underlined, or leave it plain. You can use the Font and Style dialog box, but using the toolbar or keyboard is much quicker. Follow these steps:

1. Highlight the text you want to change

   or

   Position the cursor where you want to begin typing with the character enhancement.

2. On the toolbar, click the Bold, Italic, or Underline button.

3. To remove an enhancement, click the toolbar button again. For example, to remove bold, click the bold button.

   or

   Press Ctrl+B for bold, Ctrl+I for italic, Ctrl+U for underline, or Ctrl+space bar for plain text.

To use the Font and Style dialog box, repeat step 1 then choose Forma**t**, **F**ont and Style. Select the **B**old, **I**talic, **U**nderline, or **St**rikethrough check box, then choose OK.

Changing the Default Font

You can change the font that Works uses by default. This step is useful when you find that you use another font more often than the current default font.

Tip
You can select font, font size, font style, and color at the same time in the Font and Style dialog box.

Follow these steps to change the default font:

1. Choose Format, Font and Style.

2. In the Font and Style dialog box, select a Font, Size, Color, and Style.

3. Choose Set Default then choose OK.

4. When Works prompts you to confirm the new default, choose Yes to return to the Database window.

Works uses the new default font and style for all future documents. Changing the default font does not change any fonts you have used in existing documents, however.

Using Rectangles, Borders, Colors, and Shading

In the Works Database form view, you can organize and enhance your Database input forms with rectangles, borders, colors, and shading. For example, you may want to highlight a message to the user by placing the message in a shaded, colored rectangle.

In list and report views, you can add shading but not rectangles or colors. Any shading you apply in list view also appears in report view; but shading in form view does not appear in list or report views.

Creating Rectangles in Form View

Rectangles are very useful for organizing database forms so the user can find labels and data entry areas quickly. For example, you may want to set apart two separate areas on a database form, one area for a customer's name, address, and customer identification number, and the other area for the customer's credit information.

To create a rectangle in form view:

1. Position the cursor where you want the rectangle.

2. Choose Rectangle from the Insert menu.

Works inserts a standard, square, gray-edged rectangle at the insertion point (see fig. 18.4).

Fig. 18.4

When you first create a rectangle, Works inserts a grayed rectangle at the insertion point.

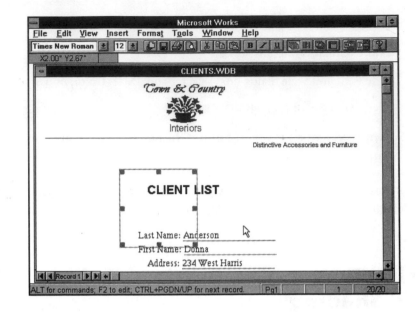

Sizing and Moving Rectangles

After inserting a rectangle, you can change its size or move the rectangle anywhere on the form. Follow these steps to resize a rectangle with the mouse:

1. Click the rectangle. Works displays resize handles around the object.

2. Move the mouse cursor onto a resizing handle. The cursor becomes a box and double arrow labeled with the word RESIZE.

3. Drag the handles to the new size.

To move a rectangle with the mouse, follow these steps:

1. Click the rectangle. Works displays resize handles around the object.

2. Move the mouse cursor onto the object until the word DRAG appears under the arrow.

3. Drag the object to the new location.

To move a rectangle with the keyboard, follow these steps:

1. Highlight the rectangle by moving the cursor onto the rectangle with the arrow keys.

When you move the cursor onto the object, resizing handles appear.

 2. Choose Position Selection from the **E**dit menu.

    The mouse cursor becomes a double arrow labeled with the word DRAG.

 3. Use the arrow keys to move the object to a new position.

 4. Press Enter to drop the object in the new location.

Figure 18.5 shows the form label CLIENT LIST enclosed in a rectangle.

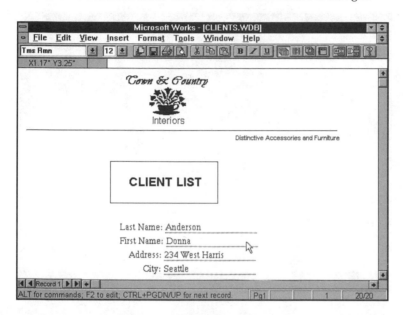

Fig. 18.5
A database label
formatted in a
rectangle.

IV

Databases

Note

The *Snap to Grid* feature makes positioning objects easier. (Snap to Grid is available only in Form view.) With Snap to Grid turned on, Works automatically aligns objects with the nearest invisible vertical and horizontal gridlines. Invisible gridlines are positioned .08" apart horizontally and in increments of one line vertically, measured at the height of the current font. With Snap to Grid turned off, you can position objects more precisely, in increments of a hundredth inch (.01").

To turn Snap to Grid on or off, choose **S**nap to Grid from the Forma**t** menu.

Creating a Border

After you create a rectangle, you must size and move the rectangle to achieve the effect you want. With the border feature, Works places a correctly formatted border around a database label or other object—you don't need to move or resize the border.

You can use borders to quickly format labels and other objects. You can use rectangles in any size for special effects. Figure 18.6 shows a label formatted with a rectangle and a border.

Fig. 18.6
A database label formatted with a rectangle and double-line border.

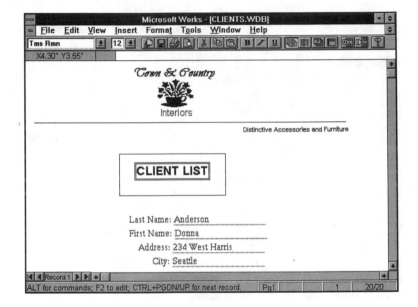

Follow these steps to create borders:

1. Select the object you want to format with a border.

   To select more than one object, hold down Control and click each object.

2. From the Format menu, choose order.

   Works displays the Border dialog box (see fig. 18.7).

3. From the Line Style list box, select a style for the border.

4. To change the border's color, select a color from the Color drop-down list box.

5. Choose OK.

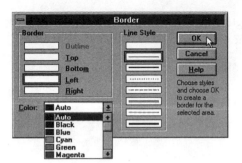

Fig. 18.7
The Border
dialog box.

Works adds the border to any elements you selected.

Deleting a Border

You easily can remove a border if, for example, you decide the border is unnecessary or unattractive. Follow these steps:

1. Click the bordered object to select it.

   To select more than one object, hold down Control and click each object.

2. From the Format menu, choose **B**order.

3. In the **Li**ne Style list box, select the empty line style.

4. Choose OK.

Works removes the border from the elements you selected.

Using Bring to Front and Send to Back

When you create an object such as a rectangle or drawing, Works places it on top of any other existing objects. For example, in figure 18.6, a database label was formatted first with a rectangle, then a border. The label border is layered on top of the rectangle. Clicking the label selects the label and its border, not the rectangle. Before you can select the rectangle, you must select the label and send it to the back.

Follow these steps to bring an object to the front or send it to the back:

1. Select the object.

2. Choose **S**end to Back from the Forma**t** menu.

   or

   Choose **Br**ing to Front from the Forma**t** menu.

You now can select the front object by clicking it or moving the cursor onto the object with the arrow keys.

Using Color and Shading

Earlier in this chapter, you learned to apply color to fonts and borders. In this section, you learn to add color and shading to labels, fields, and field names, or to an entire database form.

Follow these steps:

1. Select the element you want to format with color and/or shading. To select more than one object, hold down Control and click each object.

   or

   To add color and/or shading to an entire database form, do not select any objects.

2. From the Format menu, choose **P**atterns.

   Works displays the Patterns dialog box (see fig. 18.8).

Fig. 18.8
The Patterns
dialog box.

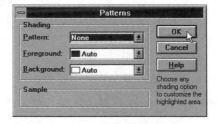

Tip
Choosing a foreground color and the default background color (white) creates a much lighter color than if you select a background color and the default foreground color (black).

3. Choose **P**attern and select a pattern from the drop-down list.

4. Choose **F**oreground and select a foreground color.

5. Choose **B**ackground and select a background color.

   Works displays your choices of pattern and colors in the example box.

6. Choose OK.

Works applies the pattern and colors to the objects you selected or to the entire form if you did not select any objects.

> **Note**
>
> The foreground color applies to the lines in the pattern. The background color applies to the spaces between the lines in the pattern. If you select a solid pattern, only the foreground color appears.

The field names in figure 18.9 were formatted with shading and borders using the preceding steps and the steps given earlier in this chapter under "Creating a Border."

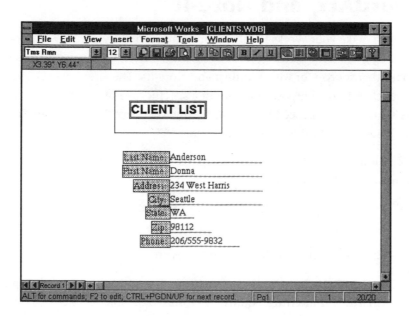

Fig. 18.9
Field names formatted with shading and borders.

Removing Color and Shading

You can remove color and shading from a rectangle, form, or other object. Follow these steps:

1. Select the objects from which you want to remove color and shading

or

To remove color and shading from the entire form, don't select any objects.

2. From the Format menu, choose **Patterns**.

3. From the **Patterns** drop-down list, select None.

4. Choose OK.

Works removes color and shading from the selected objects or the form.

Using Microsoft Draw, ClipArt, WordArt, and Note-It

You can make your Works Database forms more visually attractive by enhancing them with drawings from the Works ClipArt library, with pictures from other sources, or with WordArt and Note-Its. These features can provide visual clues to the purpose of a form or a specific area of a form. To learn how to use these options, see Chapter 24, "Using Microsoft Draw and ClipArt," and Chapter 25, "Using WordArt and Note-It."

The following steps briefly review the procedure for inserting ClipArt, WordArt, or a Note-It note:

1. Position the cursor where you want to insert the ClipArt, WordArt, or Note-It note.

2. Choose **I**nsert then choose Clip**A**rt, **W**ordArt, or Not**e**-It.

3. Follow the steps in the appropriate sections of Chapter 14, "Creating Charts," for inserting a drawing, WordArt, or Note-It note.

From Here...

In this chapter, you learned about enhancing Works database forms with labels, descriptive text, fonts, rectangles, borders, colors, and shading. To expand your knowledge of enhancing Works database forms, see the following chapters:

■ In Chapter 19, "Entering and Editing Data," you learn how to type data and save records. In addition, you learn to copy and move information and hide records.

- In Chapter 24, "Using Microsoft Draw and ClipArt," you learn about inserting and editing drawings in documents. You also learn about using clip art.

- In Chapter 25, "Using WordArt and Note-It," you learn how to add WordArt and Note-Its to decorate your documents and create pop-up reminders and hints.

IV

Databases

Chapter 19

Entering and Editing Data

In Chapters 16, 17, and 18, you learn how to create and customize database forms. After you design and save a form, you can begin entering information in the database.

Entering Information in a Works Database

To store information in a Works database, you first create a database form and type the information in the fields. Creating forms is discussed in Chapter 17, "Creating and Editing a Database Form." After you finish entering information in the fields for the current record, you can save the information by saving the record. Or, you can tell Works to add a new, empty record to the database so you can fill in the record and save it.

You can type information in fields in Form view or List view. In Chapter 26, "Using the Works Tools Together," you learn how to save data from other applications in a Works Database.

A Works Database field may contain numbers or text. To find out how to format number and text fields, see "Aligning Data in Text Fields" and "Formatting Numbers in Fields" in Chapter 17, "Creating and Editing a Database Form."

In this chapter, you learn about the following topics:

- Entering data in database fields

- Editing data in a field

- Adding new records to a database

- Copying and moving data between fields

- Copying and moving fields and records

- Hiding fields and records

Entering Data in the Form

Typing information in a Works Database form is easy. You use the following steps in Form or List view:

1. Highlight the field.

   To highlight a field in Form view, click the field. In List view, click the fields name. Or using the keyboard, press the arrow or tab keys to move the highlight into the field. In Form view, don't highlight the field name. The field is to the right of the field name. In List view, the field is in the column under the fields title at top of the column. Figure 19.1 shows a database record with the Address field highlighted.

Fig. 19.1
A database record with the Address field highlighted.

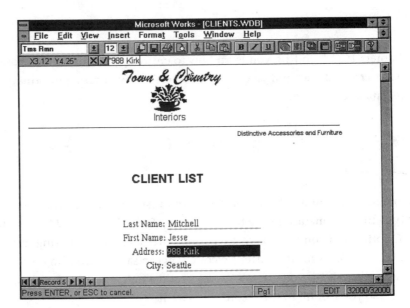

2. Type the data.

3. Move to the next field by clicking the next field or pressing Tab or using the arrow keys. You can move to the previous field by clicking the previous field or pressing Shift+Tab or using the arrow keys.

Editing Data in a Field

After you type data in a Works database form, you can make changes to the information in a field. You can make changes in Form view or List view, and your changes take effect in both views.

Works enables you to insert new data in a field or edit existing data in the field. To replace the information in a field, follow these steps:

1. Highlight the field and type the new entry.

When you type the first character of the new entry, Works deletes the old entry and begins inserting your new keystrokes.

2. After you finish typing the new entry, press Enter or click the Enter box on the formula bar. (The Enter box is the check mark at the left end of the data entry area on the formula bar.)

To make changes to an existing field entry, follow these steps:

1. Highlight the field.

2. Click the formula bar or press F2.

Works moves the cursor into the data entry area of the formula bar.

3. Use the editing keys to edit the entry. Table 19.1 shows the keystrokes and mouse actions you can use to edit information in a Works Database field.

4. Press Enter or click the Enter box.

Table 19.1 Data Editing Keystrokes and Mouse Actions		
Action	**Mouse**	**Keyboard**
Move to beginning of line	Click beginning of line	Home
Move to end of line	Click end of line	End
Left one character	Click left one character	Left arrow
Right one character	Click right one character	Right arrow
Move insertion point	Click to correct position	Arrow keys
Highlight characters	Drag mouse pointer	Shift+arrow keys
Delete highlighted characters		Delete

Clearing Data from a Field

In the preceding section, you learned how to edit information in a field and replace field data. You also can clear information from one or more fields, including fields that contain formulas. Follow these steps:

Tip
To reverse the effect of choosing Clear Field entry, choose **Edit**, **Undo** or press Ctrl+Z before you choose another command.

1. In Form view or List view, highlight the field or fields you want to clear.

2. Choose Clear Field Entry from the Edit menu or press Delete.

   Works clears the field entry. If you previously applied formatting commands to the field (for example, right alignment), Works retains the formatting.

Creating New Records

After you have entered data in the last field of the last record in Form view, press Tab. Works moves the cursor to the first field of a new record (see fig. 19.2). In List view, you must move the highlight to the first field of the next record.

Fig. 19.2
Pressing Tab in the last field of the last record in Form view moves the highlight to the first field in a new, blank record.

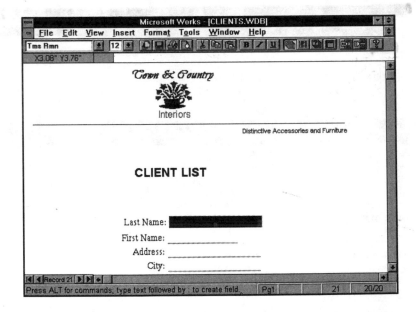

You can add a new record in Form view with the mouse. In the status bar, click the second right-pointing arrow. Works moves the insertion point to the first field in a new, blank record at the end of the file. To add a new record *before* the record that is currently displayed in Form view or List view, click the Insert Record toolbar button.

In List view, you can insert a new record anywhere in a database by following these steps:

1. Highlight the record below the row where you want to insert the new record. Then from the **I**nsert menu, choose **R**ecord/Field. Works displays the Insert dialog box (see fig. 19.3).

2. Choose **R**ecord.

3. Choose OK. Works inserts a new record above the highlighted row.

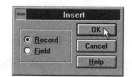

IV

Databases

Tip
To add more than one record in a single step, follow step 1 but highlight the same number of existing records as the number of new records you want to add.

Fig. 19.3
To insert a new record in List view, use the Insert dialog box.

To insert a new record anywhere in a database in Form view, follow these steps:

1. Move the cursor to the record before the position where you want to insert a new record.

2. From the Insert menu, choose Record.

   Works inserts a new, blank record and places the insertion point in the first field.

Deleting Records

You quickly can remove records in Form or List view. When you delete a record, Works renumbers all the remaining records.

Follow these steps to delete a record in List view:

1. Highlight any data in the record you want to delete.

2. From the **I**nsert menu, choose **D**elete Record/Field.

3. In the Delete dialog box, choose **R**ecord.

4. Choose OK.

   Works deletes the record immediately, without asking for confirmation.

Follow these steps to delete a record in Form view:

Tip

To restore a record
you deleted in
Form or List view,
before you choose
other program
commands, choose
Undo Delete
Record from the
Edit menu; or
press Ctrl+Z.

1. Display the record you want to delete.

2. Choose **D**elete Record from the **I**nsert menu.

Works deletes the record immediately, without asking for confirmation.

Using Formulas To Enter Data in Fields

Works enables you to perform math calculations on numbers in fields. When
Works performs the calculation you specified, it inserts the result in the field
that contains the formula. For example, figure 19.4 shows a database form
with a calculated field.

Fig. 19.4

Works calculates a
formula when you
type information
in fields used in
the calculation.

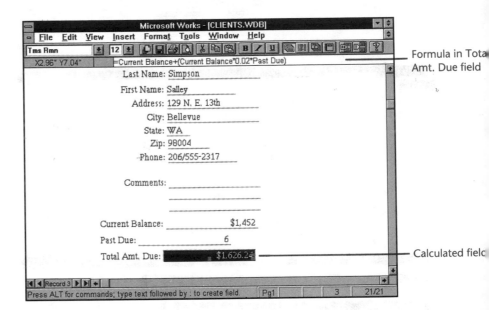

Notice in figure 19.4 that the field named Total Amt. Due is highlighted and
the formula used to calculate the amount due appears in the formula bar:

```
=Current Balance+(Current Balance*0.02*Past Due)
```

As the figure shows, when you type the Current Balance and the Past Due
amounts, Works automatically inserts the result of the formula in the Total
Amt. Due field. For a full description of writing formulas, see "Using Math
Formulas and Functions" in Chapter 20, "Expanding Your Database Skills."

Follow these steps to create a formula in a field in Form or List view:

1. Highlight the field where you want to create a formula.

2. Type an equals sign (=), then type the formula.

   As you type, the formula appears in the field and in the formula bar.

3. Press Enter.

   Works calculates the formula and inserts the results in the field. After you create a formula, Works calculates the formula in the field for each record you display.

Clearing Formulas

The steps to clear a formula from a field are different from the steps to clear a field entry.

To clear a formula from a field in Form view, follow these steps:

1. Highlight the field.

2. From the **E**dit menu, choose Cl**e**ar Formula.

   Works removes the formula from that field in all the records in the database.

Inserting Numbers or Dates in Multiple Records

In List view, Works can automatically enter a series of numbers or dates into adjacent records. For example, you can tell Works to insert a series of dates five days apart into adjacent records for the period 10/15/93 to 10/14/96. This procedure is very useful for numbering invoices, parts lists, and so on.

To number or date several records sequentially, follow these steps:

1. In List view, type a starting date or number in the first field of the series.

   Figure 19.5 shows the number 1 entered in the Employee # field in the first record of a database.

2. Press Enter or click the Enter box in the formula bar (the box with a check mark).

3. Highlight the fields in which you want to insert the series of dates or numbers.

Fig. 19.5
To begin number-
ing or dating
adjacent records,
type the first
number of the
series in the first
record.

	Address	City	State	Zip	Phone	Next Contact	
						1/1/94	
1	Harris	Seattle	WA	98112	206/555-9832		1/1/94
2	129 N. E. 13th	Bellevue	WA	98004	206/555-2317		1/6/94
3	Drive	Renton	WA	98553	206/555-5374		1/11/94
4	Point Rd.	Lynnwood	WA	98342	206/555-9781		1/16/94
5	Ave.	Seattle	WA	98109	206/555-9921		1/21/94
6	Ave.	Redmond	WA	98052	206/555-7888		1/26/94
7	Rd.	Bellevue	WA	98007	206/555-6781		1/31/94
8	456 Terry Ave.	Kent	WA	98331	206/555-2231		2/5/94
9	889 Dillon Ave.	Seattle	WA	98109	206/555-4096		2/10/94
10	N.E.	Lynnwood	WA	98342	206/555-9970		2/15/94
11	Ave.	Redmond	WA	98052	206/555-2992		2/20/94
12	Rd.	Kent	WA	98331	206/555-7714		2/25/94
13	View	Seattle	WA	98114	206/555-8541		3/2/94
14	Road	Redmond	WA	98052	206/555-7747		3/7/94
15	S.E.	Langley	WA	98312	206/555-8338		3/12/94
16	Drive	Tukwila	WA	98131	206/555-2210		3/17/94
17	Ave.	Redmond	WA	98052	206/555-8176		3/22/94
18	7342 King St.	Seattle	WA	98109	206/555-1976		3/27/94
19	Ave.	Bellevue	WA	98004	206/555-1454		4/1/94
20	Pl.	Tukwila	WA	98131	206/555-3198		4/6/94
21							

Press ALT to choose commands, or F2 to edit.   1   32000/32000

4. From the **E**dit menu, choose **Fi**ll Series.

   Works displays the Fill Series dialog box (see fig. 19.6).

Fig. 19.6
Use the Fill Series
dialog box to
insert numbers,
dates, weekdays,
months, or years.

5. Choose a unit: **N**umber, **D**ay, **W**eekday, **M**onth, or **Y**ear.

6. Type a numeric interval in the **S**tep by text box.

   For example, if you want to number a series of records in intervals of
   10, type **10** in the **S**tep by text box. To number the adjacent records
   in descending order, type a negative number.

7. Choose OK.

   Works numbers the records.

Figure 19.7 shows the results of numbering the first 10 records in increments
of 10.

	Client No.	Last Name	First Name	Address	City	State	Zip	Pho
1	1200	Anderson	Donna	Harris	Seattle	WA	98112	206/555-9
2	1210	Simpson	Salley	129 N. E. 13th	Bellevue	WA	98004	206/555-2
3	1220	Hawkins	James	Drive	Renton	WA	98553	206/555-5
4	1230	Steele	Michael	Point Rd.	Lynnwood	WA	98342	206/555-9
5	1240	Mitchell	Jesse	Ave.	Seattle	WA	98109	206/555-9
6	1250	Connors	Matthew	Ave.	Redmond	WA	98052	206/555-7
7	1260	Swanson	Teresa	Rd.	Bellevue	WA	98007	206/555-6
8	1270	Lindsey	Jason	456 Terry Ave.	Kent	WA	98331	206/555-2
9	1280	Adams	Heidi	889 Dillon Ave.	Seattle	WA	98109	206/555-4
10	1290	Pryor	Jessica	N.E.	Lynnwood	WA	98342	206/555-2
11	1300	Meyers	Tim	Ave.	Redmond	WA	98052	206/555-2
12	1310	Hobart	Doug	Rd.	Kent	WA	98331	206/555-7
13	1320	Bell	Randy	View	Seattle	WA	98114	206/555-8
14	1330	Stein	Garth	Road	Redmond	WA	98052	206/555-7
15	1340	Harris	Robert	S.E.	Langley	WA	98312	206/555-8
16	1350	Rogers	Paula	Drive	Tukwila	WA	98131	206/555-2
17	1360	Pender	Sara	Ave.	Redmond	WA	98052	206/555-8
18	1370	Kessler	Allison	7342 King St.	Seattle	WA	98109	206/555-1
19	1380	Davidson	Betty	Ave.	Bellevue	WA	98004	206/555-1
20	1390	Spicer	Janet	Pl.	Tukwila	WA	98131	206/555-3
21								

Fig. 19.7
The Fill Series feature can automatically insert numbers in fields.

IV

Databases

Troubleshooting

When I try to remove a formula, Works removes the formula only from the current record.

To remove a formula from all fields in a database in List view, be sure to highlight all field entries in the database. To highlight all entries, click the field name; or move the highlight into the field and press Shift+F8.

I need to remove the results of a formula from just one record in a database. Is that possible?

To remove the field contents that Works enters when it calculates a formula, without removing the formula from any other records in the database, just type the new entry in the field.

Copying and Moving Data

You can copy and move information to another location in a Works Database, or you can copy and move Database information to another Works application. Copying leaves the original information and inserts a copy at a new location. Moving deletes the original information and inserts it at a new location.

For example, you can copy data from one record to another, or you can copy an entire record into a Works Word Processor document. To find out how to copy and move information between applications, see Chapter 26, "Using the Works Tools Together." The following sections describe copying and moving information within the Database.

Copying and Moving Data in a Field

You can copy or move the information you enter in a field. Before you can copy or move the information, you must highlight it. To highlight a field's contents in Form or List view, click the field data entry area, or move the highlight into the field with Tab or with the arrow keys.

You can also highlight more than one field and copy or move the contents of the selected fields in one step. To highlight more than one field with the mouse in Form view, hold down the Ctrl key and click each field. (You cannot do this in List view.) To highlight a series of fields in Form view or List view, click the first field, then hold down Shift and click the last field in the series.

You can select the contents of multiple fields and copy or paste them into multiple fields elsewhere, but be careful, since copying or moving information into fields that already contain data may produce undesirable results. You can also move or copy an entire record into a new record, as described later in this chapter in "Copying and Moving Records."

To copy or move the field contents you have selected, follow these steps:

1. To *copy* the information in a field, highlight the information, and then choose **C**opy from the **E**dit menu; press Ctrl+C; or click the Copy toolbar button.

   or

   To *move* the information, choose Cu**t** from the **E**dit menu; press Ctrl+X; or click the Cut toolbar button.

2. Highlight the field where you want to insert the cut or copied information.

3. From the **E**dit menu, choose **P**aste; or press Ctrl+V; or click the Paste toolbar button.

Works inserts the copied or cut information into the highlighted field, replacing any existing field contents.

> **Note**
>
> Moving records may leave empty records behind. You should delete these records to avoid undesirable results when printing the database.

Using Drag and Drop in List View

In List view, you can move Database information quickly with the mouse. This method is called *drag and drop*. Drag and drop does not work in Form view.

To use drag and drop, first select the information you want to move or copy. For example, to select a database record, click its number. Or to select an entire field, click its name.

To move the selected information, move the mouse cursor onto one of the borders of the selection until the mouse cursor displays the word DRAG (see fig. 19.8).

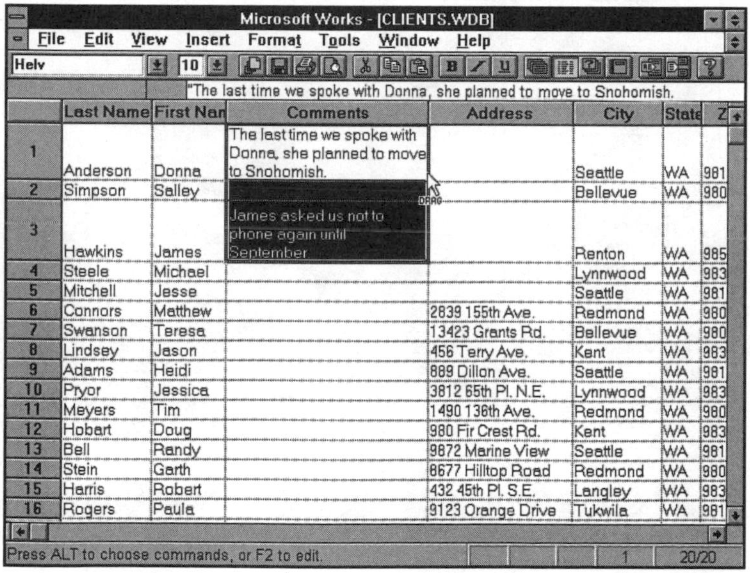

Fig. 19.8
When you move the cursor onto the border of a selection, the cursor displays the word DRAG.

You then click the mouse button and drag the selection to a new location. While you drag, the mouse cursor displays the word MOVE (see fig. 19.9). If you hold down Ctrl while you drag, Works copies the selection and the mouse cursor displays the word COPY (see fig. 19.10).

Fig. 19.9
When you drag a selection, the mouse cursor displays the word MOVE.

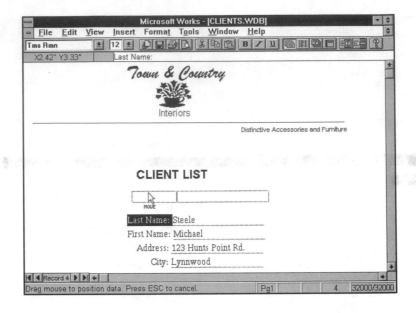

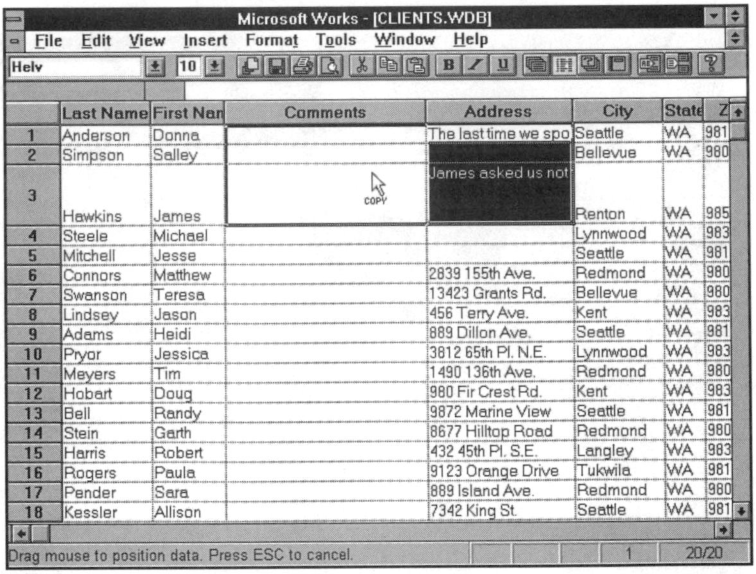

Fig. 19.10
If you hold down the Ctrl key while dragging a selection, the mouse cursor displays the word COPY.

When you release the mouse button, Works inserts the moved or copied information.

If you move field contents vertically, Works inserts the field contents in the record(s) above the record that contains the mouse cursor. If you move field

IV

Databases

contents horizontally, Works inserts the selection in the field to the left of the field that contains the mouse cursor. To cancel a drag-and-drop operation after you begin dragging a selection, press Esc. Works restores the highlight at the original location.

> **Note**
>
> The drag-and-drop method of copying and moving information with the mouse does not work to move information in Form view, but you can use it while designing a form. Drag and drop *does* work with field contents in List view, however.

Tip

To undo a drag-and-drop operation, before you perform any other actions, choose **U**ndo Drag and Drop from the **E**dit menu; or press Ctrl+Z.

Copying and Moving Fields and Records

In the previous sections, you learned to copy and move information in fields. You can also copy and move entire fields and records. For example, you may find it helpful to place several records next to each other in List view in order to view them without scrolling.

Copying and Moving Fields

Works lets you copy and move fields while you design a form or later, after you have entered information in your database. Moving fields is especially useful. For example, you might discover that you enter information in certain fields always but seldom enter information in other fields. By placing the most-used fields adjacent to each other, you can enter data without having to move over seldom-used fields.

Figures 19.11 and 19.12 show the results of exchanging the positions of the First Name and Last Name fields by using the following steps:

1. In List view, select the First Name field.

2. Choose Cu**t** from the **E**dit menu; or click the Cut toolbar button; or press Ctrl+X.

3. Select the Last Name Field.

4. Choose **P**aste from the **E**dit menu; click the Paste toolbar button; or press Ctrl+V.

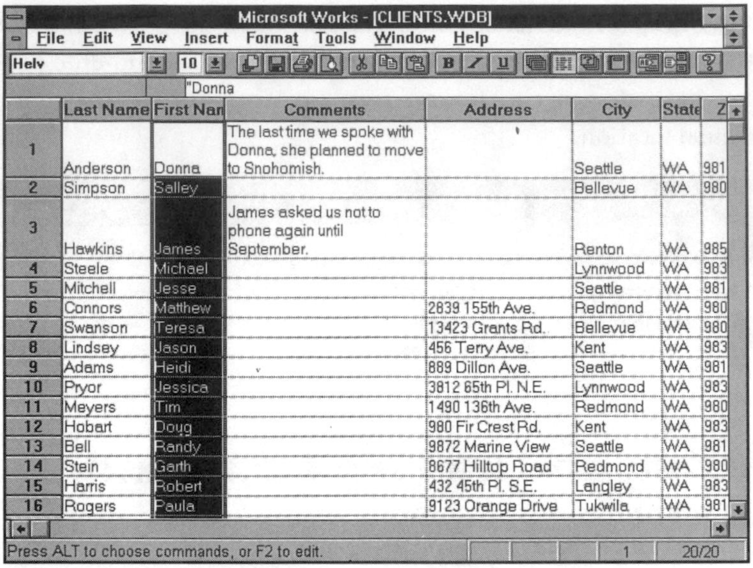
Microsoft Works - [CLIENTS.WDB]
File Edit View Insert Format Tools Window Help
Helv 10
"Donna
Last Name First Nar Comments Address City State Z
1 Anderson Donna The last time we spoke with Donna, she planned to move to Snohomish. Seattle WA 981
2 Simpson Salley Bellevue WA 980
3 Hawkins James James asked us not to phone again until September. Renton WA 985
4 Steele Michael Lynnwood WA 983
5 Mitchell Jesse Seattle WA 981
6 Connors Matthew 2839 155th Ave. Redmond WA 980
7 Swanson Teresa 13423 Grants Rd. Bellevue WA 980
8 Lindsey Jason 456 Terry Ave. Kent WA 983
9 Adams Heidi 889 Dillon Ave. Seattle WA 981
10 Pryor Jessica 3812 65th Pl. N.E. Lynnwood WA 983
11 Meyers Tim 1490 136th Ave. Redmond WA 980
12 Hobart Doug 980 Fir Crest Rd. Kent WA 983
13 Bell Randy 9872 Marine View Seattle WA 981
14 Stein Garth 8677 Hilltop Road Redmond WA 980
15 Harris Robert 432 45th Pl. S.E. Langley WA 983
16 Rogers Paula 9123 Orange Drive Tukwila WA 981
Press ALT to choose commands, or F2 to edit. 1 20/20

Fig. 19.11
The First Name field highlighted.

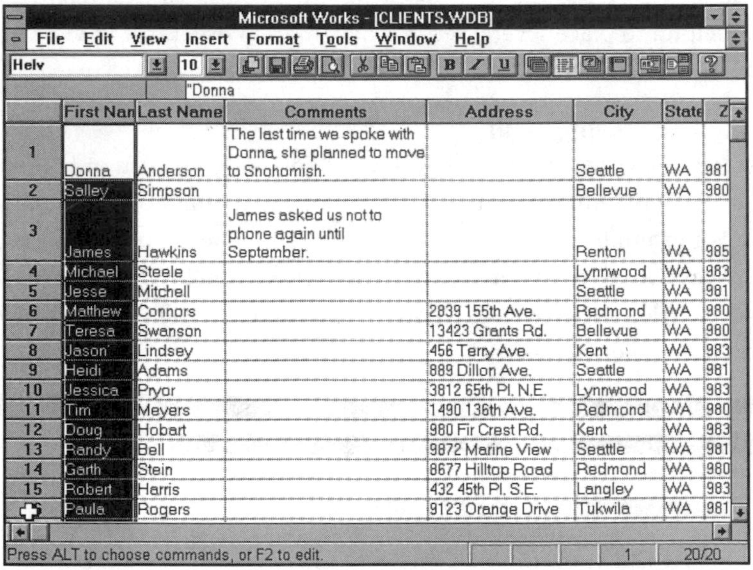
Microsoft Works - [CLIENTS.WDB]
File Edit View Insert Format Tools Window Help
Helv 10
"Donna
First Nar Last Name Comments Address City State Z
1 Donna Anderson The last time we spoke with Donna, she planned to move to Snohomish. Seattle WA 981
2 Salley Simpson Bellevue WA 980
3 James Hawkins James asked us not to phone again until September. Renton WA 985
4 Michael Steele Lynnwood WA 983
5 Jesse Mitchell Seattle WA 981
6 Matthew Connors 2839 155th Ave. Redmond WA 980
7 Teresa Swanson 13423 Grants Rd. Bellevue WA 980
8 Jason Lindsey 456 Terry Ave. Kent WA 983
9 Heidi Adams 889 Dillon Ave. Seattle WA 981
10 Jessica Pryor 3812 65th Pl. N.E. Lynnwood WA 983
11 Tim Meyers 1490 136th Ave. Redmond WA 980
12 Doug Hobart 980 Fir Crest Rd. Kent WA 983
13 Randy Bell 9872 Marine View Seattle WA 981
14 Garth Stein 8677 Hilltop Road Redmond WA 980
15 Robert Harris 432 45th Pl. S.E. Langley WA 983
Paula Rogers 9123 Orange Drive Tukwila WA 981
Press ALT to choose commands, or F2 to edit. 1 20/20

Fig. 19.12
The First Name field is now in the first column.

Copying and Moving Records

You can copy or move an entire Works Database record. Moving records is useful when you want to group two or more records together so you can scroll quickly between them in Form view or view them together in List view. Copying a record is useful when you want to create a new record with very minor changes to an existing record.

To copy or move a record in Form view, follow these steps:

1. Display the record you want to copy or move.

2. To *copy* the record, choose Copy Record from the Edit menu; or press Ctrl+Shift+C.

    or

    To *move* the record, choose Cut Record from the Edit menu; or press Ctrl+Shift+X.

3. Display the record before which you want to insert the copied or cut record.

4. From the Edit menu, choose Paste Record; or press Ctrl+V.

    Works inserts the copied or moved record before the displayed record.

To copy or move a record in List view, follow these steps:

1. Highlight the record or records you want to copy or move.

    To highlight a record in List view, click its record number; or move the highlight into the record and choose Select Record from the Edit menu. To highlight more than one adjacent record, drag across the record numbers.

2. To copy the record, choose Copy from the Edit menu; or press Ctrl+C

    or

    To move the record, choose Cut from the Edit menu; or press Ctrl+X.

3. Select the record before which you want to copy or move the record.

4. From the Edit menu, choose Paste Record; or press Ctrl+V.

Works inserts the copied or moved record before the displayed record.

Tip
To insert additional copies of the cut or copied record, move to the location where you want to insert another copy and again choose Edit, Paste Record; or press Ctrl+V.

Troubleshooting

I am trying to copy a record in Form view and insert the copy immediately so that Works places it next to the original, but it doesn't work. What am I doing wrong?

You cannot copy the displayed record and immediately insert a copy next to the original. (This appears to be an oversight on the part of the Works programmers.) You must paste the copy at a location not adjacent to the original, and then cut and paste the record before the original record.

I sometimes begin copying information with drag and drop, and then change my mind and decide to move the information instead. Is there a way to do that? Inserting the copy and deleting it is awkward.

To toggle between copying and moving the selection, before you release the mouse button, press or release the Ctrl key.

Hiding Fields and Records

When you display a database on-screen in Form or List view, Works shows you the fields, field labels, and any other elements such as labels, lines, and drawings. In List view, you can hide fields to keep other people from reading the information in the field, to temporarily display fewer fields on-screen, or to display fields together.

In Form view, hiding field names is useful when you want to display the contents of several fields together. For example, you can display the contents of the First Name and Last Name fields together on one line, without their field labels. Also, if field names on a form are not helpful, you can hide or replace them.

You also can hide entire records in Form or List view. You then can print only the records that appear. This step is very useful when you want to print selective records that you cannot retrieve using a database query as described in Chapter 21, "Retrieving Database Information."

Hiding Field Names in Form View

Figure 19.13 shows the result of hiding the State and Zip field names in Form view and placing the City, State, and Zip fields on the same line. The final line of the address now is easier to read: Seattle WA 98112. To achieve this result, you use the following steps:

1. Highlight the field name you want to hide.

2. From the Format menu, choose Show Field Name.

Works hides the field name. Show Field Name is a toggle. To turn field names back on, repeat steps 1 and 2.

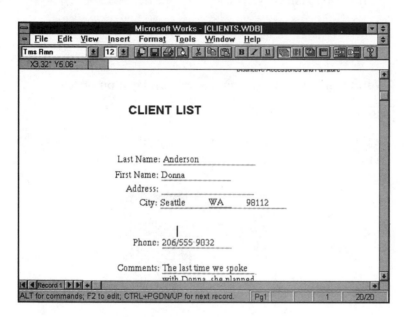

Fig. 19.13
A form with State and Zip fields hidden.

Hiding Fields in List View

Hiding a field in List view is easy. With the mouse, you drag the right border of the field's name to the left until the field disappears. To hide a field with the keyboard, follow these steps:

1. Move the highlight into the field you want to hide.

2. From the Format menu, choose Field Width.

Works displays the Field Width dialog box (see fig. 19.14).

Fig. 19.14
Use the Field
Width dialog box
to hide a field.

3. Type **0** in the **W**idth text box then choose OK. Works hides the field.

To redisplay a hidden field, follow these steps:

1. From the **E**dit menu, choose **G**o To; or press F5.

   Works displays the Go To dialog box (see fig. 19.15).

2. In the **N**ames list box, select the hidden field you want to display.

3. Choose OK.

   Works highlights the field but doesn't display it on-screen.

4. From the Forma**t** menu, choose Field **W**idth.

5. In the Field Width dialog box, type the field width you want in the **W**idth text box. Then choose OK.

Fig. 19.15
Use the Go To
dialog box to
redisplay a hidden
field.

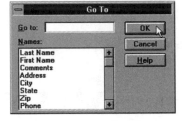

Works redisplays the field.

Hiding Records

Hiding records is useful when you want to print selected records that don't meet the standard Works Database query criteria, as described in Chapter 21, "Retrieving Database Information."

To hide a record, follow these steps:

1. In Form view, display the record you want to hide.

   or

   In List view, highlight the record or records you want to hide.

2. From the **V**iew menu, choose Hi**d**e Record.

   Works hides the selected record(s).

3. To redisplay hidden records, choose Show All Records from the View menu.

   Works displays all the hidden records.

From Here...

Tip
After you hide records, you still can tell your total number of records, displayed and hidden. For example, if 16 records appear out of a total of 25 records, the record count indicator at the right end of the status bar shows 16/25.

In this chapter, you learned how to enter database information. You also learned how to make changes to existing information and how to copy and move field contents and records. Finally, you learned how to hide and display fields and records. To learn more about related commands, see the following chapters:

- See Chapter 20, "Expanding Your Database Skills," to find out how to sort and print records, use dates, times, math formulas and functions, protect your data, and format data in fields.

- See Chapter 21, "Retrieving Database Information," when you need to retrieve information from a database using specific criteria (for example, retrieving only the records where the state is *WA*).

- See Chapter 22, "Creating a Database Report," to learn how to print database information in neatly formatted lists.

Chapter 20

Expanding Your Database Skills

This chapter could appropriately have been named "Database Housekeeping," because it covers tasks that you perform frequently but don't fit among the three main database functions of creating forms, entering data, and printing reports.

Now that you have learned how to create database forms and enter data, you will probably find that you sometimes need to arrange the information in alphabetical or numerical order according to the data stored in a field. For example, the U.S. Postal Service may require you to sort address labels in zip order for a bulk mailing. You also need to know how to print records. And you may find it useful to have Works insert the current date and/or time in database fields or perform math calculations. Finally, Works can protect your database forms, fields, and field entries so that you and other users don't accidentally or deliberately change the information or the form design.

In this chapter, you learn how to:

■ Sort database records

■ Print database records

■ Use dates and times in database fields

■ Use math formulas and functions

■ Protect your data and form designs

Sorting Database Records

Sorting arranges the records in a database in alphabetical, numerical, or date or time order. You can arrange the records in a sales contact database alphabetically on the Region, Last Name, and First Name fields, for example, in order to print a list of sales contacts by region, with the contact names for each region sorted by last and first name. Works can sort on up to three fields in a database form.

Figure 20.1 shows a database in List view with the Last Name and First Name fields in random, unsorted order.

Fig. 20.1
A database with
the Last Name and
First Name fields
in unsorted order.

	Last Name	First Name	Address	City	State	Zip	Phone
1	Anderson	Donna	234 West Harris	Seattle	WA	98112	206/555-9832
2	Simpson	Salley	129 N. E. 13th	Bellevue	WA	98004	206/555-2317
3	Hawkins	James	9810 Crest Drive	Renton	WA	98553	206/555-5374
4	Steele	Michael	123 Hunts Point Rd.	Lynnwood	WA	98342	206/555-9781
5	Mitchell	Jesse	988 Kirkland Ave.	Seattle	WA	98109	206/555-9921
6	Connors	Matthew	2839 155th Ave.	Redmond	WA	98052	206/555-7888
7	Swanson	Teresa	13423 Grants Rd.	Bellevue	WA	98007	206/555-6781
8	Lindsey	Jason	456 Terry Ave.	Kent	WA	98331	206/555-2231
9	Adams	Heidi	889 Dillon Ave.	Seattle	WA	98109	206/555-4096
10	Pryor	Jessica	3812 65th Pl. N.E.	Lynnwood	WA	98342	206/555-9970
11	Meyers	Tim	1490 136th Ave.	Redmond	WA	98052	206/555-2992
12	Hobart	Doug	980 Fir Crest Rd.	Kent	WA	98331	206/555-7714
13	Bell	Randy	9872 Marine View	Seattle	WA	98114	206/555-8541
14	Stein	Garth	8677 Hilltop Road	Redmond	WA	98052	206/555-7747
15	Harris	Robert	432 45th Pl. S.E.	Langley	WA	98312	206/555-8338
16	Rogers	Paula	9123 Orange Drive	Tukwila	WA	98131	206/555-2210
17	Pender	Sara	889 Island Ave.	Redmond	WA	98052	206/555-8176
18	Kessler	Allison	7342 King St.	Seattle	WA	98109	206/555-1976
19	Davidson	Betty	4512 N.E. 60th Ave.	Bellevue	WA	98004	206/555-1454
20	Spicer	Janet	3312 S. E. 40th Pl.	Tukwila	WA	98131	206/555-3198
21							

To sort a database, follow these steps:

1. With the database displayed in either Form or List view, from the T**o**ols menu, choose So**r**t Records.

   Works displays the Sort Records dialog box (see fig. 20.2).

Fig. 20.2
Use the Sort
Records dialog box
to sort on up to
three fields at a
time.

Works automatically inserts name of first field here

2. From the drop-down list in the **1**st Field options box select the name of the field to sort by; or type the name of a field in the text box.

3. Choose Ascend **A** or Descend **B** to sort the database records by that field in ascending or descending order.

> **Note**
>
> Works sorts text without regard for capitalization. For example, BELL is placed after Allen in an ascending sort.

4. Optionally, enter the names of up to two more fields to sort by in the **2**nd Field and **3**rd Field options boxes, and select the Ascend **C**, Descend **D**, Ascend **E**, or Descend **F** options to specify the sort order.

5. Choose OK.

Works sorts the records according to the criteria you specified. Figure 20.3 shows the database in figure 20.1 sorted in ascending order by Last Name (**1**st Field) and First Name (**2**nd Field). Notice that the records for Gary Adams and Heidi Adams are sorted first on the Last Name, then on the First Name, so that Gary Adams is above Heidi Adams in the sorted database.

Sorted on last name and then first name

	Last Name	First Name	Address	City	State	Zip	Phone
1	Adams	Heidi	889 Dillon Ave.	Seattle	WA	98109	206/555-4096
2	Anderson	Donna	234 West Harris	Seattle	WA	98112	206/555-9832
3	Bell	Randy	9872 Marine View	Seattle	WA	98114	206/555-8541
4	Connors	Matthew	2839 155th Ave.	Redmond	WA	98052	206/555-7888
5	Davidson	Betty	4512 N.E. 60th Ave.	Bellevue	WA	98004	206/555-1454
6	Harris	Robert	432 45th Pl. S.E.	Langley	WA	98312	206/555-8338
7	Hawkins	James	9810 Crest Drive	Renton	WA	98553	206/555-5374
8	Hobart	Doug	980 Fir Crest Rd.	Kent	WA	98331	206/555-7714
9	Kessler	Allison	7342 King St.	Seattle	WA	98109	206/555-1976
10	Lindsey	Jason	456 Terry Ave.	Kent	WA	98331	206/555-2231
11	Meyers	Tim	1490 136th Ave.	Redmond	WA	98052	206/555-2992
12	Mitchell	Jesse	988 Kirkland Ave.	Seattle	WA	98109	206/555-9921
13	Pender	Sara	889 Island Ave.	Redmond	WA	98052	206/555-8176
14	Pryor	Jessica	3812 65th Pl. N.E.	Lynnwood	WA	98342	206/555-9970
15	Rogers	Paula	9123 Orange Drive	Tukwila	WA	98131	206/555-2210
16	Simpson	Salley	129 N. E. 13th	Bellevue	WA	98004	206/555-2317
17	Spicer	Janet	3312 S. E. 40th Pl.	Tukwila	WA	98131	206/555-3198
18	Steele	Michael	123 Hunts Point Rd.	Lynnwood	WA	98342	206/555-9781
19	Stein	Garth	8677 Hilltop Road	Redmond	WA	98052	206/555-7747
20	Swanson	Teresa	13423 Grants Rd.	Bellevue	WA	98007	206/555-6781
21							

Press ALT to choose commands, or F2 to edit.   1   32000/32000

Fig. 20.3
A database sorted in ascending order on the Last Name and First Name fields.

You can repeat a sort quickly within the same Works session by using the same sort criteria. For example, you can re-sort a database after adding new records in unsorted order. To repeat a sort, follow these steps:

1. From the **T**ools menu, choose So**r**t Records.

Works displays the Sort Records dialog box with the sort options you chose previously.

2. Choose OK.

Works re-sorts the database using the same sort criteria.

Troubleshooting

I'm planning a database and would like to create a field that will hold mixed information: dates, text, and numbers. But I want to be able to sort the field. Is that possible?

Works can create orderly lists from this kind of mixed information, because Works automatically groups mixed data in the following order: text, time, number, date. For example, if you specify an ascending sort, all of the text entries appear first in the sorted list, and they are sorted in ascending order, followed by all the time entries, and so on. In a descending sort, Works groups mixed data in the reverse order: date, number, time, text.

I would like to sort my database on more than three fields, but the standard sort procedure doesn't allow that.

Sort the database twice, using the least important criteria for the first sort, and the most important criteria for the second sort. For example, suppose you want to sort a database on five fields: Amount Due, Credit Rating, Last Name, First Name, Zip. Amount Due is the most important sort field, followed by Credit Rating. Sort the database first on the three least important fields, and then sort the database again and specify Amount Due in the **1**st Field text box and Credit Rating in the **2**nd Field text box.

Printing Database Records

Regardless of the kinds of databases you create, you will almost certainly want to print some of the information stored in the database from time to time. Printing database information uses similar steps to printing with the Works Word Processor. Before you can create printed database documents, you must know how to set up header and footer margins; the source, size, and orientation of the paper you are printing on; page numbering and footnote options; and other standard settings for your particular printer. (You learn how to create Word Processor document headers, footers, and footnotes in Chapter 8, "Adding Headers, Footers, Footnotes, and Bookmarks to a Document.")

While setting page parameters, you can preview the printed results, just as you can preview a Word Processor document. In the following sections, you learn how to specify page settings.

Note

The settings you choose in the Page Setup dialog box affect only the current document.

Setting Margins

Page margins are the white space that surrounds the text on the printed page. To set page margins, follow these steps:

1. From the **F**ile menu, choose Pa**g**e Setup.

   Works displays the Page Setup dialog box (see fig. 20.4).

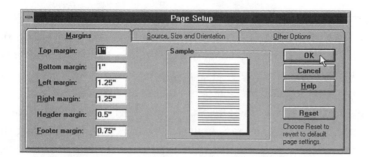

Fig. 20.4
Use the Page Setup dialog box to print your database records in Form or List view.

2. In the appropriate margin boxes on the **M**argins tab, type the settings you want to use.

3. When all margin settings are correct, choose OK.

Works automatically reformats your database form or list using the new margin settings.

> ### Note
>
> In Form view, the margin settings are shown on-screen. For example, if you set a top margin of 6" and the database form now extends onto a second page, Works inserts a page break at the corresponding point of the form in the form view screen. In List view, your changes are not reflected in the Works Database window. You must use Print Preview to view the effects of your changes. (See "Previewing a Document" later in this chapter.)

If you decide to include a header or footer in your document, you can change the header and footer margins in the Page Setup dialog box. (See "Creating Headers and Footers" later in this chapter.)

> **Note**
>
> If you commonly work with centimeters or another unit of measure other than inches, you can change the Works default units setting. Choose T**o**ols, **O**ptions, and, in the Units box, choose a unit of measure, and then click OK. Notice that the unit of measure you choose applies to *all* tools in Works.

Setting Paper Source, Size, and Orientation

Before you can print your database, you must tell Works which paper source to use, the size of the paper you are printing on, and the direction you want the print to appear on the page. To change the paper source, paper size, and print orientation, you use the Page Setup dialog box shown in figure 20.5. In the figure, the Source, Size and Orientation tab is selected and the default settings appear. The page in the Sample area reflects the current paper size and orientation settings.

Fig. 20.5

The Source, Size and Orientation options include paper source, size, and orientation settings for the current document.

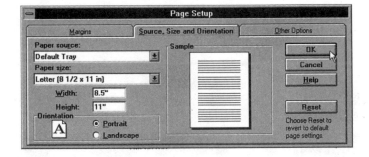

Depending on the type of printer you are using, you can choose the correct paper source (such as the default paper tray, second paper tray, or envelope feeder) from the Paper Sou**r**ce drop-down list. The Paper S**i**ze list offers a variety of standard paper and envelope sizes. Choose a size from the list or enter the correct size in the **W**idth and Hei**g**ht boxes.

To change source, size, and orientation settings, follow these steps:

1. From the **F**ile menu, choose the Pa**g**e Setup command. The Page Setup dialog box appears.

2. In the dialog box, choose the **S**ource, Size and Orientation tab. The dialog box shown in figure 20.5 appears.

3. Select a paper source from the Paper sou**r**ce drop-down list.

4. Select a paper size from the Paper Size drop-down list, or specify a custom size in the **W**idth and Hei**g**ht boxes.

5. Select a paper orientation by clicking either the **P**ortrait or **L**andscape option button. The Sample area of the dialog box reflects the settings you choose.

6. When all settings are correct, choose OK.

Setting Other Page Options

The third tab in the Page Setup dialog box is **O**ther Options (see figures 20.6 and 20.7). With your database displayed in Form view, you use the settings on this tab to specify the page number on the first page of the document, whether you want field lines printed and page breaks inserted, and whether you want Works to print the entire form or field entries only.

With a database displayed in List view, you use the **O**ther Options tab to number the first page and to tell Works whether to print gridlines and record and field labels.

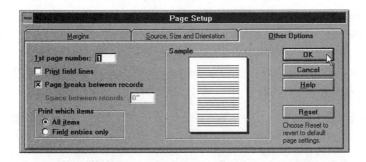

Fig. 20.6
The Page Setup, Other Options tab in Form view displays settings for first page number, field lines, page breaks, and printing of entire forms or field entries.

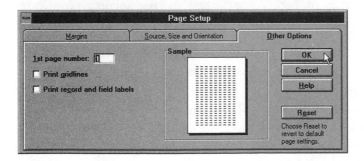

Fig. 20.7
The Page Setup, Other Options tab in List view displays page settings for printing first page number, gridlines, and record and field labels.

The page number on the first printed page of your document can be a number other than 1. To start page numbering with the number 5, for instance, enter 5 in the **1**st page number box.

With a database displayed in List view, you can tell Works to Print **g**ridlines. Works prints the database just as it appears with gridlines turned on, showing field contents separated by gridlines.

In List view, you can also choose Print re**c**ord and field labels. Works then prints the database just as it appears in List view, with field labels at the tops of the field columns and record labels at the left of record rows.

You can use the Page Setup dialog box to choose special options for printing reports. These options are discussed in the section "Printing Reports" in Chapter 22, "Creating a Database Report."

Previewing a Document

One of the most important steps you can take before printing database information is to *preview* it. Previewing enables you to see on-screen how your document will look on the printed page. When you preview a document, Works displays a full-page view, one page at a time, of the document. This is your chance to see that margins are the appropriate size, line spacing is appropriate, page breaks are correct, header and footer text is positioned correctly, inserted objects appear in the proper locations, and so on. All these elements appear on the preview screen.

To preview a document, choose **F**ile, Print Pre**v**iew. The current database appears in a preview screen like the one shown in figure 20.8.

The actual text displayed in the preview screen can be difficult to read because it is reduced, but reading the text isn't the important consideration here; checking the document's layout is.

If you think you spot a problem in the layout, you can zero in on a particular location. Notice that the mouse pointer changes to a magnifying glass when it is pointed anywhere on the page. To magnify an area, point to the area you want to enlarge and click it; or click the Zoom **I**n button. Works magnifies the area. To magnify the area further, click the Zoom **I**n button again. To return to the full-page view, click the area, or choose Zoom **O**ut. You can scroll the zoomed display with the horizontal and vertical scroll bars.

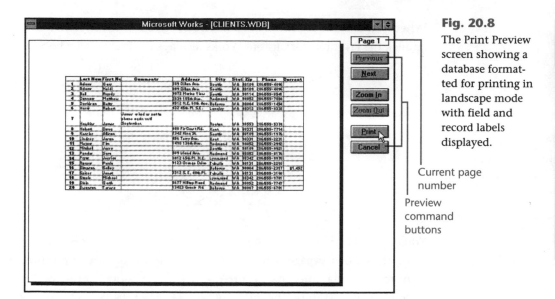

Fig. 20.8
The Print Preview screen showing a database formatted for printing in landscape mode with field and record labels displayed.

Current page number

Preview command buttons

If your document is longer than one page, display the page you want to preview by clicking the **P**revious or **N**ext button, or use the Page Up and Page Down keys on the keyboard. When you're ready to print the document, you can print directly from the preview screen by clicking the **P**rint button. This button displays the Print dialog box. You learn how to use the Print dialog box in the next section.

Printing

If you have access to more than one printer on your computer, you need to select the correct printer in the Printer Setup dialog box before you can print database information (see fig. 20.9). To display the Printer Setup dialog box, choose **F**ile, Printer Setup. The printer that is currently selected is highlighted in the Printer Setup dialog box. To choose a different printer, highlight the name, and then choose OK.

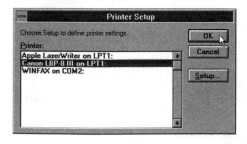

Fig. 20.9
Use the Printer Setup dialog box to choose a printer if more than one printer is attached to your computer.

When you're ready to print a document, choose **F**ile, **P**rint; or press Ctrl+P; or click the Print toolbar button. Works displays the Print dialog box shown in figure 20.10.

Fig. 20.10
Use the Print dialog box to specify the number of copies and the pages you want to print.

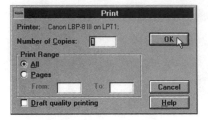

You use the Print dialog box to specify the number of copies you want to print, the particular pages you want to print, and the quality of printing you want to use. The printer that is currently selected is shown at the top of the dialog box. If the printer shown is not correct, select the correct printer using the **P**rinter Setup command on the **F**ile menu.

Notice that a **P**review command button is available in the Print dialog box. If you forget to preview a document before choosing the **P**rint command on the **F**ile menu, you can choose the **P**review button in the Print dialog box. The **T**est button is used when you merge documents (see Chapter 27, "Creating and Printing Form Letters, Envelopes, and Mailing Labels"). Table 20.1 describes the options in the Print dialog box.

Table 20.1 Options in the Print Dialog Box	
Option	**Description**
Number of **C**opies	The default setting is 1; to print more than one copy of the current document, enter a number.
Print Range: **A**ll	The default setting is to print all pages of the current document.
Print Range: **P**ages	To print selected pages, choose the Pages option button, and then enter the first page to print in the **F**rom box and the last page to print in the **T**o box.
Draft quality printing	If your printer is capable of printing at draft quality, choose this setting to print more quickly but at a lower print quality.

To print a database, follow these steps:

1. Open the database you want to print.

2. From the **F**ile menu, choose the Pa**g**e Setup command to specify print margins, paper source, size, orientation, and other print settings.

3. Preview the database using **F**ile, Print Pre**v**iew; or by clicking the Print Preview toolbar button.

4. Choose **F**ile, **P**rint; or press Ctrl+P; or click the Print toolbar button.

   Works displays the Print dialog box (refer to fig. 20.10).

5. Choose the appropriate print settings, and then choose OK.

To print a single record in form view, follow these steps:

1. Display the record you want to print.

2. Choose **F**ile, **P**rint; press Ctrl+P; or click the Print toolbar button.

3. Choose C**u**rrent Record Only.

4. Choose OK.

Works prints the displayed record.

You can print more than one record on a page to save paper and produce a more compact printout. To print several records on one page, follow these steps:

1. In form view, choose **F**ile, Pa**g**e Setup.

2. Choose **O**ther Options.

3. Clear the Page **b**reaks between records check box.

4. In the S**p**ace between records box, type the space you want Works to insert between records on the page.

5. Choose OK.

When you print the database, Works prints the records continuously, without inserting a page break between records.

Tip

To hide records in database List view that you don't want to print, see "Hiding Records" in Chapter 19, "Entering and Editing Data."

Tip

To print a blank record, press Ctrl+End in Form view to display a blank record, then follow steps 1 through 4 above.

IV

Databases

Removing Extra Space

When you print a database, Works inserts a sufficient space in the printout for the entire length of each field. For example, if field entries are formatted flush left, Works adds space to the right of the entry in the printout; or if a field entry is formatted flush right, Works adds space to the left of the entry in the printout.

You can tell Works to eliminate extra space from fields when it prints a database. This can be useful for printing addresses. For example, you can tell Works to eliminate extra space from the three fields City, State, and Zip. With field labels hidden, Works prints the field contents on the same line, with no extra spaces between field contents. To achieve this effect, you use the slide to left command.

To slide a field to the left in form view, follow these steps:

1. Highlight the field or label you want to slide to the left.

2. From the Format menu, choose **A**lignment.

3. Select **S**lide to left.

4. Choose OK.

To preview the effect of using the slide to left command, choose **F**ile, Print Pre**v**iew; or click the Print Preview toolbar button (see fig. 20.11).

Fig. 20.11
To display several fields on the same line with extra spaces removed from the fields, use the slide to left command.

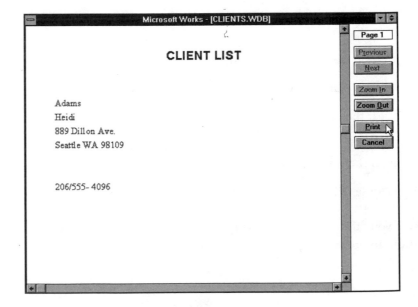

Using Page Breaks

When you print a Works database in Form view, just one record is printed on each page. But you can tell Works to fit as many records as possible on each printed page.

> **Note**
>
> Page breaks that you insert in Form or List view do not affect the way Works prints forms in the other view. In List view, Works automatically prints as many records as will fit within the current margins of each page. But you can insert vertical and horizontal page breaks in List view, as described later in this section.

You can specify exactly where Works inserts page breaks when it prints a database in form view. This might be useful, for example, when you want to print the name and address section of a single database form on one page, and the credit account status on a separate page.

To insert a page break in Form view, follow these steps:

1. Move the insertion point to where you want to insert a page break.

2. From the **I**nsert menu, choose Page **B**reak.

Works inserts a page break above the insertion point. The page break appears as a single line across the form.

Follow these steps to delete a page break in Form view:

1. Move the insertion point immediately beneath the page break.

2. Choose **I**nsert, Delete Pa**g**e Break.

To insert a page break in List view, follow these steps:

1. To insert a horizontal page break, highlight the record below which you want the page break.

   or

   To insert a vertical page break, highlight the field to the right of where you want the page break.

2. Choose **I**nsert, Page **B**reak.

Works inserts a dashed page break line above the record or to the left of the field.

You can also insert page breaks in List view with the Insert Page Break dialog box by following these steps:

1. Move the highlight into the record or field where you want to insert a page break. Don't select the entire record or field.

2. Choose **I**nsert, Page **B**reak.

    Works displays the Insert Page Break dialog box (see fig. 20.12).

Fig. 20.12
You can use the
Insert Page Break
dialog box to
insert a page
break in List view.

3. Choose **R**ecord or **F**ield.

4. Choose OK.

Works inserts a page break above the record or to the right of the field.

To delete a page break in List view, follow these steps:

1. Highlight the record below or the field to the right of the page break.

2. Choose **I**nsert, Delete Pa**g**e Break.

    Works removes the page break.

Displaying Forms as They Will Be Printed

The letter spacing that Works uses to display a form on-screen may be slightly different from the letter spacing that is used to print the form. Normally, the differences are slight and won't cause problems. In rare cases, however, you may need to view letter spacing exactly as a form will be printed. This might be the case, for example, if you intend to print database forms on preprinted paper forms.

To display a form as it will appear when printed, from the **V**iew menu choose F**o**rmat For Printer.

Works displays the form on-screen and uses the same letter spacing that will be used to print the form with the currently selected printer.

Creating Headers and Footers

When you print a database, it can be quite useful to add descriptive text at the top or bottom of each printed page. For example, when you drop a big stack of printed database forms, it's convenient to have page numbers printed on each form.

Follow these steps to create a header or footer:

1. From the **V**iew menu, choose **H**eaders and Footers.

    Works displays the Headers and Footers dialog box (see fig. 20.13).

Fig. 20.13
Use the Headers and Footers dialog box to add text to the top and bottom of each printed database page.

2. Type the header and/or footer text in the **H**eader and **F**ooter boxes.

3. To tell Works not to print a header or footer on page 1 of the printout, select **N**o header on 1st page and/or N**o** footer on 1st page.

4. Choose OK.

When you print the database, Works adds the header or footer at the top or bottom of the printout.

> **Note**
>
> Works doesn't display headers and footers on-screen. To preview the text and position of headers and footers, use **F**ile, Print Pre**v**iew; or click the Print Preview toolbar button.

Using Special Header/Footer Codes and Numbering Pages

Works can automatically print the page number, file name, date, or time in a header or footer. You can also format text in a header or footer flush left, flush right, or centered. For example, you might want to print the author's name flush left in a header, and print the database name centered, and the current date flush right. To print page numbers, etc., and format header/footer text, you type special codes in the **H**eader or **F**ooter text box in the Headers and Footers dialog box.

You can use the following special codes:

Purpose	Code
Page number	&p
File name	&f
Current date	&d
Date in long format	&n
Current time	&t
Print an ampersand character	&&
Left align the characters that follow	&l
Right align the characters that follow	&r
Center the characters that follow	&c

When you insert a page number code in a header or footer, you tell Works where to print the page number.

To insert a page number and specify the page number position, follow these steps:

1. From the **V**iew menu, choose **H**eaders And Footers.

2. Select H**e**ader and/or **F**ooter and type the text for the header and/or footer.

3. In the H**e**ader and **F**ooter text boxes, type one or more of the following codes along with the header/footer text, and then choose OK.

Page number position	Code
Centered at top of page	&c&p in the Header box
Centered at bottom of page	&c&p in the Footer box
Flush right at top of page	&r&p in the Header box
Flush left at top of page	&l&p in the Header box
Flush right at bottom of page	&r&p in the Footer box
Flush left at bottom of page	&l&p in the Footer box

Figure 20.14 shows a database record displayed in the Print Preview, formatted with the following header:

&lACCOUNTING DEPT.&cCLIENTS DATABASE&r&d.

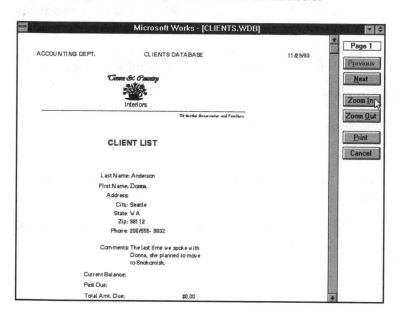

Fig. 20.14
A database record formatted with header alignment and date codes.

To remove header or footer information like page numbers from a database printout, follow these steps:

1. From the **V**iew menu, select H**e**aders and f**o**oters.

2. Delete the codes and the related text in the **H**eader or **F**ooter box.

3. Choose OK.

Changing the Starting Page Number

When you print database records, you may need to number your pages starting with a number other than one. This might be the case, for example, when you insert a database printout in the middle of a word processed report.

To set a new page number, follow these steps:

1. From the **F**ile menu, choose Pa**g**e Setup.

2. Choose the **O**ther Options tab.

3. In the **1**st page number box, type a new page number for the first page.

4. Choose OK.

Works begins numbering the pages of the database with the number you specified.

Changing Header and Footer Margins

After previewing or printing your database, you may discover that the header or footer is too close or too far from the body of the database information, or from the top or bottom of the page. Or you may want to set different left and right margins for the header than for the body of the printout.

To change header and footer margins:

1. From the File menu, choose Page Setup.

2. Choose the Margins tab.

3. In the Header Margin and Footer Margin boxes, type the new margin settings.

   Notice that Works does not reflect your header and footer margin settings in the Sample graphic.

4. Choose OK.

Removing Headers and Footers

When you create a header or footer and then decide to print the database without a header or footer, follow these steps to delete the header and/or footer from the database:

1. Choose View, Headers and Footers.

2. Highlight any text in the Header or Footer box and press Delete.

3. Choose OK.

Troubleshooting

When I create a two-line header, it prints immediately above the top line of text. Is there a way to insert extra space between the header and the body text?

In the Margins tab box, check that the top and bottom page margins are large enough to accommodate a header and/or footer. For example, for a footer margin of 1.5 inches, the Bottom margin must be larger than 1.5 inches.

I want to print a database using a header that prints a message above a specific column. How can I do that?

Follow the steps in the previous section, "Changing Header and Footer Margins." You may need to fine-tune the margin settings with print preview. Choose **F**ile, Print Pre**v**iew; or click the Print Preview toolbar button.

Using Dates and Times

With the Works Database, you can store four kinds of data: text, numbers, dates, and times. When you type a date or time in a field in a date or time format that Works recognizes, Works automatically interprets the field as a date or time field when you sort the field or use it in a formula.

> **Note**
>
> The Works Database can accept dates in the range January 1, 1900 to June 3, 2079. Dates and times outside this range are interpreted as text.

To type a date or time in a Works Database field, follow these steps:

1. Type the date or time in a format that Works can recognize.

2. Click the Enter box in the formula bar; or press Enter.

Works converts the date to the default date format, MM/DD/YY, and aligns it flush-right in the field. For example, if you type November 30, 1993, Works reformats the date as 11/30/93.

You can change the format that Works applies when it accepts a date in a field by following these steps:

1. Highlight the field or data you want to change.

2. From the Forma**t** menu, choose **N**umber.

   Works displays the Number dialog box. Formatting number fields was discussed in the section "Formatting Numbers in Fields" in Chapter 17, "Creating and Editing a Database Form."

3. Choose **D**ate or **T**ime.

   Works displays the available formats in the Date or Time list box.

Tip
To save keystrokes when entering dates in a date field for the current year, type only the month and day. Works automatically inserts the year. For example, when you type 11/1 during 1994, Works inserts 11/1/94.

4. Choose a Date or Time format.

5. Choose OK.

Works applies the new format to the field.

To enter the current date or time in a field, follow these steps:

1. Move to the field where you want to insert the date or time.

2. To insert today's date, press Ctrl+; (semicolon).

   or

   To insert the time, press Ctrl+Shift+; (semicolon).

3. Press Enter; or click the Enter box in the formula bar.

Tip

To enter dates and times in international formats, you must change the country selection in the International dialog box of the Windows Control Panel.

Note

The current date and time is only as accurate as your computer's clock. When you enter a date and time with the hot keys as described above, the date and time do not change automatically the next time you open the file.

Troubleshooting

I formatted a field with a time format, but Works changes the format when I enter data. What's happening?

To retain the date or time format for a field, don't enter text or numeric data in the field, or Works changes the data type to match the most recently entered data. Formulas then interpret the field's data as text or numeric.

Works is suddenly displaying some sort of cryptic code in a date field. How can I restore the dates?

Works uses numeric codes to interpret numeric and date fields. If you change the format of a field that contains dates or times, Works displays the numeric code for the date in the field. For example, if a field contains the date 11/1/94 and you format the field as a percentage, Works displays 3463900.00%. To restore the date, switch back to the date format.

Using Math Formulas and Functions

You learned how to type a math formula in a field in the section "Using Formulas in Fields" in Chapter 19, "Entering and Editing Data." This section gives more detailed information for using math formulas and functions.

You can use a formula to perform a math calculation and insert the results in a field, or to insert a "most likely" data entry in a field. For example, you can multiply the Price field and the Quantity field and insert the results in the Amount field. Or, you can use a math formula to insert "Seattle" in the City field. This would be useful if you expect most of the entries in the City field to be "Seattle."

Using a Math Formula to Perform a Calculation

When you type a formula in a database field in Form view or List view, Works automatically inserts the formula in the field for all records in the database. When you display a new record and enter data in fields that are used by the formula, Works automatically enters the results in the field that contains the formula. You don't have to re-enter the formula for each new record.

When you display a new, blank record and begin entering data, you don't see the formula in the field; but when you highlight the field, Works displays the formula in the formula bar.

> **Note**
>
> Formulas can refer to any number of fields, but a formula can refer only to fields in the same form and database.

Follow these steps to enter a formula in a field in Form view or List view:

1. Move the highlight to the field where you want to type the formula.

2. Type an = (equal sign) followed by the formula.

3. Press Enter.

For example, you might type =price*quantity in a field named Amount, where Price and Quantity are fields in the same database form. When you type new data in the Price and Quantity fields, Works automatically calculates the formula and inserts the results in the Amount field. If you don't type anything in the Price and Quantity fields, Works inserts 0 in the Amount field.

Tip
To perform math calculations on a field in more than one record, use a database report. For example, you can use a report to calculate the sum of all the entries in the Amount field in a database. (See Chapter 22, "Creating a Database Report," for more information.)

Using a Formula to Enter "Most Likely" Data

You can use a math formula to type the "most likely" data in a field. For example, if you know that most of the entries in the City and State fields will be "Seattle" and "WA," you can use a math formula to insert these words in the fields automatically. If the city and state are different (for example, "Portland" and "OR"), you can simply type over the data that the formula proposes.

Follow these steps to create a formula that inserts "most likely" data:

1. Move to the field where you want to insert the formula.

2. Type = (equal sign) followed by the "most likely" data.

   For example, in the City field, type ="Seattle", and in the State field, type ="WA".

> **Note**
>
> You must enclose proposed text data in double quotes, as shown. You don't need to enclose numbers, dates, or times in double quotes, however.

3. Press Enter.

   Works inserts the "most likely" data in each record in the database.

Using Functions

Works contains 76 built-in mathematical formulas that you can apply to the field entries in a database. These built-in formulas are called functions.

Tip
To display descriptions of the Works math functions on-screen, from the **Help** menu choose **S**earch for Help on.... Type **functions**, then choose **S**how Topics. Select Alphabetical List of Works Functions and choose **G**o To.

Functions perform calculations or enter data without requiring you to type complex formulas or long text. For example, you can use the AVG (average) function to calculate the average of the contents of the fields Distance1, Distance2, and Distance3. In the field where you want Works to insert the average, type =AVG(Distance1,Distance2,Distance3). When you enter data in the distance fields, Works calculates the average and inserts the results in the field where you typed the formula with the AVG function.

To enter a formula that uses a function, follow these steps:

1. Move to the field where you want to type a formula.

2. Type = (equal sign) followed by the function you want to use.

For example, type =avg. Works doesn't distinguish between upper- and lowercase letters when you type function names.

3. In parentheses, type the names of the fields that you want the function to use, separated by commas.

   For example, type =avg(Distance1,Distance2,Distance3).

4. Press Enter.

Protecting Your Data

If the Works Database has one fault, it's that users can too easily make accidental or deliberate changes to a form design. For example, if you use the mouse to move around in a form, you can accidentally drag a field label to a new location. With the keyboard, you can also quite easily delete part or all of a field label.

You can prevent yourself and others from making unwanted changes by protecting fields and field entries. You can protect either field labels and field entries, or you can protect a form design in Form view.

Protecting Fields

Protecting data is a two-step process involving locking and protecting. Works automatically locks every new field that you create on a database form. To protect a field, you leave the field locked and protect it as described in this section. To protect certain fields and leave others unprotected, you turn off locking for the fields you don't want protected, and turn on protection for the fields you do want to protect.

> **Note**
>
> If you leave a field locked and turn protection on, you cannot change the information in the field, format it, or unlock it. You must first turn off protection.

Follow these steps to lock or unlock a field:

1. Highlight one or more fields you want to unlock or lock.

2. Choose Format, Protection.

   Works displays the Protection dialog box (see fig. 20.15).

Fig. 20.15
Use the Protection
dialog box to
protect field labels,
data, or entire
forms.

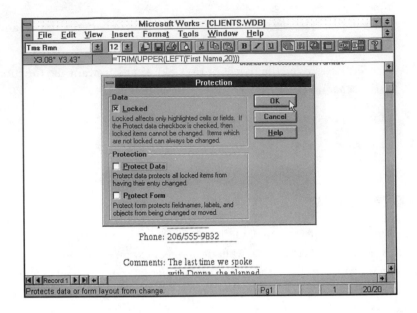

3. To lock the selected fields, choose **L**ocked.

4. Choose OK.

5. To protect the data in the selected fields, choose **P**rotect Data.

6. Choose OK.

Works protects the parts of the form you selected in steps 5 and 6.

Protecting Forms

When you protect a database in Form view, Works gives you the option to protect the entire form, including fields, labels, and objects. This option is not available in List view, because labels and fields are much less likely to be changed accidentally in List view.

Follow these steps to protect a form design:

1. In Form view, choose Forma**t**, P**r**otection.

   Works displays the Protection dialog box (refer to fig. 20.15).

2. To protect the form design, including field names, labels, and objects, choose P**r**otect Form.

3. Choose OK.

Tip
With protection turned on, Tab and Shift+Tab move the highlight to the next and previous unlocked fields.

> **Note**
>
> When you protect a form design, you cannot change, move, copy, or delete field names, labels, or objects on the form.

From Here...

In this chapter, you learned how to sort and print database records. You also learned to use dates, times, and math formulas and functions in database fields. Finally, you learned how to protect fields, field entries, and form designs from changes and deletions. To learn how to perform related Works Database tasks, see the following chapters:

- See Chapter 21, "Retrieving Database Information," when you need to retrieve information from a database using specific criteria (for example, retrieving only the records where the state is "WA").

- See Chapter 22, "Creating a Database Report," to find out how to print database information in neatly formatted lists.

Chapter 21

Retrieving Database Information

So far, in the chapters on the Works Database, you have learned how to create forms and enter information in a database. But once you build a database and store information, how do you get the information out again? Suppose, for example, that you want to print a list of all the people in your database who have birthdays in December, or all the distributors who stock left-threaded brass bolts with square heads. In this chapter, you learn how to retrieve information from a database using find and replace and queries.

Using Wild Cards

You use a wild card in a Find or query operation to represent one or more characters. For example, you can use a wild card to retrieve all records where the last name begins with Steve*. The asterisk wild card would retrieve Steve, Steves, Stevenson, and Stevensen.

You can use two wild cards: the question mark (?) and the asterisk (*).

The question mark wild card stands for a single character. For example, to find Allan and Allen, type **All?n**.

The asterisk wild card stands for any number of characters. For example, whole* finds whole, wholesome, and wholesale.

In this chapter, you learn how to:

- Perform simple find and replace operations

- Create simple database queries

- Edit, save, and copy queries

- Create advanced queries by using selection criteria

Using Find and Replace

The simplest way to locate information in a database is with the Find command. In List view, you can also find specific information and replace it. For example, you could find records where the Company field is "Smith Co." and replace it with "Clark Industries, Inc."

Using Find

Use Find when you simply want to locate all the records that contain a search term. For example, you might want to look at all the records where a field named Paid contains the entry "No."

Follow these steps to use the Find command in form or list view:

1. From the Edit menu, choose **Find**.

Works displays the Find dialog box (see fig. 21.1).

Fig. 21.1
Use the Find dialog box to search for one or all records that match the search term.

2. In the Find What text box, type the characters you want to search for.

3. Select Next record or All records.

If you choose Next record, Works finds the next record where any field entry matches the search string, but it does not retrieve any other records that match.

If you choose All records, Works retrieves all the records where any field's entry matches the search string.

4. Choose OK.

If you choose Next record, Works moves the highlight to the first field that contains the search string. If you choose All records, Works retrieves all the records that contain the search string. Figure 21.2 shows a database in List view after searching for the search term "Seattle" with All records selected. Notice that Works retrieved all the records where the City is Seattle. If you

Tip
You can add a toolbar button that displays the Find dialog box. Choose Tools, Customize Toolbar, and in the Customize Toolbar dialog box select the Edit options. Drag the button with binoculars onto the toolbar, then choose OK.

had chosen Next **r**ecord, Works would have displayed all the records in the database and moved the highlight into the first field containing the search term "Seattle."

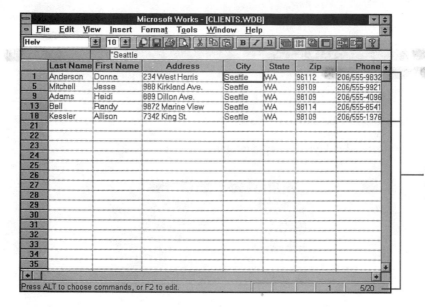

Fig. 21.2
The result of searching for "Seattle" with **A**ll records selected.

Works displays the five records found

Tip
To find records where a specific field contains the search term, in List view highlight the field, and then use the **F**ind command.

After performing a search, you can display all the records that Works did not select by choosing S**w**itch Hidden Records from the **V**iew menu. Works displays the records that *do not* contain the search term (see fig. 21.3).

Fig. 21.3
After choosing S**w**itch Hidden Records from the **V**iew menu, Works displays the records that do not contain the search term "Seattle."

	Last Name	First Name	Address	City	State	Zip	Phone
2	Simpson	Salley	129 N. E. 13th	Bellevue	WA	98004	206/555-2317
3	Hawkins	James	9810 Crest Drive	Renton	WA	98553	206/555-5374
4	Steele	Michael	123 Hunts Point Rd.	Lynnwood	WA	98342	206/555-9781
6	Connors	Matthew	2839 155th Ave.	Redmond	WA	98052	206/555-7888
7	Swanson	Teresa	13423 Grants Rd.	Bellevue	WA	98007	206/555-6781
8	Lindsey	Jason	456 Terry Ave.	Kent	WA	98331	206/555-2231
10	Pryor	Jessica	3812 65th Pl. N.E.	Lynnwood	WA	98342	206/555-9970
11	Meyers	Tim	1490 136th Ave.	Redmond	WA	98052	206/555-2992
12	Hobart	Doug	980 Fir Crest Rd.	Kent	WA	98331	206/555-7714
14	Stein	Garth	8677 Hilltop Road	Redmond	WA	98052	206/555-7747
15	Harris	Robert	432 45th Pl. S.E.	Langley	WA	98312	206/555-8338
16	Rogers	Paula	9123 Orange Drive	Tukwila	WA	98131	206/555-2210
17	Pender	Sara	889 Island Ave.	Redmond	WA	98052	206/555-8176
19	Davidson	Betty	4512 N.E. 60th Ave.	Bellevue	WA	98004	206/555-1454
20	Spicer	Janet	3312 S. E. 40th Pl.	Tukwila	WA	98131	206/555-3198

Tip
To repeat the previous search, press F7.

To tell Works to display all records after performing a search, from the **V**iew menu, select Show **A**ll Records. Works displays all the records in the database.

Using Replace

Works not only can locate records that contain a search term, it can automatically replace the search term with an entry that you specify. For example, it can replace "Seattle" with "Redmond" in all records where the City field contains "Seattle." Follow these steps to find and replace text or numeric values in list view:

1. From the **E**dit menu, choose Rep**l**ace.

   Works displays the Replace dialog box (see fig. 21.4).

Fig. 21.4
Use the Replace dialog box to automatically change the contents of a field.

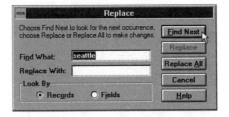

2. In the Fi**n**d What box, type the field entry you want to find and replace.

   As with the Find command, you can use wild card characters, as described earlier in the section "Using Find."

3. In the Re**p**lace With box, type the characters with which you want Works to replace the found item.

   You cannot use wild card characters in the Re**p**lace With box.

4. If you choose Rec**o**rds, Works replaces the search term moving from left to right through one record at a time. If you choose F**i**elds, Works replaces the search term moving from top to bottom one field at a time.

Tip
To replace a search term with nothing (to delete the search term), type the search term in the Fi**n**d What box, but leave the Re**p**lace With box empty.

5. To locate the next single record that contains the Fi**n**d What term, choose **F**ind Next. Choose **R**eplace to perform the replacement for that record, and choose **F**ind Next again.

   or

   To automatically find and replace throughout the database without stopping, choose Replace **A**ll.

6. When you finish replacing, choose Close.

> **Note**
>
> Be careful when using Replace. You cannot undo a replace command.

Working with Queries

A query lets you perform much more complex searches than Find. Use Find, as described earlier in the section "Using Find," to perform simple searches—for example, to find a person's birthday.

There are times, however, when Find isn't sufficiently powerful, for example when you need to look at the records where the Purchase Date is greater than or equal to 12/15/94, the Amount Due is more than $100, and the city is Seattle.

When you perform a query, Works searches all the records in the database, including any hidden records. Just as with Find, it displays the records that match the query and hides the records that do not match.

With a query, you can use a wide range of search criteria to retrieve records. Here are a few examples:

- *Exact matches.* For example, you can retrieve only the records where the purchase amount is exactly $97.57.

- *Partial matches.* For example, you can retrieve records where the Component field contains the words "switch," "switching," or "switcher."

- *"Greater than" or "less than."* For example, you can select records where the Zip code is greater than 98000 but less than 99000.

- *By range criteria.* For example, you can select records where the Birthdate field is between 1/1/42 and 1/1/50.

- *By more than one field entry.* For example, you can retrieve records where the Product field contains "crusher," and the Sales Territory field contains "Southeast Florida."

- *By non-matches.* For example, you can select records for people who have not purchased an Acme Juice-O-Matic.

Works provides powerful search tools. You can even query your database using calculations. For example, you can find the records where Current Date minus Purchase Date is greater than 90 days.

Creating Simple Queries

In a simple query, you tell Works which fields to compare and how you want them compared. Figures 21.5 and 21.6 show a database in List view before and after using a query to retrieve all records where the Zip field entry is greater than 98300 and the Last Name field entry begins with a letter greater than "M" (falls within the last half of the alphabet).

Fig. 21.5

The database before the query.

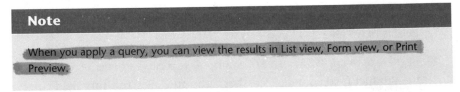

Figures 21.5 and 21.6 show a database before and after using a query to locate records with Zip greater than 98300 and Last Name beginning with a letter in the last half of the alphabet.

> **Note**
>
> When you apply a query, you can view the results in List view, Form view, or Print Preview.

Follow these steps to create a new query:

1. From the **T**ools menu, choose **C**reate New Query.

Works displays the New Query dialog box and automatically names the
query for you (see fig. 21.7).

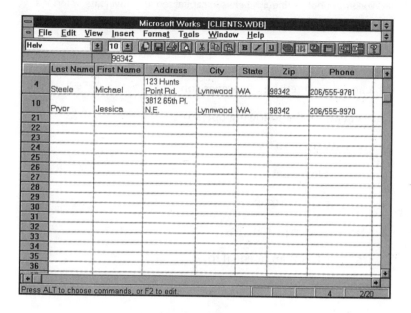

Fig. 21.6
The database after
the query.

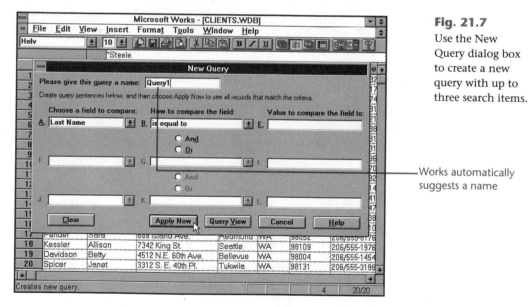

Fig. 21.7
Use the New
Query dialog box
to create a new
query with up to
three search items.

Works automatically
suggests a name

2. Type a new name for the query, if desired.

3. Under the Choose a Field to Compare heading, from the **A** drop-down
list, select the field you want to use for the first query criterion.

> **Note**
>
> Works does not distinguish between capitalized and lowercase letters in a query.

4. Under the How to Compare the Field heading, from the **B** drop-down list, choose the method of comparison.

   You can choose the following operators:

=	is equal to
<	is less than
>	is greater than
≠	is not equal to
≤	is less than or equal to
≥	is greater than or equal to
" "	contains

5. Under the heading Value to Compare the Field to, in the **E** box, type the information you want to compare the field to.

   For example, select Last Name Is Greater Than M to locate records where the last name begins with a letter in the second half of the alphabet.

6. To add another query sentence, choose An**d** or **O**r.

   The following table describes the effect of choosing An**d** or **O**r:

Choose	To
An**d**	Find records that match the criteria in the preceding **and** next query sentence
Or	Find all records that match the criteria in **either** the preceding **or** next query sentence

Tip
To show records that do **not** match your query, from the **V**iew menu, choose **S**witch Hidden Records.

7. To add a third query sentence, repeat steps 3 through 6.

8. Choose A**pp**ly Now.

Works displays the records that match your query.

To reapply the last query, follow these steps:

1. From the **V**iew menu, choose A**p**ply Query; or press F3.

Works displays the Apply Query dialog box (see fig 21.8).

IV

Databases

Fig. 21.8
Use the Apply
Query dialog box
to use a query that
you previously
created and saved.

2. Choose the query you want to apply.

3. Choose OK.

Works reapplies the query.

You may occasionally want to use a query and hide selective records. For example, you can use a query to retrieve the names of people on your mailing list who have birthdays in June. You can then selectively hide records of people to whom you do not want to send a birthday card. To hide an individual record, follow these steps:

1. In List view, highlight the record or records you want to hide.

or

In Form view, display the record you want to hide.

2. From the **V**iew menu, choose Hi**d**e Record.

3. To redisplay all records, from the **V**iew menu, choose Show **A**ll Records.

Tip
To show all records
again after viewing
the results of a
query, from the
View menu,
choose Show **A**ll
Records.

Naming and Saving Queries

You can name your queries and save them so that you can use them again. Works automatically saves a query when you create it, but gives each new query a cryptic name: Query1, Query2, Query3, and so on. If you don't rename a query when you create it, you can rename it later. Naming a query with a descriptive title helps you identify the query's purpose.

Follow these steps to name (or rename) a query:

1. From the **T**ools menu, choose Na**m**e Query.

Works displays the Name Query dialog box and lists the queries associated with the current database (see fig 21.9).

Fig. 21.9

Use the Name Query dialog box to name or rename your queries.

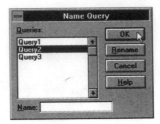

2. Select the query you want to name or rename.

3. In the **N**ame box, type a name of up to 15 characters.

4. Choose **R**ename.

   Works renames the query in the **Q**ueries list.

5. To rename other queries, repeat steps 2 through 4.

6. Choose OK.

Deleting and Copying Queries

Works automatically saves every query you create. If you don't intend to use a query later, you can delete it. A Works database can have a maximum of eight queries, so you may need to delete an existing query before Works allows you to create a new one.

Follow these steps to delete a query:

1. From the T**o**ols menu, select Delete Query.

   Works displays the Delete Query dialog box (see fig. 21.10).

Fig. 21.10

The Delete Query dialog box.

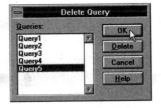

2. From the **Q**ueries list, select the one you want to delete.

3. Choose **D**elete.

4. To delete other queries, repeat steps 2 and 3.

5. Choose OK.

Caution

You cannot restore a deleted query with Undo.

You can copy queries. This is useful when you create a complex query and want to create and save another query that is slightly different, instead of starting from scratch. To learn how to edit a query, see "Creating Advanced Queries" later in this chapter. Follow these steps to copy a query:

1. From the **T**ools menu, choose Du**p**licate Query.

Works displays the Duplicate Query dialog box (see fig. 21.11).

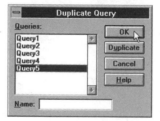

Fig. 21.11
The Duplicate
Query dialog box.

2. Select the query you want to duplicate.

3. In the **N**ame box, type a name of up to 15 characters.

4. Choose D**u**plicate.

5. For each query you want to copy, repeat steps 2 through 4.

6. Choose OK.

Creating Advanced Queries

With the Create New Query dialog box, you can perform most database queries. However, you may be unable to create complex queries with the dialog box. For example, you may need to use more than three criteria to retrieve records, or you may need to use a mathematical formula in a query. In such cases, you must use Query view.

Figure 21.12 shows a Works database form displayed in Query view. Notice that Query view looks just like a blank database form. Notice also that the Last Name field contains the formula that Works created when you defined a query with the Create New Query dialog box. In Query view, you can create complex queries by typing formulas in field entry areas.

Fig. 21.12
Use Query view to type complex formulas or use more than three query criteria.

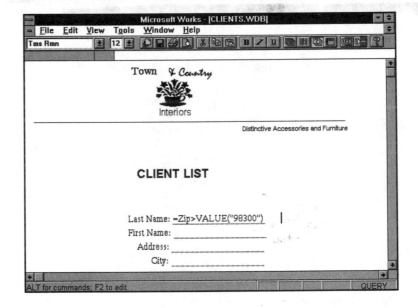

> ### Note
>
> Works places the first formula in a query in the first field in the form, the second formula in the second field, and so on, even though a formula may not apply to the field.

Each query instruction defines the text or values you want Works to look for, as shown in the following example:

Last Name:=Zip>VALUE("98300")

This query selects all records where the Zip code is greater than 98300.

Creating Queries Based on More Than Three Criteria

Works enables you to create queries easily using up to three criteria, as described earlier in this chapter in the section "Creating Simple Queries." You can create queries with more than three criteria, but you cannot use the Create New Query dialog box, as described in that section. Instead, you must type the query in Query view.

Follow these steps to create a query based on more than three criteria:

1. From the **T**ools menu, choose **C**reate New Query; or click the Query View toolbar button.

   Works displays the New Query dialog box and automatically names the query.

2. Type a new name for the query, if desired.

3. Choose **C**lear.

4. Choose Query **V**iew.

   Works switches to Query view and highlights the first field.

5. Type query instructions in the appropriate field and press Enter. Repeat for any other fields.

> **Note**
>
> When you display a saved query in List view, Works places the first query instruction in the first field, regardless of whether it has anything to do with the field or not. When you type a query in Query view, however, you must type the query in the appropriate field. For example, to see records where the Last Name is greater than M (the last name falls in the second half of the alphabet), type **=>"M"** in the Last Name field.

6. To see the results of the query, switch to List view, Form view, or Print Preview.

Retrieving Records with Exact Matching Criteria

Works can retrieve records that match a field's contents exactly. For example, you might want to view the records where the ZIP code is 98112.

Follow these steps to create an exact-match query:

Tip
You can also switch to Query view by choosing **View**, **Query**, selecting an existing query from the Query list, and choosing OK. You can then delete the existing query specification and type the new query.

1. From the **T**ools menu, choose **C**reate New Query.

   Works displays the New Query dialog box and automatically names the query.

2. Type a new name for the query, if desired.

3. Choose **C**lear.

4. Choose Query **V**iew.

   Works switches to Query view and highlights the first field.

5. Type query instructions in a field and press Enter. Repeat for any other fields.

   For example, you might want to find out which person's phone number is 206/555-1976, as shown in the following query:

   > Phone: 206/555-1976

6. To view the results of the query, switch to List view, Form view, or Print Preview.

> **Note**
>
> When you want to find just one exact match, it's usually faster to use the Find command. When you want to find exactly matching field entries for more than one field, use a query, as described in the next section, "Retrieving Records Using More Than One Field."

Retrieving Records Using More Than One Field

You may find that you sometimes need to retrieve records using more than one field in Query view. To do so, you type the criteria in the corresponding fields, as shown in the following example:

> Sponsor Last Name:
>
> Sponsor First Name:
>
> Event: Run
>
> Pledge: >50

The query in the example retrieves records for sponsors who pledged over $50 for the running event.

Retrieving Records Using "Greater Than" and "Less Than" Operators

You can use "greater than" (>) and "less than" (<) operators to retrieve records where a field's entry is above or below a certain value. The following sample queries show examples of the greater than and less than operators:

First Name:

Last Name: >"M"

    Age:

  Address:

This query uses the greater than operator (>) to retrieve records where the last name falls in the second half of the alphabet (>"M"). Notice that when you query on a text value, you must enclose the query text in double quotation marks (").

First Name:

Last Name:

    Age: <21

  Address:

This query uses the less than operator (<) to select records where the age is less than 21.

Retrieving Records Using Numeric and Alphabetic Range Criteria

To retrieve records where the field contents fall within a range, you use "greater than" and "less than" operators together with the AND logical operator. For example, in the Last Name field type:

>"A"#AND#<"N"

This query selects records where the last name falls in the first half of the alphabet: greater than A and less than N.

> **Note**
>
> You must enclose the AND and OR operators in number symbols (#AND#).

This query selects all records for screwdrivers that sell for more than $2 but less than $7 (greater than 2 and less than 7).

Part No.:

Description: "screwdriver"

Wholesale Price: >2#AND#<7

Retrieving Records Using Multiple Conditions

You can narrow the search logic of a query using the AND and OR logical operators. The following shows the effect of the AND and OR operators in a query:

#AND#   Selects records that meet ALL of the criteria

#OR#   Selects records that match ANY of the criteria

For example, the following query uses #AND# to retrieve only those records where the city is Seattle AND the sales district is 15:

First Name:

Last Name: =City="Seattle"#AND#Sales District="sw"

Sales District:

City:

Notice the syntax. When you type a complex query that refers to several fields, you can place the query in any field, but you must precede it with an equal sign (=).

The OR operator lets you select records that match ANY of several conditions. For example:

=City="Seattle"#OR#="Portland"#OR#="Snohomish#"

This query retrieves records where the city is Seattle OR Portland OR Snohomish. Again, notice the syntax.

You can combine AND and OR in a query. For example:

=City="Seattle"#OR#=State="OR"#AND#LastName="Anderson"

This query retrieves records where the city is Seattle, OR the state is Oregon, AND the last name is Anderson. In other words, it selects records for people named Anderson who live in Seattle or Oregon.

Retrieving Records That Don't Match a Condition

Sometimes you may find it helpful to look at the records that don't match a certain condition. In such cases, you can use the NOT EQUAL (<>) operator. For example:

Part No.:

Category: =Category<>"sheet metal"#AND#Cost>"9.99"

Cost:

This example retrieves records where the category is not "sheet metal" AND the cost is greater than $9.99.

Retrieving Records Using Math

Works lets you use math calculations in a retrieval. This is useful when you need to create a comparison by adding, subtracting, multiplying, dividing, or exponentiating one or more fields. You can use the following math operators:

Operator	Example
+ (addition)	=(Premium+Principle)>500 Selects records where premium plus principle is greater than $500
- (subtraction)	=(PastDue-DueDate)>30 Selects records where the past due date less the due date is greater than 30
* (multiplication)	=(Cost*Qty)<1000 Selects records where cost times quantity is less than $1000
/ (division)	=(Pledge/Miles)>25 Selects records where pledge per mile is greater than $25
^ (exponentiation)	=side^2<200 Selects records where the area of a square is less than 200

> **Note**
>
> As these examples show, you can group conditions in parentheses. For example, in the following instruction, the OR operator applies to all the conditions enclosed by parentheses:
>
> =Name="Johnson"#OR#(Age>30#AND#Sex="M"). This query retrieves records for people who are either named Johnson OR are male and over 30 years old.

Retrieving Records Using Functions

Works functions are built-in conditions that save you the trouble of typing complex formulas in a query.

The following examples show queries that use functions:

=DateDue-NOW( )>30. This query selects records where the due date is more than 30 days from today's date.

=PI( )diameter>400. This query selects records where the circumference of a circle is greater than 400.

> **Note**
>
> Notice in the examples that some functions require you to include empty parentheses after the function name, even though no function parameters are specified; for example: PI( ).

Using Date Queries

Tip
You don't have to include the current year when you type a date query. If you type only the month and day, Works assumes that the year is the current year.

You can use dates in a query using the equals, greater than, less than, and not equals operators. When you use a date in a query, you must enclose it in single quotation marks: '4/15/94'.

The following examples show dates used in queries:

DateDue-'5/15/94'>90. This query selects records where the due date falls more than 90 days after June 15, 1994.

>='1/1/94'#AND#<='7/1/94'. This query selects records where a date falls in the first six months of 1994.

=AmtDue>500#AND#(Now( )-DateDue)>90. This query selects records where the amount due is more than $500 and payment is more than 90 days overdue.

Troubleshooting

When I apply a query, Works retrieves records that aren't displayed in list view. What's the problem?

You previously applied a query or the Find or Hide Records command to hide some of the records in the database. When you apply a query to a database with hidden records, Works searches the entire database, including the hidden records, and displays all the matching records it finds. You cannot perform a query on only non-hidden records, but you can hide selected records after you apply a query. See "Hiding Fields and Records" in Chapter 19, "Entering and Editing Data."

I would like to save a query that retrieves records saved no earlier than 30 days before todays date. How can I do that?

Use the built-in Works NOW function. For example, the following statement retrieves records where the date entered in the Date field is no earlier than 30 days before today's date: =(NOW( )-Date)>=30.

From Here...

In this chapter, you learned how to retrieve information from a Works database using simple find and replace commands and basic and advanced queries. For related information, please review the following chapters:

- Chapter 22, "Creating a Database Report," tells you how to retrieve and print database information in neatly formatted lists.

- See Chapter 23, "Customizing a Report," for reports that require customized formatting and data selection, and to print reports for use with other applications.

Chapter 22

Creating a Database Report

After you enter information in a database, you occasionally need to view or print it. Works gives you five ways to look at your stored data:

■ You can display the database in Form or List view and scroll between records.

■ You can use the Find command to locate one or more records, as described in Chapter 21, "Retrieving Database Information."

■ You can use the Query command to search for records based on complex query statements, as described in Chapter 21, "Retrieving Database Information."

■ You can print the information in your database, or display it with Print Preview, as described in Chapter 20, "Expanding Your Database Skills."

■ You can create a report, as described in this chapter.

When you print or display database records by printing them, by using Print Preview, or by using Find or Query, you have little control over how Works formats the retrieved information. Works simply displays or prints the records as they appear in Form or List view. With a report, you can tell Works to print or display only the fields you want, and you can tell Works to calculate and print report statistics, such as a count of the records in the database. You can add titles, headers, and footers to a report. Figure 22.1 shows a simple printout of a database displayed in Print Preview.

In this chapter, you learn how to create basic Works Database reports. Specifically, you learn how to:

■ Create a basic Works Database report

■ Make changes to reports

■ Save, delete, and copy reports

■ Choose Page Setup options for printing reports

■ Select records to print in reports

Fig. 22.1
This figure shows a simple database report. Notice that in a report you can tell Works to include a title and report statistics, such as a count of the records in the database.

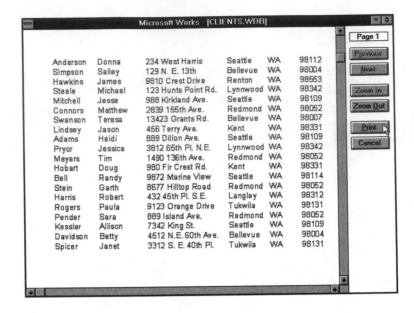

What Is a Report?

As mentioned above, a report enables you to organize and format database information before you print or view it. After you create a report that displays information the way you want, you can save the report and use it again later. You can save eight reports for each Works database.

Works enables you to create reports in two ways:

- You can create simple reports with the Tools, Report command.

- You can create complex reports in report view.

In a simple report, you tell Works which fields to include in the report and in what order. You can also have Works print a title and generate and print report statistics such as sum, count, average, minimum, maximum, standard deviation, and variance.

With complex reports, you can sort and group field entries, use calculations, add titles and notes, and change alignment and number formats. Creating complex reports is discussed in Chapter 23, "Customizing a Report."

Whether you create a simple or complex report, you can use the Find, Query, and Hide Record commands to select records, as explained in Chapter 21, "Retrieving Database Information."

Figure 22.2 shows a simple phone list report with the parts labeled.

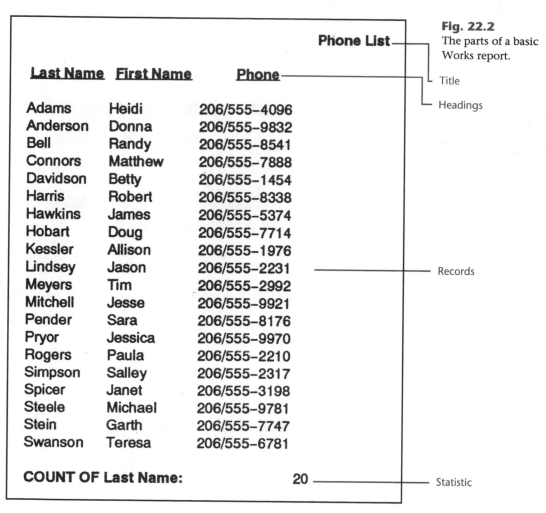

Fig. 22.2
The parts of a basic
Works report.

Creating a Basic Works Report

When you create simple reports, you use dialog boxes to specify a report title,
choose fields and field order, and choose the statistics you want Works to
include in the report. After you create a report, you can print it or preview it.

Note

If you want to select specific records to print in a report, and if you want to sort the
records before printing them, use the Find, Query, and Sort Records commands
before printing the report, as described in Chapter 21, "Retrieving Database
Information."

Follow these steps to create a basic report:

1. Display the database for which you want to create a report.

2. From the **T**ools menu, choose Create **N**ew Report.

    Works displays the New Report dialog box (see fig. 22.3).

Fig. 22.3
Use the New
Report dialog box
to create a basic
Works Database
report.

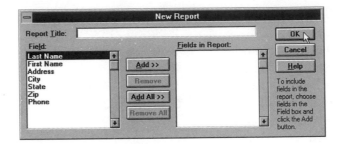

3. Type a title, if desired, in the Report **T**itle text box.

4. In the Fie**l**d text box, highlight the first field you want to include in the report.

    Works prints the first field in the leftmost column of the report.

5. Choose **A**dd.

    or

    To add all the fields in the order that they are listed in the Fie**l**d text box, choose A**d**d All.

6. Repeat steps 4 and 5 to add other fields.

7. To remove a field from the report, highlight its name in the **F**ields in Report list box and choose **R**emove. To remove all the fields and start over, choose R**e**move All.

8. Choose OK.

    Works displays the Report Statistics dialog box (see fig. 22.4).

Follow these steps to add statistics to the new report:

1. In the **F**ields in Report list box, highlight the name of the field for which you want Works to calculate statistics.

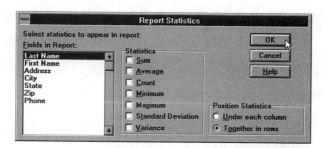

Fig. 22.4
Use the Report
Statistics dialog
box to select
statistical calcula-
tions you want
printed in a report.

2. In the Statistics area, choose the type of statistics you want Works to calculate for the highlighted field.

> **Note**
>
> Notice that all the statistics except Count apply only to numerical fields. If you choose a statistical type other than Count for a non-numerical field (for example, Last Name), the value Works calculates and prints on the report for the statistic is zero (0).

3. Repeat steps 1 and 2 for each field for which you want Works to calculate statistics.

4. In the Position Statistics area, select whether Works should print the statistics **U**nder each column or **T**ogether in rows.

5. Choose OK.

   Works displays a message box indicating that it has created the report.

6. Choose OK.

   Works displays the report definition in Report view. Figure 22.5 shows a simple report definition in Report view.

You learn more about using report view in the section "Using Report View," later in this chapter, and also in Chapter 23, "Customizing a Report."

To switch from the report definition to another view, click the Form View, List View, or Query View toolbar button; or choose **V**iew and choose **F**orm, **L**ist, or **Q**uery.

To switch to Report view from another view, you must tell Works which report you want to view. Follow these steps:

Fig. 22.5
A basic name and address report displayed in Report view.

	A	B	C	D	E	F
Title				Test		
Title						
Headings	Last Name	First Name	Address	City	State	Zip
Headings						
Record	=Last Name	=First Name	=Address	=City	=State	=Zip
Summary						

1. In Form, List, or Query view, from the **View** menu, choose **R**eport.

   Works displays the Reports dialog box (see fig. 22.6).

Fig. 22.6
Use the Reports dialog box to select a report and display its definition in Report View.

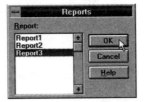

2. Highlight the name of the report you want to display.

> **Note**
>
> Notice that the reports in the Reports list box are named Report1, Report2, and Report3. These are the names that Works automatically gives reports when you first create them. You can give your reports descriptive names, as described later in this chapter in the section "Renaming, Deleting, and Copying Reports."

3. Choose OK.

   Works displays the report definition in report view.

Tip
To switch immediately to the last report definition you viewed, click the Report View toolbar button.

Using Report View

As the last step when you create a new report, Works displays the report definition in Report view. Report view is similar to List view, because the definition is laid out in rows and columns.

Notice in figure 22.7 that each row of a report definition contains a label. The
following list shows the purpose of each type of label:

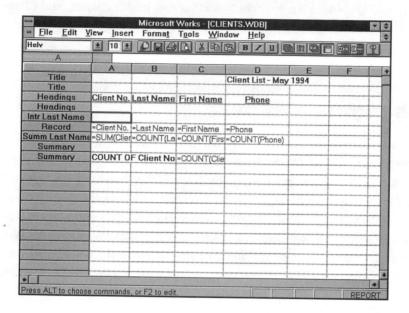

Fig. 22.7
This figure shows
the parts of a
report in Report
view.

- *Title.* A title row shows the title, if any, that Works prints at the top of
  the first page of the report.

- *Headings.* A heading row prints a field name or other text at the top of
  each column.

- *Record.* Record rows indicate which records Works prints in the report.
  For example, in figure 22.7, the Record row indicates that Works will
  print the Last Name field under the Last Name column heading, the
  First Name field under the First Name column heading, and the Phone
  field under the Phone column heading. You can use formulas and functions in the Record row to tell Works to print other kinds of data in a
  column, as described in Chapter 23, "Customizing a Report."

- *Intr <fieldname>.* This label tells Works to print a blank row or a heading
  before each group of records when you sort the report and specify
  column breaks. To learn more about this label, see Chapter 23,
  "Customizing a Report."

- *Summ <fieldname>.* You use this label to tell Works to print a statistical
  summary after each group of records when the report is sorted and you
  specify column breaks, as described in Chapter 23, "Customizing a
  Report."

■ *Summary.* The summary label indicates which statistics Works prints at the end of the report. To find out how to create statistical summaries, see "Creating a Basic Works Report" earlier in this chapter, and Chapter 23, "Customizing a Report."

The following sections describe the purpose of each row type in detail.

Changing a Report

For most purposes, a basic report works fine. (To learn how to create a basic report, see "Creating a Basic Works Report" earlier in this chapter.) Sometimes, however, you might need report features that you can't create with the New Report dialog box. In such cases, you can add features to a report by editing the report definition in Report view. For example, in the report definition you can add new title rows, create new column headings, and tell Works how to select, sort, and group database information in the report. Or, you can create a report entirely from scratch in Report view, as described in the next section, "Creating a New, Empty Report Definition."

Creating a New, Empty Report Definition

You don't have to use the New Report dialog box to create a new report. Instead, you can create a new report from scratch in Report view. To display a blank report definition in Report view, choose Tools, Create New Report, and then choose OK without typing anything in the New Report dialog box. When Works indicates it has created a new report definition, choose OK to remove the text dialog box and edit the new, empty report definition.

Editing a Report Definition

After creating a report, you can change the information that Works prints in the report. To edit a report you work in Report view. To create and edit text and commands in Report view, you use the same editing keys that you use in List view. By editing a report definition, you can change the order in which Works prints the fields and rows, change the text in the title and headings, and insert commands that use math or Works functions to calculate columns.

When you edit in Report view, you can type over existing text, add new text in blank rows and columns, or delete information from a row or column with the same cursor movement and deletion keys that you would use to edit a database in List view. For example, you might want to change the column heading Last Name to Client's Name.

Follow these steps in Report view to change an existing entry by replacing it with new text or instructions:

1. Highlight the text or instruction you want to change.

2. Type new text; or choose a command from the **I**nsert menu to insert a report instruction.

For example, you can insert a field name, field entry, or field summary.

3. Press Enter.

To change a text entry or an instruction, follow these steps:

1. Highlight the text or instruction you want to edit.

2. Click the formula bar; or press F2.

Works moves the insertion point into the formula bar.

3. Edit the entry in the formula bar by using the Works cursor movement and deletion commands for the mouse and keyboard.

Follow these steps to delete an entry:

1. Highlight the text or instructions you want to clear.

or

To clear all the information from two or more adjacent rows or columns, highlight the rows or columns.

2. Choose **E**dit, Clear; or press Del.

Works deletes the entry, but keeps any formatting intact. For example, if you formatted an instruction with a font, any new text or instructions that you type in the row or column is formatted with the same font.

Adding and Removing Rows and Columns

Works automatically inserts a blank Title row between the Title row at the top of the report and the first Headings row when you create a report. You can delete or insert rows and columns. For example, you might discover that a report title would look better with more (or less) space inserted between the title and the first row of the report.

To delete a row or column, do the following:

1. Highlight the entire row or column by clicking the row or column label.

   Works deletes the row or column immediately.

To insert a blank row or column, follow these steps:

1. Select the row above which you want to insert a blank row, or into the column to the right of where you want to insert a blank column.

2. From the **I**nsert menu, choose **R**ow/Column.

3. Choose OK.

Fig. 22.8
Use the Insert Row dialog box to choose the type of row you want to insert.

If you choose **C**olumn, Works inserts a column immediately. If you choose **R**ow, Works displays the Insert Row dialog box (see fig. 22.8).

4. Highlight the name of the row type you want to insert.

5. Choose OK.

Works inserts a new row and automatically places it first among the rows of the same type. For example, if you insert a new Summary row, Works places the new row first among the Summary rows.

Renaming, Deleting, and Copying Reports

Renaming Reports

When you first create a report, Works automatically names it Report1, Report2, Report3, and so on. Obviously, it's much easier to remember the purpose of a report if you save it under a more descriptive name. For example, you might name a school jogathon report "Pledge Tally."

Follow these steps to rename a report:

1. From the Tools menu, choose Name Report.

   Works displays the Name Report dialog box (see fig. 22.9).

Fig. 22.9
Use the Name
Report dialog box
to give your
reports descriptive
names.

2. In the Reports list box, select the report you want to rename.

3. In the Name box, type a new name of up to 15 characters.

4. Choose Rename.

5. To rename another report, highlight another report in the Name box
   and repeat steps 2 through 4.

6. Choose OK.

When you display a list of reports in a dialog box, Works lists the reports
under their new, descriptive titles.

Deleting and Copying Reports

You can delete reports that you no longer need. Each Works database can
have no more than eight reports associated with it, so you may need to delete
reports before you can create new ones.

Copying reports is also very useful. For example, you can create a complex
report and create a slight variation of it by copying and editing it instead of
starting over from scratch.

Follow these steps to delete a report:

1. From the Tools menu, choose Delete Report.

   Works displays the Delete Report dialog box (see fig. 22.10).

Fig. 22.10
Use the Delete
Report dialog box
to discard reports
that are no longer
useful.

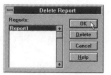

2. In the Reports list box, select the report you want to delete.

3. Choose **D**elete.

4. To delete other reports, repeat steps 2 through 3.

5. Choose OK.

Caution

Be careful when deleting reports. You cannot restore a deleted report with the Undo
command.

Follow these steps to copy a report:

1. From the **T**ools menu, choose Dupl**i**cate Report.

   Works displays the Duplicate Report dialog box (see fig. 22.11).

Fig. 22.11
Use the Duplicate
Report dialog box
to copy a report so
that you can edit
it or use it with a
different database.

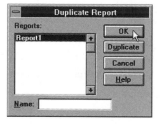

2. In the Reports list box, highlight the name of the report you want to
   copy.

3. In the **N**ame box, type a name of up to 15 characters for the copy.

4. Choose D**u**plicate.

5. To copy other reports, repeat steps 2 through 4.

6. Choose OK.

Works includes the copy whenever you display a dialog box with a list of reports.

Printing Reports

In Chapter 20, "Expanding Your Database Skills," you learned how to print a Works database. In connection with printing, you learned how to use the Page Setup dialog box to set margins, paper source, size, and orientation, and other options.

Printing a Works Database report involves the same steps as printing a database. For basic instructions for printing databases and reports, see the section "Printing Database Records" in Chapter 20, "Expanding Your Database Skills."

The only difference between printing reports and databases is that when you choose File, Page Setup from Report view, Works displays a report-specific option in the **O**ther Options tab. This option enables you to print reports without records.

Printing Reports Without Records

It is especially useful to fine-tune a report design by switching back and forth between Report view and Print Preview. Previewing or printing a report without records is much quicker, especially with large databases. The Print all but record rows option enables you to do this.

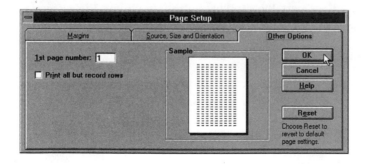

Fig. 22.12
The Other Options tab displays a report-specific option, Print all but record rows.

When you choose Print all but record rows from the Other Options tab, Works does not print any of the contents of database records in the report; instead, it prints only the introductory (Intr) and summary (Summ) row types that you specify in the report definition. To learn about using Intr and Summ, see Chapter 23, "Customizing a Report."

Follow these steps to print a report without records:

1. From the File menu, choose Page Setup.

2. Choose the Other Options tab.

3. Select Print All But Record Rows.

4. Choose OK.

5. From the File menu, select Print Preview.

Works displays the report in Print Preview without showing you any information from the database. All you see is text, titles, headings, and summary information.

Selecting Database Records to Print in a Report

Tip

To retrieve records quickly using just one search term, use Find command on the Edit menu.

In Chapter 21, "Retrieving Database Information," you learned how to retrieve selected records from a database with a query. Before you print a report, you can use a query to tell Works which records to include in the report.

For example, in a membership report, you might want to include only the names of members whose dues are over 90 days past due. Or you could print a phone list that includes members in the telephone area codes in and around the city where you live.

Follow these steps to select records for a report with a query:

1. Click the Query View toolbar button; or choose View, Query; or choose Tools, Create New Query.

2. Build the query or apply an existing query.

   Works retrieves the records according to the conditions you specified in the New Query dialog box, or in Query view.

3. Create a new report, or open an existing report as described earlier in this chapter.

IV

4. To preview the report, from the File menu choose Print Preview.

5. If you chose to print the report, from the File menu choose Print, select print options, then choose OK.

   Works prints the report, including only the records you retrieved with the Query.

From Here...

In this chapter, you learned how to create simple and complex reports. You learned how to customize a report in Report Definition view. You learned how to save, delete, and copy reports. And you learned how to use queries to select records for printing in a report. For related information, please refer to the following chapter:

■ Consult Chapter 23, "Customizing a Report," to learn how to create reports that require customized formatting and data selection, and to print reports for use with other applications.

Customizing a Report

In Chapter 22, "Creating a Database Report," you learn how to build basic Works Database reports using a "fill-in-the-blanks" approach with help from the New Report dialog box. Basic reports work fine for most purposes, but they do have limitations. For example, the New Report dialog box enables you to create only a single, centered title for a report. You cannot edit the header rows, or create column breaks, or print columns in a report using calculations.

Works provides the means for creating complex reports as well as simple ones.

Formatting a Report

After you create a standard Works Database report, you can customize it to make it more readable and attractive. For example, you can add titles, headings, and labels, and change column widths, row heights, number formats, alignment, and fonts. You can insert page breaks between sections of the report, and you can change page and margin settings.

Adding Text, Numbers, and Dates to a Report

In Chapter 22, "Creating a Database Report," you learn how to edit a report definition in Report view. (See the sections on "Using Report View" and "Changing a Report.") In this chapter, you learn about the many ways you can change a report's contents and appearance by editing the report definition.

In this chapter, you learn how to:

- Customize report formats with titles, labels, headers, and footers

- Change column width, row height, numbering format and alignment in fields

- Use special instructions for report contents and calculations

- Use fonts and set page breaks

- Use math calculations, and sort and group field entries

- Copy report output for use with other applications

For example, you can add text, numbers, or dates in the report definition so that Works prints them in the report. Follow these steps:

1. Display the report definition in Report view by selecting **View**, **R**eport; or by clicking the Report View toolbar button.

   Figure 23.1 shows a basic fundraising phone list report in Report view.

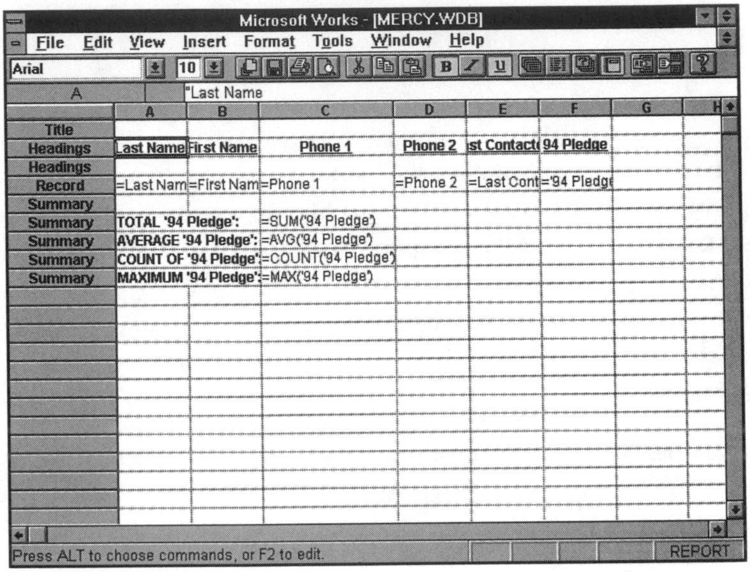

Fig. 23.1

Use Report view to customize a basic Works Database report with text, formatting, and calculation commands.

2. Move the highlight to where you want to type an entry.

3. Type the entry.

   For example, to insert a title in the report in figure 23.1, move the highlight into column E and type a title: for example, **Pledge Contacts**. (See fig. 23.2.)

4. Press Enter.

Tip

To replace an existing entry, highlight it and type the new entry.

Later in this chapter, in the section on "Using Fonts," you learn how to format text in a report definition using any fonts that are available with your printer.

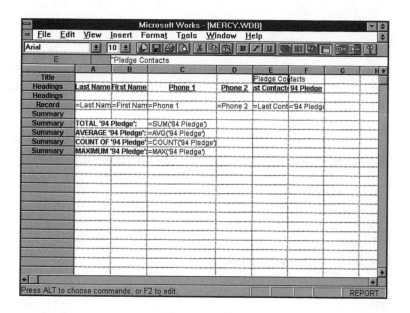

Fig. 23.2

To insert text in a report definition, highlight a cell and type the text, then press Enter.

IV

Databases

Changing Column Width and Row Height

Works displays a report definition using the same column width and row height that it uses to display a database in List view. The default column width is often not wide enough to hold text or formulas without spilling over into adjacent cells. If there is information in the column to the right, Works may hide part of the information you type, as shown in column E in figure 23.2.

You can change column width and row height to accommodate long information. Remember, though, in Report view, you are looking at the structure of a report, not the field contents that are printed in the report. Although you can change column widths and row height to view information in Report view, you should only do so temporarily. When you finish making changes to a report definition, adjust the columns and rows to the width and height you want Works to use for the columns in the actual report.

Follow these steps to change column width or row height in Report view:

1. Drag the column or row border to the desired width or height.

   or

   Highlight the column or row you want to change by clicking the row or column label.

2. From the Format menu, choose Column **W**idth or Row **H**eight.

3. Type a width between 1 and 79 or a height between 4 and 409.

4. Choose OK.

Works adjusts the row height or column width. Figure 23.3 shows the effect of changing the width of column E. Notice that you can now read the heading in column E.

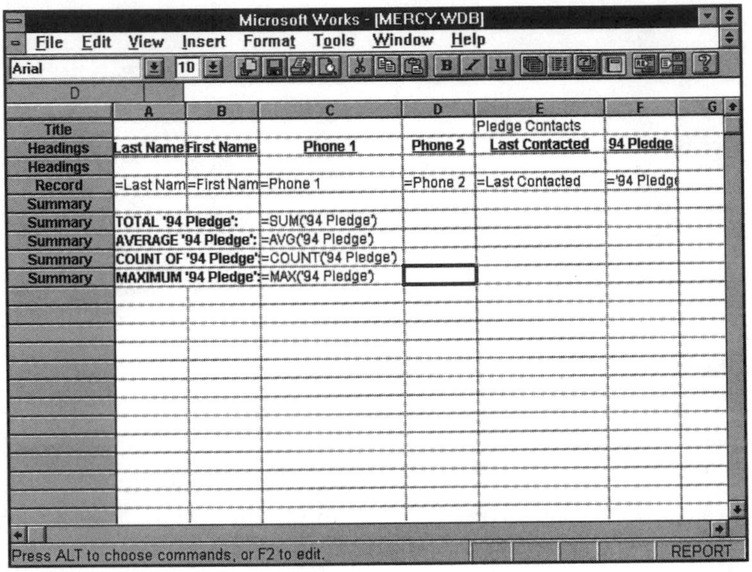

Fig. 23.3
Drag column or row borders to make room for long information.

Changing a Number Format

In Chapter 17, "Creating and Editing a Database Form," you learn how to change the number format of a field in a database form. (Refer to the section on "Changing Number Formats.") Similarly, you can change the number format that Works applies when it prints information in a report. For example, you can format currency amounts with dollar signs and two decimal places, and long numbers with comma separators after every third digit.

Tip
When you create a field that contains mixed text and numbers, you should format the field as text if you want Works to group text and numbers separately when you sort the field.

Caution

When you want to sort on a ZIP code field in your database form, format it as text. Otherwise, Works formats codes that begin with zero improperly. For example, if you format the ZIP code field with the default general format, Works formats 02091 as 2091. Also, it treats 10-digit ZIP codes as math formulas: when you type 98000-2000, for example, it calculates a subtraction and inserts 96000.

Follow these steps to change a field's number format in a report:

1. In Report view, highlight the entry or entries you want to format.

   For example, to apply the currency format to the Summary row that contains AVERAGE '94 Pledge':=AVG('94 Pledge'), click the Summary row title to select the row, then continue with step 2.

2. Choose Forma**t**, **N**umber.

   Works displays the Number dialog box, which is exactly the same as the Number dialog box that appears when you format fields in a database form, as described in Chapter 17, "Creating and Editing a Database Form." (See fig. 23.4.)

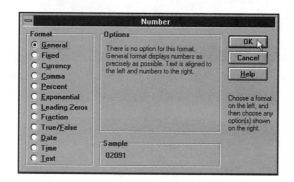

Fig. 23.4
Use the Number dialog box to format field contents in a report.

3. Choose the number format you want.

4. If you choose a number format and Works displays additional options for that choice, choose one of the additional options.

To see a list of descriptions of the available number types and how they display numbers, see "Formatting Numbers in Fields" in Chapter 17, "Creating and Editing a Database Form."

Note

In figure 23.4 with 02091 selected in a ZIP code field and the **G**eneral option selected, the Sample box displays 02091. This is incorrect. With **G**eneral selected, Works deletes leading zeros in ZIP codes; therefore you should format ZIP code fields as text.

You can change the default number of decimal places that Works proposes for the various number formats in the Number dialog box. Follow these steps:

1. Choose Tools, Options.

2. Choose Default number of decimals and type the number of decimals you want Works to propose for the fixed, currency, comma, percent, and exponential number formats.

3. Choose OK.

Works changes the default number of decimals until you change the default again.

Changing Alignment in a Report Field

Report columns are sometimes easier to read when Works aligns the column contents flush left, flush right, or centered, depending on the type of data in the column. For example, text is easier to read when formatted flush left, and numbers are easier to read formatted flush right. This is the alignment that Works applies by default, but you can change the alignment for any column in Report view.

You also can have Works wrap long text in the specified column width.

Follow these steps to change report field alignment:

1. In Report view, highlight the field or entry you want to change.

2. Choose Format, Alignment.

   Works displays the Alignment dialog box (fig. 23.5).

Fig. 23.5
Use the Alignment dialog box to align text and numbers horizontally and vertically in a cell and to wrap long text.

3. Choose **G**eneral, **L**eft, **R**ight, **C**enter, **F**ill, or Center **a**cross selection.

Use the **F**ill option to copy a row heading into empty cells to the right or left of the heading. Select the heading and the empty cell or cells, and choose **F**ill in the Alignment dialog box.

4. To align text vertically, choose **T**op, **C**enter, or **B**ottom.

When you align text vertically, Works moves the text or numbers to the top, bottom, or center of a cell. In figure 23.6, the **T**op vertical alignment option was selected for the Address Line 2 field. Notice that the field contents for the second record, 234 West Harris, is aligned at the top of the cell.

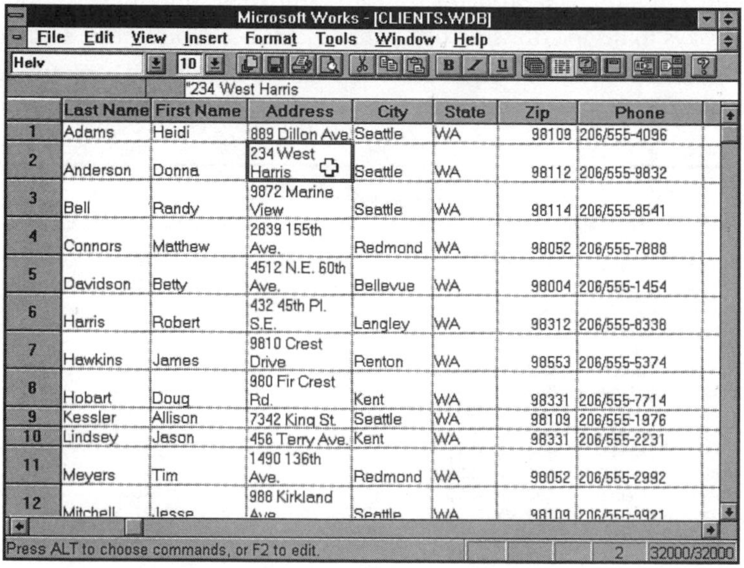

Fig. 23.6
Use field alignment to make column contents more readable in your reports.

5. To wrap text in the selected field, choose **W**rap text.

6. Choose OK.

In figure 23.6, notice that **W**rap text is turned on for the Business Name and Address Line 1 fields.

Tip
Works only wraps
text. It does not
wrap numbers,
dates, times, per-
centages, or other
values.

Note

To make your reports readable, format *all* columns with the **T**op, **W**rap text, and **G**eneral alignment options. To quickly align an entire report with the **T**op option, choose **E**dit, Select **A**ll, then choose Forma**t**, **A**lignment, **T**op, **W**rap text, **G**eneral, OK. View the effects of your changes in Print Preview, then adjust field widths as needed.

Choosing Fonts and Font Sizes, Styles, and Colors

When you create a report using the New Report dialog box, Works uses the default Works Database font for the report title, column headings, and report text. The resulting report is visually dull. If you are preparing a report for a formal presentation, you probably want to improve its appearance. One of the best ways to begin "dressing up" your reports is by formatting text with fonts. Figures 23.7 and 23.8 show the same report, before and after formatting the title with a larger, more decorative bold font.

Fig. 23.7
A report with a
10-point Arial
normal font used
for the title.

		Pledge Contacts			
Last Name	**First Name**	**Phone 1**	**Phone 2**	**Last Contacted**	**94 Pledge**
Albright	Henry	602/222-8686		34487	2500
Athelsen	Harold	602/395-3294		34395	10000
Bannon	Bella	602/813-8892		34410	4500
Black	Dick	602/777-1243		34226	450
Clearwater	Hollis	602/329-4888		34516	10000
Conner	Betsy	602/854-2830		34335	500
Emsworth	Clarence	602/777-1243		34226	450
Fleming	Garth	602/777-1243		34226	450
Foreman	Helen	602/482-5631		34516	25000
Foster	Nancy	602/482-5631		34516	25000
Mallory	Alicia	602/231-9856		34516	750
Mallory	Denice	602/329-4888		34516	10000
McGilloway	Kerry	602/854-2833		34318	5000
Megander	Orelle	602/813-8892		34410	4500
Novak	Bruce	602/813-8892		34410	4500
O'Hara	Doreen	602/395-4446		34487	15000
Ollander	Samantha	602/482-5631		34516	25000
Orden	Gary	602/854-2833		34318	5000
Porter	L. Janice	602/329-4891		34486	5000
Seligman	Anders	602/329-4888		34516	10000
Trant	Phillida	602/854-2830		34335	500
Van Slyke	Gene	602/444-6666	602/444-68˙	34530	1000
Walton	Alice	602/854-2830		34335	500
Watkins	Orlo	602/329-4832		34486	2500
Whiting	Decker	602/854-2833		34318	5000

TOTAL '94 Pledge': 173100
AVERAGE '94 Pledge' 6924
COUNT OF '94 Pledge 25
MAXIMUM '94 Pledge' 25000

Pledge Contacts

Last Name	First Name	Phone 1	Phone 2	Last Contacted	94 Pledge
Albright	Henry	602/222-8686		34487	2500
Athelsen	Harold	602/395-3294		34395	10000
Bannon	Bella	602/813-8892		34410	4500
Black	Dick	602/777-1243		34226	450
Clearwater	Hollis	602/329-4888		34516	10000
Conner	Betsy	602/854-2830		34335	500
Emsworth	Clarence	602/777-1243		34226	450
Fleming	Garth	602/777-1243		34226	450
Foreman	Helen	602/482-5631		34516	25000
Foster	Nancy	602/482-5631		34516	25000
Mallory	Alicia	602/231-9856		34516	750
Mallory	Denice	602/329-4888		34516	10000
McGilloway	Kerry	602/854-2833		34318	5000
Megander	Orelle	602/813-8892		34410	4500
Novak	Bruce	602/813-8892		34410	4500
O'Hara	Doreen	602/395-4446		34487	15000
Ollander	Samantha	602/482-5631		34516	25000
Orden	Gary	602/854-2833		34318	5000
Porter	L. Janice	602/329-4891		34486	5000
Seligman	Anders	602/329-4888		34516	10000
Trant	Phillida	602/854-2830		34335	500
Van Slyke	Gene	602/444-6666	602/444-68'	34530	1000
Walton	Alice	602/854-2830		34335	500
Watkins	Orlo	602/329-4832		34486	2500
Whiting	Decker	602/854-2833		34318	5000

TOTAL '94 Pledge': 173100
AVERAGE '94 Pledge' 6924
COUNT OF '94 Pledge 25
MAXIMUM '94 Pledge' 25000

Fig. 23.8
The same report with a 16-point Arial bold font used for the title.

IV

Databases

Follow these steps to change the font for information in a report:

1. Highlight the information you want to change.

   For example, move the highlight into the cell that contains the report title.

2. Click the Font box arrow on the toolbar and select a new font from the drop-down list, then click the font size arrow and select a size from the drop-down list.

   or

   Choose Format, Font and Style. The Font and Style dialog box appears. Select a font, size, color, and style, then choose OK.

To learn more about using fonts, see "Using Fonts" in Chapter 18, "Enhancing a Database Form." You use the same steps and dialog boxes to apply fonts in Report view and in Form view.

Tip
You can display fonts in color if you have a color monitor, even if you don't have a color printer. You might want to display fonts in color, for example, if you present the report to others on your monitor.

To change the default font and style that Works uses for all new report definitions, follow steps 1 and 2 in the previous section. In the Font and Style dialog box, choose the font, size, color, and style for the default font, then choose **S**et Default. Choose **Y**es to confirm your choice, then choose OK. Works uses the new default font for each new database report, for databases that you design in List view, and for new spreadsheets, until you change the default again. Existing reports and spreadsheets are not changed.

You can set a separate default font for database forms and for Works Word Processor documents. To set the default font for database forms, see "Using Fonts" in Chapter 18, "Enhancing a Database Form."

Creating a Page Break in a Report

Page breaks enable you to divide report contents logically. For example, you can insert page breaks to tell Works to print each group in a sorted report on a separate page. You can also insert a column page break to have Works print the columns to the right of the page break on a new page.

When you create a report that is too wide for the paper you are printing on, Works automatically prints as many columns as fit on the first page and prints the remaining columns on subsequent pages. You can use a column page break to tell Works which columns to print on each page. For example, you might prefer to have columns 1 through 3 printed on page 1, columns 4 and 5 on page 2, and columns 6 through 10 on page 3.

Row page breaks work differently, depending on where you insert them. For example, if you insert a page break between two Summ <fieldname> rows, Works inserts a page break after it prints each summary group for the field. (You learn about the Summ <fieldname> row function later in this chapter, in the section on "Selecting Data and Using Calculations.")

Tip
To insert a page break between the groups in a sorted report, insert a Summ <fieldname> row as described later in this chapter under "Sorting and Grouping Report Data," then insert a horizontal page break.

Follow these steps to insert a page break in a report:

1. In Report view, highlight the row below the row or the column to the left of the column where you want to insert a page break.

2. Choose **I**nsert, Page **B**reak.

   Works inserts the page break. To see how the page break affects the report, display the report with Print Preview.

3. To remove a page break, place the highlight in the row below or column to the right of the page break, then choose **I**nsert, Delete Pa**g**e Break.

IV

Creating Report Headers and Footers and Numbering Pages

As with a Works Word Processor document, you can create headers and footers that print on each page of a report. A report header or footer can contain text such as the report title and author, the page number, the date, and so on.

Follow these steps to create a header or footer:

1. In Report view, from the **V**iew menu, choose **H**eaders and Footers.

   Works displays the Headers and Footers dialog box (fig. 23.9).

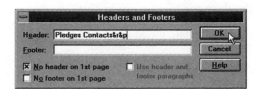

Fig. 23.9
Use the Headers and Footers dialog box to print a header and/or footer on each report page.

2. In the **H**eader and **F**ooter text boxes type the text for the header and/or footer, including the date, time, file name, page number or special characters to align text. Refer to the section on Using Special Header/Footer Codes and Numbering Pages in Chapter 20,"Expanding Your Database Skills," for a detailed explanation of the codes.

3. Choose **N**o header on 1st page or N**o** footer on 1st page to omit the header or footer from the first page of the report.

> **Note**
>
> Notice that the Use header and footer paragraphs option is grayed, because it can only be used in the Works Word Processor.

4. Choose OK.

You might occasionally have to change the page number that Works uses for the first page of a report. This might be necessary, for example, if you insert the report in a word processor document that someone else has created using a different application. Follow these steps to change the starting page number of the report:

1. From Report view, choose **F**ile, Pa**g**e Setup.

   2. Choose the **O**ther Options tab.

   3. In the **1**st Page Number box, type the page number for the first page of the report.

   4. Choose OK.

Works numbers the report beginning with the page number you typed.

To format headers or footers attractively, you can change the header or footer margins. For example, you might want to print a flush-left report title and flush-right page number in a header, and print this information using margins a little bit wider than the body of the report.

Follow these steps to change the header and footer margins:

   1. From the **F**ile menu, choose Pa**g**e Setup.

   2. Choose the **M**argins tab.

   3. In the **M**argins text boxes, type the new margin settings.

   4. Choose OK.

To remove headers and footers from a report, follow these steps:

   1. From the **V**iew menu, choose **H**eaders and Footers.

   2. Highlight the text in the H**e**ader or **F**ooter box and press Del.

   3. Choose OK.

Sorting and Grouping Report Data

Works gives you two ways to sort the records that it prints in a report:

■ You can display and sort the records in a database in Form or List view, then display or print the report. Works then displays or prints the records in the order you sorted them. You learned to use this method in the section on "Sorting Database Records" in Chapter 20, "Expanding Your Database Skills."

■ You can also specify sorting as part of the report definition. When you choose this option, Works automatically sorts the database according to your specifications before it displays or prints the report. You learn how to use this method in this section.

When you sort the columns in a report by inserting sort commands in the report definition, Works saves your sort preferences with the report. When you print or display the report again after entering or deleting records, Works automatically reapplies the sort you specified.

When you sort a report, you can tell Works to group the sorted records. For example, you can sort the report in ascending order by '94 Pledge and tell Works to insert a group break every time the pledge amount changes. If you specified summary information, Works calculates and prints summary data for each group, and also at the end of the report, as shown in figure 23.10.

Pledge Contacts

Last Name	First Name	Phone 1	Phone 2	Last Contacted	'94 Pledge
Foreman	Helen	602/482-5631		7/1/94	$25,000.00
Foster	Nancy	602/482-5631		7/1/94	$25,000.00
Ollander	Samantha	602/482-5631		7/1/94	$25,000.00
	3	3	3		$75,000.00
O'Hara	Doreen	602/395-4446		6/2/94	$15,000.00
	1	1	1		$15,000.00
Clearwater	Hollis	602/329-4888		7/1/94	$10,000.00
Mallory	Denice	602/329-4888		7/1/94	$10,000.00
Seligman	Anders	602/329-4888		7/1/94	$10,000.00
Athelsen	Harold	602/395-3294		3/2/94	$10,000.00
	4	4	4		$40,000.00
Porter	L. Janice	602/329-4891		6/1/94	$5,000.00
McGilloway	Kerry	602/854-2833		12/15/93	$5,000.00
Orden	Gary	602/854-2833		12/15/93	$5,000.00
Whiting	Decker	602/854-2833		12/15/93	$5,000.00
	4	4	4		$20,000.00
Bannon	Bella	602/813-8892		3/17/94	$4,500.00
Megander	Orelle	602/813-8892		3/17/94	$4,500.00
Novak	Bruce	602/813-8892		3/17/94	$4,500.00
	3	3	3		$13,500.00
Albright	Henry	602/222-8686		6/2/94	$2,500.00
Watkins	Orlo	602/329-4832		6/1/94	$2,500.00
	2	2	2		$5,000.00
Last Name	First Name	Phone 1	Phone 2	Last Contacted	'94 Pledge
	3	3	3		$1,500.00
Black	Dick	602/777-1243		9/14/93	$450.00
Emsworth	Clarence	602/777-1243		9/14/93	$450.00
Fleming	Garth	602/777-1243		9/14/93	$450.00
	3	3	3		$1,350.00

Fig. 23.10
When you sort and group data, Works inserts summary information for each group, and also at the end of the report.

Notice in figure 23.10 that because the report included summary fields for count and total before it was sorted and grouped, Works automatically calculated and printed totals and counts for the subgroups after the report was sorted and grouped.

Figure 23.11 shows the report definition that was used to print the report shown in figure 23.10. You learn about the rows labeled Summ '94 Pledge in this section. Works automatically inserts a Summ <fieldname> row when you sort and group a report.

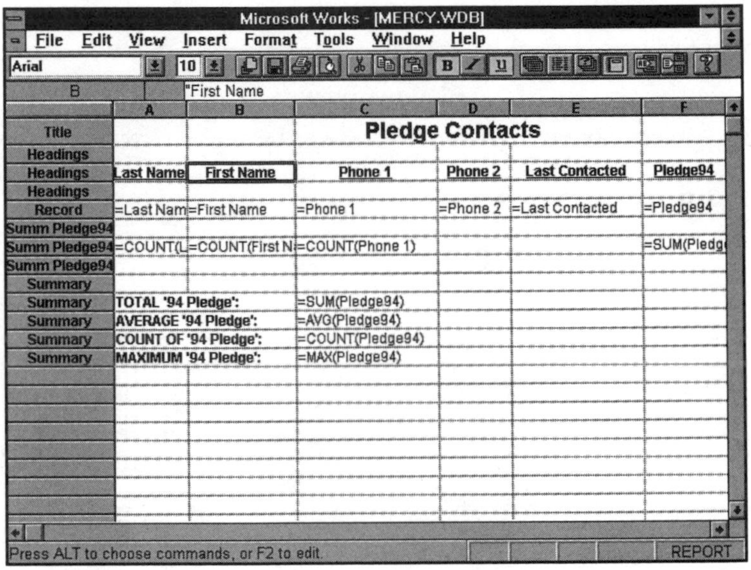

Fig. 23.11
The report definition that was used to create the report in figure 23.10.

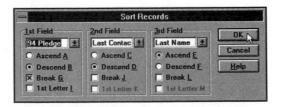

For a full discussion of the rules that Works uses when it sorts database records, see "Sorting Database Records" in Chapter 20, "Expanding Your Database Skills."

Follow these steps to sort a report and group the sorted records:

1. Display the report definition and choose Tools, Sort Records.

   Works displays the Sort Records dialog box (fig. 23.12).

Fig. 23.12
Use the Sort Records dialog box to sort a report on as many as three fields and specify sort breaks.

Figure 23.12 shows the settings that were used to sort the report shown in figure 23.10. The report was sorted first in descending order by the amount of the donor's '94 Pledge. A group break was specified for each time the pledge amount changed. Notice in figure 23.10 that Works grouped the donors who gave $25,000, $15,000, and $10,000, and so on.

2. Select **1**st Field and type or select from the drop-down list the name of the field you want Works to sort first.

3. Select Ascend **A** or Descend **B** to determine the sort order for the first sort field.

4. If you want Works to group records each time the contents of the first sort field change, select Break **G**.

5. If you select Break **G** to group records, you then have the option of selecting 1st Letter **I**. With this option selected Works groups records when the first letter in the sort field changes.

> **Note**
>
> Works breaks report groups first letter only for text fields. If you choose 1st Letter, Works creates a new group *only* when the first letter of the group changes. This is useful for creating phone lists and other alphabetic references. If you don't choose 1st Letter, Works creates a new group when *any part* of the sort field changes.

6. Repeat steps 1-5 for the **2**nd Field and **3**rd Field, if you want to sort on more than one field.

7. Choose OK.

Works sorts the records and, if you choose group breaks, inserts Summ <fieldname> rows for each break.

Notice that in figure 23.11 two empty Summ Pledge94 rows were deliberately inserted to separate the groups and make the report more legible. To insert an empty row, place the cursor in the row above which you want to insert the empty row, then choose **I**nsert, **R**ow/Column, and choose **R**ow, then choose the row **T**ype and choose OK. Works inserts an empty row above the row that contains the highlight.

Selecting Fields and Using Calculations

So far in this chapter, you have learned how to change the formatting that Works applies to a report. To change the report format, you applied commands with a report definition displayed in Report view.

In this section you find out how to use the report definition to tell Works which field contents to print in a report. For example, you might want to add a field titled Amount Due. You also learn how to create report columns based on math calculations on database fields. For example, you might want to create the field named Amount Due based on the formula: '94 Pledge minus Amount Paid.

Inserting a Field Name Label

The most basic change you can make to the contents of a Works database report definition is to add a field to the report. To have Works print the contents of a field, you add a new field name label in a headings row, then add a field entry instruction, as described in the next section, "Adding a Field Entry Instruction." In figure 23.11, notice that a Headings row contains the field labels, and a Record row contains field entry instructions.

You can also use field names in calculation formulas, as described later in this chapter in the section on "Adding a Calculation Formula."

Follow these steps to add a field name label:

1. In Report view, move the highlight to the cell in which you want to insert the field name.

   For example, you can highlight an empty cell in a Headings row.

   > **Caution**
   >
   > If you highlight a cell that already contains a heading, Works overwrites the heading when you insert the new field.

2. Choose **I**nsert, Field **N**ame.

   Works displays the Insert Field Name dialog box (fig. 23.13).

Fig. 23.13
Use the Insert Field
Name dialog box
to add a new
field to a report
definition.

3. Choose the field name you want to insert.

4. Choose OK.

Works inserts the field name.

Adding a Field Entry Instruction

A field entry instruction is different from a field label. A field label merely
prints the name of a field in the report, but a field entry instruction prints all
the database entries from the field in the report.

Follow these steps to add a field entry instruction:

1. Move the highlight to where you want the instruction.

   Field entry instructions are usually put in Record rows to tell Works to
   print the field contents in the body of the report.

2. From the **I**nsert menu, choose Field Entr**y**.

   Works displays the Insert Field Entry dialog box, which is the same as
   the Insert Field Name dialog box (see fig. 23.13) except for its title.

3. Choose **F**ields and select the field whose contents you want printed in
   the report.

4. Choose OK.

Works inserts the field name formatted as a field entry formula, for example:
=Date Entered. When Works prints the report, it inserts the entries from the
database field.

> **Note**
>
> If a field contains an object such as a drawing, Works does not print the object in the
> report; instead, it prints <<object>>.

Tip
You don't have to
use the Insert Field
Entry dialog box to
insert field entry
instructions; you
can simply type
them directly in a
report definition
cell. For example,
type =DATE to
print the Date
field.

Adding a Calculation Formula

In a report definition, you can tell Works to calculate the results of a formula or Works function and insert the results in a field column in the report.

Observe the following rules for placement of formulas in a report definition:

- For a simple calculated field, insert the formula in a Record row.

- For a formula you want Works to apply to a field for each sorted field group, insert a formula in a Summ <fieldname> row. (You must first sort the report as described earlier in this chapter under "Sorting and Grouping Report Data.")

- For a formula you want Works to apply to a field for the entire report, place the formula in a Summary row.

You can use the following built-in functions in calculated fields. Notice that these functions are the same ones that Works inserts in the report definition when you specify report statistics from a dialog box, as described under "Creating a Basic Works Report" in Chapter 22, "Creating a Database Report."

- *SUM.* Totals the values in a numeric field. For example: SUM(Amt. Due).

- *AVG.* Averages the values in a numeric field. For example: AVG(Pledge94).

- *COUNT.* Counts the number of entries in a field. For example: COUNT(Stock No.).

- *MAX.* Finds the largest value in a numeric field. For example: MAX(Annual Income).

- *MIN.* Finds the smallest value in a numeric field. For example: MIN(Diameter).

- *STD.* Calculates the standard deviation for a numeric field. For example: STD(Acreage).

- *VAR.* Calculates the variance for a numeric field. For example: VAR(Dept. Sum).

Follow these steps to add a calculation formula:

1. If necessary, add a Summ <fieldname> row or a Summary row for the calculation.

> **Note**
>
> To add a Summ <fieldname> row, you must sort the report as described earlier in this chapter under "Sorting and Grouping Report Data," and you must include at least one sort break. You can add a Summ <fieldname> row only if you have a sort break in the report.

2. Move the highlight to where you want to insert the calculation.

3. Choose Insert, Field Summary.

   Works displays the Insert Field Summary dialog box (fig. 23.14).

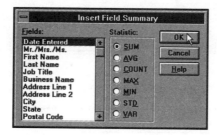

Fig. 23.14
Use the Insert Field Summary dialog box to insert summary calculations in a report definition.

4. Select Fields and select a field name.

5. Select a calculation option.

   Example: Choose SUM to total the amounts in the Amt. Due field.

6. Choose OK.

   Works inserts the calculation formula. Figure 23.15 shows the result of choosing the Amt. Due field and the SUM calculation formula.

Performing Arithmetic Calculations

You don't have to use the Works built-in functions in a calculated report column. You can calculate column contents by using arithmetic operations on fields. For example, you could use the following formula to calculate the interest on an Amt. Due field and insert the results in a Current Balance field in the report: =Amt. Due*.035*Past Due.

Fig. 23.15
Works inserts a
calculation using
the field name and
function you
selected.

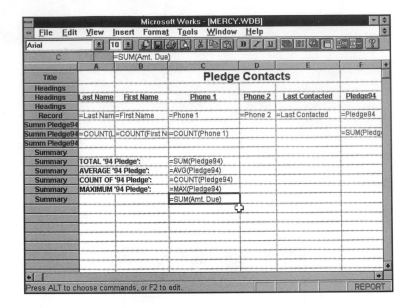

You can use the following Works math operators in a report definition:

Operator	Purpose
+	Addition
–	Subtraction
*	Multiplication
/	Division
^	Exponentiation

Follow these steps to insert a math calculation in a report field:

1. If necessary, add a Record row, a Summ <fieldname> row, or a Summary row.

To add a Summ <fieldname>, sort and group the report as described earlier in this chapter under "Sorting and Grouping Report Data." To add a Record row or a Summary Row, see "Changing a Report" in Chapter 22, "Creating a Database Report."

2. Move the highlight to the cell in which you want to insert the calculated field.

3. Type the math formula.

For example, type =Pledge94-Amt. Paid

4. Press Enter.

Works inserts the formula in the cell. When you preview or print the report, Works displays the results of the math calculation in the field column. Figures 23.16 and 23.17 show a report definition and previewed report that include a field titled Amt. Due. Notice in the report definition in figure 23.16 that the formula for the field is: =Pledge94 –Amt. Paid. In figure 23.17 Works calculated the formula and inserted the results in the column labeled Amt. Due.

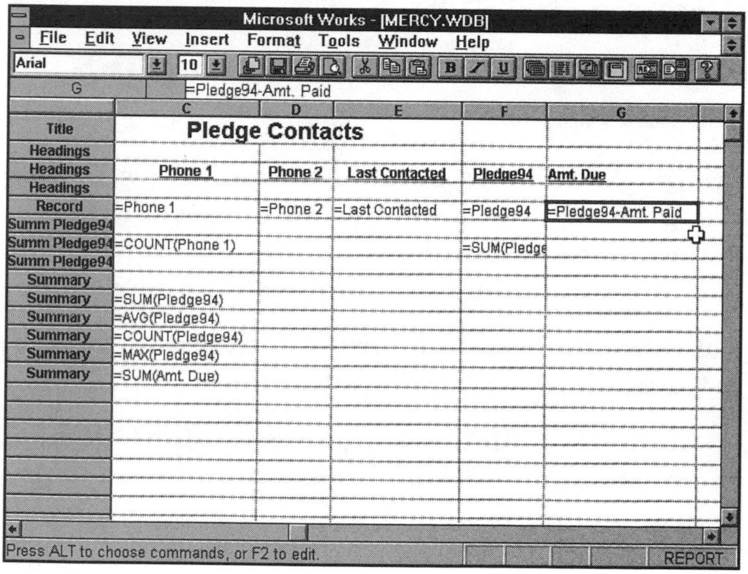

Fig. 23.16
Type a math formula in a report definition cell to print the calculated results in a report column.

Fig. 23.17
When you print a report, Works calculates math formulas and inserts the results in the corresponding columns.

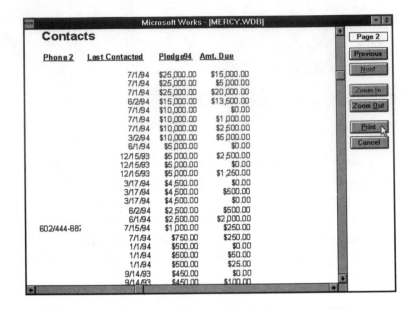

Using Report Output in Another Application

You can copy a Works Database report to another application. For example, you can insert formatted report contents in a Works Word Processor or Works Spreadsheet document. When you copy a report to the Word Processor or Spreadsheet, Works uses the following formatting guidelines:

- In the Word Processor, Works separates report columns with tabs and ends rows with paragraph marks.

- In the Spreadsheet, Works places report rows in spreadsheet rows and report columns in spreadsheet columns.

Figure 23.18 shows a Works Database report that was copied to a Word Processor document, and figure 23.19 shows the same report copied to a Spreadsheet document.

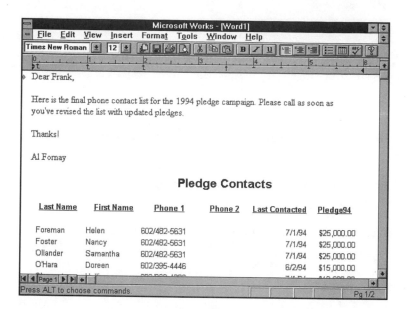

Fig. 23.18
Copy report
output to a Word
Processor docu-
ment to use it in
a letter or word-
processed report.

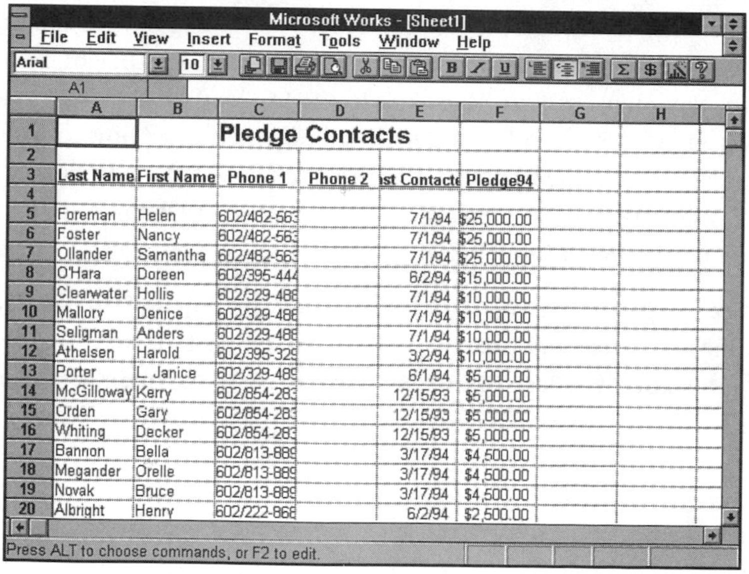

Fig. 23.19
When you copy
report output to
a Spreadsheet
document, Works
places the report's
contents in
spreadsheet rows
and columns.

Follow these steps to copy a report into another Works tool or Windows
application:

1. Display the report definition in Report view.

2. Highlight the part of the report whose output you want to copy.

> **Note**
>
> If nothing is highlighted, Works copies the entire report.

3. From the Edit menu, select Copy Report Output.

4. Switch to the Works module or other Windows application document in which you want to insert the report.

5. From the Edit menu, choose Paste; or press Ctrl+V; or click the Paste toolbar button.

   Works pastes the report output into the document.

From Here...

In this chapter, you learned how to create complex reports by editing a report definition in Report view. Specifically, you learned how to add titles, headings, and labels to a report, change column width, row height, number formats, alignment, and use fonts. You learned to set page breaks and page margins and to create headers and footers. You also learned how to specify fields, sort and group report output, and create calculated report fields. Finally, you learned how to export reports for use in other applications. You can find related information in the following chapter:

■ See Chapter 26, "Using the Works Tools Together," to find out how to link and embed information between the Works tools so that Works automatically reflects any changes you make to the original document.

Part V

Enhancing Documents

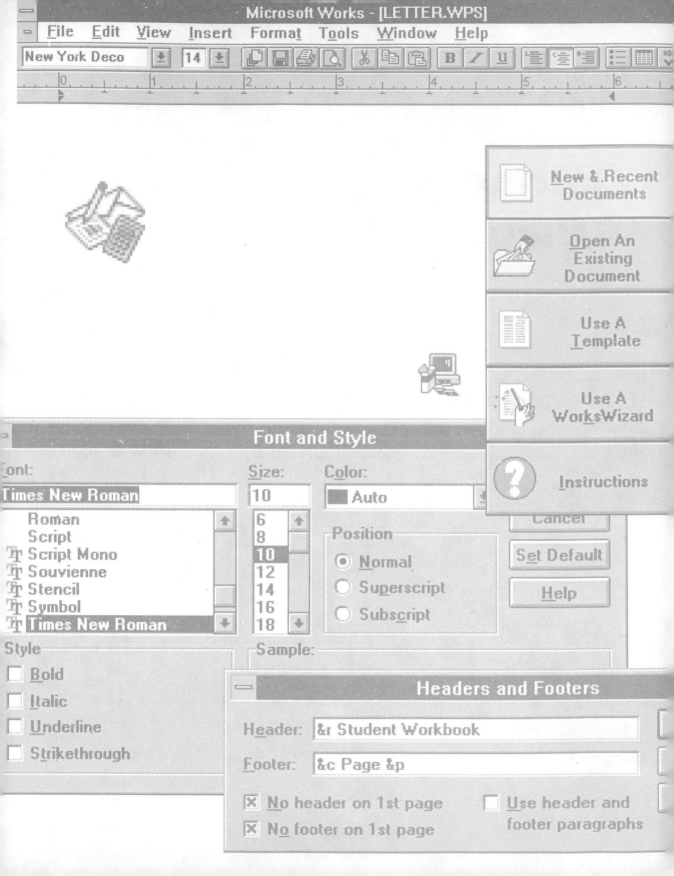

Microsoft Works - [LETTER.WPS]

File Edit View Insert Format Tools Window Help

New York Deco   14

New &.Recent Documents

Open An Existing Document

Use A Template

Use A WorksWizard

Instructions

Font and Style

Font:
Times New Roman

Roman
Script
Script Mono
Souvienne
Stencil
Symbol
Times New Roman

Size:
10

6
8
10
12
14
16
18

Color:
Auto

Cancel

Set Default

Help

Position
● Normal
○ Superscript
○ Subscript

Style
☐ Bold
☐ Italic
☐ Underline
☐ Strikethrough

Sample:

Headers and Footers

Header: &r Student Workbook

Footer: &c Page &p

☒ No header on 1st page
☒ No footer on 1st page

☐ Use header and footer paragraphs

Chapter 24

Using Microsoft Draw and ClipArt

For each of the tools in Works, you have learned how to enhance the appearance of the documents you create by changing fonts and point sizes of text, aligning and formatting text in special ways, adding color, borders, patterns, and so on. But nothing enhances a document more than a picture. Works provides the means for you to include pictures in your word processor documents and database forms using Microsoft Draw or ClipArt.

Chapter 1, "Introducing Works for Windows," explains that Microsoft Draw is a special drawing tool included with Works that enables you to create your own color drawings. The ClipArt Gallery, also included in Works, is a collection of prepared drawings that span a wide variety of categories; you simply select the drawing you want and insert it in your file. Use Microsoft Draw or ClipArt to add humor, draw attention, or illustrate a point in a document or form.

Inserting Drawings in Documents and Forms

The word processor and database parts of this book introduce you to working with pictures, or *inserted objects*, as they are called in Works. Specifically, in Chapter 7, "Working with Tables, Columns, and Inserted Objects," and Chapter 17, "Creating and Editing a Database Form," you learn how to work with inserted objects in a word processor document and database form. You

In this chapter, you learn how to perform the following tasks:

■ Insert drawings in word processor documents and database forms

■ Create, save, and change a drawing using Microsoft Draw

■ Select a ClipArt drawing to insert

■ Size, modify, and delete a ClipArt drawing

learn how to position an object, size it, and format surrounding text. What you don't learn in these chapters is how to create and insert the object itself.

Before you can insert an object from Microsoft Draw or the ClipArt Gallery, you first must open a word processor document or a database form. From either of these types of files, you have access to Microsoft Draw and ClipArt via the **I**nsert menu, shown in figure 24.1. The bottom portion of the menu includes the ClipArt and Drawing commands. This particular menu is from the word processor tool, but the same commands appear on the **I**nsert menu in the database tool.

Fig. 24.1
The **I**nsert menu gives you access to Microsoft ClipArt and Draw.

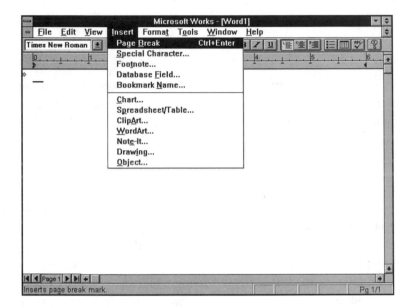

Before inserting an object, you place the insertion point or highlight where you want to insert the object in your file. Then you choose the command you want to use.

When you choose the Drawing command from the **I**nsert menu, Works starts up Microsoft Draw in a separate window on-screen. You create your drawing, then insert it by returning to your document or database form.

When you choose the ClipArt command from the **I**nsert menu, Works displays the ClipArt Gallery dialog box from which you select a ClipArt file to insert. After you select a file, the ClipArt Gallery dialog box closes and Works copies the ClipArt file into your document.

Creating and Saving a Drawing

After you display the Microsoft Draw window on-screen, you're ready to create a drawing. Microsoft Draw is a separate application program that has its own set of menus and drawing tools. In figure 24.2, you see how the window looks on-screen after you choose the Drawing command from the Insert menu.

Microsoft Draw window

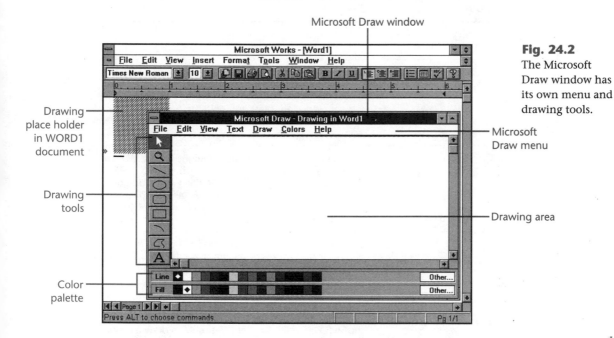

Fig. 24.2
The Microsoft Draw window has its own menu and drawing tools.

V

Enhancing Documents

The Draw window appears on top of the document window from which you chose the command—in this case, the WORD1 document window. The grayed area that appears in the document window acts as a place holder for the drawing you create. This place holder is a reminder to you that Works will place a drawing in your document at this location.

> **Note**
>
> Don't be concerned about the size of the grayed area—at this point it is simply a place holder and not representative of the size of the drawing you create. After you create the drawing, you can size it appropriately for your document.

Using the Drawing Tools

Along the left side of the Microsoft Draw window is a toolbox of drawing tools. You use these tools to select and draw objects. Techniques for using each of the tools are described in Table 24.1.

Table 24.1 Microsoft Draw Drawing Tools	
Tool	**Purpose**
	Selects objects.
	Enlarges or reduces your view of an entire drawing. To enlarge, click the Zoom tool, then click the drawing repeatedly until it is the size you want. To reduce your view of a drawing, press and hold the Shift key, then click the Zoom tool repeatedly until the drawing is the size you want.
	Click and drag to draw a single straight line. To draw a line at any angle of 45° increments (0°, 45°, 90°, 135°, and so on), press and hold the Shift key while dragging the line tool. To draw a line at any angle for which the center point is constrained, press and hold the Ctrl key while dragging the line tool.
	Click and drag to draw an ellipse. To draw a circle, press and hold the Shift key while dragging this tool. To draw a circle constrained to its center point, press and hold the Ctrl key while dragging this tool.
	Click and drag to draw a rectangle with rounded corners. To draw a square with rounded corners, press and hold the Shift key while dragging this tool. To draw a rectangle with rounded corners for which the center point is constrained, press and hold the Ctrl key while dragging this tool.
	Click and drag to draw a rectangle. To draw a square, press and hold the Shift key while dragging this tool. To draw a rectangle for which the center point is constrained, press and hold the Ctrl key while dragging this tool.
	Click and drag to draw a pie-wedge-shaped object. To constrain the center point, hold the Ctrl key while dragging this tool. To draw a 45° angle with arc, hold down the Shift key while dragging this tool.
	Click and drag to make a freeform drawing.
	Click, then type up to 255 letters on a single line of text.

To draw a line, circle/ellipse, rectangle/square, rounded rectangle/square, or arc, follow these steps:

1. Click the drawing tool you want to use.

2. Move the crosshair mouse pointer to the location where you want to draw the object.

3. Press the Shift or Ctrl keys as indicated in Table 24.1 to draw specialized objects. Click and drag the mouse until you're satisfied with the shape of the object.

4. Release the mouse button. Four frame handles appear at the outer corners of the object.

5. Click in any blank area of the drawing area or click the Arrow tool to deselect the object.

Using the *freeform* tool, you can draw open objects or closed polygons, or open or closed freehand drawings. You also can combine straight lines and freehand drawing in one object. Examples are shown in figure 24.3. To draw polygons consisting of straight lines, you click and release the mouse button at each vertex of the polygon. To draw freehand shapes, you drag the freeform tool then release the mouse button where you want the line or shape to end. The freeform tool remains in effect until you complete an object by double-clicking or pressing Enter.

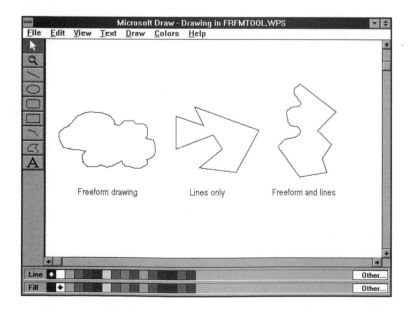

Fig. 24.3
Objects drawn with the freeform tool.

To draw an open or closed polygon, use these steps:

1. Select the freeform tool.

2. Move the crosshair mouse pointer to the location where you want the object to begin.

3. Click the mouse button, then release it.

4. Move the crosshair to the point where you want the first line to end and the connecting line to begin.

5. Click the mouse button, then release it.

6. Repeat steps 4 and 5, clicking the mouse button at each vertex.

7. To make the object an open polygon, double-click after you draw the last line or press Enter. To make the object a closed polygon, move the mouse pointer near or to the point where you began drawing, then click the mouse button. Works draws a straight line connecting the last line to the first.

8. Click on the arrow tool or anywhere in a blank area of the screen to deselect the object.

To draw an open or closed freehand shape, use these steps:

1. Select the freeform tool.

2. Move the crosshair mouse pointer to the location where you want the object to begin.

3. Click and drag the mouse in any direction, drawing the shape you want.

4. To leave the object open, double-click after you finish drawing or press Enter. To close the object, move the mouse pointer near or on the point where you began drawing, then click the mouse button. Works draws a straight line, connecting the beginning of the shape to the end of the shape.

5. Click on the arrow tool or anywhere in a blank area of the screen to deselect the object.

> **Note**
>
> While drawing freehand shapes, you can pause at any point by releasing the mouse button. Before beginning to draw again, position the crosshair in its location before you paused, then click and drag to continue drawing. To mix straight lines and freehand shapes in the same drawing, alternate between clicking the mouse and dragging the mouse.

Selecting Objects

Before you can make any changes to an object—move, copy, delete, resize, or enhance it—you first must select it. You select an object by clicking the Arrow tool, then clicking anywhere on the border of the object. When you select an object, Works displays four black squares that form a rectangle surrounding the object (see fig. 24.4). The black squares, called *resize handles,* enable you to adjust the size of the object. The handles also indicate that an object is selected.

Resize handle

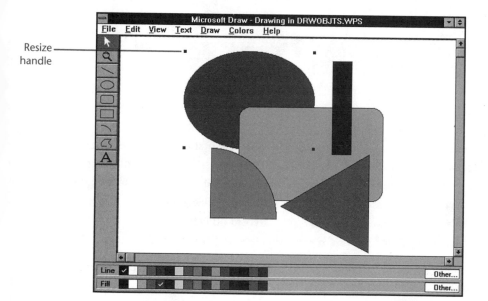

Fig. 24.4
The visible resize handles indicate the ellipse is selected.

V

Enhancing Documents

> **Note**
>
> When you enter text in a drawing, Works considers text an object. You can select text just like any other type of object.

You can select multiple objects at the same time by pressing and holding the Shift key as you click each object individually. After you have selected all the objects you want to include, release the Shift key. Figure 24.5 shows a group of objects selected.

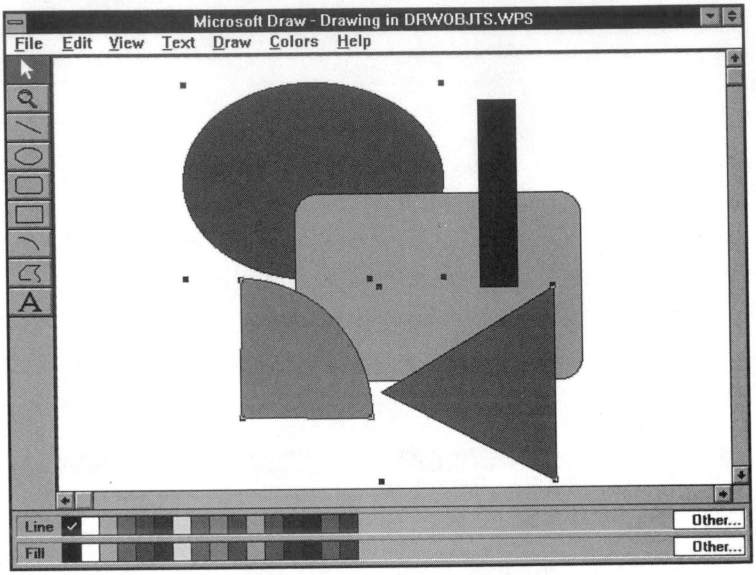

Fig. 24.5
Select multiple objects by holding the Shift key as you click. Here, the ellipse, arc, and triangle are selected.

Tip
When you want to select *all* objects in a drawing, choose the Select **A**ll command on the **E**dit menu, or press Ctrl+A. This command is particularly useful when you want to clear the current drawing and start over.

Tip
To group several objects together to treat them as a single object, select the objects and choose **D**raw **G**roup, or press Ctrl+G. To ungroup grouped objects, select **D**raw, **U**ngroup or press Ctrl+H.

Another way to select multiple objects is to draw a selection box around them. Select the Arrow tool from the toolbar, then click and drag the crosshair pointer from the upper left corner of the first object to the lower left corner of the last object you want to include in the selection. As you drag the mouse, a selection box in the form of a dashed rectangle defines the area you cover. When you release the mouse button, Draw selects all objects that you fully enclosed in the selection box. You can add objects to the selection by pressing and holding the Shift key as you click additional objects.

If you select the wrong object, you can easily cancel the selection by clicking any blank part of the drawing area. If you have selected multiple objects and want to remove one object from the selection, hold down the Shift key and click again on the object you want to remove. Works removes only the object you click from the selection.

Using Color in a Drawing

Color is one of the most important aspects of a drawing. Using Draw, you can change the line color or the fill color of objects. In this context, *line* refers to individual lines, the frame or outline of objects and text, and the foreground of a pattern. (You learn about using patterns later in this chapter.) *Fill* refers to the interior portion of a closed object or the background of a pattern. Available colors are shown on the color palette at the bottom of the Draw window (see fig. 24.6). A diamond marker on the palette indicates the default colors Draw uses for line (black) and fill (white). When an object is selected, a check mark indicates the line and fill colors that the object uses.

Fig. 24.6
Select a Line and
Fill color for all
objects and text in
a drawing.

To change the line or fill color of an object, select the object, then click a color in the appropriate palette. A check mark appears on the color you select as long as the object still is selected. When you cancel the selection, the diamond markers return to the color palette, indicating the default colors.

You also can select a line and fill color *before* you draw an object. Click the Arrow tool or click any blank area of the drawing palette to make sure no objects are selected. Select the line and fill colors you want to use for all new objects you draw. Diamond markers appear on the colors you select, indicating these colors now are the default colors. Click a drawing tool and begin drawing. The new colors you select remain in effect until you select new default colors.

Entering and Editing Text in a Drawing

To add text to a drawing, you click the Text tool. When you move the mouse pointer into the drawing area, the pointer changes to a vertical bar insertion point. Click the drawing area where you want the text to appear, then begin typing. You can type up to 255 characters on a single line of text (Draw does not wrap text). After you finish entering text, press Enter or click in any blank portion of the drawing area to select the text you typed. Click again in any blank portion of the drawing area or click the Arrow tool to cancel the selection.

If you create a particularly long text object and realize it contains an error, you can correct the error without retyping the entire entry. To edit the text, select the text object, then choose the E**d**it Text command from the **E**dit menu. When you choose this command, the insertion point is visible at the beginning of the text entry. (You can also double-click the character you want to edit to place the insertion point at that location.) Use the arrow keys to move the insertion point to the character you want to correct. Use the Del or Backspace keys to erase the error, then retype.

The default font and size used when you create a text object is System 12. To change the font or size of an existing text object, you use the **F**ont and **S**ize commands on the **T**ext menu. Follow these steps:

1. Select the text for which you want to change the font or size. Works displays the resize handles for the object.

2. From the **T**ext menu, choose the **F**ont command. A list of fonts appears.

3. Highlight the font you want to use, then press Enter. Works places a check mark next to the font and returns to the drawing, changing the font of the selected text.

4. From the **T**ext menu, choose the **S**ize command. A list of available point sizes appears.

5. Select a point size from the list or specify a custom size by choosing the **O**ther option and entering the point size. Works places a check mark next to the size and returns to the drawing, changing the point size of the selected text.

6. Click the Arrow tool or any blank portion of the drawing area to cancel the text selection.

The fonts used in figure 24.7 are Harem, Lucida Blackletter, Desdemona, Coronet, and Exchequer Script. These fonts appear in a variety of point sizes.

You also can change the default font and size. When you change the default font and size, all new text you type conforms to the font and size you specify until you select a new font and size. To change the default font and size, click the Arrow tool or click in any blank portion of the drawing area to make sure no objects are selected. Then make your choices using the **F**ont and **S**ize commands on the **T**ext menu. Works places a diamond marker next to the font and size you select, indicating they are now the default settings. Now when you enter new text, it appears in the new default font and size.

Fig. 24.7
Draw offers a wide
variety of fonts
and point sizes.

Saving Your Drawing in Your Document

After you complete your drawing and you are ready to insert it in your document, you use the Exit and Return to [*file name*] command on the File menu. When you choose this command, the Draw window closes and Works automatically inserts the drawing in the database form or word processor file you are using.

If you choose, you can insert intermediate versions of a drawing into a database form or word processor file as you are working. This process is called *updating* and ensures that your document includes at least the previous version of your drawing. When creating a complex drawing, updating is an important feature that prevents you from losing your drawing should your equipment fail or a power failure occur. To update a document at any point, choose the Update command from the File menu in Draw.

Editing a Drawing

Just as you can edit text in a document, you can edit an inserted drawing. Editing includes changing the pattern or line style used in an object; copying, moving, and deleting objects; rearranging the order of objects; and sizing, rotating, and flipping objects.

Troubleshooting

I drew a selection box around several objects to select all of them, but some of the objects I included were not selected.

When you draw a selection box using the Arrow tool, you must completely enclose all objects you want to select. Any objects that are only partially enclosed in the selection box are not included in the selection.

I changed the fill color of an object to red. Now all new objects I draw are filled with red.

You changed the default fill color instead of changing the color of a single object. To restore the default fill color of white, click the Arrow tool to make sure no objects are selected. Then click the white square in the fill color palette. The diamond on the white square indicates white is the default color for all new objects you draw.

When I try to draw any type of object or enter text, nothing shows on-screen except resize handles. What's wrong?

You changed the default line color to white, which matches the default fill color as well as the screen background, so your objects are not visible on-screen. To recover the objects you drew, choose the Select **A**ll command from the **E**dit menu, then change the default line color back to black (or any other color that's visible on a white background).

Changing Your View of a Drawing

Changing your view of a drawing can help you see portions up close, or you can view an entire drawing that is too large to appear entirely on-screen. This feature is called *Zoom*. You can use the **V**iew menu or the Zoom tool on the drawing toolbox to change your view of a drawing. The **V**iew menu, shown in figure 24.8, indicates that you can reduce a drawing to 25% **S**ize, **5**0%, or **7**5%. You also can enlarge a drawing to **2**00%, **4**00%, or **8**00%. Just select the percentage you want to use from the **V**iew menu. When you want to return to 100%, or full-size view, choose the **F**ull Size command from the **V**iew menu.

To change your view of a drawing using the Zoom tool, click the tool to select it. The mouse pointer changes to a magnifying glass with a + (plus) symbol inside. Click anywhere in the drawing area to zoom to 200%. Click a second time to zoom to 400% or click a third time to zoom to 800%.

To reduce your view of a drawing, select the Zoom tool, then press and hold the Shift key. The magnifying glass mouse pointer now has a – (minus) symbol inside. Click anywhere in the drawing area until the drawing appears in the size you want.

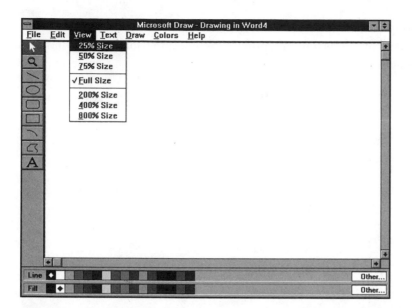

Fig. 24.8
The View menu
enables you to
enlarge or reduce
your view of a
drawing.

Note

The zoom feature in Draw does not alter the size of the drawing, only your *view*
of the drawing. To learn how to change the actual size of the drawing, see this
chapter's section "Resizing, Rotating, and Flipping Objects."

Selecting Line Styles and Patterns

Whenever you draw an object such as a circle or rectangle, an *outline* defines
the object. By default, Draw uses a solid line the width of one point to define
objects. However, you can increase the line width or change the line style
(to dotted, dashed, and so on) using the **L**ine Style command on the **D**raw
menu. The **L**ine Style command displays a submenu that lists line style
choices. If you prefer to set a custom line width, choose the **O**ther option and
enter a point size in the dialog box that appears. Examples of line styles and
point sizes are shown in figure 24.9.

As with fonts, sizes, and colors, you can change the line style for an existing
object or the default settings for all new objects you create. To change an
existing object, first select the object, then select a line style using the **L**ine
Style command from the **D**raw menu. While the object is selected, a check
mark appears next to the line style that the object uses. To change the default
line style, click the Arrow tool to make sure no objects in the drawing are

V

Enhancing Documents

selected, then select a new line style. On the **L**ine Style submenu, diamond markers appear next to the current line style and width choices, indicating the default settings.

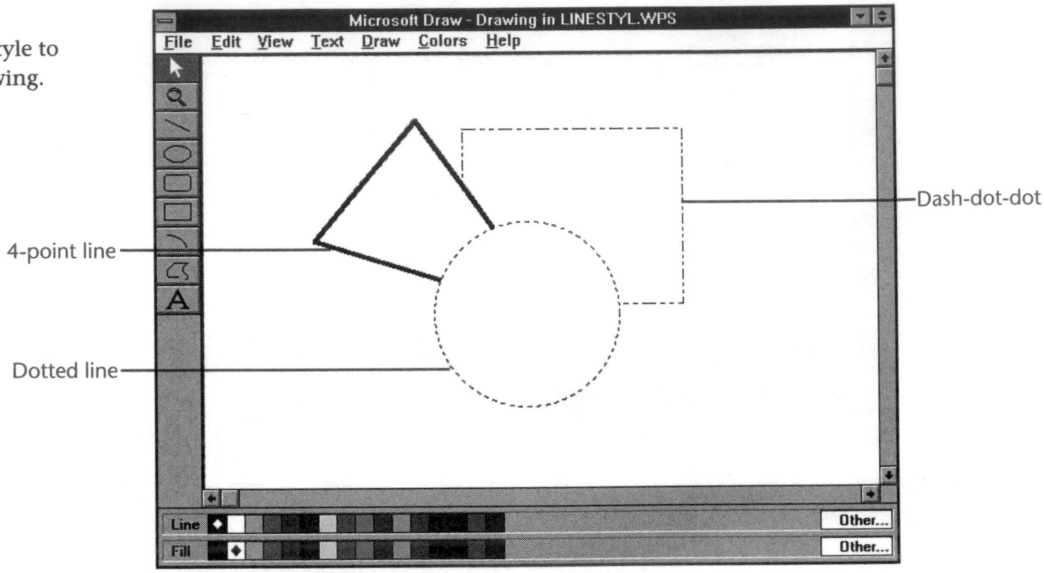

Fig. 24.9
Select a line style to
suit your drawing.

Earlier in this chapter, you learned how to fill an object with a color from the color palette. You also can fill an object with a two-color pattern (see fig. 24.10). Available patterns appear when you choose the **P**attern command from the **D**raw menu.

To fill an object with a pattern, select the object, then select a pattern style from the **P**attern submenu. If you are using the default line and fill colors, Draw makes the pattern background white and the pattern foreground black. To change the colors used in the pattern, select the object, then select line and fill colors from the color palette. Draw changes the black and white to the colors you select.

Moving, Copying, and Deleting Objects

In a text document, you frequently move, copy, and delete words, phrases, sentences, and entire paragraphs. In a drawing, moving, copying, and deleting objects are common tasks as well, and you use the same commands and keystrokes as for text.

To move an object, select it and drag it in any direction to a new location. After you have properly positioned the object, release the mouse button.

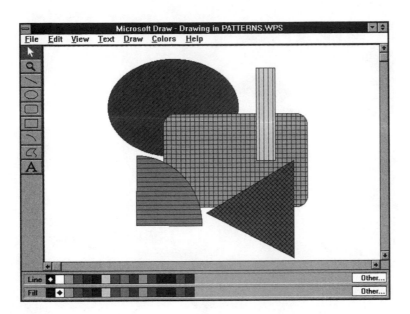

Fig. 24.10
Dress up an object
by filling it with a
pattern rather than
a solid color.

To copy an object, select it, then choose the **C**opy command on the **E**dit
menu. Keyboard shortcuts for the **C**opy command are Ctrl+C and Ctrl+Insert.
This command does not remove or change the selected object, but Works
places a copy of the object on the clipboard. To insert a copy of the object,
choose the **P**aste command on the **E**dit menu. Keyboard shortcuts for the
Paste command are Ctrl+V and Shift+Insert. Draw pastes a copy of the object
near the original object. You then can move the object to a new location if
you want.

To delete an object, begin by selecting the object, then choose the Cl**e**ar command on the **E**dit menu. The keyboard shortcut for the Cl**e**ar command is
the Del key.

You can move, copy, and delete more than one object at a time if you want.
To move a group of objects, select all objects, then drag them to a new position and release the mouse button. To copy or delete multiple objects, select
all objects, then use the **C**opy or **D**elete commands on the **E**dit menu, or use
the appropriate keyboard shortcuts.

Rearranging the Order of Objects

If you draw multiple objects in succession and overlap each one, each new
object you draw appears on top of the previous one, as shown in figure 24.11.

Tip
When you are
moving, copying,
or deleting a large
number of objects,
you can select all
objects in an area
quickly by enclos-
ing them in a
selection box. See
"Selecting Objects"
earlier in this
chapter.

V

Enhancing Documents

Fig. 24.11
When objects over-
lap, the most recent
object appears on
top of the previous
object.

First object drawn —

Last object drawn —

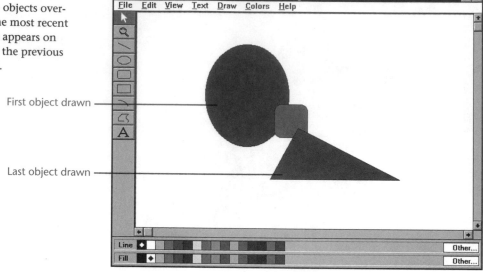

You can change the order in which Works stacks objects by using the Bring
to **F**ront and Send to **B**ack commands on the **E**dit menu. The Bring to
Front command brings the selected object to the top of the stack; the Send
to **B**ack command sends the selected object to the bottom of the stack. In
figure 24.12, objects were rearranged using either of the two commands. The
keyboard shortcut for the Bring to **F**ront command is Ctrl+=; the shortcut
Ctrl+- sends the selected object to the back.

Fig. 24.12
You can restack
objects using the
Bring to Front
and Send to Back
commands.

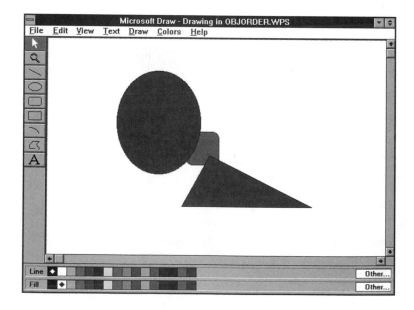

Resizing, Rotating, and Flipping Objects

By now you are familiar with the four resize handles that appear each time you select an object. Resizing an object is as easy as dragging a resize handle in the direction you want to enlarge or shrink the object. For example, to increase or decrease the width of an object, select the object, then press and hold the Shift key as you drag any of the resize handles to the left or right. Release the mouse button when the object is the width you want. To increase or decrease the height of an object, select the object, then press and hold the Shift key as you drag a resize handle up or down.

Microsoft Draw also enables you to rotate an object to the right or left 90°. In effect, *rotating* an object turns an object on its side. An example is shown in figure 24.13.

Tip
You can change an object's height and width at the same time by dragging a resize handle diagonally. If you press and hold the Shift key while dragging, you maintain the object's height-to-width proportions.

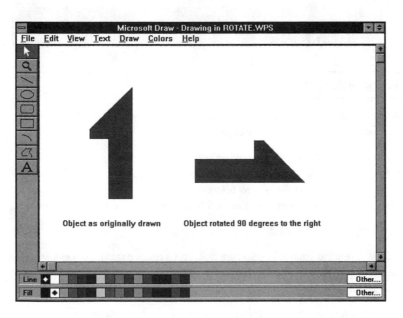

Fig. 24.13
Rotating turns an object on its side.

To rotate an object to the right or left, select the object, then choose the Rotate/Flip command on the **D**raw menu. From the submenu that appears, choose the Rotate **L**eft or Rotate **R**ight command.

Flipping enables you to create a mirror image of an object. You can flip an object vertically to turn it upside down or horizontally to turn it backward. To flip an object, select the object, then choose the R**o**tate/Flip command on the **D**raw menu. From the submenu that appears, choose the Flip **H**orizontally or Flip **V**ertically command. An example is shown in figure 24.14.

V

Enhancing Documents

Fig. 24.14
Flipping makes a
vertical or hori-
zontal mirror of
an object.

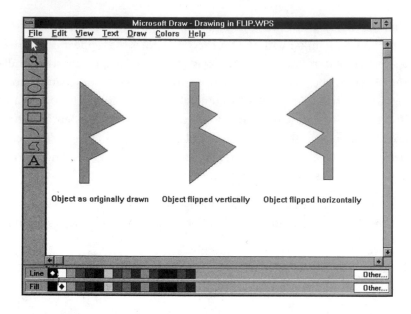

Troubleshooting

When I try to select and copy an object, nothing happens—I don't see the copy of the selected object on-screen, only the original object.

If you are using an enlarged view when you copy an object—especially 400% or 800%—you may not see the copy of the object on-screen because the view is too large. Switch back to full-size view before copying. When you use full-size view, Draw pastes the copy on-screen very close to (often overlapping) the original object.

When I try to move an object, Draw resizes the object instead. Why?

If Draw is resizing your object, you are dragging a resize handle. To move an object, click and drag it all in one step. If the object is already selected, click inside the object and drag it to a new location rather than clicking a handle.

I want to rotate (or flip) several objects as a single unit. Will Draw let me do this?

Yes, but you need to group the objects first. Select all objects you want to group, then choose the **G**roup command on the **D**raw menu. Draw encloses all objects within the boundaries of four resize handles. You now can manipulate the objects as a single unit. You can edit the object in any way, including using the R**o**tate/Flip command on the **D**raw menu. To separate the objects after you finish, choose the **U**ngroup command on the **D**raw menu.

Using ClipArt

For users who are uncertain of their drawing ability, ClipArt is a tremendous feature of Works. Even for the adept artist, ClipArt can be useful when you are in a hurry. Available directly from within a database form or word processor file, the ClipArt Gallery includes pictures that fall into a wide range of categories. Just select the ClipArt file you want to use and insert it in your document.

Choosing a ClipArt File

To select a ClipArt file, move the highlight or insertion point in your database form or word processor document to the location where you want to insert a picture. Then choose the Clip**A**rt command on the **I**nsert menu. Works displays the ClipArt Gallery dialog box shown in figure 24.15.

At the top of the dialog box is a list of categories. The box below the **c**ategory box displays a sample of all ClipArt files in the current category. Figure 24.15 shows a selection of ClipArt files in the Miscellaneous category. Use the scroll bar to see a sample of each file in a category. If you prefer to scroll through the entire selection, you can select the All Categories option in the category list box.

Fig. 24.15
Use the ClipArt Gallery dialog box to select a ClipArt file.

When you find a ClipArt file you want to use, click the file to select it, then choose OK. Works closes the ClipArt Gallery dialog box and returns to your database form or document, pasting a copy of the ClipArt file at the insertion point. Figure 24.16 shows a ClipArt file used as the logo for Town & Country Interiors' letterhead.

Fig. 24.16
Use ClipArt to create a logo for your company stationery.

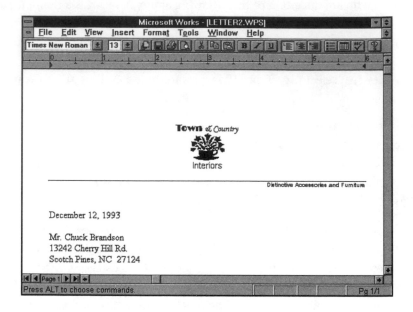

Sizing and Arranging ClipArt

ClipArt files usually are quite large—they often cannot appear completely within the document window. Click anywhere in the picture to select it, then resize the picture to suit your document.

Resizing objects, such as ClipArt files, is covered in detail in Chapter 7, "Working with Tables, Columns, and Inserted Objects." Refer to that chapter for specific instructions about resizing by using the frame's resize handles or by indicating a specific size in the Picture/Object dialog box. That chapter also discusses how to arrange the text surrounding an inserted object. For help sizing and arranging a ClipArt file in a database form, refer to Chapter 17, "Creating and Editing a Database Form."

Deleting ClipArt

To delete a ClipArt file from a database form or word processor document, select the picture, then press the Del key, click the Cut button on the toolbar, or select the Cut command on the Edit menu. In a word processor document, Works automatically reformats the surrounding text. In a database form, surrounding fields remain unchanged.

From Here...

In this chapter you learned how to enhance documents using drawings and ClipArt files. Refer to the following chapter for related information:

■ Chapter 25, "Using WordArt and Note-It," explains how to enhance documents with stylized text and pop-up notes.

Chapter 25

Using WordArt and Note-It

WordArt is an application accessible from within Works that enables you to dress up your documents with stylized text. You can use WordArt to create an impressive company logo for your letterhead or an eye-catching title for your newsletter. Or you can use WordArt to create a distinctive first character that begins a new section or paragraph in a document. You select a font and size for the text then curve, slant, bend, or rotate the text and add shadows, borders, color, or shaded patterns.

Note-It is a handy tool that enables you to annotate your documents in a distinctive and unique way by creating pop-up notes. Accessible from within Works, Note-It can be used to add instructions for working with a document, insert a reminder to yourself, include additional information on a particular topic, or include a note to a colleague. Note-It inserts an *icon* (a picture of a notepad, envelope, file folder, or other item) in your document to mark the location of the note. Just double-click the icon to pop up the note.

This chapter covers the following topics:

- Using the WordArt toolbar and menus

- Creating and editing WordArt text

- Adding special effects to WordArt text

- Sizing, moving, and deleting WordArt text

- Creating a note with Note-It

- Reading, editing, and deleting a note

V

Enhancing Documents

Adding WordArt and Notes to a Document or Form

Just like drawings and ClipArt files, WordArt and Note-It notes are objects you can insert in a word processor document or a database form. To use WordArt or Note-It, follow these steps:

1. Open a word processor document or database form.

2. Position the insertion point where you want to place the object.

3. From the Insert menu, choose the WordArt or Note-It command.

Creating WordArt Text

When you choose the **W**ordArt command from the **I**nsert menu, Works displays the Enter Your Text Here dialog box shown in figure 25.1. In the dialog box, the sample text Your Text Here is highlighted. When you begin entering your own text, this sample text disappears. Just above the dialog box is a grayed frame in your document that acts as a place holder for the WordArt you create.

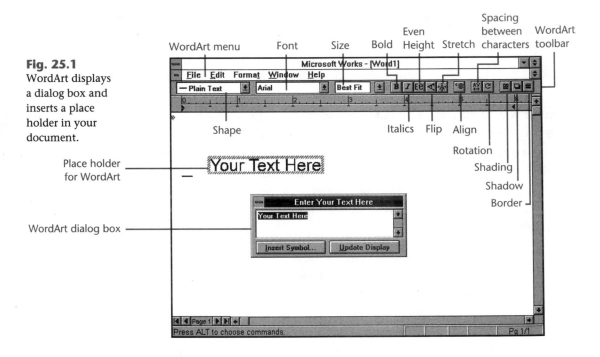

Fig. 25.1
WordArt displays a dialog box and inserts a place holder in your document.

Examining the WordArt Toolbar and Menus

When you choose the **W**ordArt command, notice that the menus and toolbar change to reflect WordArt commands. The **F**ile and **W**indow menus are identical to those in the Works word processor and database tools. The **H**elp menu displays help topics on WordArt only. To change the font, size, shape, or add special effects to your WordArt text, you use the buttons on the toolbar. The following text describes the toolbar buttons. Examples of special effects are shown in this section or later in the chapter.

■ *Shape.* Click this button to display the Shape drop-down list. After you select a shape, your WordArt text follows the shape. For example, if you select a wave or semicircle, your text bends to form the shape of a wave or semicircle.

■ *Font.* Select a font from the displayed list. The available fonts are the same as those found in the word processor and database tools.

■ *Size.* Select a point size from the displayed list. Choose the Best Fit option if you want Works to select the best point size to fit the WordArt frame.

■ *Bold.* Change the WordArt text to bold. This button toggles this feature on and off.

■ *Italic.* Change the WordArt text to italic. This button toggles this feature on and off.

■ *Even Height.* Make the letters in WordArt—including upper- and lower-case—all the same height (see fig. 25.2). This button toggles this feature on and off.

Fig. 25.2
WordArt can display characters at an even height, regardless of capitalization.

■ *Flip.* Click this button to turn each letter on its side (see fig. 25.3). This button toggles this feature on and off.

■ *Stretch.* Click this button to make your text fill the WordArt frame horizontally and vertically. This button toggles this feature on and off. When the feature is off, WordArt text aligns center.

Fig. 25.3
WordArt flips
individual
characters on
their side.

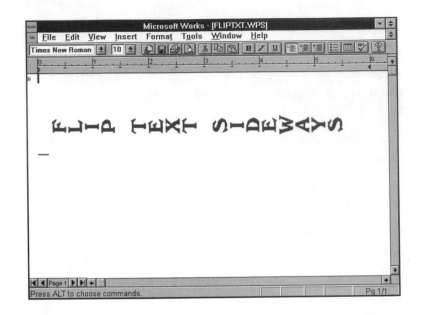

 ■ *Align.* Select an alignment style to align the text within the WordArt frame. If you don't select a style, WordArt automatically uses the Center alignment style.

 ■ *Spacing Between Characters.* Display a dialog box that enables you to control the space between characters in WordArt. You can move characters closer together or farther apart.

 ■ *Rotation.* Display a dialog box that enables you to rotate text by degrees and adjust the angle or arc of the text.

 ■ *Shading.* Display the Shading dialog box in which you select a two-color shaded pattern and the foreground and background colors to apply to WordArt characters.

 ■ *Shadow.* Display a drop-down list of shadow styles for individual characters in your WordArt text (see fig. 25.4). To select a color for the shadow, click the More button to display a Shadow dialog box (see fig. 25.13 later in the chapter).

 ■ *Border.* Display the Border dialog box in which you select a border style and color. Note that in this context, border refers to a character border, not a frame border. When you select a border style or color, Works borders individual characters.

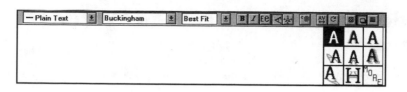

Fig. 25.4
The Shadow drop-
down box displays
shadow styles.

Creating and Editing WordArt Text

When you're ready to add WordArt to a document or database form, follow these steps:

1. Open the word processor file or database form to which you want to add WordArt text.

2. Place the insertion point at the location where you want to insert the WordArt text.

3. From the **I**nsert menu, choose the **W**ordArt command. The Enter Your Text Here dialog box opens (refer to fig. 25.1).

4. Type your text in the dialog box. Press Enter if you want to begin a new line.

5. Click the appropriate toolbar buttons to add special effects to the text.

6. After you finish, click in the document where you want to continue working. Works closes the Enter Your Text Here dialog box and displays your WordArt text in your document or database form.

7. To save the WordArt text in your document or database form, use the **S**ave or Save **A**s command on the **F**ile menu then continue working as usual.

From your database form or word processor document, you can return to the Enter Your Text Here dialog box at any time to change text or special effects of your WordArt text. Just double-click the WordArt text in your document or database form and WordArt displays the dialog box. To change the text, click where you want to position the insertion point then delete or retype existing text. Click the **U**pdate Display button to view the changes in your document. To change any special effects, click the appropriate toolbar buttons.

Tip
If the Enter Your Text Here dialog box obstructs your view of the WordArt in your document, drag the title bar to move the dialog box out of the way.

V

Enhancing Documents

Adding Special Effects to WordArt Text

In the preceding section, you learned about the special effects you can apply to WordArt text. Some special effects—such as font, size, bold, italic, even height, flip, stretch, and alignment—are self-explanatory. When you click the appropriate button, Works immediately applies the special effect to the WordArt text without displaying a dialog box.

This section describes and illustrates how to apply the special effects that require you to choose options or respond to a dialog box. These effects include shaping, spacing, rotating, shading, shadowing, and bordering. The important thing to remember when working with special effects is to *experiment*. Try different fonts with different effects. Explore how combinations of shapes and other effects change your WordArt—the possibilities are almost limitless. The examples in this section only introduce you to the possibilities.

As you add special effects to WordArt, you may see the Size Change dialog box shown in figure 25.5. This box appears whenever the special effect you are using requires you to resize the WordArt frame. To display the WordArt text accurately, you may need to resize the frame. Choose **Yes** to resize the frame and continue working.

Fig. 25.5
Choose **Yes** in the Size Change dialog box to display your WordArt text accurately.

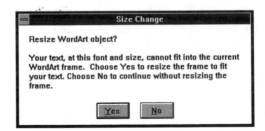

Wrapping Text in a Shape

Shaping text is one of the most important features of WordArt. Some word processors enable you to shade or shadow text, but few enable you to bend text to a particular shape. After you enter your text in the Enter Your Text Here dialog box, you can apply a shape or an angle by clicking a shape in the Shape drop-down list, shown in figure 25.6. (Click the Shape button to display the drop-down list.)

Shape button

Shape drop-down list

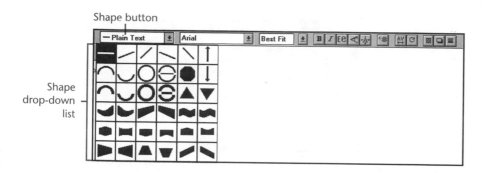

Fig. 25.6
Select a shape or
an angle for your
WordArt from the
Shape drop-down
list.

In figure 25.7, you see three examples of WordArt that conform to shapes. The first example uses the Slant Up shape, the second uses the Wave 1 shape, the third uses the Fade Down shape.

Controlling Spacing

You can control the space between characters in WordArt by clicking the Spacing Between Characters button on the toolbar or choosing the **S**pacing Between Characters command on the Forma**t** menu. Using either method, the Spacing Between Characters dialog box shown in figure 25.8 opens.

Tip
To display the
name of a shape,
you must select a
shape from the
Shape drop-down
list. The name is
then displayed in
the Shape button
on the toolbar.

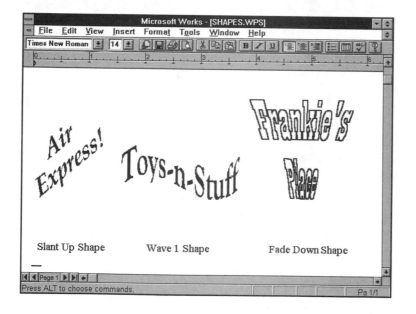

Fig. 25.7
Examples of
WordArt shapes.

V

Enhancing Documents

Fig. 25.8

The Spacing
Between Charac-
ters dialog box.

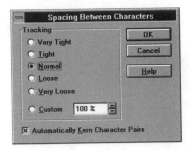

In the dialog box, *tracking* refers to the space between all characters in the
WordArt frame. For instance, if you choose the Very Tight option, the characters in your WordArt text move as close together as possible (60% of their
normal spacing). If you prefer, you can use the Custom box to enter a
specific tracking percentage. Examples of tracking percentages are shown
in figure 25.9.

Fig. 25.9

Examples
of tracking
percentages.

Kerning refers to the space between pairs of characters. Because of their
shapes, certain characters typed next to one another often look like they are
spaced too far apart. For instance, when you type the letters **Ti**, the stem on
the T can cause a large space between the two characters depending on the
font you use. Kerning moves the two characters closer together. To have
WordArt automatically kern pairs of characters for you, choose the Automatically **K**ern Character Pairs check box.

Rotating and Sliding WordArt Text

You can *rotate* WordArt text to the right or left by clicking the Rotation button on the toolbar or choosing the **R**otation and Effects command on the Format menu. Using either method, a Special Effects dialog box opens. The **R**otation setting always appears in this dialog box. The other settings vary depending on the shape you have chosen for your WordArt text. If you have chosen an arc shape, the **A**rc Angle setting appears, as shown in figure 25.10. This setting enables you to adjust the curve of the arc. If you have chosen any shape other than an arc (such as a slant or straight line), the **S**lider setting appears in place of the Arc Angle setting. The **S**lider enables you to adjust the slant of characters.

For shapes other than the arc, this box is called Slider.

Fig. 25.10
The Special Effects dialog box.

Experiment with the **R**otation setting to see how it affects the shape you are using. Increasing the rotation rotates the WordArt text to the right; decreasing the rotation rotates the WordArt text to the left.

Shading WordArt Text

To enhance WordArt text, you can add *shading* to individual characters. When you click the Shading button on the toolbar or choose the S**h**ading command on the Format menu, the Shading dialog box shown in figure 25.11 opens.

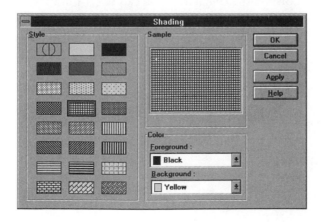

Fig. 25.11
Use the Shading dialog box to apply a shade pattern and color to WordArt.

V

Enhancing Documents

From the **S**tyle box, select a shading style. From the Color box, select **F**ore-ground and **B**ackground colors. The Sample area displays the choices you make. Choose the A**p**ply button to apply the selected shading to your WordArt. If you aren't satisfied with the way the shading looks, select a different pattern of colors then choose the A**p**ply button again. When you're happy with the results, choose OK to close the Shading dialog box. An example of shaded WordArt is shown in figure 25.12.

Fig. 25.12
Apply a shade pattern to dress up your WordArt text.

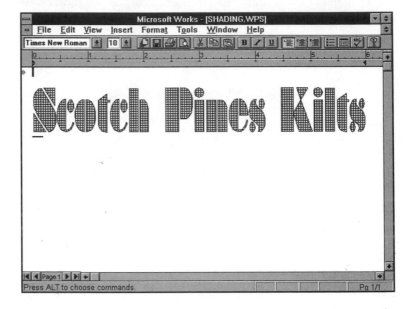

Shadowing and Bordering WordArt Text

Shadowing is a technique that adds depth to WordArt text by creating the illusion of light cast on the characters. You can select from several different styles of shadows, and you can specify the shadow's color rather than simply using gray.

The Shadow dialog box is shown in figure 25.13. Display this box by choosing the Shado**w** command on the Forma**t** menu. You also can display this dialog box by clicking the Shadow toolbar button (which displays a drop-down list of shadow styles), then selecting the More option from the drop-down list. To add a shadow to text, select a shadow style and color, then choose the OK button.

Fig. 25.13
Select a shadow
style and color
from the Shadow
dialog box.

Bordering is a special effect that makes characters stand out by outlining each character individually. You specify the thickness of the border using the Border dialog box shown in figure 25.14. The default border color is the background color defined in the Shading dialog box. To change the border color, select a color from the **C**olor drop-down list in the Border dialog box.

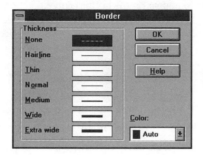

Fig. 25.14
Select a border
style and color
from the Border
dialog box.

Examples of shadows and borders are shown in figure 25.15.

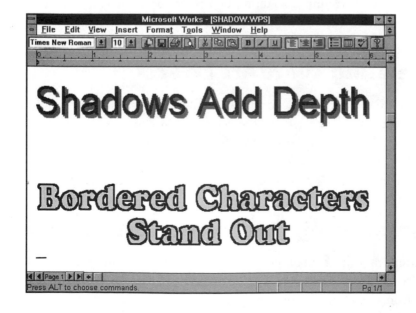

Fig. 25.15
Shadows add
depth to WordArt
and borders make
characters stand
out.

Tip
Works immedi-
ately applies shad-
ows and borders to
your WordArt
characters when
you choose op-
tions in the dialog
boxes. To see how
your choices look,
move the dialog
box out of the way
if it obstructs your
view.

V

Enhancing Documents

Troubleshooting

How can I change the color of WordArt characters?

Although you don't apply a shade, you use the Shading dialog box to change the color of characters. In the dialog box, select a foreground or background color, then instead of applying a shading pattern, click the solid color in the top row in the Style box (refer to fig. 25.11).

I can't get my text to conform to the Button Pour and Button Curve shapes shown earlier in figure 25.6.

The Button Pour and Button Curve shapes require three lines of text in the Enter Your Text Here dialog box. Type the text you want to appear on the top curve, then press Enter and type the text you want to appear on the middle line. Press Enter again then type the text you want to appear on the bottom curve.

Sizing and Positioning WordArt

When you return to your word processor document or database form, WordArt text appears in the position of the insertion point. You can move or resize WordArt just like you can any other inserted object (such as a Microsoft Draw drawing or ClipArt). Working with inserted objects is discussed in detail in Chapter 7, "Working with Tables, Columns, and Inserted Objects," and Chapter 17, "Creating and Editing a Database Form." Refer to these chapters for specific instructions about moving, copying, and sizing inserted objects.

Deleting WordArt Effects

To delete WordArt from a document or database form, click the WordArt text to select it. You can delete the selected object by choosing the Cut command on the Edit menu, by pressing the Delete key on the keyboard, or by pressing Ctrl+X. If you delete WordArt by mistake, immediately choose the Undo command on the Edit menu or press Ctrl+Z to restore the WordArt.

Annotating Documents Using Note-It

Documents often contain notes of one sort or another, and the notes are always visible within the text of the document. Using Note-It, you can insert an icon, or picture, in a document rather than the note itself. When you want to read the note, you double-click the icon to pop up the note; otherwise, the note stays hidden.

The Note-It feature is especially useful for including instructions for using a document, inserting a reminder to yourself, or adding a comment for a colleague to read. An example of a note is shown in figure 25.16. In the figure, one note is closed, the other note is popped up (open).

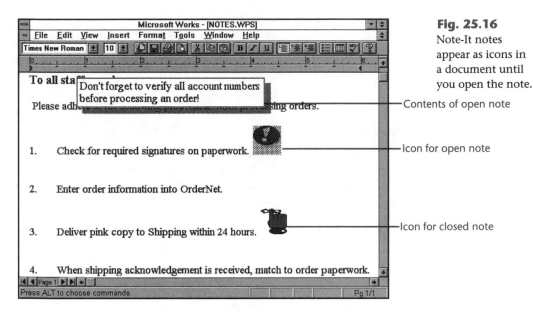

Fig. 25.16
Note-It notes appear as icons in a document until you open the note.

Contents of open note

Icon for open note

Icon for closed note

Creating a Note

To create a Note-It note in a document or database form, follow these steps:

1. From the **I**nsert menu, choose the Not**e**-It command to display the Note-It dialog box shown in figure 25.17.

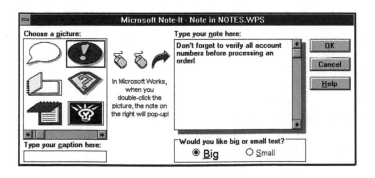

Fig. 25.17
Use the Note-It dialog box to select a note icon and enter the note text.

2. In the Choose a **P**icture box, select the picture you want to use as your note icon. Be sure to use the scroll bar to view all the icons—a wide variety of icons is available. Select the picture that best suits your needs, such as the string on the index finger for a Reminder note or the amber traffic light for a Caution note.

3. To add a note caption, enter the text in the Type Your **C**aption Here box.

4. Enter the text for your note in the Type Your **N**ote Here box.

5. Choose **B**ig or **S**mall for the font size of the pop-up note.

6. Choose OK to close the dialog box.

Reading a Note

To read a note, double-click the note icon in the document. The note icon becomes shaded, and the note text pops up in a small frame near the top of the document window. After you finish reading the note, click anywhere in the document or press Enter to close the note.

Editing a Note

You can edit the text of a note any time by following these steps:

1. Select the Note-It icon.

2. From the **E**dit menu, choose the Edit Note-It **O**bject command. Then choose the **E**dit option from the submenu.

    The Microsoft Note-It dialog box opens. Your note text appears in the Type Your **N**ote Here box, and your caption (if you included one) is shown in the Type Your **C**aption Here box. The note icon you are using is selected.

3. To edit your note text or caption, click the appropriate box then use the arrow keys to move to the characters you want to change or retype.

4. To change the Note-It icon, select a different picture from the Choose a **P**icture box.

5. When you're satisfied with the changes, choose OK.

Deleting a Note

You delete a Note-It note the same way you delete WordArt, ClipArt, or a Microsoft Draw drawing. First, select the Note-It icon. Then choose the Cu**t** command on the **E**dit menu, press the Delete key on the keyboard, or press Ctrl+Z. If you delete a Note-It note by mistake, immediately choose the **U**ndo command on the **E**dit menu to restore the note.

From Here...

This chapter completes the section on Microsoft Draw, ClipArt, WordArt, and Note-It. You have learned about all the tools in Works; now you're ready to learn how to use the tools together and communicate with other computers. Refer to the following chapters:

- In Chapter 26, "Using the Works Tools Together," you learn how to copy information from one tool to another.

- Chapter 27, "Creating and Printing Form Letters, Envelopes, and Mailing Labels," explains how to use a database document in combination with a word processor document to automatically address form letters and mailing labels.

- Chapter 28, "Communicating with Other Computers," teaches you how to communicate through your computer with the outside world.

V

Enhancing Documents

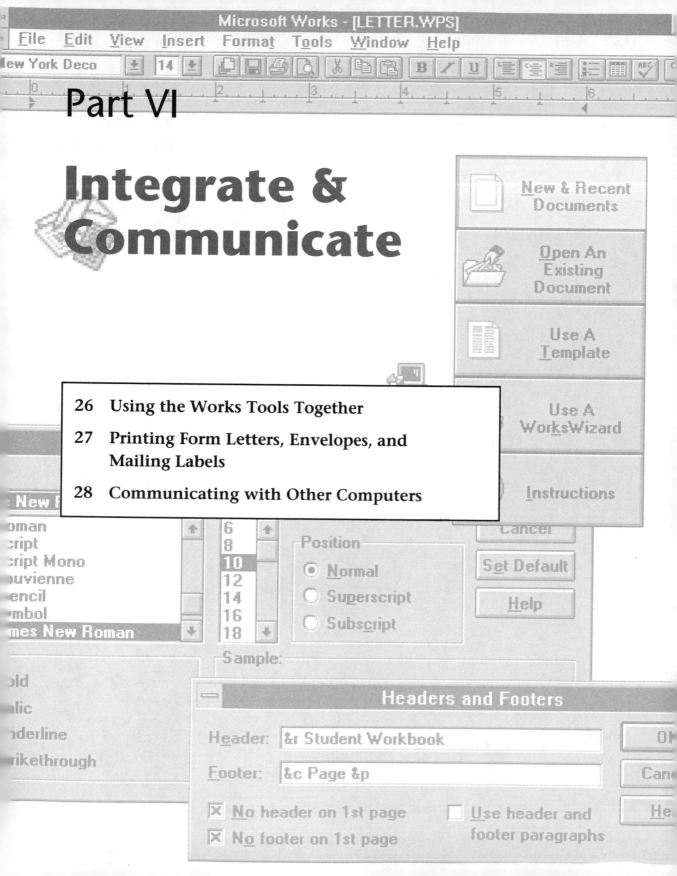

Part VI

Integrate & Communicate

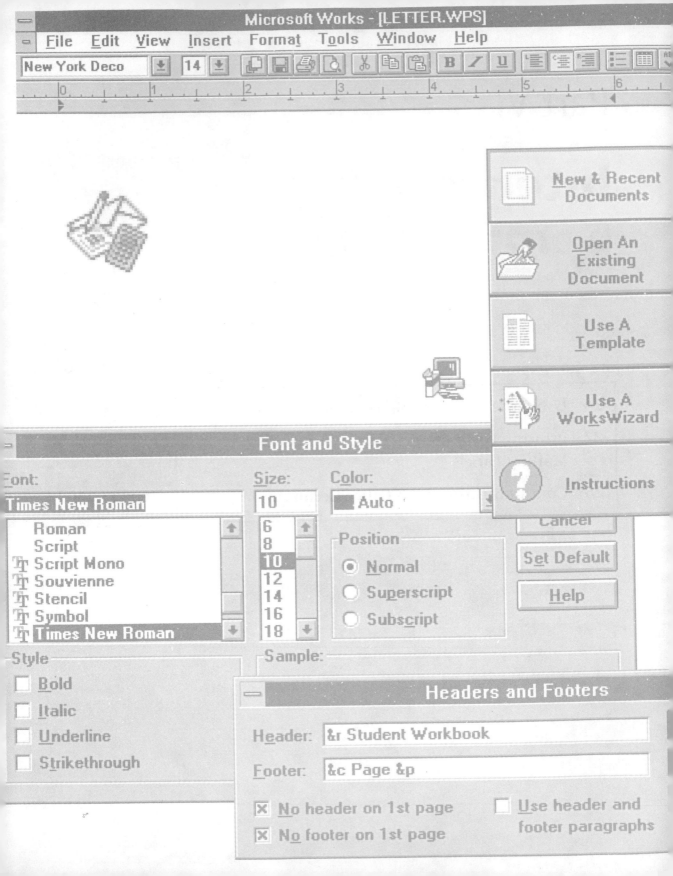

Microsoft Works - [LETTER.WPS]

File Edit View Insert Format Tools Window Help

New York Deco | 14 |

0   1   2   3   4   5   6

New & Recent Documents

Open An Existing Document

Use A Template

Use A WorksWizard

Instructions

Font and Style

Font:

Times New Roman

- Roman
- Script
- Script Mono
- Souvienne
- Stencil
- Symbol
- **Times New Roman**

Size:

10

6
8
10
12
14
16
18

Color:

Auto

Position
- ● Normal
- ○ Superscript
- ○ Subscript

Cancel

Set Default

Help

Style
- ☐ Bold
- ☐ Italic
- ☐ Underline
- ☐ Strikethrough

Sample:

Headers and Footers

Header: &r Student Workbook

Footer: &c Page &p

☒ No header on 1st page

☒ No footer on 1st page

☐ Use header and footer paragraphs

Chapter 26

Using the Works Tools Together

If you use more than one of the Works tools, there's a good chance that at some time you'll want to transfer information from one tool to another. For example, you may want to include a spreadsheet chart or database report in a letter. Or you may want to create a drawing or other illustration with another application and include it in a Works letter or database form.

In Chapter 23, "Customizing a Report," you can find out about transfering data between Works tools by exporting a report. In the Works Database, you can copy a report and insert it into another Works tool document. This is described in the section "Using a Report with Other Applications" in Chapter 23, "Customizing a Report."

Because the Works Word Processor is used more often to transfer information than the Database or Spreadsheet, the figures in this chapter are based on Word Processor documents. However, you should also be aware that you can use exactly the same steps to copy, link, or embed information into a Works database form or report or into a Works spreadsheet.

Copying and Moving Information

Copying and pasting is the simplest way to transfer information into a Works Word Processor document. Choose this method if you don't expect the transferred information to change, or if you don't need the same information in more than one document.

In this chapter, you learn how to do the following:

- Copy and paste with the Windows Clipboard

- Link with Dynamic Data Exchange (DDE)

- Embed with Object Linking and Embedding (OLE)

- Move and resize objects

- Wrap text around an object

VI

Integrate & Communicate

When you copy information, you switch to the source application and highlight the information you want to copy. You then copy the information to the Windows Clipboard, switch to the destination document, and insert the information. If you cut the information from the source document instead of copying it, Works deletes the original information, effectively moving it instead of copying it.

Moving and copying information between applications is essentially the same as moving and copying in or between documents in the Word Processor, Spreadsheet, or Database. (See "Moving and Copying Text" in Chapter 5, "Editing a Document"; "Editing Cell Entries" in Chapter 10, "Creating, Saving, and Printing a Spreadsheet"; and "Editing Database Information" in Chapter 19, "Entering and Editing Data.")

Caution

When Typing Replaces Selection is turned on in the Options dialog box (choose **To**ols, **O**ptions) and you highlight text before copying or moving information, Works replaces the highlighted information when you insert the copied or moved text. To restore the deleted text, immediately choose **E**dit, **U**ndo or press Ctrl+Z.

Transferring Information with Drag and Drop

Works lets you transfer information quickly with the mouse using the *drag-and-drop* method. You can drag and drop data from one location to another in the same document, between two documents you create in the same application, or between different applications. You can also use drag and drop to link information.

Follow these steps to drag and drop:

1. To copy or move information between documents created with the same or different applications, open the documents and arrange them so that you can see both documents.

2. In the destination document, move the insertion point to where you want to insert the information.

3. Switch to the source document, and highlight the information you want to copy or move.

4. To copy, move, or link the information, use one of the following methods:

To move information within a single document, click the highlighted information and drag it to the new location. In the Works Spreadsheet or Database, click the selection border and drag.

To move information to another Works document or Windows application, click the highlighted information and hold Shift while you drag it to the new location. In the Works Spreadsheet or Database, click the selection border and hold down Shift while you drag.

To copy information within a single document, click the highlighted information and hold Ctrl while you drag it to the new location. In the Works Spreadsheet or Database, click the selection border and hold down Ctrl as you drag.

To copy information to another Works document or Windows application, click the highlighted information and hold Ctrl while you drag it to the new location. In the Works Spreadsheet or Database, click the selection border and hold Ctrl while you drag.

To link information to another Works document or Windows application, click the highlighted information and hold Ctrl and Shift while you drag it to the new location. In the Works Spreadsheet, click the selection border and hold Ctrl and Shift while you drag.

Caution

If the cursor changes to a circle with a diagonal line, you cannot move, copy, or link the information because it is the wrong type or because the application does not support drag and drop or linking.

---

5. Release the mouse button.

Works inserts the information.

Note

To undo a drag-and-drop copy, move, or link, choose **E**dit, **U**ndo immediately after you use drag and drop. If you copied or moved information to another application, choose **E**dit, **U**ndo in the destination document, and then choose **E**dit, **U**ndo in the Works Word Processor document.

VI

Integrate & Communicate

Figure 26.1 shows two documents in the Works document window: a letter named LETTER.WPS and a spreadsheet titled INCMSTMT.WKS. The figure shows the spreadsheet and document prior to a drag and drop. Notice that the entire spreadsheet has been selected using the **E**dit, Select **A**ll command.

Fig. 26.1
To copy or move information using drag and drop, display both documents and highlight the information in the source document.

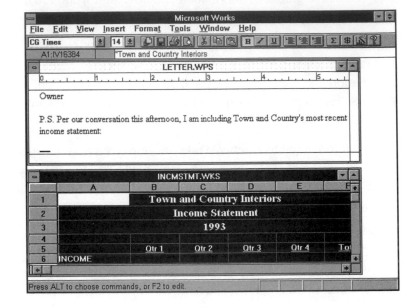

Figure 26.2 shows the Word Processor document after the spreadsheet was copied to the insertion point.

Transferring Information with the Menus

Sometimes it's easier not to use drag and drop to transfer information, but instead, it is easier to use the **C**opy, Cu**t**, and **P**aste commands in the **E**dit menu, or the Copy, Cut, and Paste toolbar buttons. For example, using drag and drop to move several pages of information with the mouse may be less convenient than using menu commands. If you accidentally click outside the selection or press a key, Works un-highlights the selection, and you have to start over.

To copy or move information with the menus, follow these steps:

1. Open the source document.

2. Highlight the text or object you want to copy.

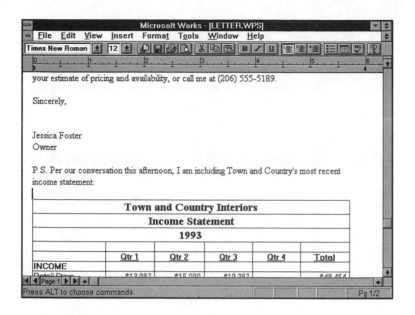

Fig. 26.2
The document after drag and drop has copied the spreadsheet into the document.

3. To copy the selection, choose **E**dit, **C**opy, or press Ctrl+C; or click the Copy toolbar button.

or

To move the selection, choose **E**dit, Cu**t**, or press Ctrl+X; or click the Cut toolbar button.

4. To copy or move the information to another location in the same document, move the insertion point where you want to insert the copy.

or

To copy or move to another document, open the destination document and move the insertion point where you want to insert the copy.

5. Choose **E**dit, **P**aste, or press Ctrl+V; or click the Paste toolbar button.

Works inserts the information at the insertion point.

6. To insert another copy, repeat steps 4 and 5.

Figures 26.3 and 26.4 show a Works Word Processor document and a Works Database form before and after copying the drawing in the letter into the database form.

VI

Integrate & Communicate

Fig. 26.3
A drawing ready
to be copied
from a Word
Processor letter
to a Database
form.

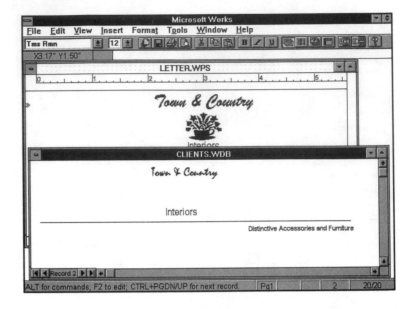

Fig. 26.4
The drawing
copied from the
Word Processor
letter to the
Database form.

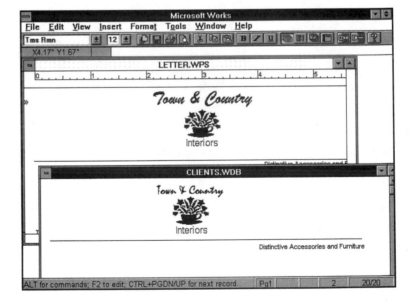

Understanding Linking and Embedding

Linking and embedding are ways to transfer information between Works documents when you expect the source of the information to change. With linking, you copy the information and Works automatically updates the information when the source changes. With embedding, you can edit the source information without leaving your document. You can link or embed information into a Works document from any Windows program that supports linking with Dynamic Data Exchange (DDE) or embedding with Object Linking and Embedding (OLE).

The following guidelines help you make the decision to use linking or embedding:

- When you want to transfer information into a Works document and you expect the source information to change or if you need to include the information in several Works documents, use linking. You can then edit the source information, and Windows automatically changes the information wherever you inserted a linked copy.

- If you don't expect to copy the information to other documents, but you do need to edit the information, you should choose embedding. When you edit embedded information, Windows automatically opens the source application and displays the embedded object, ready for you to edit. When you close the source application, Windows returns you to the Works document screen that contains the object.

Linking

Works automatically updates a linked object whenever the source object changes, but you can turn off this feature and update the object manually. For example, you might want to update linked payroll spreadsheet information in a Word Processor document just once a month, when payroll figures are completed.

You can also switch the source of a linked object. For example, if you link a drawing that you created with Microsoft Draw, you can change the link to a different drawing. Windows then automatically updates the linked object in any destination documents to reflect the new drawing.

Figure 26.5 shows a Works spreadsheet that was copied and linked into a Word Processor document.

Figure 26.6 shows the same spreadsheet and letter after the amount for Retail Store income in Qtr 1 was changed from $13,987 to $14,542 in the spreadsheet. Notice that Works has automatically changed the number and the column total in the letter as well.

VI

Integrate & Communicate

Fig. 26.5
To link objects, copy them to the destination document with the Paste Link command.

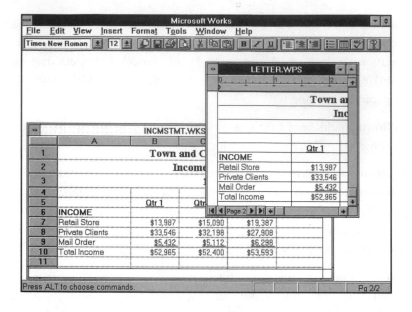

Fig. 26.6
Works can change a linked object, such as a spreadsheet, automatically when you change the source document.

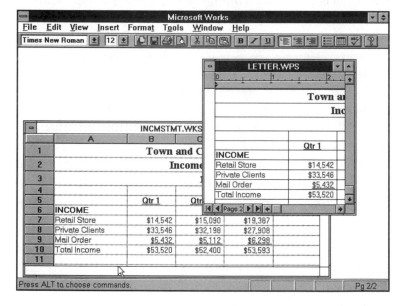

Use the following steps to link information:

1. Open the Works tool or Windows application that contains the information you want to link, and display the source document.

> **Note**
>
> You must name and save the source document before you can link information from it.

2. Highlight the information you want to link.

   For example, highlight a spreadsheet or spreadsheet cell(s), a drawing, a word processor table, or cells in a database displayed in List view.

3. Choose **E**dit, **C**opy in the source application, or press Ctrl+C, or click the Copy toolbar button.

4. Move to the location in the document where you want to insert the linked information.

5. Choose **E**dit, Paste **S**pecial.

   Works displays the Paste Special dialog box (see fig. 26.7).

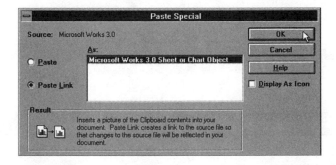

Fig. 26.7
Use the Paste Special dialog box to insert linked information.

6. Choose Paste **L**ink.

> **Note**
>
> If Paste Link is not available, the other application may not be able to create a link or may not support DDE (Dynamic Data Exchange).

7. Choose OK.

   Works inserts the linked information.

You can also insert not just a portion of information from a source file, but the entire file. For example, you might want to link a standard contract document from the Works Word Processor into other Word Processor documents. When you change the standard contract, all the contracts change. Use the following steps to link an entire file:

1. Open the document where you want to insert the information, and choose **I**nsert, **O**bject.

   Works displays the Insert Object dialog box (see fig. 26.8).

Fig. 26.8
Use the Insert Object dialog box to insert and link an entire file.

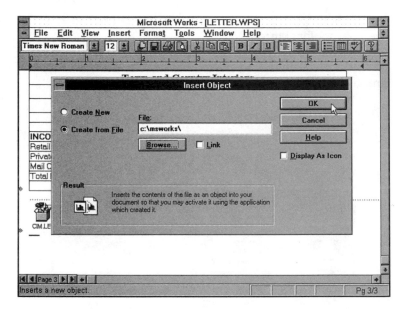

2. In the Insert Object dialog box, choose Create from **F**ile.

3. In the Fil**e** text box, enter the name of the file to which you want to link.

   or

   Choose **B**rowse, and use the Browse dialog box to find the file you want. Choose OK to return to the Insert Object dialog box.

4. To have Works display the file as an icon, choose the **D**isplay as Icon check box.

   If you select **D**isplay as Icon, Works displays and prints the file as an icon. To display the actual contents of the linked file, do not select **D**isplay as icon.

5. Choose OK.

   Works runs the application that was used to create the source document, and displays the source document.

6. Make any desired changes to the source document.

7. To return to the destination document, click outside the source application.

Works inserts the file into your destination document as an icon. Figure 26.9 shows an icon that Works inserts when you copy an entire database record into a Word Processor document.

Fig. 26.9
To display a linked file as an icon, select **D**isplay as Icon in the Insert Object dialog box.

Linking Spreadsheet Information

One of the most popular uses for linking is to display spreadsheets, spreadsheet ranges, and spreadsheet charts in Word Processor documents. Because this is such a common use of linking, this section gives the exact steps to link a Works Spreadsheet worksheet or chart.

Follow these steps to link a Works Spreadsheet chart:

1. Open the spreadsheet that contains the chart you want to link.

   > **Note**
   >
   > You must save the spreadsheet before you can link the chart.

2. Switch to the Word Processor document and move the insertion point where you want to insert the chart.

3. Choose **I**nsert, **C**hart.

   Works displays the Insert Chart dialog box (see fig. 26.10).

4. Select **U**se Existing Chart.

Fig. 26.10
Use the Insert
Chart dialog box
to select a chart
and insert it.

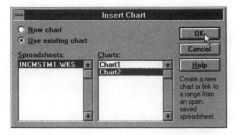

5. From the **S**preadsheets list box, select the spreadsheet where you
   created the chart.

> **Note**
>
> You must open a spreadsheet in step 1 before Works includes it in the **S**pread-
> sheets list box.

6. In the **C**harts list box, highlight the chart you want to insert.

7. Choose OK.

Works inserts the chart in the destination document (see fig. 26.11).

Fig. 26.11
You can insert
linked spreadsheet
charts and spread-
sheet ranges in a
Works Word
Processsor
document.

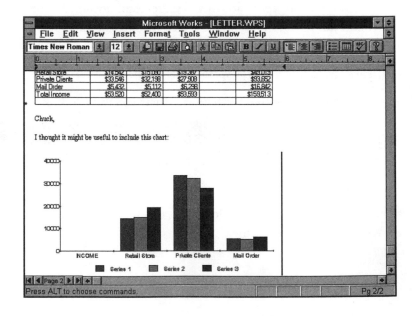

> **Note**
>
> The document in figure 26.11 is displayed in 75% zoom view in order to show more information.

The steps to linking a spreadsheet range are similar to linking a chart:

1. Open the spreadsheet that contains the range of cells you want to link.

   > **Note**
   >
   > You must save the spreadsheet and name the range of cells before you can link it.

2. In the Word Processor document, move the insertion point where you want to insert the spreadsheet cells.

3. Choose **I**nsert, **Sp**readsheet/Table.

   Works displays the Spreadsheet/Table dialog box (see fig. 26.12).

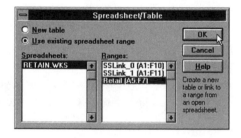

Fig. 26.12
Use the Spreadsheet/Table dialog box to link a range of spreadsheet cells.

4. Select **U**se Existing Spreadsheet range.

5. From the **S**preadsheets list box, select the name of the spreadsheet you want to link.

   > **Note**
   >
   > You must open the spreadsheet in step 1 or Works does not list it in the **S**preadsheets list box.

6. From the **R**anges list box, select the spreadsheet range you want to link.

7. Choose OK.

Works inserts the spreadsheet range in your document at the insertion point (see fig. 26.13).

Fig. 26.13
Linking a
spreadsheet range
is a good way to
draw attention to
a particular aspect
of a spreadsheet
that may change
over time.

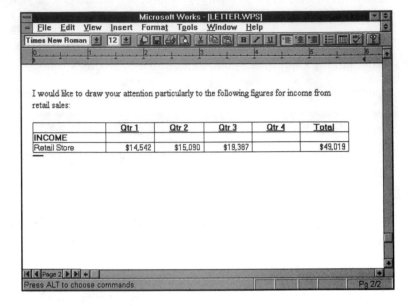

Editing Linked Objects

After you insert linked data in a Works document, you can make changes to the data in the source application. Works then automatically reflects the changes in the destination document, or you can update the link manually at some later time. For example, you might want to wait until you finish a complex series of changes before you take the time to update the link.

Follow these steps to edit linked information:

Tip
To select an object
that has text wrap-
ping around it,
move the cursor
above or below the
object, then press
the up- or down-
arrow.

1. In the destination document, double-click the object you want to edit.

   or

   Use the arrow keys to move the insertion point to the left of the object. Press Shift+right-arrow to select the object. Works displays sizing boxes around the object's borders. Choose **E**dit, [Object Name] Object. For example, for a linked spreadsheet range, the **E**dit menu displays Linked Works Sheet or Chart **O**bject. Choose **E**dit from the submenu (see fig. 26.14).

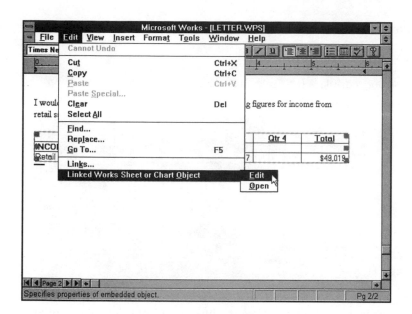

Fig. 26.14
To make changes
to a linked object,
choose **E**dit from
the submenu.

Works opens the source application and displays the linked object. For example, if the linked object is a Works Spreadsheet cell range, Works opens the Spreadsheet and highlights the range.

2. Make any desired changes to the source information.

3. Save the source document.

or

If you are editing the object in another Windows application, choose **F**ile, E**x**it.

Works changes the linked information in the destination document. Works also reflects your changes when it updates other occurrences of the linked information in other documents.

Updating Linked Objects Manually

Sometimes, it is convenient to update linked objects manually, instead of letting Works update them each time they change. Works takes a moment to update an object, and this may interfere with your work flow, especially if you are making frequent changes and switching back and forth between the source and destination documents.

Follow these steps to switch between automatic and manual link updating:

1. Choose **E**dit, Lin**k**s.

   Works displays the Links dialog box (see fig. 26.15).

Fig. 26.15
Use the Links
dialog box to
switch between
automatic and
manual link
updating.

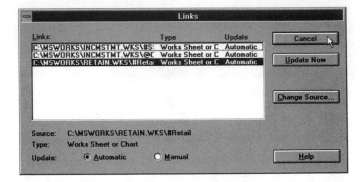

2. In the **L**inks list box, select the link you want to update manually.

3. Select **M**anual or **A**utomatic as appropriate.

   Works displays Manual or Automatic in the Update column of the Links list box.

4. Choose Close.

Works no longer updates the link automatically. To update the link manually, follow these steps:

1. Choose **E**dit, Lin**k**s.

2. In the Links dialog box, choose the link you want to update (refer to fig. 26.15).

3. Choose **U**pdate Now.

Works reflects any changes you made since the last update.

Note

Works can update all links automatically whenever you open a document that contains links. Works asks whether you want the links updated. Choose Yes to update the links, or choose No to bypass updating and open the document.

Reconnecting a Link or Changing the Source of a Link

When you change the name of a source document, Works breaks any links from that document to other documents. If you want to continue updating the linked data, you must reconnect the link. You can also change the source of a link at any time. For example, you might decide to choose a different spreadsheet chart as the source of a link.

Follow these steps to reconnect or change the source of a link:

1. Choose **E**dit, Lin**k**s.

   Works displays the Links dialog box (refer to fig. 26.15).

2. Choose the link whose source you want to change.

3. Choose **C**hange Source....

   Works displays the Change Source dialog box (see fig. 26.16).

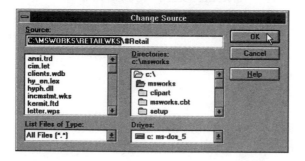

Fig. 26.16
Use the Change Source dialog box to reconnect a link or change the source of a link.

4. In the **S**ource text box, type the path for the source file or spreadsheet range to which you want to reconnect or change the link.

   or

   Choose a new source from the list of file names.

> **Note**
>
> Notice in figure 26.16 that Works displays the name of a spreadsheet range after the source spreadsheet's file name: `C:\MSWORKS\RETAIL.WKS\#Retail`.

5. Choose OK.

6. In the Links dialog box, choose Close.

VI

Integrate & Communicate

If you have other links to the same source file, Works asks you to confirm that you want to change the source file for all of the linked data.

Embedding

Embedding lets you make changes to objects in a Works tool using the source application, without leaving the tool. For example, you can embed a drawing that you create with Microsoft Draw. When you need to make changes to the drawing, you can open Microsoft Draw and edit the drawing without leaving Works. When you link information such as a Works spreadsheet, the spreadsheet is saved as a separate document; but when you embed a spreadsheet, Works saves the information with the document where you embedded it.

Embedding is convenient for sharing documents between users. Both users must have the source application if they want to edit embedded information, but they don't have to have the source application in order to view documents that contain embedded objects. With linking, all users must not only have the source application, but they must have the source document and must save the linked source data in subdirectories with the same names as the original user created.

To summarize:

- Use link when the same information changes frequently in several documents.

- Use embedding when you don't need to place information in several documents, and you want to edit the information without leaving a Works tool.

Follow these steps to embed an object:

1. In the Works document, move the insertion point where you want to insert the object.

2. Select **I**nsert.

3. Choose the type of object:

> **C**hart
>
> **Sp**readsheet/Table
>
> Clip**A**rt

WordArt

Not**e**-It

Draw**i**ng

Object

4. Follow the steps given in the detailed descriptions in the sections that follow.

Inserting a Chart

Choosing **I**nsert, **C**hart displays the Insert Chart dialog box (see fig. 26.17).

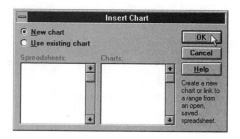

Fig. 26.17
Use the Insert
Chart dialog box
to insert an
existing chart or a
new chart.

To insert an existing chart, from the Insert Chart dialog box, choose **U**se Existing Chart, a spreadsheet from the **S**preadsheets list box, a chart from the **C**harts list, and choose OK. Works inserts the chart in the document.

To insert a new chart, follow these steps:

1. From the Insert Chart dialog box, choose **N**ew chart and choose OK.

Works displays a message box saying: `To Create a Chart, type your data for the chart, select the data, and then press the chart button.`

2. Press Escape, or click in the underlying Works document.

Works embeds a spreadsheet in your document at the insertion point (fig. 26.18).

3. Create the new spreadsheet in the embedded spreadsheet.

Works replaces the current Works tool menu commands with the Spreadsheet commands.

Tip
To move the
spreadsheet win-
dow, click an edge
and drag it.

VI

Integrate & Communicate

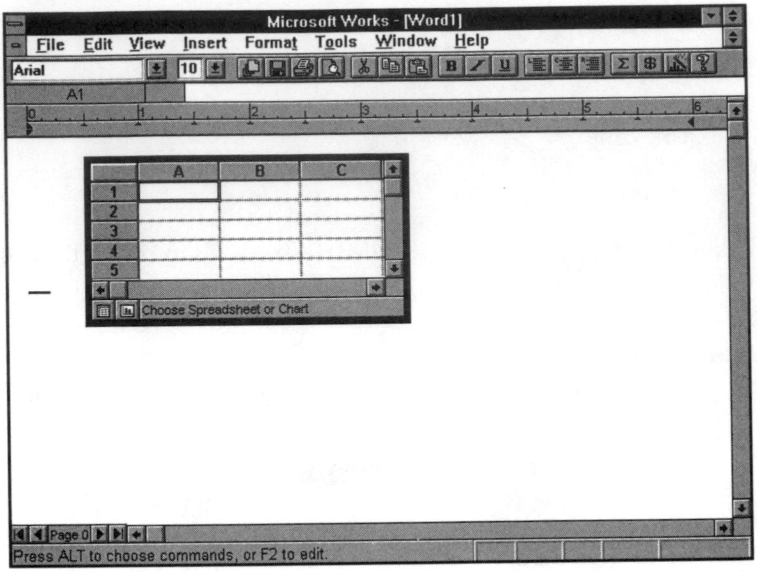

Fig. 26.18
Use the spread-
sheet window to
insert a new
spreadsheet from
which Works will
create a chart.

4. To embed a spreadsheet from the new data, click the spreadsheet button.

   or

   To embed a chart from the data, select the cells from which you want to create the chart, and click the chart button.

   If you click the chart button, Works displays the New Chart dialog box. To learn how to use the New Chart dialog box, see Chapter 14, "Creating Charts."

5. To return to the underlying Works tool, exit New Chart dialog box. Then click outside the spreadsheet, or press Esc.

Now that the chart is embedded, you can edit it without leaving your Works document. Follow these steps:

1. Double-click the chart.

   Works activates the chart window and replaces the current Works tool's menu commands with chart commands.

2. To change the spreadsheet values on which the chart is based, click the Spreadsheet button in the chart window to display the spreadsheet and make changes.

or

To change the chart design, choose Tools, Create New Chart, make any changes in the New Chart dialog box, and choose OK.

3. If you changed spreadsheet values in step 2, highlight the values that you want included in the new version of the chart, and click the Chart button.

4. To return to the underlying Works document, click outside the chart window, or press Esc.

Inserting a Spreadsheet or Table

Choosing Insert, Spreadsheet/Table displays the Spreadsheet/Table dialog box, which is exactly the same as the Insert Chart dialog box, except for its title (refer to fig. 26.17). To insert a spreadsheet or table, follow the steps given earlier for inserting a chart, but in step 4, click the spreadsheet button, and when you finish creating the spreadsheet, return to the underlying Works document by clicking outside the spreadsheet or by pressing Esc.

Inserting ClipArt, WordArt, Note-It, or a Drawing

From the Insert menu, choose ClipArt, WordArt, Note-It, or Drawing to start one of these tools. Follow these steps to embed one of these types of objects:

1. In your Works document, move the insertion point to where you want to insert the object.

2. Choose Insert, and the command for the object you want to insert: ClipArt, WordArt, Note-It, or Drawing.

   Works starts the corresponding tool.

3. Create or open and select the object you want to embed.

4. To return to the underlying Works document, use one of the following methods:

   If the application opened a separate window, choose File; then choose Exit, Exit and Return, Quit, or Return.

   If the application replaced the underlying Works tool's menus and toolbar, click outside the object; or press Esc.

   If the application is in a dialog box, as with Note-It, choose OK.

VI

Integrate & Communicate

If Works asks whether you want to update the object, choose Yes to add your changes or choose No to abandon your changes. If Works asks whether you want to update the document, choose Yes to insert the new version of the object.

Inserting an Object

Choosing **I**nsert, **O**bject displays the Insert Object dialog box (see fig. 26.19).

Fig. 26.19
Use the Insert Object dialog box to embed objects that are available with applications that support OLE (Object Linking and Embedding).

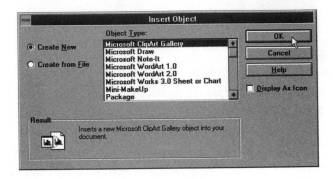

Follow these steps to create and embed other objects:

1. In your Works document, move the insertion point to where you want to embed the object.

2. From the **I**nsert menu, choose **O**bject. The Insert Object dialog box appears.

3. In the Insert Object dialog box, choose one of the following options:

   To create a new object, choose Create **N**ew. From the Object **T**ype list box, select the type of object you want to embed.

   To insert an existing file as an object, choose Create From **F**ile. Works displays a text box where you can type a file name. Type the file name or use the **B**rowse function to locate the file. To link the object instead of embedding it, choose the **L**ink check box.

Caution

In order to link or embed an existing file, the application that created the file must support OLE (Object Linking and Embedding). To link an existing file, the source application must support DDE (Dynamic Data Exchange).

---

4. Choose OK.

   Works starts the application you selected.

5. Open or create the object you want.

6. Return to your Works document by using one of the following methods:

   If the application opened a separate window, choose **F**ile, then choose E**x**it, E**x**it and Return, **Q**uit, or **R**eturn.

   If the application replaced the underlying Works tool's menus and toolbar, click outside the object or press Esc.

   If the application is in a dialog box, as with Note-It, choose OK.

Editing an Embedded Object

After embedding an object, you can open the object's source application and make changes without leaving the currently active Works tool. Follow these steps:

1. Double-click the object you want to edit.

   or

   Use the arrow keys to place the insertion point to the immediate left of the object, press Shift+right arrow, choose **E**dit, [Object Name] Object, and then choose **E**dit from the submenu.

2. Make the changes.

3. To return to your Works document, follow one of these steps:

   If the application opened a separate window, choose **F**ile, then choose E**x**it, E**x**it and Return, **Q**uit, or **R**eturn.

   If the application replaced the underlying Works tool's menus and toolbar, click outside the object or press Esc.

   If the application is in a dialog box, as with Note-It, choose OK.

VI

Integrate & Communicate

Moving and Resizing Objects

After you embed or link an object in a Works document, you can move it or change its size without disturbing the active embedding or linking function. To change an object's size with the mouse, click it and drag one of the object's sizing handles.

To change an object's size using exact measurements, follow these steps:

1. Click the object or move the insertion point to the immediate left of the object, and press Shift+right arrow.

   Works displays sizing handles around the object.

2. Choose Format, Picture/Object.

   Works displays the Picture/Object dialog box (see fig. 26.20).

Fig. 26.20
Use the Picture/ Object dialog box to format a picture or other object in your document.

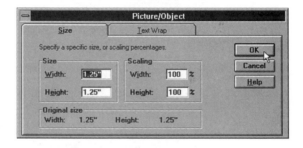

3. Choose the **S**ize tab.

4. Enter new dimensions for the object in the Size area for **W**idth and H**e**ight, or enter a percentage in the Scaling area for W**i**dth and Hei**g**ht.

5. Choose OK.

   Works changes the object's size.

To move an object with the mouse, click it and drag the object to the new location, or select the object with the keyboard by moving the insertion point to the immediate left of the object, pressing Shift+right-arrow, and dragging the object to the new location.

To move a selected object with the keyboard, choose **E**dit, Cu**t** or press Ctrl+X. Move the insertion point to where you want to place the object, and choose **E**dit, **P**aste or press Ctrl+V.

Wrapping Text Around an Object

When you place an object in a Works document, you can choose how Works formats text around the object. You have three choices:

- You can place the object "in-line," as if it were text. When you choose this option, Works automatically adjusts the line height to accommodate the object. If you insert, delete, or move text, Works moves the object just as it would move text.

- You can place the object in a paragraph by itself. When you choose this object, Works treats the object as a paragraph. You can enter text above and below the object, but Works does not run text around the sides of the object. The object moves with nearby text as if it were a paragraph of text.

- You can specify an exact (absolute) position for the object on the page. Regardless of any changes to the text on the page, Works keeps the object in exactly the same position on the page. Text wraps around the object.

Follow these steps to tell Works how you want text wrapped around an object:

1. Select the object by clicking it.

   or

   Select the object by moving the insertion point to the immediate left of the object and pressing Shift+right arrow.

2. Choose Format, Picture/Object.

3. Choose the **T**ext Wrap tab (see fig. 26.21).

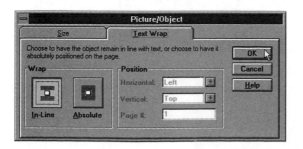

Tip
To see how text wraps around an object in the Works Word Processor, switch to Page Layout view, choose **V**iew, Pa**g**e Layout; or switch to Print Preview, choose **F**ile, Print Pre**v**iew.

Fig. 26.21
Use the Text Wrap tab to tell Works how to wrap text around a linked or embedded object.

4. Works selects **In**-Line by default. To change the text wrap setting, choose **A**bsolute.

   If you choose **In**-Line, Works treats the object as if it were a character. If you edit the surrounding text, the object moves with the text. If you choose **A**bsolute, Works anchors the object at the location you specify with the H**o**rizontal, **V**ertical, and **P**age # options, and wraps text around the sides of the object.

   If you choose **A**bsolute, continue with step 5; otherwise, choose OK to return to the document.

5. Choose H**o**rizontal, and then choose Left, Center, or Right.

   or

   In the Horizontal text box, delete Left and enter the exact distance from the left edge of the page where you want to place the left edge of the object.

6. Choose **V**ertical, and then choose Top, Center, or Bottom.

   or

   In the Vertical text box, delete Top and enter the exact distance from the top edge of the page where you want to place the top edge of the object.

Tip
To print an object in a header or footer on each page of the document, specify a Vertical position that places the object in the header or footer area of the page.

7. To tell Works to print the object on a specific page, enter a page number in the **P**age # text box.

8. Choose OK.

If your document is not displayed in Page Layout view, Works displays a message and asks whether you want to switch to Page Layout view now. Choose Yes to switch to Page Layout view, or choose No to remain in the current view.

Works positions the object on the page as you specified.

From Here...

In this chapter, you learned how to move, copy, embed, and link information from one Works document to another or from another Windows application to a Works document. The next chapters discuss the following:

- Chapter 27, "Creating and Printing Form Letters, Envelopes, and Mailing Labels," discusses how to create and print a form letter and how to print mailing labels and envelopes.

- Chapter 28, "Communicating with Other Computers," discusses choosing communications settings, saving a communications file, starting a communications session, and sending and receiving files.

VI

Integrate & Communicate

Chapter 27

Printing Form Letters, Envelopes, and Mailing Labels

If you have created a Works database that contains names and addresses, you can print form letters with the Works Word Processor. (This process is sometimes called *merge printing* or *mail merge*.) Works inserts in each copy of the form letter the name and address from one record in a database. You can use Database tools to sort and select addresses for the form letters. You can also print form letters from names and addresses you have saved with the Microsoft Profit program.

Works can also use Works database information to print envelopes and mailing labels, or Works can print a single envelope or label using a name and address in a document displayed on-screen.

Creating a Form Letter

Before you can print form letters, you must do two things:

■ You must create a Works database that contains the names and addresses you want to print on the form letter, one name and address per form letter.

■ You must type the form letter in the Word Processor and insert codes, called *placeholders*, that tell Works where to print the merged information from a Works database. For example, you could insert placeholders

In this chapter, you learn how to:

■ Create and print a form letter

■ Print mailing labels

■ Print envelopes

VI

Integrate & Communicate

that tell Works to first print the First Name database field, then the Last Name field, followed by the Company, City, State, ZIP, and Country fields.

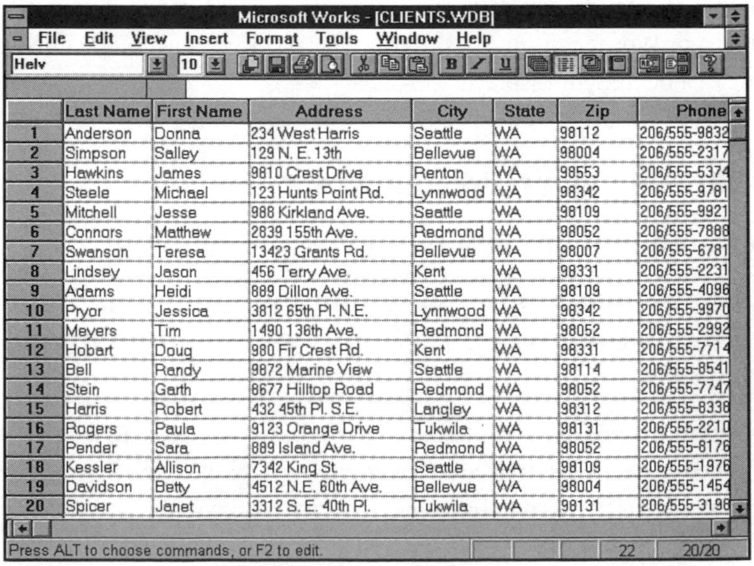

Figure 27.1 shows a form letter with placeholders inserted for the name, address, and greeting; figure 27.2 shows a Works database in List view; and figure 27.3 shows several letters printed from the database and form.

Fig. 27.1 A form letter with placeholders inserted for the name, address, and greeting.

	Last Name	First Name	Address	City	State	Zip	Phone
1	Anderson	Donna	234 West Harris	Seattle	WA	98112	206/555-9832
2	Simpson	Salley	129 N. E. 13th	Bellevue	WA	98004	206/555-2317
3	Hawkins	James	9810 Crest Drive	Renton	WA	98553	206/555-5374
4	Steele	Michael	123 Hunts Point Rd.	Lynnwood	WA	98342	206/555-9781
5	Mitchell	Jesse	988 Kirkland Ave.	Seattle	WA	98109	206/555-9921
6	Connors	Matthew	2839 155th Ave.	Redmond	WA	98052	206/555-7888
7	Swanson	Teresa	13423 Grants Rd.	Bellevue	WA	98007	206/555-6781
8	Lindsey	Jason	456 Terry Ave.	Kent	WA	98331	206/555-2231
9	Adams	Heidi	889 Dillon Ave.	Seattle	WA	98109	206/555-4096
10	Pryor	Jessica	3812 65th Pl. N.E.	Lynnwood	WA	98342	206/555-9970
11	Meyers	Tim	1490 136th Ave.	Redmond	WA	98052	206/555-2992
12	Hobart	Doug	980 Fir Crest Rd.	Kent	WA	98331	206/555-7714
13	Bell	Randy	9872 Marine View	Seattle	WA	98114	206/555-8541
14	Stein	Garth	8677 Hilltop Road	Redmond	WA	98052	206/555-7747
15	Harris	Robert	432 45th Pl. S.E.	Langley	WA	98312	206/555-8338
16	Rogers	Paula	9123 Orange Drive	Tukwila	WA	98131	206/555-2210
17	Pender	Sara	889 Island Ave.	Redmond	WA	98052	206/555-8176
18	Kessler	Allison	7342 King St.	Seattle	WA	98109	206/555-1976
19	Davidson	Betty	4512 N.E. 60th Ave.	Bellevue	WA	98004	206/555-1454
20	Spicer	Janet	3312 S. E. 40th Pl.	Tukwila	WA	98131	206/555-3198

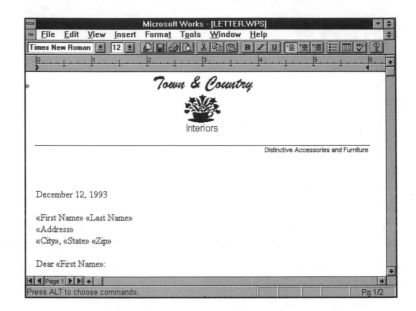

Fig. 27.2 A Works database in List view.

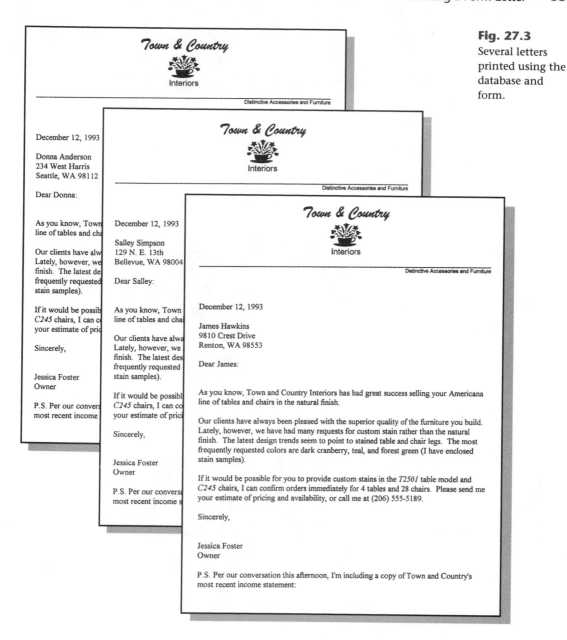

Fig. 27.3
Several letters
printed using the
database and
form.

The first step in printing form letters is to create the database and letter that
you will use. Next, in the form letter, you insert placeholders that tell Works
where to print database information in the letters. Follow these steps:

1. Create the database that contains the information you want to print in
   the form letters, and make sure it has been saved.

VI

Integrate & Communicate

2. Create a Word Processor document that contains the form letter, and be sure to save the letter.

3. In the Word Processor document, move the insertion point to where you want the first placeholder.

   For example, move the insertion point to where you want to insert the First Name field.

Tip

If you want to use names and addresses stored with Microsoft Profit, choose **I**nsert and choose a Database/Profit Field.

4. Choose **I**nsert, Database **F**ield.

   Works displays the Insert Field dialog box (see fig. 27.4).

Fig. 27.4

Use the Insert Field dialog box to insert placeholders in a form letter.

5. To select the database to use with the form letter, choose Data**b**ase.

   Works displays the Choose Database dialog box (see fig. 27.5).

Fig. 27.5

Use the Choose Database dialog box to select a database for printing form letters.

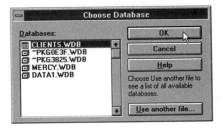

6. From the **D**atabases list box, select the database you want to use with the form letter.

> **Note**
>
> Works can print records from only one database at a time in a form letter. To switch databases, repeat steps 4 through 6. Works prompts you to confirm that you want to attach a new database to the form letter.

7. To locate databases that aren't listed, choose **U**se Another File.

8. In the Use Another File dialog box, select a file in the File **N**ame list box, then choose OK.

Works displays the Insert Field dialog box again (refer to fig. 27.4).

Follow these steps to use the Insert Field dialog box to add placeholders to the form letter:

1. In the **F**ields list box of the Insert field dialog box, choose the first field for which you want to print information in the form letter.

2. Choose **I**nsert.

   Works inserts the placeholder in the letter without closing the dialog box.

3. Repeat steps 1 and 2 for each field you want to insert.

4. Choose Clos**e**.

5. In the Word Processor document, move the field placeholders to their correct locations.

Tip

Don't worry if the placeholder isn't positioned where you want the field to print. When you return to your document, you can move the placeholders to the correct locations.

For example, figure 27.1 shows placeholders for a name, address, and greeting formatted with a comma between the <<City>> and <<State>> fields.

Note

You can copy, move, and delete placeholders like any other text. You can format placeholders with fonts and character enhancements such as italics or boldfacing. And you can copy placeholder chevrons to insert new placeholders without using the Insert Field dialog box. However, you cannot format placeholders with left and right pointed brackets (<<>>). Placeholders must be enclosed in chevrons.

Printing Form Letters

When you print a form letter, Works prints one copy of the letter for each record in the database you attached to the letter, as described in the preceding section, "Creating a Form Letter." In each letter, Works replaces each field

VI

Integrate & Communicate

placeholder with the corresponding field contents from one database record. For example, Works replaces the <<First Name>> placeholder with "Donna" and the <<Last Name>> placeholder with "Anderson".

Follow these steps to print form letters:

1. Display the Word Processor form letter document.

   The document must contain placeholders and be associated with a database. To learn how to create a form letter and insert placeholders, see the preceding section on "Creating a Form Letter."

2. If you want to print only selected records from the database, open the database associated with the letter and use a Query or the Find or Hide Records command to display only the selected records.

   To find out how to use Query, Find, and Hide Records, see Chapter 21, "Retrieving Database Information."

3. From the **F**ile menu, choose **P**rint.

   Works displays the Print dialog box with special options for printing form letters (see fig. 27.6).

Fig. 27.6
Use special merge-printing options in the Print dialog box to print form letters.

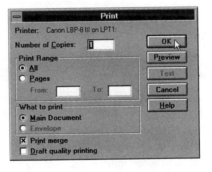

Notice in figure 27.6 that Works automatically detected a form letter and displayed and selected the Print Merge check box.

4. Choose OK to print the form letters.

   Works prints the letters, inserting information from one database record in each copy of the letter.

Tip
To print the form letter without merging information from a database, deselect the Print merge check box.

Follow these steps to preview merge-printed letters before you print them:

1. Display the Word Processor form letter document.

2. If you want to preview only selected records from the database, open the database associated with the letter and use a Query or the Find or Hide Records command to display only the selected records.

To find out how to use Query, Find, and Hide Records, see Chapter 21, "Retrieving Database Information."

3. From the **F**ile menu, choose **P**rint.

Works displays the Choose Database dialog box (refer to fig. 27.5).

4. Follow the steps for choosing a database as described in the preceding section on "Creating a Form Letter."

5. Choose **F**ile, **P**rint, **P**review.

Works displays the Choose a Database dialog box (refer to fig. 27.5).

6. Choose a database in the File **N**ame list box, then choose OK.

Works asks if you want to merge all records.

7. Choose OK.

Works displays the first page of the first merged form letter in the Print Preview screen.

8. To print the merged letters, choose **P**rint; or choose Cancel or press Escape to return to the form letter document.

Printing Mailing Labels

In the preceding sections of this chapter, you learned how to print form letters by inserting information from a Works database into a Word Processor document. In a very similar fashion, you can tell Works to print names and addresses from a database on labels. Printing labels is simpler than printing form letters, however, because Works includes formatting information for printing on most popular mailing label sizes. You can also create your own customized label definitions.

VI

Integrate & Communicate

Once you select or customize a mailing label definition, Works can print a few test labels to ensure that you have selected the proper label definition and that the labels are inserted properly in the printer.

> **Note**
>
> You can insert placeholders in a Word Processor document for labels or envelopes, but not both.

Printing mailing labels involves four steps:

- Designate the database that contains the information you want to print on labels.

- In a Word Processor document, insert placeholders for the database information you want to print on each label. For example, insert placeholders for <<First Name>> and <<Last Name>>.

- Choose a preset label size, or customize a label definition.

- Print the labels. Optionally, you can preview the merge-printed labels and print a few test labels to make sure the labels print correctly.

Follow these steps to print labels:

Tip
You can print labels that contain information other than names and addresses. For example, you might print product labels that contain each product's name and price from a database of product descriptions.

1. Create the database that contains the information you want to print on the labels.

2. Display the Word Processor document for which you want to print mailing labels.

3. From the Tools menu, choose Envelopes and Labels.

4. Select the Mailing Labels tab.

   Works displays the Mailing Labels tab (see fig. 27.7).

5. Choose Fields.

   Works expands the Mailing Labels tab to include options for selecting fields (see fig. 27.8).

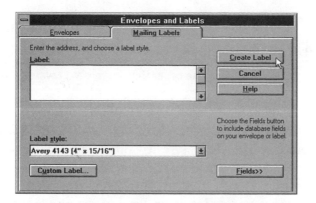

Fig. 27.7
Use the **M**ailing Labels tab to select or create a label definition.

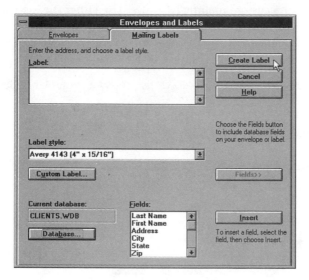

Fig. 27.8
Choosing **F**ields adds options for inserting field placeholders.

6. If the Current Database box says None, or if you want to switch to a different database, choose Data**b**ase. If Works prompts you to confirm the switch, choose OK. Use the Choose Database dialog box (refer to fig. 27.5) to select a database, then choose OK to return to the **M**ailing Labels tab.

or

If you want to use the database shown in the Current Database box, skip this step.

7. In the **F**ields List box, choose the first field name you want to use as a placeholder for your labels.

8. Choose **I**nsert.

   Works inserts the placeholder in the **L**abel text box.

9. Repeat steps 7 and 8 for the other field names you want to print.

10. Choose **L**abel and make any changes to the labels.

   For example, you can type text to include on each label (such as **Season's Greetings!**), or use Cu**t**, **C**opy, and **P**aste (Ctrl+X, Ctrl+C, Ctrl+V) to move placeholders. Press Shift+Enter to end each line.

Without leaving the Mailing Labels tab, you can choose either a preset mailing label size or a custom mailing label size. Use either the next steps or the subsequent steps.

From the Mailing labels tab, choose a preset mailing label size:

1. From the Label **S**tyle drop-down list, select a preset label size.

2. **C**reate Label to insert the label definition at the top of your document (see fig. 27.9).

Fig. 27.9
When you choose a label type, Works inserts the label placeholders at the top of your document.

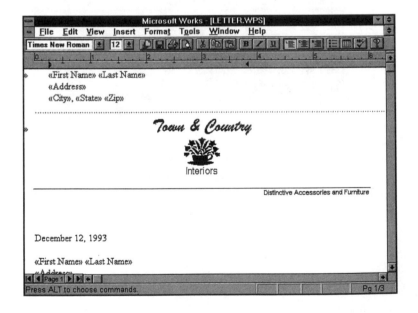

From the Mailing labels tab, choose a custom mailing label size:

1. Choose the Custom Label to display the Custom Labels dialog box (see fig. 27.10).

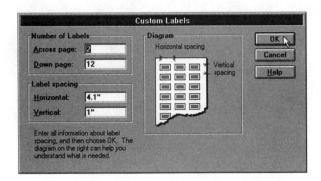

Fig. 27.10
Use the Custom Labels dialog box to design your own label definitions.

2. In the **A**cross Page text box, type the number of labels you want Works to print across the page. Then, in the **D**own Page text box, specify the number of labels to print down the page.

3. In the **H**orizontal text box, type the horizontal spacing for the label definition. Then, in the **V**ertical text box, type the vertical spacing.

4. Choose OK.

VI

Integrate & Communicate

Works displays the Custom Labels dialog box (see fig. 27.11).

Fig. 27.11
Use the Custom Labels dialog box to design your own label definitions.

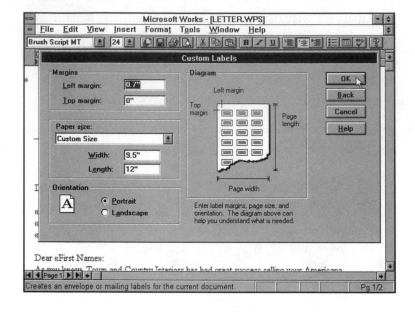

5. Type custom measurements in the **L**eft Margin and **T**op Margin text boxes.

Refer to the sample Diagram to see the effect of margin and paper size settings.

Tip
If you discover that you need to adjust the number of labels on the page, choose **B**ack to return to the first Custom Labels dialog box.

6. From the Paper S**i**ze drop-down list, select a standard paper size.

or

Type custom measurements in the paper size **W**idth and L**e**ngth text boxes.

7. Choose **P**ortrait or L**a**ndscape.

8. Choose OK to return to the Mailing Labels tab of the Envelopes and Labels dialog box.

9. Choose **C**reate Label.

Works returns you to your document and inserts the label definition at the top of the file.

Changing a Label Definition

After you insert a label definition in a Word Processor document, you may discover that you need to change the definition. For example, you may decide to print labels using a different label size. Follow these steps to change the existing label definition:

1. Open the document that contains the label definition.

2. To make simple changes to the placeholders and any text that prints on the labels, edit the label definition at the top of the document.

3. To choose a different label size, paper size, or to create a custom label definition, from the Tools menu, choose **E**nvelopes and Labels. Then select the **M**ailing Labels tab. Make the desired changes, following the steps given earlier in this section. For example, choose a different standard label type, choose different field placeholders, or change the page size. When you finish making changes, from the Mailing Labels tab, choose **C**hange Label.

   Works inserts the new definition at the top of the document, replacing the previous definition.

Previewing and Printing Labels

After you create a label definition, as described earlier in this section, you are ready to print labels. Because labels may not print correctly if you position the label stock incorrectly in the printer, or if you choose the wrong label definition, it's a good idea to preview the label definition and test-print a few labels before you proceed to the final print run.

Follow these steps to preview mailing labels:

1. Open the document that contains the label definition.

2. From the **F**ile menu, choose **P**rint.

3. Select Mailing Labels.

4. Choose **P**review.

   Works displays the Choose Database dialog box.

5. Select **D**atabases and select the database from which you want to print mailing label information.

6. Choose OK.

Works shows you the mailing labels in the Print Preview screen (see fig. 27.12).

Fig. 27.12
Use Print Preview to check that labels will print correctly.

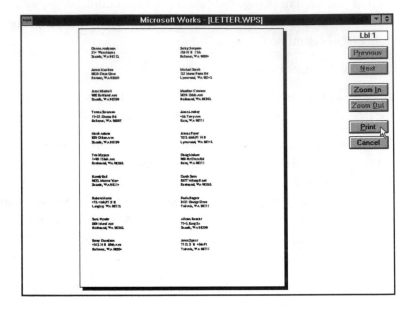

7. To return to the mailing label document, choose Cancel; or press Esc.

Print preview lets you see whether your labels are formatted correctly, but it doesn't show you if they print correctly on the label stock. For example, the label text may print too close to the left edge of each label.

To fine-tune the placement of printed label text, test-print a few labels by following these steps:

1. Load a sheet of plain paper into your printer.

2. Open the mailing label document.

3. From the **F**ile menu, choose **P**rint.

4. Select Maili**n**g Labels.

5. Choose T**e**st.

6. In the Choose Database dialog box, choose the database for the labels.

7. Choose OK.

Works prints one or two test rows of labels, depending on your label definition (see fig. 27.13).

Donna Anderson 234 West Harris Seattle, WA 98112	Salley Simpson 129 N. E. 13th Bellevue, WA 98004
James Hawkins 9810 Crest Drive Renton, WA 98553	Michael Steele 123 Hunts Point Rd. Lynnwood, WA 98342

Fig. 27.13
Test print a few labels to make sure Works prints labels in the proper position.

Works displays the Test Label Printing dialog box, where you can choose to **P**rint all the labels, choose **T**est to print another test, choose **A**djust to make changes to the label definition, or choose Cancel to return to your document.

To print mailing labels using a label definition you've previously created, follow these steps:

1. Load the labels into the printer.

2. Open the mailing label document.

3. From the **F**ile menu, choose **P**rint.

4. In the Print dialog box, leave Pr**i**nt Merge selected, and select any other print options.

   Printing is described in detail under "Printing a Document" in Chapter 4, "Creating, Saving, and Printing a Document."

5. Choose OK.

6. In the Choose Database dialog box, select the database that contains the information you want to print on the labels.

   If the database you named is not currently open, Works asks whether you want to merge all records.

Tip
To print the document without merging database records, clear the Print Merge check box. Works prints the document and includes the placeholders.

VI

Integrate & Communicate

7. Choose OK to merge all records.

or

To print only some of the records from the database, choose Cancel, then open the database and use the Find, Hide Records, or Query commands to display the records you want to print; then repeat steps 1 through 7.

Works prints the labels. To cancel printing choose Cancel or press Esc.

Printing Envelopes

Works makes it easy to print an envelope using an address in a Word Processor document. You can also print one envelope for each name and address in a Works database. When you tell Works to print a single envelope from a name and address in a document, you can save the envelope definition with the document, making it easy to print the envelope next time. Or you can save the envelope-printing instructions in a different document and print only the envelope later.

Caution

A Word Processor document can include instructions for printing envelopes or labels, but not both.

Works can print envelopes using your printer's manual feed or envelope bin, or using form-feed envelopes that are attached to continuous paper.

Preparing a Single Envelope

Works can print a single envelope, using an address in an on-screen document, and an optional return address.

Follow these steps to prepare a single envelope from an address in a Word Processor document:

1. Display the document that contains the address you want to print.

2. Highlight the address you want to print on an envelope.

3. From the Tools menu, choose Envelopes and Labels.

Works displays the Envelopes and labels dialog box with the **E**nvelopes tab automatically selected (see fig 27.14).

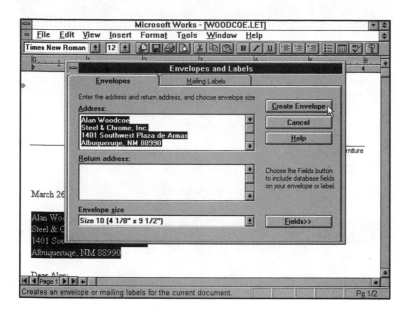

Fig. 27.14
When you highlight an address and choose T**o**ols, **E**nvelopes and Labels, Works automatically displays the **E**nvelopes tab and inserts the address in the **A**ddress box.

4. Select **R**eturn address and type a return address, if any.

To print the address on preprinted envelopes, omit the return address.

5. From the Envelope **S**ize drop-down list, select a standard envelope size.

6. Choose **C**reate Envelope.

Works places the envelope definition at the top of your document, separated from the rest of the text by a nonremovable page break (see fig. 27.15).

To print the envelope, follow the directions under "Previewing and Printing Envelopes" later in this chapter.

Creating an Envelope Definition

Merge-printing envelopes from database information involves three steps:

■ Create a database with address information you want to print on the envelopes.

■ Insert database field placeholders in a Word Processor document.

■ Preview and print the envelope.

VI

Integrate & Communicate

Fig. 27.15
When you create an envelope from an address in a Word Processor document, Works inserts the envelope definition at the top of the document.

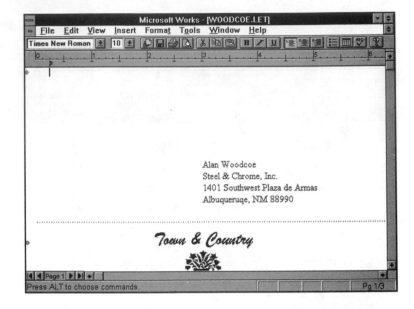

Follow these steps to insert database field placeholders for merge-printing envelopes:

1. Display the Word Processor document for which you want to merge-print envelopes.

2. From the T**o**ols menu, choose **E**nvelopes and Labels.

3. Choose the **E**nvelopes tab.

   Works displays the Envelopes and Labels dialog box with the **E**nvelopes tab selected (see fig. 27.16).

Fig. 27.16
Use the **E**nvelopes tab in the Envelopes and Labels dialog box to insert field placeholders for merge-printing envelopes.

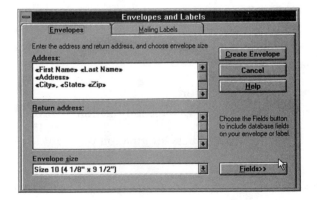

Note

If your document already has placeholders for printing labels, Works warns you that inserting envelope placeholders will replace the label placeholders. Choose **Y**es to replace the old placeholders.

4. Choose **F**ields.

Works displays extra options on the **E**nvelopes tab for inserting field placeholders (see fig. 27.17).

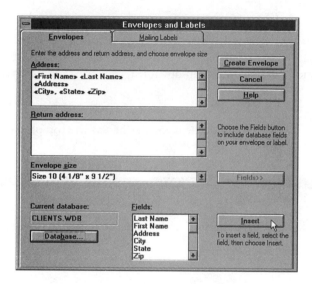

Fig. 27.17
Select **F**ields from the **E**nvelopes tab to select the database fields you want to merge-print on envelopes.

5. If the Current database box displays None, or if you want to use a different database, choose Data**b**ase and select a database in the Choose Database dialog box.

or

If the Current database box displays the name of the database you want to use, proceed to step 6.

6. Select **A**ddress and move the highlight to where you want to insert a placeholder.

7. Choose **F**ields and highlight the first field for which you want to insert a placeholder.

8. Choose **I**nsert.

Works inserts the placeholder in the **A**ddress box.

9. Repeat steps 6 through 8 for each field you want to print on the envelopes.

10. Select **R**eturn Address, and type the return address, if any.

> **Note**
>
> In the **A**ddress and **R**eturn Address boxes, be sure to include any desired text, spaces, or punctuation for the placeholders. For example, add a comma between the City and State placeholders:
>
> **<<City>>, <<State>> <<Zip>>**

11. From the Envelope **S**ize drop-down list, select a standard envelope size.

12. Choose Create Envelope.

Works inserts the placeholders you defined at the top of your document (see fig. 27.18).

Fig. 27.18
When you create an envelope definition, Works inserts the placeholders at the top of the document.

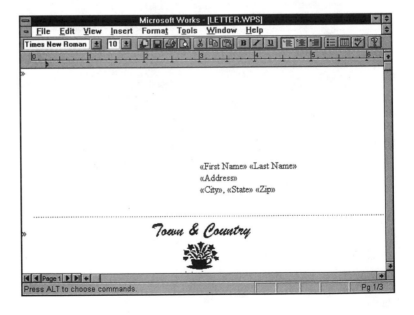

Modifying an Envelope Definition

You may decide to send the same letter to several different addresses. You can use the form letter method described earlier in this chapter, or you can use the File, Save As command to save the letter under a different name, then type a new address for the letter. If you previously created an envelope definition, you need to modify the envelope.

Follow these steps to modify an existing envelope definition:

1. Display the document that contains the envelope definition.

2. Make any changes to the address you want to print on the envelope.

3. Select the address. Then, from the **E**dit menu, choose **C**opy; or press Ctrl+C.

4. From the T**o**ols menu, choose **E**nvelopes and Labels.

5. Choose the **E**nvelopes tab.

   Works displays the Envelopes tab with the old address in the **A**ddress box (see fig. 27.19).

6. Select **A**ddress and press Delete to remove the old address.

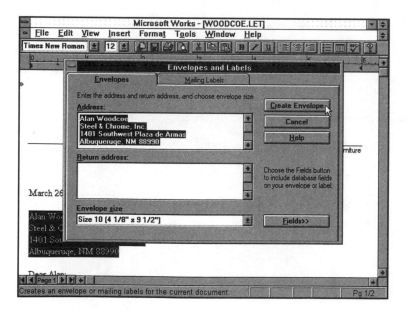

Fig. 27.19
The old address is displayed in the Address box.

7. Press Ctrl+V to insert the new address.

8. Make any changes to the **R**eturn Address and Envelope **S**ize.

9. Choose **C**hange Envelope.

Works replaces the old envelope address with the new one.

Previewing and Printing Envelopes

After you insert an envelope address in a document, as described earlier in this chapter on "Preparing a Single Envelope," you can preview and print the envelope.

To find out how to merge-print envelopes, see the previous section "Creating an Envelope Definition."

Follow these steps to preview and print envelopes:

1. Insert a single envelope in your printer, load envelopes in your printer's envelope bin, or load form-feed envelopes.

2. If your printer has an envelope feeder, from the **T**ools menu, choose **O**ptions. Then select Printer's Envelope Feeder Is Installed and choose OK.

3. From the **F**ile menu, choose **P**rint; or press Ctrl+P.

   Works displays the Print dialog box. Works detects the envelope definition in your document and automatically selects the E**n**velope radio button.

4. Choose P**r**eview.

   Works displays the envelope in Print Preview (see fig. 27.20).

5. Choose **P**rint to print the envelope.

   Or press Esc or choose Cancel to return to your document without printing.

Tip
To adjust the position of the address, in the **E**nvelopes tab of the Envelopes and Labels dialog box, add or remove blank lines and use paragraph indents in the **A**ddress and **Re**turn address text boxes.

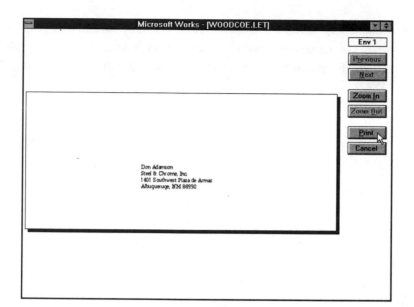

Fig. 27.20
Use Print Preview
to ensure that
Works positions
the address
correctly on an
envelope.

From Here...

In this chapter, you learned how to create and print form letters and labels.
You also learned how to merge-print envelopes and print single envelopes
using addresses in the body of a Word Processor document. For related information, see the following chapters:

- Chapter 4, "Creating, Saving, and Printing a Word Processing
  Document." In this chapter, you learn how to create and print
  Word Processor documents.

- Chapter 5, "Editing a Document." In this chapter, you learn how to
  make changes to the text in Word Processor documents.

- Chapter 17, "Creating and Editing a Database Form." This chapter tells
  you how to lay out a database form and create data entry fields.

- Chapter 19, "Entering and Editing Data." In this chapter, you learn how
  to type data and save records. In addition, you learn how to copy and
  move information and hide records.

- Chapter 20, "Expanding Your Database Skills." See this chapter to find
  out how to sort and print records, use dates and times, math formulas
  and functions, protect your data, and format data in fields.

VI

Integrate & Communicate

■ Chapter 21, "Retrieving Database Information." Consult this chapter when you need to retrieve information from a database using specific criteria (for example, retrieving only the records where the state is "WA").

Chapter 28

Communicating with Other Computers

If your computer system has a modem, you have access to a whole world of information via the telephone lines. You can connect to other computers, fax modems, MCI mail boxes, and online news and information services like CompuServe and America Online. You can log on to other computers to read information, capture information that you're reading, or you can send and receive files.

What You Can Do with Communications

The communications tool in Works is a software application that enables you to connect your computer to another computer so that you can share and exchange information. You can connect to a large computer shared by hundreds of users or to another personal computer. In either case, the other computer must be equipped with a modem and communications software. In the case of a personal computer, the communications software doesn't have to be Works. It can be an application as simple as the Terminal application in Microsoft Windows, or it can be a more sophisticated communications application like Crosstalk, produced by Digital Communications Associates, Inc.

Whether you are connecting to a large computer system at your office, a large computer that runs an online information service like CompuServe, or a colleague's personal computer, the operator of the other computer has complete control over which programs and files you have access to on that

In this chapter, you learn about the following topics:

- What you can do with communications

- Communications terminology

- The communications menus and toolbar

- Choosing communications settings

- Saving a communications file

- Starting a communications session

- Capturing text

- Sending and receiving files

VI

Integrate & Communicate

computer. Once you have the authority to connect to another computer, the communications software in Works provides the tools for you to perform any of the following tasks.

- *Use your computer as a terminal.* The hundreds of users connected to a large computer system access the computer through a *terminal*, which is nothing more than a keyboard and a screen. When you use the communications tool in Works to connect your computer to a large computer, you are using your computer as if it were a terminal directly connected to the large computer. You have access to all programs and files on the computer that you are authorized to use. When you use your computer to connect to a computer information service such as CompuServe, you are using your computer as a terminal. Likewise, when you use your computer to connect to a large computer at your office to read and send electronic mail or edit a file, you are using your computer as a terminal.

- *Send and Receive Files.* Often you might want to share some of your computer files with business or academic colleagues who are users on large computer systems or who have personal computers. Using the communications tool in Works, you can send a file stored on a disk, and you can receive a file from a user on another computer and save the file on your computer. Sending and receiving files is different from simply reading electronic mail or information from an online information service.

- *Capture Text.* There may be times when you want to save on your computer all of the information you receive from another computer, even if you are just reading files. For example, if you are gathering the latest stock quotes from Dow Jones for a report you are writing, you can save that information in a file on your computer so you can use it later in a Works document. This is called "capturing" text. Works saves the captured text in a file called *capture.txt* or any other file name that you specify.

Terms You Need To Know Before Using Communications

Many new users are intimidated by computer communications when they hear terms like *stop bits*, *parity*, *protocol*, and *baud*. It's true that computer communications is a topic with terminology all its own. But familiarity with this terminology will help you feel more comfortable with communications and get you started more quickly. You don't need to understand the intricacies of how computers actually communicate; you just need to recognize some terms and know which settings to use when you prepare to communicate with another computer. Following is a list of general communications terms. Throughout this chapter you learn additional terms where appropriate.

- *Modem.* A hardware device that converts a computer's digital signals into analog signals used by telephone lines, then converts the signals back again so that computers can "talk" to one another across telephone lines. You must have a modem connected to your computer in order to communicate with other computers. There are two types of modems, internal and external. Internal modems are computer cards that plug into a slot inside your computer. External modems are boxes that sit outside your computer. For both types of modems, you plug your telephone cord into the modem. Another cord connects your modem to your telephone jack so that the modem acts as an intermediary between your phone and your computer.

> **Note**
>
> To communicate with another computer, *both* computers must have modems.

- *Port.* There are two types; a physical connector on the back of your computer or a slot inside your computer. An example of a physical connector on the back of your computer is a printer port, into which you plug your printer cable. A port inside your computer is used for plugging in computer cards such as internal modems and communications cards. Before using communications, you must know which port is your communications port (usually COM1, COM2, COM3, or COM4).

VI

Integrate & Communicate

■ *Host computer.* The computer to which you establish a connection via your computer. A host can be a large computer or a personal computer.

■ *Mainframe computer.* A large computer that supports sometimes hundreds of multiple users and can run dozens of programs at one time. Mainframe computers are almost always connected to a computer network, making them accessible to many more users provided those users have authority to access the computer.

■ *Computer network.* Computers that are connected to one another for the purpose of sharing information are *networked.* Users on one networked computer have immediate access to all other computers on the network. Computers in a network can be physically connected, but most often are connected via direct telephone lines, fiber optic cable, or satellite. Networked computers can be located in a single building, a single city, or hundreds (even thousands) of miles apart from each other.

■ *Online Information Service.* A service available only by computer that provides information on a variety of topics such as news, weather, travel, and investments. Some even include shopping services. CompuServe and America Online are two popular online services that provide a wide variety of information. To access an online information service, you join the membership and pay a monthly fee. The monthly fee gives you a specific amount of connect time each month. Depending on the service, you are charged an additional fee for additional connect time.

■ *Terminal Emulation.* A terminal is a keyboard and screen connected to a computer. Some mainframe computers respond only to certain types of terminals, so if you want to connect to that computer, your computer must *emulate* the particular type of terminal the computer recognizes.

■ *Transfer Protocol.* A set of agreed-upon rules that two computers use when communicating with one another to check for and correct errors during transmission. When transferring (sending or receiving) files to or from another computer, you must specify a single protocol that both computers use. (There are half a dozen or so standard transfer protocols.)

■ *Baud Rate.* The speed at which computers transfer data, such as 1200 baud, 2400 baud, or 9600 baud. (The higher the number, the faster the rate.) The baud rate you set must match the baud rate of the computer to which you are connected, and you can only set a baud rate that your modem supports. Most modems support 1200, 2400, and 9600 baud.

- *Parity.* Parity is a setting that some computers use to determine whether characters are being transmitted accurately. Typical settings are even, odd, or none.

- *Data Bits.* Data bits define the number of bits used to represent a single character. Typical settings are 7 or 8.

- *Stop Bits.* Define the number of bits used to signal the end of a character. Typical settings are 1 or 2.

- *Handshake.* A protocol that controls the flow of information between two computers. The computers send Continue and Pause signals to one another when they're ready to receive more information and when they need to pause. Both computers must use the same handshake in order to communicate, or use none at all.

- *ASCII file.* A file that contains only text characters that are part of the ASCII code. All formatting (such as bold, italic, tabs, and so on) is stripped out of an ASCII file.

- *Binary file.* A file in a format readable only by the computer. Rather than containing text, each character in the file is represented in its binary code (combinations of zeros and ones).

- *Communications session.* The time during which you are connected to another computer via your telephone line.

Getting Started with Communications

To use the Communications tool in Works, open the Startup dialog box by clicking the Startup button on the toolbar or by choosing the Create New File command on the File menu. When the Startup dialog box appears, click the Communications icon to open a new communications file. The communications window appears inside of the Works window and is titled COMM1. An example is shown in figure 28.1.

VI

Integrate & Communicate

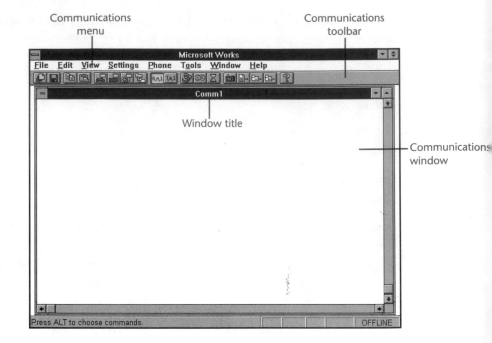

Fig. 28.1
The Communications window.

As you've seen in all of the other Works tools, each tool has a unique menu bar and toolbar.

Examining the Communications Menus

In the Communications tool, most of the menus are very different from those in other tools because the nature of the application is very different. The emphasis is on communicating with other computers rather than on creating documents. As such, the **F**ile menu includes the familiar create, open, and save commands, but you won't find any printer, page setup, or print commands. The **E**dit menu enables you to select, copy, and paste text. On the **V**iew menu, you find only one command, Tool**b**ar, which turns on or off the display of the toolbar.

You use the **S**ettings menu to set all of your phone, communication, terminal, transfer, and modem settings before you begin a communications session. The **P**hone menu lets you dial, pause, and hang up your phone during a communications session. The T**o**ols menu is used primarily for sending and receiving files or text. You also use this menu to customize the communications toolbar.

The **W**indow menu is similar to those in the other Works tools. It enables you to arrange open windows on-screen and switch between open documents. And finally, the **H**elp menu gives you access to online help for communications and any other tool in Works.

Examining the Communications Toolbar

The communications window has its own toolbar as well. You can customize the toolbar, just like you can in other Works tools. For instructions on customizing the toolbar, refer to Chapter 2, "Getting Started with Works for Windows."

The toolbar buttons are described in Table 28.1. To use a button, simply click it. If the button requires that you take some action before clicking the button, Works displays a message telling you what to do.

Table 28.1 Communications Toolbar Buttons	
Button	**Description**
	Displays the Works Startup dialog box.
	Saves the active communications file.
	Copies the selected text to the Clipboard.
	Pastes the contents of the Clipboard into the active communications file at the location of the insertion point.
	Displays the **C**ommunications tab in the Settings dialog box, in which you define communication settings.
	Displays the **T**erminal tab in the Settings dialog box, in which you define terminal settings.
	Displays the **P**hone tab in the Settings dialog box, in which you define phone settings.
	Displays the **T**ransfer tab in the Settings dialog box, in which you define transfer settings.
	Automatically changes your communication settings to 8 data bits, no parity, and 1 stop bit.
	Automatically changes your communication settings to 7 data bits, even parity, and 1 stop bit.

(continues)

Button	Description
Table 28.1 Continued	
	Displays the Easy Connect dialog box, in which you can enter the phone number and service name of the computer you want to dial.
	Dials the current phone number to establish a connection. If you are already connected, clicking this button disconnects your connection.
	Pauses your communications session.
	Saves the text you are receiving as a file.
	Lets you send an ASCII (text) file to the computer to which you are connected.
	Lets you send a binary file to the computer to which you are connected.
	Receives a binary file and saves it.
	Displays the Learning Works dialog box, from which you can access help, tutorials, WorksWizards, and CueCards.

Setting Up Your Computer for Communications

Before you begin to communicate with another computer, you need to know some of the standard communication settings required by the computer to which you are connecting. For example, you must know parity bits, stop bits, data bits, baud rate, handshake, transfer protocol, and terminal emulation settings required by the other computer. You also need to know the phone number to dial to establish the connection.

If you are connecting to an information service such as CompuServe, this information is available in the membership packet you receive. If you are connecting to a large computer at a specific business or organization, the computer's operations staff can provide you this information. In all cases, you need to know your user name on the host computer, and in most cases, a password is required.

If you can't find all of the communications settings, don't worry. In some cases you can guess which settings to use. For some settings, you have a choice between only two options, so your chances of guessing correctly are fifty-fifty. You know you need to change some settings if the information you see on-screen doesn't make sense or contains a lot of "garbage" characters.

Choosing Phone Settings

Phone settings refers to the phone number of the computer you are dialing and the dialing instructions you want to use. To specify phone settings, you choose the **P**hone command on the **S**ettings menu or click the Phone button on the toolbar. Works displays the Settings dialog box shown in figure 28.2. Notice that the Settings dialog box is tabbed; the **P**hone tab is selected.

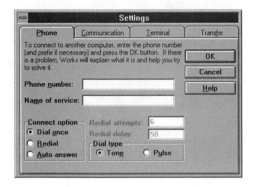

Fig. 28.2
Choose the Phone tab in the Settings dialog box to specify phone settings.

Use the following steps to specify phone settings:

1. From the **S**ettings menu, choose the **P**hone command; or click the Phone Settings button on the toolbar. The dialog box shown in figure 28.2 appears.

2. In the Phone **N**umber box, type the phone number to dial, including a prefix, if required. You can type parentheses or dashes if you want. Enter a comma to cause your modem to pause for a dial tone before continuing to dial.

3. In the Na**m**e of Service box, enter the service, company, or organization's name.

4. In the Connect Option box, select Dial **O**nce, **R**edial, or **A**uto Answer. If you select **R**edial, set the number of Redial attempt**s** and Redial **D**elay.

Tip
A prefix is any number, such as a 9, a 1, or an area code, that you must dial before dialing a phone number.

VI

Integrate & Communicate

Tip

The Auto Answer setting tells Works to answer all incoming calls. Use this setting when you expect another computer to call you.

5. In the Dial Type box, select Ton**e** or P**u**lse.

6. When all settings are correct, choose OK.

Once you specify phone settings, Works can later use the information to automatically dial the phone number and establish a connection to the other computer.

Choosing Communication Settings

Communication settings define the rules by which your computer communicates with the computer you are connecting to. To set communication settings, you choose the **C**ommunication command on the **S**ettings menu or click the Communication button on the toolbar. Works displays the Communication tab in the Settings dialog box, shown in figure 28.3.

Fig. 28.3

Use the Communication tab in the Settings dialog box to define communication settings.

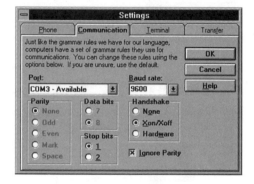

To choose communication settings, follow these steps:

1. From the **S**ettings menu, choose the **C**ommunication command; or click the Communication button on the toolbar. The dialog box shown in figure 28.3 appears. (If the Settings dialog box is already displayed but a different tab is chosen, simply click the **C**ommunication tab.)

2. From the Po**r**t list, select the port to which your modem is connected.

3. From the **B**aud Rate list, select a baud rate.

4. In the Parity box, select a setting, or use the default setting, **N**one. If you want Works to ignore parity, select the **I**gnore Parity check box.

5. In the Data Bits box, select either **7** or **8**.

6. In the Stop Bits box, select either **1** or **2**.

7. In the Handshake box, select a setting. **X**on/Xoff is the most common setting used for communicating by modem. Choose N**o**ne if the other computer doesn't use a handshake.

8. When all settings are correct, choose OK.

Choosing Terminal Settings

Terminal settings determine how your computer displays on-screen the information it receives from another computer. To set terminal settings, you choose the **T**erminal command on the **S**ettings menu or click the Terminal button on the toolbar. The Terminal tab in the Settings dialog box is shown in figure 28.4.

Tip
The Hard**w**are setting is used only when your computer is directly connected by a cable to the computer with which you are communicating.

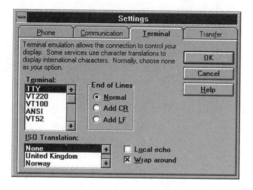

Fig. 28.4
Use the Terminal tab in the Settings dialog box to define terminal settings.

To set terminal settings, follow these steps:

1. From the **S**ettings menu, choose the **T**erminal command; or click the Terminal Settings button on the toolbar. The dialog box shown in figure 28.4 appears.

2. From the T**e**rminal list, select a terminal emulation. This is the type of terminal emulation required by the computer you are connecting to.

3. In the End of Lines box, select **N**ormal, Add C**R**, or Add **L**F if you are having trouble with text overlapping or not aligning correctly at the left margin. In most cases, you can use the **N**ormal setting. If some of the lines of text you are receiving don't begin at the left margin, select the Add C**R** option to add a carriage return at the end of each line. If lines of text are overwriting each other, select the Add **L**F option to move each new line of text to the next line.

VI

Integrate & Communicate

Tip

You can add Local
Echo and Wrap
Around buttons to
your toolbar for
these options. For
instructions on
customizing the
toolbar, refer
to Chapter 2,
"Getting Started
with Works for
Windows."

4. If you are connecting to an information service that transmits in a foreign language, select the appropriate language from the ISO Translation
   list. Otherwise, you should use the default None setting.

5. If you want to use Local Echo or **W**rap Around, select these check
   boxes.

   Local Echo is a setting that causes the characters you type to the host
   computer to be "echoed" back on your screen. Use this option when
   the characters you type don't appear on-screen. Turn this option off if
   you see two of every character on-screen. The **W**rap Around option
   adds a carriage return and line feed to the end of each line on your
   screen. Turn this option on if characters are overwriting one another
   at the end of each line.

6. When all terminal settings are correct, choose OK.

Choosing Transfer Settings

If you are transferring files (sending or receiving) during your communications session, you need to specify transfer settings. Sending and receiving files
does *not* include reading or capturing information from an online information service. Sending and receiving means actually sending a file stored on a
disk to the host computer and vice versa. For instance, a sales person in a
branch office might send an annual business plan to a headquarters office.

To specify transfer settings, choose the Transfer command on the **S**ettings
menu, or click the Transfer button on the toolbar. The Transfer tab in the
Settings dialog box is shown in figure 28.5.

Fig. 28.5

Before sending or
receiving files, use
the Transfer tab in
the Settings dialog
box to choose
settings.

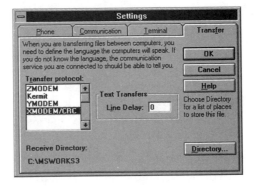

Follow these steps to specify transfer settings:

1. From the **S**ettings menu, choose the **T**ransfer command; or click the Transfer button on the toolbar. The dialog box shown in figure 28.5 appears. (If the Settings dialog box is already displayed but a different tab is chosen, simply click the Trans**f**er tab.)

2. From the **T**ransfer Protocol list, select the protocol that both computers use to transfer files.

3. If you are sending an ASCII (text) file that the receiving computer can't receive as quickly as it is being sent, enter a number representing tenths of a second in the **Li**ne Delay box. For example, enter **6** to have Works pause six tenths of a second after each line of text it sends.

4. To specify a default directory other than the one shown in which to save files you receive, click the **D**irectory button. Then choose a directory from the dialog box that appears and click OK.

5. When all transfer settings are correct, choose OK.

Choosing Modem Settings

Earlier in this chapter you learned that you need to know which port your modem is connected to before you can communicate with another computer. If you don't know the correct port, use the Modem Setup dialog box shown in figure 28.6 to have Works determine the correct port for you. Display this dialog box by choosing the Modem command on the **S**ettings menu.

Tip
If you use the Modem Setup dialog box frequently, you can add a Modem button to the communications toolbar. Refer to Chapter 2, "Getting Started with Works for Windows," for instructions on customizing the toolbar.

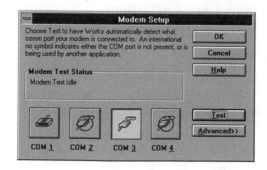

Fig. 28.6
Use the Modem Setup dialog box to determine the port your modem is connected to.

In the dialog box, the communications port (COM1, COM2, COM3, or COM4) currently selected is highlighted. Ports that are not available display the international No symbol. Click the Test button to have Works determine to which port your modem is connected. After several seconds, the Modem Test Status box displays the result and Works automatically selects the correct communications port.

To change the name of your modem or any of the commands it uses, click the **A**dvanced button in the Modem Setup dialog box. This button displays the Modem Settings dialog box in which you can enter or edit modem commands and results. Refer to your modem manual for specific instructions on modem settings. When modem settings are correct, choose OK to return to the Modem Setup dialog box, and then choose OK again.

Troubleshooting

I sent a text file to a friend but when she received the file, some of the text was missing.

Your friend's computer was not receiving the file as quickly as it was being sent. Try sending the file again, but specify a delay in the Transfer Settings dialog box (refer to figure 28.5).

Saving a Communications File

With the exception of transfer settings, all the settings you just read about in the previous section are required before you can connect to another computer. (Transfer settings are required only if you are sending or receiving files.) If you regularly connect to several different online information services, or perhaps a mainframe computer at your office, the communications settings for each computer are likely to be slightly different.

To avoid having to reset communication settings each time you connect to a different host computer, you can save the settings you specify in a communications file. For instance, if one of the services you connect to is CompuServe, you might save the required settings in a file called COMPUSRV.WCM. Or if you regularly use your computer to log on to a mainframe computer at your office, you might save the appropriate communications settings in a file called OFFICE.WCM. To save a communications file, choose the Save As command from the File menu. When you want to connect to a specific computer, just recall the communications file using the **O**pen command on the **F**ile menu.

Starting and Ending a Communications Session

When you start a communications session, Works automatically connects you to the host computer you specify. In the case of a mainframe computer system, the host computer prompts you for your user name and password once the telephone connection is established. This is called *logging in* to a computer. After your login information is accepted, the host computer displays its own menu. From this point on, you must use the commands the host computer recognizes to navigate the programs and files available to you on that computer. To log off of the host computer, you must also use the correct exit command (such as Logout, Quit, Exit, or Off) the host computer recognizes.

If you are connecting to a personal computer, your access to programs and files on that computer is dependent upon the operator of that computer and the communications software his or her computer is running. In some cases, a password may be required.

When you have a saved communications file for the computer to which you are connecting, follow these steps to start and end a communications session:

1. Open the communications file for the host computer to which you want to connect.

2. Works displays a message asking whether you want to connect to the other computer. Choose OK to have Works automatically begin dialing and establish the connection.

3. When the connection is established, the host computer prompts you for your user name and password.

4. Log off of the host computer by using the correct exit command for the host.

If you do not have a saved communications file for the computer to which you are connecting, start a new communications file and specify the correct communications settings. Then choose the Easy **C**onnect command on the **P**hone menu, or click the Easy Connect tool on the toolbar. When the Easy Connect dialog box appears, verify that the phone number is correct, and then click OK. Works begins dialing the host computer.

Capturing Text

When you capture text during a communications session, Works saves all information that you receive in a file called CAPTURE.TXT or any other file name that you specify. Use this feature when you want to incorporate information that you gather from online information services or other computers into Works documents, or when you want an accurate record of what occurred during a communications session.

To capture text, choose the **C**apture Text command on the T**o**ols menu, or click the Capture Text button on the toolbar. You can choose this command before you establish a connection, or at any time during a communications session. At whatever point you choose the command, Works begins recording the information received on your computer.

When you choose the **C**apture Text command on the T**o**ols menu, or the Capture Text button on the toolbar, the button is highlighted. To stop capturing text at any time during a communications session, choose the End **C**apture Text command on the T**o**ols menu. The capture button on the toolbar is no longer highlighted.

Use the following steps to have Works capture text for you. You can begin capturing text before you connect to another computer or anytime after the connection is already established.

1. From the T**o**ols menu, choose the **C**apture Text command, or click the Capture Text button on the toolbar. The Capture Text dialog box shown in figure 28.7 appears.

Fig. 28.7
In the Capture
Text dialog box,
supply a file name
for captured text.

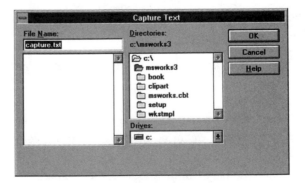

2. In the File **N**ame box, enter the name of the file you want to use, or use the default CAPTURE.TXT file name.

3. To save the file in a directory other than C:\MSWORKS
(or C:\MSWORKS3, as shown in the figure), select a directory
from the **D**irectories list box.

4. To save the file on a different disk drive, select a drive from the Dri**v**es
list.

5. When all settings are correct, choose OK. To remind you that you are
capturing text, Works highlights the Capture Text button on the
toolbar. Once you establish a connection to another computer, the
CAPT indicator appears on the status bar in the communications
window.

6. To stop capturing text, click the Capture Text button on the toolbar;
or choose the End **C**apture Text command from the T**o**ols menu. The
Capture Text button is no longer highlighted and the CAPT indicator is
removed from the status bar.

Sending and Receiving Files

Sending and receiving files is a common task when using the communications tool in Works. The following sections describe the required settings
and procedures for sending and receiving files.

Sending Files

Most files you create on your computer are either *binary* files or *text* files.
A binary file contains special formatting. (Tabs, bold or centered text, dollar
signs and commas used to display numbers in a spreadsheet, are all special
formatting.) Works files with a file type of .WPS, .WKS, .WDB, or .WCM are
binary files because they contain special formatting. Most files you create by
using other software programs are also binary files, because they usually contain formatting.

When you want to send a binary file to another computer, you use the **S**end
File command on the T**o**ols menu, or click the Send Binary File button on the
toolbar. The other computer automatically saves the file on the disk when
the file is received.

To send a binary file to another computer, use these steps:

1. Make sure your phone, communication, terminal, transfer, and modem settings are correct for the computer to which you are connecting. You must use the same transfer protocol used by the other computer.

2. Connect to the other computer using the Easy **C**onnect or **D**ial command from the **P**hone menu, or the Easy Connect or Dial button on the toolbar.

3. From the **T**ools menu, choose the **S**end File command; or click the Send Binary File button on the toolbar. Works displays the Send File dialog box shown in figure 28.8.

Fig. 28.8
Use the Send File dialog box to specify the file to send.

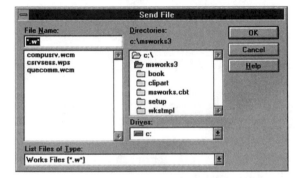

4. In the dialog box, select the correct disk drive, directory, and file name for the file you want to send, and then choose OK. Works begins transmitting the file. (You don't see the file on-screen.) During the transfer, Works displays a message indicating the status of the transfer.

You can cancel transmission of a binary file at any time by pressing the Esc key. Works displays a message asking you to confirm that you want to cancel the transmission. Choose OK.

In contrast to binary files, text files—or ASCII files, as they are often called—contain no formatting, and the file type is usually .TXT.

To send a text file to another computer, follow these steps:

1. Make sure your phone, communications, terminal, transfer, and modem settings are correct for the computer to which you are connecting. You must use the same transfer protocol used by the other computer.

2. Connect to the other computer using the Easy **C**onnect or **D**ial command on the **P**hone menu, or the Easy Connect or Dial button on the toolbar.

3. From the T**o**ols menu, choose the Send **T**ext command; or click the Send Text button on the toolbar. Works displays the Send Text dialog box shown in figure 28.9.

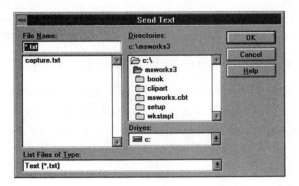

Fig. 28.9
Use the Send Text dialog box to choose a text file to send to another computer.

4. In the dialog box, select the correct disk drive, directory, and file name for the file you want to send, and then choose OK. Works begins transmitting the file. (You don't see the file on-screen.) During the transfer, Works displays a message indicating the status of the transfer.

Just as when you send a binary file, you can cancel sending a text file at any time by pressing the Esc key. Works displays a message asking you to confirm that you want to cancel the transmission. Choose OK.

Sending Text

Sometimes you don't want to send an entire file to another computer, you just want to send text. For instance, you might want to send a few pages of a document to a colleague on another computer. To do so, you use the **C**opy and **P**aste commands in Works. If the text is formatted, the formatting is not sent to the other computer, only the text.

To send text by copying it, use these steps:

1. In Works, open the file that contains the text you want to send.

2. Create a new communications file, or use the saved file for the computer to which you are connecting.

VI

Integrate & Communicate

3. Make sure your phone, communications, terminal, transfer, and modem settings are correct for the computer to which you are connecting.

4. Connect to the other computer using the Easy **C**onnect or **D**ial command on the **P**hone menu.

5. Using the **W**indow menu, switch to the Works file that contains the text you want to send.

6. In the file, select the text you want to send, then choose the **C**opy command from the **E**dit menu; or click the Copy button on the toolbar.

7. Switch back to your communications document window.

8. From the **E**dit menu, choose the **P**aste command. Works automatically sends the pasted text to the other computer. If the document contains any special formatting, it is not sent; only the text of the document is sent.

Receiving Files

You can receive a binary or a text file from another computer just as easily as you can send one. The other computer must use the same transfer protocol you are using in Works, and you must notify someone at the host computer when you are ready to receive the file.

Use the following steps to receive a file:

1. Make sure your phone, communications, terminal, transfer, and modem settings are correct for the computer to which you are connecting. You must use the same transfer protocol used by the other computer.

2. Connect to the other computer using the Easy **C**onnect or **D**ial command from the **P**hone menu.

3. Contact the user on the other computer who is sending you the file to let him or her know you are ready to receive a file. If you are receiving a file from an information service, choose the file, then choose the menu option and press the key sequence that enables you to transfer the file to your computer.

4. From the **T**ools menu, choose the **R**eceive File command; or click the Receive Binary File button on the toolbar. Works displays the Receiving File dialog box shown in figure 28.10.

Fig. 28.10
The Receive File
dialog box updates
you constantly on
the status of the
transfer.

5. If you are using the Xmodem protocol, enter a file name in the Receive
   Dir box, and then choose OK. (If you are using any other protocol,
   Works saves the file with the same file name used on the other computer.) Works begins transmitting the file. (You don't see the file on-
   screen.) During the transfer, Works displays a message indicating the
   status of the transfer.

At any point during the transfer, you can cancel receiving a file by pressing
the Esc key. Works displays a message asking you to confirm that you want
to cancel the transmission. Choose OK.

From Here...

This chapter completes *Using Microsoft Works 3 for Windows*. At this point,
you have a working knowledge of all the Works tools and understand how
to integrate information from various tools into a single document.

■ If you want to include functions in your database and spreadsheet files,
  refer to Appendix B, "Works for Windows Functions," which describes
  each function and includes examples.

VI

Integrate & Communicate

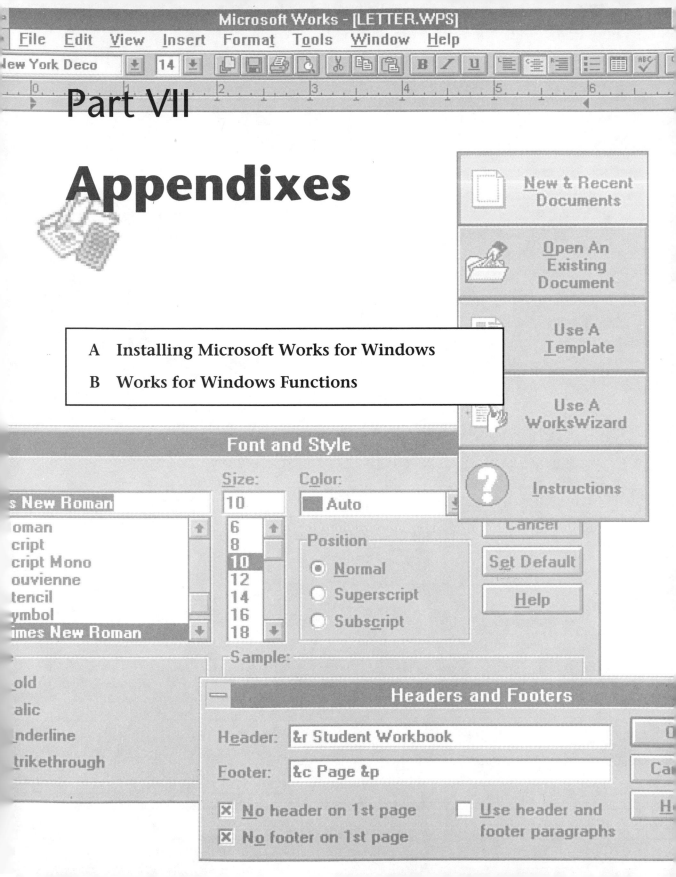

Part VII

Appendixes

A   Installing Microsoft Works for Windows

B   Works for Windows Functions

Microsoft Works - [LETTER.WPS]

File Edit View Insert Format Tools Window Help

New York Deco | 14

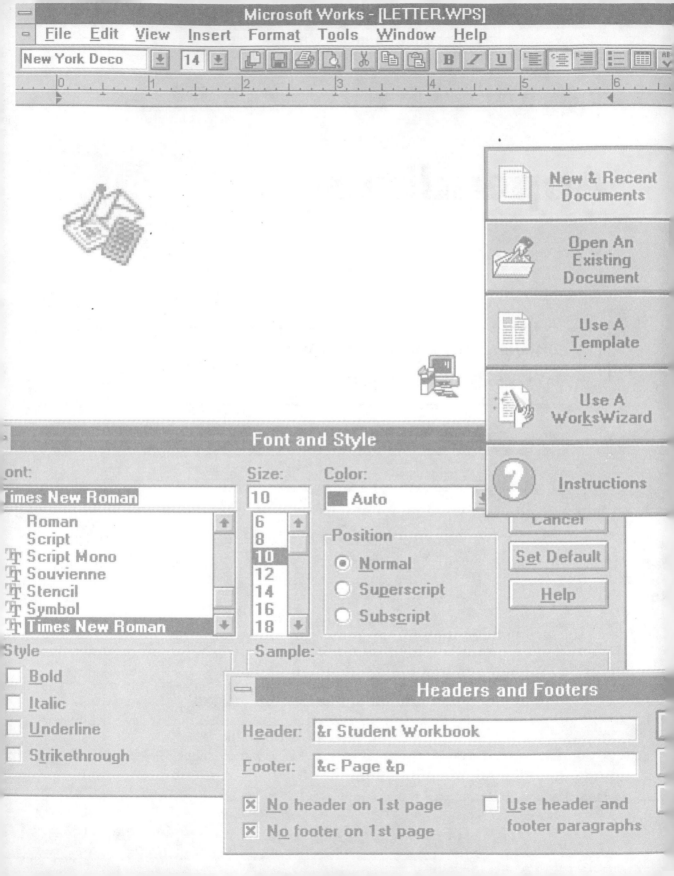

New & Recent Documents

Open An Existing Document

Use A Template

Use A WorksWizard

Instructions

Font and Style

Font:

Times New Roman

Roman
Script
Script Mono
Souvienne
Stencil
Symbol
Times New Roman

Size:

10

6
8
10
12
14
16
18

Color:

Auto

Position
- Normal
- Superscript
- Subscript

Cancel

Set Default

Help

Style
- Bold
- Italic
- Underline
- Strikethrough

Sample:

Headers and Footers

Header: &r Student Workbook

Footer: &c Page &p

- No header on 1st page
- No footer on 1st page

- Use header and footer paragraphs

Appendix A

Installing Microsoft Works for Windows

To install Microsoft Works for Windows, you must have Microsoft Windows installed on your computer. Make sure that your computer is turned on and ready to use before beginning installation. Follow these steps:

1. Start Windows as you normally do. The Windows Program Manager window is displayed. If the window isn't open, double-click the Program Manager icon.

2. Insert the Microsoft Works for Windows 3.0 disk 1 in drive A or B.

3. Choose **F**ile, **R**un to display the Run dialog box.

4. In the **C**ommand Line box, enter a:setup (or b:setup if you are using drive B). Windows begins copying the Microsoft Works Setup files to your hard disk. After a few seconds, the Microsoft Works 3.0 Setup welcome dialog box is displayed. Choose OK to continue.

5. In the Name and Organization Information dialog box, enter your name and organization, if appropriate, in the proper boxes and choose OK. In the next dialog box, confirm that the information you typed is correct by choosing OK. Choose **C**hange to correct errors.

6. Setup displays the serial number of your software. Write down the serial number and store it in a safe place, and choose OK.

7. The next dialog box tells you that the program will be installed in the C:\MSWORKS directory. Choose OK to use this directory, or choose the Change Directory button to enter a different directory.

8. In the next dialog box, select the type of installation (complete, minimal, or custom) that best suits your needs, and choose OK.

9. At this point, the Setup program prompts you to remove and insert additional Works distribution disks. Follow the instructions given on-screen until the installation is complete.

As part of the installation process, the Works startup icon and the Microsoft Works Setup icon are automatically installed in the Microsoft Works for Windows program group or other program group you specify. Should you ever need to reinstall a Works component or install additional components, use the Microsoft Works Setup icon.

Appendix B

Works for Windows Functions

This appendix lists all the functions included in Microsoft Works for Windows. The functions appear in alphabetical order, showing the function name, syntax, usage, and an example. Each function consists of a function name and *arguments*. The arguments represent the numbers or text that the function operates on. The *syntax* refers to the order in which the arguments must appear and the placement of parentheses. The PMT function shown below illustrates the elements of a typical function and its syntax. Enter each function exactly as the syntax shows.

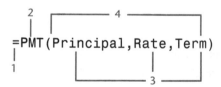

```
    2  ┌──── 4 ────┐
    |  |           |
  =PMT(Principal,Rate,Term)
    |        |     |      |
    1        └──── 3 ─────┘
```

1. Equal sign signifies the beginning of a formula

2. PMT is the function name

3. Principal, Rate, Term are three separate arguments

4. Parentheses enclose the arguments

ABS
Syntax: `ABS(x)`

Usage: Returns the absolute value of x, which can be a value or a reference to a cell that contains a number.

Example: `=ABS(-12)` returns 12.

ACOS
Syntax: `ACOS(x)`

Usage: Returns the arccosine of x, which is the angle whose cosine is x. The value of ACOS is returned in radians. x must be in the range from –1 through 1.

Example: `=ACOS(-.05)` returns `1.6208172`.

AND
Syntax: `AND(logical1,logical2,...)`

Usage: This function returns 1 (TRUE) if all arguments (logical1, logical2, etc.) are true and returns 0 (FALSE) if one or more arguments are false. You may include up to 14 arguments (logical1...logical14). Arguments themselves must be logical values or must reference cells that contain logical values.

Example: The function `=AND(3*5=15, 20/4=5)` returns TRUE because both arguments are true.

ASIN
Syntax: `ASIN(x)`

Usage: Returns the arcsine of x, which is the angle whose sine is x. The value of ASIN is returned in radians. x must range from –1 through 1.

Example: `=ASIN(-.3)*180/PI()` returns –30 degrees).

ATAN
Syntax: `ATAN(x)`

Usage: Returns the arctangent of x, which is the angle whose tangent is x. The value of ATAN is returned in radians.

Example: `=ATAN(3)*180/PI()` returns `71.565051` degrees.

ATAN2

Syntax: `ATAN2(x coordinate,y coordinate)`

Usage: This function computes the angle for which the tangent is defined by the x and y coordinates. One of the arguments must be a number other than zero.

Example: `=ATAN(A5,B5)` where A5 is 1.87092 and B5 is 1.24531, returns the value of `0.5872733`.

AVG

Syntax: `AVG(RangeReference0,RangeReference1,...)`

Usage: Calculates the average of the values specified in RangeReference. The value of RangeReference may be a number, a cell reference, a range reference, or a formula. Blank cells in a cell reference are considered to be 0. Blank cells in a range reference are ignored, and all text references are treated as 0.

Example: `=AVG(20,31,A5:A8)` where cells A5:A8 contain the values 12, 4, 22, and 32 returns the value `20.166667`.

CHOOSE

Syntax: `CHOOSE(Choice,Option0,Option1,...)`

Usage: This function uses the value of *Choice* to select an Option from the list of arguments. For example, if Choice is 2, CHOOSE returns the value of the third argument, *Option2*. If Choice is 0 or is greater than the number of options available in the list of arguments, the function returns the error value ERR.

Example: `=CHOOSE(C20,12,24,19)` returns the value of 24 if C20 holds the value of 1.

COLS

Syntax: `COLS(RangeReference)`

Usage: Calculates the number of columns within RangeReference.

Example: If the range B12:G25 is named Sales, the function `=COLS(Sales)` returns 6.

COS

Syntax: `COS(x)`

Usage: This function calculates the cosine of x when x is an angle measured in radians.

Example: `=COS(0.785)` returns `0.7073883`.

COUNT

Syntax: `COUNT(RangeReference0,RangeReference1,...)`

Usage: Counts the number of cells in RangeReference. COUNT adds 1 for every cell in RangeReference that holds a number, formula, text, ERR, and N/A. RangeReference can be numbers, cell references, range references, or formulas. When using range references, blank cells are ignored. With cell references, blank cells add 1 to the count.

Example: When the values in cells F4:F8 are 1, 5, (blank), (blank), and 4, the function `=COUNT(F4:F8)` returns 3.

CTERM

Syntax: `CTERM(Rate,FutureValue,PresentValue)`

Usage: Calculates the number of periods required for an initial investment (PresentValue) earning a fixed rate per compounding period (Rate) to grow to a future value (FutureValue). The Rate is the interest rate for a single compounding period, so if the interest rate is 9 percent annually, divide the rate by 12 to find the monthly rate.

Example: You put $12,000 into an investment account that has an annual interest rate of 9 percent and interest is compounded monthly. Use this function to determine how long it takes to double your investment.

`=CTERM(9.0%/12,24000,12000)` returns `92.76` periods (almost 8 years).

DATE

Syntax: `DATE(Year,Month,Day)`

Usage: This function calculates the serial number for the day specified by the Year, Month, and Day arguments. Serial numbers are integers ranging from 1 to 65534 that represent all the dates from January 1, 1990 to June 3, 2079.

The value for Year must be a number ranging from 0 (1900) to 179 (2079), the value for Month must be a number from 1 to 12, and the number for Day must be a number from 1 to 31. If you enter a value outside of these ranges, DATE adjusts the value to the correct date. If Year, Month, and Day are not a valid date in the Works range of dates, ERR is returned.

Example: =DATE(93,3,28) returns the serial number 34056 representing the date March 28, 1993.

DAY

Syntax: Day(DateNumber)

Usage: This function returns the day of the date when DateNumber is a serial number or is an integer ranging from 1 to 31.

Example: =DAY(34056) returns 28, the day of the date represented by the serial number 34056.

DDB

Syntax: DDB(Cost,Salvage,Life,Period)

Usage: Calculates the depreciation amount in a specific period using the double-declining balance method. Cost is the amount paid for the asset; Salvage is the value of the asset at the end of its working life. Life refers to the number of time periods (usually years) that you intend to use the asset. Period is the specific time period for which you want to find the depreciation amount.

Example: If you purchase capital equipment for $25,000 that has a usable life of 10 years and a salvage value of $3,000, the function returns $2,048, the depreciation amount for the fifth year, based on the function =DDB(25000,3000,10,5).

ERR

Syntax: ERR()

Usage: Returns the error value ERR. Use this function to force a cell to display ERR whenever a specified condition exists or to disallow unacceptable values in a cell.

Example: If you want cell C12 to contain values higher than zero, you could use the function =(IF(C12<=0,ERR(),C12)) to display ERR if the value in C12 is 0 or less. If the value is greater than zero, the function displays the actual value in C12.

EXACT

Syntax: `(TextValue0,TextValue1)`

Usage: This function compares two text values and returns 1 (TRUE) if TextValue0 and TextValue1 are exact matches and 0 (FALSE) if they are not exact matches. The function is case-sensitive; for example, Sales and SALES are not exact matches.

Example: If cells C3 contains Sales and D12 contains SALES, the function `=EXACT(C3,D12)` returns `0` (FALSE).

EXP

Syntax: `EXP(x)`

Usage: Returns e raised to the power of x (where e is 2.718282...). Use the exponentiation operator (^) to compute the powers of other bases. EXP is the inverse of LN.

Example: `=EXP(3)` returns `20.085537`.

FALSE

Syntax: `FALSE()`

Usage: The FALSE( ) function returns the value 0, the Boolean value for false. Use this function to check for errors.

Example: The function `FALSE()` returns `0`.

FIND

Syntax: `FIND(FindText,SearchText,Offset)`

Example: Use this function to find one string of text within another. The function returns the number of the character at which the FindText begins. This function differentiates between uppercase and lowercase letters.

The FindText argument is the text you want to find; SearchText is the text that contains the text you want to find. Both the FindText and SearchText arguments can be a cell reference that contains text, or the text itself, enclosed in quotation marks. The Offset argument is the character where you want to start the search. To start at the beginning, make this argument 0.

Example: If cell B3 contains the value "Profit and Loss Statement" the function `=FIND("Loss",B3,0)` returns 11.

FV

Syntax: `FV(Payment,Rate,Term)`

Usage: Calculates the future value of an ordinary annuity of equal payments, earning a fixed interest rate per term, compounded over several terms. The assumption is that the first payment occurs at the end of the first period.

Example: If you deposit $2,000 in your savings account every year for 8 years, how much money is in the account at the end of 8 years if the interest rate of 8.55 is compounded annually?

> `=FV(2000,8.55%,8)` returns 21700.499, or $21,700.50.

HLOOKUP

Syntax: `HLOOKUP(LookupValue,RangeReference,RowNumber)`

Usage: The function HLOOKUP (horizontal lookup) searches the top row of the specified RangeReference until it finds the number that matches LookupValue. It then moves down that column by the number of rows specified in the RowNumber argument. The entry found in that cell is the value returned.

The error value ERR is displayed if RowNumber is negative or is greater than or equal to the number of rows in RangeReference.

Example: `=HLOOKUP(36.1,B3:E19,3)`.

HOUR

Syntax: `HOUR(TimeNumber)`

Usage: Returns the number for the hour of the time represented by TimeNumber. HOUR returns an integer from 0 through 23. TimeNumber can be a number like 8:21:33 or 0.3483, the serial number for the same time.

Example: `=HOUR('8:21:33')` returns 8.

IF

Syntax: `IF(Condition,ValueIfTrue,ValueIfFalse)`

Usage: This function determines whether the value specified in Condition is true or false and then returns either ValueIfTrue or ValueIfFalse.

Example: If C24 contains the value $123.88, and D24 contains the value $329.99, the function `=IF(C24>D24,C24,0)` returns 0 because the condition is false.

INDEX

Syntax: `INDEX(RangeReference,Column,Row)`

Usage: This function finds the data contained in a specified cell. Within the RangeReference, the function returns the value in the cell at the intersection of the specified Column and Row.

If either Column or Row is negative or is greater than or equal to the number of rows or columns in RangeReference, Works returns the error value ERR.

Example: If you enter INDEX(C2:F5,3,2), Works returns the value in cell F4 (three columns to the right of C2 and two rows below C2).

INT

Syntax: `INT(x)`

Usage: This function returns the integer for x by deleting the digits to the right of the decimal point.

Example: `=INT(32.87891)` returns 32.

IRR

Syntax: `IRR(Guess,RangeReference)`

Usage: This function finds the internal rate of return for the cash flow series specified in RangeReference. The internal rate of return is the interest rate received for an investment of payments and received income by you. The Guess argument is the interest rate you guess to be close to the interest rate found by the IRR function.

Example: Suppose you put $1,000 into an investment and expect your income from the investment in years 2 through 6 to be $500, $600, $700, $–1,000, and $400. (These figures appear in cells A5:F5, with cell A5 showing –$1,000 since that is the amount you invested.) You expect the yield over the 6 years to be about 12 percent. Using these figures, the IRR function below finds the actual internal rate of return to be 0.1309899, or 13.10 percent.

   `=IRR(.12,A5:F5)` returns `0.1309899`.

ISERR

Syntax: `ISERR(x)`

Usage: This function allows you to test if the value in the referenced cell is the error value ERR. The function returns the logical value 1 (TRUE) if x is the error value ERR; otherwise, the function returns the logical value 0 (FALSE).

Example: If C19 contains the error value ERR, the function =ISERR(C19) returns 1.

ISNA
Syntax: ISNA(x)

Usage: This function allows you to test if a value in the referenced cell is the error value N/A. The function returns the logical value 1 (TRUE) if x is the value N/A; otherwise, the function returns the logical value 0 (FALSE).

Example: If C19 contains the value N/A, the function =ISNA(C19) returns 1.

LEFT
Syntax: LEFT(TextValue,Length)

Usage: This function returns the leftmost character or characters in the text string specified as TextValue. Length specifies how many characters you want the function to return.

Example: If cell C21 holds the text value "Figures based on 1992 data," the function =LEFT(C21,3) returns Fig.

LENGTH
Syntax: LENGTH(TextValue)

Usage: This function returns the number of characters in the string of text specified in the TextValue argument.

Example: If cell C21 holds the text value "Figures based on 1992 data," the function =LENGTH(C21) returns 26.

LN
Syntax: LN(x)

Usage: This function returns the natural logarithm of x. Natural logarithms are based on the mathematical constant e, 2.71828... The value for x must be a positive integer.

Example: =LN(85) returns 4.4426513.

LOG
Syntax: LOG(x)

Usage: The LOG function returns the base 10 logarithm of x, which must be a positive number.

Example: =LOG(25) returns 1.39794.

LOWER

Syntax: `Lower(TextValue)`

Usage: This function converts all uppercase letters in TextValue to lowercase.

Example: If cell B3 contains the text value "Sales Forecast," the function `=LOWER(B3)` returns `sales forecast`.

MAX

Syntax: `MAX(RangeReference0,RangeReference1,...)`

Usage: The MAX function returns the largest number contained in RangeReference. The RangeReference may be numbers, cell references, range references, or formulas. When RangeReference refers to a single cell, a blank cell is treated as 0. When RangeReference refers to a range, blank cells are ignored. In each type of reference, text is treated as 0.

Example: With values of 23, 26, 98, 87, and 38 in cells D12 through D16, the function `=MAX(D12:D16)` returns 98.

MID

Syntax: `MID(TextValue,Offset,Length)`

Usage: The MID function returns a specific number of characters (Length) from a text string (TextValue), starting with the number you specify (Offset).

Example: If cell B2 contains the value Quarterly Report, the function `=MID(B2,10,6)` returns `Report`.

MIN

Syntax: `MIN(RangeReference0,RangeReference1,...)`

Usage: The MIN function returns the smallest number contained in RangeReference. The RangeReference arguments can be numbers, cell references, range references, or formulas. In cell references, blank cells are treated as 0. In range references, blank cells are ignored. In each type of reference, text is treated as 0.

Example: With values of 23, 26, 98, 87, and 38 in cells D12 through D16, the function `=MIN(D12:D16)` returns 23.

MINUTE

Syntax: MINUTE(TimeNumber)

Usage: This function returns the number for the minute represented by TimeNumber, an integer ranging from 0 through 59. TimeNumber can be a number like 8:21:33 or 0.3483, the serial number for the same time.

Example: =MINUTE('12:32:33') returns 32.

MOD

Syntax: MOD(Numerator,Denominator)

Usage: This function returns the remainder (modulus) of after the numerator is divided by the denominator. MOD returns an ERR value if Denominator is equal to 0.

Example: =MOD(13,3) returns 1.

MONTH

Syntax: MONTH(DateNumber)

Usage: Returns the number for the month represented by DateNumber. The DateNumber is a serial number, an integer ranging from 1 to 31, or a cell reference.

Example: =MONTH(34056) returns 3, the month of the date represented by the serial number 34056.

N

Syntax: N(RangeReference)

Usage: This function returns the entry in the first cell in RangeReference as a value. If the cell contains text, the value 0 (zero) is returned.

Example: If cells C3:E3 contain the entries =D3-E3, 300, and 100, the function N(C3:E3) returns 200.

NA

Syntax: NA()

Usage: Returns the numeric value of N/A, which indicates that information is not available. Use NA( ) as a place holder for empty cells to avoid including empty cells in calculations.

Example: NA()

NOT

Syntax: `Not(Logical)`

Usage: This function reverses the value of the argument you specify in *Logical*. The *Logical* argument is a value or expression that can be evaluated as TRUE or FALSE. If FALSE, NOT returns 1 for TRUE. If TRUE, NOT returns 0 for FALSE.

Example: `=NOT(3*5=15)` returns `0` (FALSE).

NOW

Syntax: `NOW()`

Usage: The NOW function returns the date and time number for the current date and time. This value is updated each time the spreadsheet is recalculated. The integer portion of NOW( ) is the date number, and the decimal fraction is the time number.

Use the **Date** or **Time** format in the Number dialog box to display the actual date or time. (Display the **Number** dialog box by choosing the Number command on the Format menu.)

Example: If the current date is November 8, 1992 and the current time is 5:20 p.m., the function `=NOW()` returns `33915.7238`.

NPV

Syntax: `NPV(Rate,RangeReference)`

Usage: The NPV function returns the net present value of an investment based on a series of cash flows (RangeReference) and a discount rate (Rate). The net present value of an investment is the value today of a series of payments you make in the future (negative values) and income you receive in the future (positive values). The Rate argument is the rate of discount over the length of one period. The RangeReference argument must refer to a single cell or to a portion of a single row or column; the range cannot be more than one row or column.

The NPV function operates on the assumption that payments occur at the *end* of periods of equal length. If the payments occur at the beginning of the period, you must modify the formula as shown in the examples below.

Example: Suppose you are considering an investment where you pay $8,000 and receive income of $3,000, $4,000, and $5,000 in subsequent years.

The values –8000 (negative because you are paying this amount), 3000, 4000, and 5000 appear in cells D10:G10. You assume a discount rate of 10 percent per year.

If the payment of $8,000 occurs at the end of the first period, the function =NPV(10%,D10:G10) returns the result of 1626.9381, or $1,626.94, the net present value of the investment.

Suppose that the payment of the $8,000 occurs at the beginning rather than the end of the first period, and you expect to receive income of $3,000, $4,000, and $5,000 in years 1, 2, and 3. You don't include the –8,000 in the RangeReference because it occurs at the beginning of the first period. Instead, you add the –8000 to the calculation. In this case, the function =NPV(10%,E10:G10)+D10 returns 1789.6319, or $1,789.63, the net present value of the investment.

OR

Syntax: `OR(logical0,logical1,...)`

Usage: The OR function returns 1 (TRUE) if one or more of the arguments is true and returns 0 (FALSE) if all of the arguments are false.

Example: `=OR(1+1=1,1+2=2,1+3=2)` returns `0` for FALSE because all arguments are false.

PI

Syntax: `PI()`

Usage: Returns the number 3.14159..., an approximation of the mathematical constant pi.

Example: When you use PI( ) in a formula, Works inserts 3.14159... in the formula. The formula `=1+PI()` returns `4.14159`.

PMT

Syntax: `PMT(Principal,Rate,Term)`

Usage: The PMT function calculates the periodic payment for a loan or an investment. The Principal is the amount of the loan or investment; the Rate is the fixed interest rate that compounds over a given Term. In the PMT function, Works assumes that payments occur at the end of equal periods.

Example: If you want to borrow $15,000 to pay for a car over a 48-month period at 9 percent interest per year, the function `=PMT(15000,9%/12,48)` returns 373.27564, or $373.28, the amount of the monthly payment. Note that the 9 percent interest rate is divided by 12 because the interest is compounded monthly.

PROPER

Syntax: PROPER(TextValue)

Usage: This function capitalizes the first letter in a text string. When the text string contains characters other than letters (such as a comma or blank space), the letter that follows the character is also capitalized.

Example: =PROPER("foreign sales by quarter") returns Foreign Sales By Quarter.

PV

Syntax: PV(Payment,Rate,Term)

Usage: The PV function returns the present value of an annuity of equal payments that earns a fixed interest Rate compounding over the term of the annuity. Works assumes that the first payment is made at the end of the first period.

Example: Suppose you were to receive $10,000 every year for the next five years. You expect the annual inflation rate over the next five years to be 9 percent. The function =PV(10000,9%,5) returns 38896.513, or $38,896.51, the present value of the $50,000 annuity.

RAND

Syntax: RAND()

Usage: This function returns a random number in the range from 0 to 1 but not including 1. A random number is generated every time the spreadsheet is recalculated.

Example: =RAND()

RATE

Syntax: RATE(FutureValue,PresentValue,Term)

Usage: The Rate function calculates the fixed interest rate per compounding period needed for an investment at present value to grow to a future value over the term.

Example: You purchase a business property for $350,000 and expect to sell it for $750,000 after 5 years. The annual rate of return for this investment is .1646586, or 16.47 percent based on the formula =RATE(750000,350000,5).

REPEAT

Syntax: `Repeat(TextValue,Count)`

Usage: Use the Repeat function to repeat a text string the number of times you specify.

Example: If cell C1 contains the value "Important!" the function `=REPEAT(C1,5)` returns `Important! Important! Important! Important! Important!`.

REPLACE

Syntax: `REPLACE(OldText,Offset,Length,NewText)`

Usage: The Replace function replaces a text string you specify (OldText) with a new text string (NewText). You specify the number of characters to replace (Length) and the character at which to begin replacing text (Offset). The first character in OldText is zero. Enclosed OldText and NewText arguments in quotation marks.

Example: The function `=REPLACE("1,2,3,4,5,6,7,8",1,13,"...")` returns `1...8`.

RIGHT

Syntax: `RIGHT(TextValue,Length)`

Usage: The Right function returns the rightmost character in the specified TextValue. Use the Length argument to specify how many characters to return.

Example: If cell F19 contains the value "Based on 1992 Data," the function `=RIGHT(F19,4)` returns the value `Data`.

ROUND

Syntax: `ROUND(x,NumberOfPlaces)`

Usage: This function rounds x to the specified number of places either to the left or right of the decimal point. When NumberOfPlaces is a positive number, x is rounded to the right of the decimal point. When NumberOfPlaces is a negative number, x is rounded to the left of the decimal point. When NumberOfPlaces is zero, x is rounded to the nearest integer. NumberOfPlaces can range from −14 to 14.

Example: `=ROUND(36312.12,-3)` returns `36000`.

ROWS

Syntax: ROWS(RangeReference)

Usage: Returns the number of rows in RangeReference.

Example: =ROWS(C9:F20) returns 12.

S

Syntax: S(RangeReference)

Usage: The S function returns the text entry in the first cell in the specified cell range. If the first cell is blank, Works returns an empty cell.

Example: If cells A1:B4 contain the strings "First," "Second," "Third," and "Fourth," the function =S(A1:B4) returns First.

SECOND

Syntax: SECOND(TimeNumber)

Usage: This function returns the number for the seconds represented in TimeNumber, an integer ranging from 0 through 59. TimeNumber can be a number like 8:21:33 or 0.3483, the serial number for the same time.

Example: =SECOND('09:32:14') returns 14.

SIN

Syntax: SIN(x)

Usage: Returns the sine of the angle of x when x is expressed in radians. When x is expressed in degrees, multiply it by PI( )/180.

Example: SIN(45*PI()/180) returns 0.7071068.

SLN

Syntax: SLN(Cost,Salvage,Life)

Usage: The SLN function uses the straight-line depreciation method to calculate the amount of depreciation for one period. Cost is the amount you paid for an asset; Salvage is the amount you expect to obtain when you sell the asset at the end of its life; Life is the number of periods you expect to use the asset.

Example: A computer system that costs $325,000 is expected to have a useful life of 8 years and a salvage value of $20,000. The depreciation for one year is 38125, or $38,125 based on the function =SLN(325000,20000,8).

SQRT

Syntax: `SQRT(x)`

Usage: Returns the square root of x. If x is negative, the function returns the error value ERR.

Example: `=SQRT(144)` returns `12`.

STD

Syntax: `STD(RangeReference0,RangeReference1,...)`

Usage: The STD function returns an estimate for the standard deviation of a population based on the numbers supplied as RangeReference. The values in RangeReference may be numbers, cell references, range references, or formulas. Blank cells are ignored in range references. Blank cells are treated as 0 in cell references. Text is treated as 0 in any of the references.

Example: If cells B3:B8 contain the values 1321, 1431, 1992, 1762, 1283, and 1298 the formula `STD(B3:B8)` returns the standard deviation of `268.99`.

STRING

Syntax: `STRING(x,DecimalPlaces)`

Usage: The String function converts the value of x to a text entry and adds the number of decimal places you specify.

Example: If cell D29 contains the value 492, the function `=STRING(D29,2)` returns `492.00`.

SUM

Syntax: `SUM(RangeReference0,RangeReference1,...)`

Usage: The SUM function calculates the total of all values in RangeReference. The values in RangeReference may be numbers, cell references, range references, or formulas. Blank cells are ignored in range references. Blank cells are treated as 0 in cell references.

Example: When the cells B2, D3, D4, and D5 contain the values 10, 20, 30, and 40, respectively, the function `=SUM(B2,D3:D5)` returns `100`.

SYD

Syntax: `SYD(Cost,Salvage,Life,Period)`

Usage: The SYD function calculates depreciation for a specific period using the sum-of-the-year's-digits depreciation method. Cost is the amount you paid for the asset, Salvage is the amount you expect to get when you sell the asset at the end of its life, Life is the number of periods (usually measured in years) you expect to use the asset, and Period is the period of time for which you want to find the depreciation amount.

Example: A computer system that costs $325,000 is expected to have a useful life of 8 years and a salvage value of $20,000. The depreciation for year 8 is `8472.222222`, or $8,472.22 based on the function `=SYD(325000,20000,8,8)`.

TAN

Syntax: `TAN(x)`

Usage: Returns the tangent of the angle of x when x is expressed in radians. When x is expressed in degrees, multiply it by PI( )/180.

Example: `=TAN(45*PI()/180)` returns 1.

TERM

Syntax: `TERM(Payment,Rate,FutureValue)`

Usage: The TERM function calculates the number of compounding periods necessary for a series of equal payments earning a fixed interest rate per period to grow to a future value.

Example: You contribute $150 each month to your child's college fund account. You earn 11 3/4-percent interest, compounded monthly. To find out how long it takes to save $15,000 use the function `=TERM(150,11.75%/12,15000)`, which returns `70.06087355`, or 70.06 months, approximately 5.8 years.

TIME

Syntax: `TIME(Hour,Minute,Second)`

Usage: The TIME function returns a serial number for the time specified by the Hour, Minute, and Second arguments. Hour is a number ranging from 0 through 23. Minute and Second are numbers ranging from 0 through 59. If either Minute or Second is outside the specified range of 0 through 59, TIME adjusts the number to the correct time.

Example: `=TIME(8,45,15)` returns `.3647569`, the serial number for 8:45:15 a.m.

TRIM

Syntax: `TRIM(TextValue)`

Usage: This function removes all spaces from the specified text entry except for single spaces between words.

Example: If cell B3 contains the title "1993   Quarterly   Forecast," the function =TRIM(B3) returns 1993 Quarterly Forecast.

TRUE

Syntax: TRUE()

Usage: The TRUE function returns the logical value 1 (TRUE). Use TRUE() rather than 1 to create more readable logical formulas.

Example: If cell C3 holds the value 45, the function =IF(45-10=35,TRUE(),FALSE()) returns 1.

UPPER

Syntax: Upper(TextValue)

Usage: This function converts all lowercase letters in TextValue to uppercase.

Example: If cell B3 contains the text value "sales forecast," the function =UPPER(B3) returns the value SALES FORECAST.

VALUE

Syntax: Value(TextValue)

Usage: The VALUE function converts a number entered as a text entry into a value. A number entry must be a value in order to be used in mathematical calculations.

Example: If cell D19 contains the time 8:55 a.m. entered as text, the function =VALUE(D19) converts the entry to the value 0.3715278, the serial number for the time of 8:55 a.m.

VAR

Syntax: VAR(RangeReference0,RangeReference1,...)

Usage: The VAR function calculates the variance among the numbers specified in RangeReference. RangeReference may be numbers, range references, cell references, or formulas. Blank cells are ignored in range references. Blank cells are treated as 0 in cell references. Text is always treated as 0.

Example: If cells B3:B8 contain the values 1200, 1220, 1201, 1218, 1230, and 1211, the formula VAR(B3:B8) returns 113.22.

VLOOKUP

Syntax: VLOOKUP(LookupValue,RangeReference,ColumnNumber)

Usage: VLOOKUP searches the leftmost column in RangeReference until it finds the number that matches LookupValue. VLOOKUP then moves across that row by the number of columns specified in the ColumnNumber argument. The entry found in that cell is the value returned.

The error value ERR is displayed if ColumnNumber is negative or is greater than or equal to the number of columns in RangeReference.

Example: =VLOOKUP(1992,B3:F19,3)

YEAR

Syntax: YEAR(DateNumber)

Usage: Returns the number for the year represented by DateNumber. The DateNumber is a serial number, an integer ranging from 1 to 31, or a cell reference.

Example: =YEAR(34056) returns 93, the year of the date represented by the serial number 34056.

Index

Symbols